# Colloids in Drug Delivery

# Colloids in Drug Delivery

*Editor*

Lino Messana

scitus academics

**Colloids in Drug Delivery**
Edited by **Lino Messana**

ISBN: 978-1-68117-699-4
Library of Congress Control Number: 2016958854


SCITUS Academics LLC,
616, Corporate Way, Suite 2, 4766,
Valley Cottage, NY 10989

www.scitusacademics.com



Printed in United States of America on Acid Free Paper

# Preface

In the past ten years, nanomedicine, or medicine using nanometric devices, has emerged as a thrilling field that helps to solve a variety of problems linked to unsatisfactory therapeutic reactions of so-called old drugs. This dissatisfaction results from insufficient biodistribution after application of a drug, which results in a limited therapeutic response but also many side effects on healthy organs. The biodistribution of drugs in a nanoobject that serves as a vector can be modified to adjust its therapeutic effectiveness.

This book, Colloids in Drug Delivery, gives a comprehensive overview of existing colloidal nanovectors: liposomes, polymer micelles, polymer vesicles, polymer nanoparticles (NPs) and dendrimers. Their characteristics, advantages and disadvantages are described and discussed in order to treat many diseases. Colloidal drug delivery systems offer a variety of therapeutic advantages in the treatment of a variety of difficult conditions, enabling researchers to cross barriers that previously prevented efficient treatment while offering better and more specific absorption.

This book offers contemporary research in the field by leading experts and scientists from around the world who examine this rapidly developing science's entire spectrum. It provides an overview of a wide range of colloidal drug delivery systems with a special focus on vesicular and particulate systems that are used in research and may be useful as drug carrier systems or possibly active biomolecules or possibly as therapeutic cell carriers. This particular system class is popular due to excellent drug targeting, sustained and controlled release behaviour, higher drug molecular trapping efficiency, enzyme degradation or drug hydrolysis prevention and improved therapeutic efficacy. These characteristics are helped in the selection of suitable carrier systems for drug, cell and gene delivery in different fields. All those involved in research, development and manufacture of drugs will find this book a valuable tool.

# Table of Contents


| | | |
|---|---|---|
| Chapter 1 | Niosomes as Carrier in Dermal Drug Delivery | 1 |
| Chapter 2 | Dual Cross-Linked Carboxymethyl Sago Pulp-Gelatine Complex Coacervates for Sustained Drug Delivery | 33 |
| Chapter 3 | Nanoemulsion: an advanced mode of drug delivery system | 59 |
| Chapter 4 | Colloidal Microgels in Drug Delivery Applications | 71 |
| Chapter 5 | Rapid Detection and Identification of Overdose Drugs in Saliva by Surface-Enhanced Raman Scattering Using Fused Gold Colloids | 95 |
| Chapter 6 | Structural Versatility of Bicellar Systems and Their Possibilities as Colloidal Carriers | 117 |
| Chapter 7 | Etodolac Containing Topical Niosomal Gel: Formulation Development and Evaluation | 161 |
| Chapter 8 | Formulation and Evaluation of Optimized Oxybenzone Microsponge Gel for Topical Delivery | 181 |
| Chapter 9 | Fliposomes: pH-Sensitive Liposomes Containing a *trans*-2-morpholinocyclohexanol-Based Lipid That Performs a Conformational Flip and Triggers an Instant Cargo Release in Acidic Medium | 203 |

**Chapter 10** **Influence of the Vehicle on the Penetration of Particles into Hair Follicles** **243**

**Chapter 11** **Semi-solid Sucrose Stearate-Based Emulsions as Dermal Drug Delivery Systems** **255**

**Index** **303**

# Chapter 1

# Niosomes as Carrier in Dermal Drug Delivery

**Yahya Rahimpour[1] and Hamed Hamishehkar[2]**

[1] *Biotechnology Research Center and Student Research Committee, Tabriz University of Medical Sciences, Tabriz, Iran*

[2] *Pharmaceutical Technology Laboratory, Drug Applied Research Center, Tabriz University of Medical Sciences, Tabriz, Iran*

## 1. INTRODUCTION

Colloidal vesicular carriers such as liposomes or niosomes have been extensively applied in drug delivery systems due to unique advantages. These vesicles can act as drug reservoirs and the rate of drug release can be modified by changing of their composition. These lipid carriers can encapsulate both hydrophilic drugs (by loading in inner space) and hydrophobic drugs (in lipid area). Because of their potential to carry a variety of drugs, these lipid vesicles have been widely used in various drug delivery systems like drug targeting, controlled release and permeation enhancement of drugs (Akhilesh et al., 2011). Dermal (topical) delivery defines a targeting to the pathological sites within the skin with the least systemic absorption. Drug localization in this case is a crucial issue in the treatment of dermatological problems such as skin cancer, psoriasis, alopecia and acne, where the origin of disease is located in the skin (Brown et al., 2006). Topical drug administration has been initiated since long time to accomplish several functions on different skin levels (skin surface, epidermis, dermis and hypodermis). But, several limitations have been associated with the conventional topical preparations e.g. low percutaneous penetration because of the barrier function of the stratum corneum, the outermost layer of the skin, (Rubio et al., 2011) and absorption to the systemic circulation (Dubey et al., 2012). The scientific reports nowadays offer several systems that can be able to deliver drugs through the skin (Higaki et al., 2005). Recently niosomes are becoming popular in the field of topical drug delivery due to its outstanding characteristics like enhancing the penetration of drugs, providing a sustained pattern of drug release and ability to carry both hydrophilic and lipophilic drugs (Sathali et al., 2010). This chapter deals with the potential of niosome in topical delivery system focusing on its clinical approach. Skin represents a multilayered effective barricade to the penetration of drugs. The outer layer of skin, stratum corneum, provides a rate limiting step during percutaneous absorption of drug. Drug transfer across the stratum corneum is mainly a passive process, and thus the physicochemical properties of a permeant have a key role in its capability to penetrate and diffuse across the membrane. Compounds can penetrate through the stratum corneum via three routes: intercellular, transcellular (paracellular), and transappendageal (figure 1). Once it has transferred through the epidermis, a compound may be carried away by the dermal blood circulation or to be transported to deeper tissues. The relative significance of these penetration pathways will be largely dependent on the physicochemical characteristics of the drug molecules, particularly the partition and diffusion coefficients into the protein or lipid regions (Barry, 1991).

For successful dermal or transdermal delivery, a reversible overcoming of skin barrier is required. Therefore, many strategies have been assessed to overcome the barrier function of the stratum corneum and to improve drug transport into the skin (Ghafourian et al., 2004; Rahimpour et al., 2012). Targeting of topically administered drugs to the different skin layers and appendages is becoming a main center of interest for many pharmaceutical research groups studying in dermatology (Nounou et al., 2008). The carrier is one of the most important entities required for successful targeted drug delivery (figure 2). Carriers will enable a drug to reach the desired pharmacological site of action at a controlled rate and to have a sustained duration of action. Consequently, as a vehicle for active substances and targeting to skin layers, surfactant based carriers such as niosomal systems are gaining more interest.

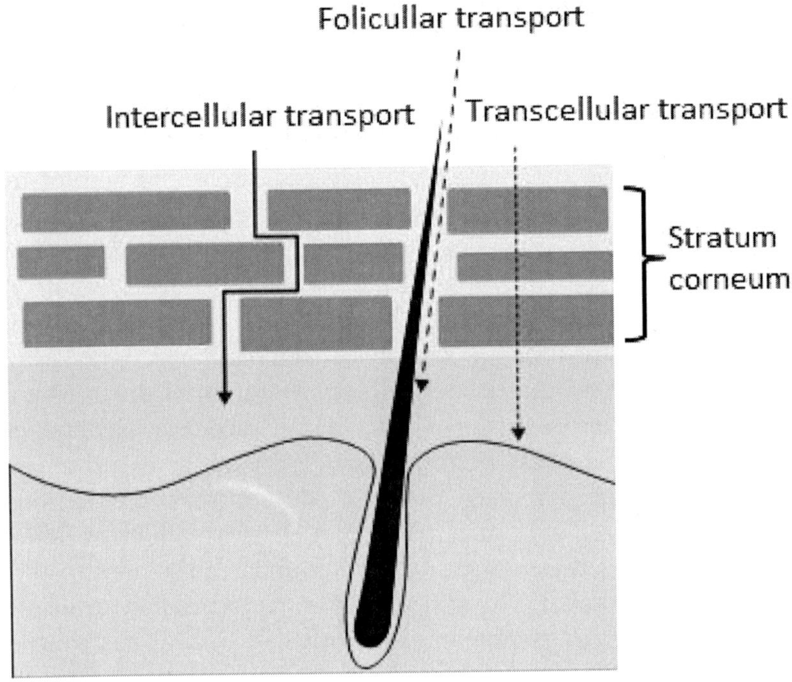


**Figure 1.** Possible pathways for delivery of compounds across the stratum corneum adapted from reference (Gašperlin et al., 2011).

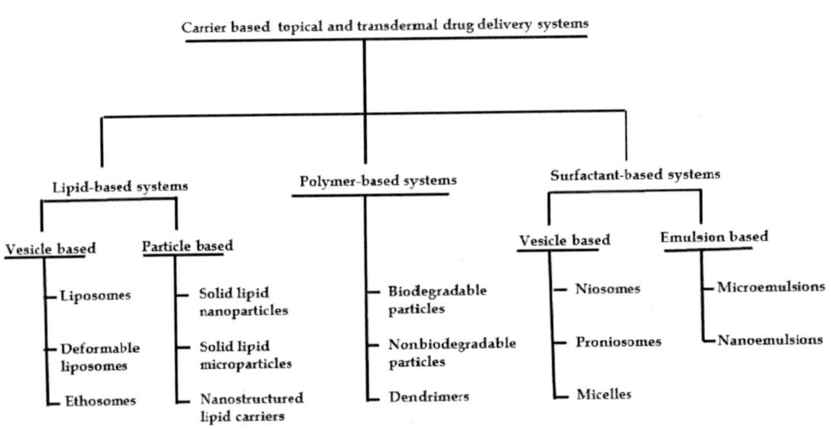


**Figure 2.** Carriers for topical and transdermal drug delivery adapted from reference (Venuganti et al., 2009).

# 2. NIOSOME

Niosomes are microscopic lamellar structures composed of non-ionic surfactants and cholesterol. The niosomes have amphiphillic bilayer structure in a way that polar region is oriented outside and inside the vesicles where the hydrophilic drug will be entrapped and non-polar region is formed within the bilayer where hydrophobic drug can be entrapped (Khan et al., 2011). The formation of vesicular system based on hydration of mixture of a single-alkyl chain nonionic surfactant and cholesterol was firstly reported in 1979 (Handjani-Vila et al., 1979). Niosomes might be produced by various types of nonionic surfactants including polyglycerol alkyl ethers, crown ethers, ester-linked surfactants, glucosyldialkyl ethers, polyoxyethylene alkyl ethers, Brij, Tweens and Spans. Nonionic surfactants used to prepare niosomes carry no charge and are relatively nontoxic and mild to use (Azeem et al., 2009).

## 2.1. TYPES OF NIOSOMES

### 2.1.1. PRONIOSOMES

Proniosome is a dry granular product that can be able to form a niosome suspension after hydration (Hu et al., 2000). Proniosomes are developed to overcome the disadvantage of vesicular system. Proniosome are prepared based on the simple scheme that a mixture of surfactant/alcohol/aqueous phase can be used to prepare a concentrated proniosome gel, which can instinctively be converted to a stable niosomal dispersion by dilution with excess aqueous phase (Perrett et al., 1991).

Carrier + surfactant = Proniosomes

Proniosomes + water = Niosomes

---

### 2.1.2. ASPASOMES

Mixture of acorbyl palmitate, cholesterol and highly charged lipid diacetyl phosphate leads to the construction of vesicles named aspasomes. Aspasomes are first hydrated with water/aqueous solution and then sonicated to attain the niosomes. Aspasomes are suggested to improve the transdermal permeation of drugs. Aspasomes have also been used to reduce disorders caused by reactive oxygen species due to its intrinsic antioxidant property (Gopinath et al., 2004; Rajera et al., 2011).

### 2.1.3. VESICLES IN WATER AND OIL SYSTEM (V/W/O)

In this system suspension of aqueous niosomes (v/w) are emulsified into the oily phase at 60°C to form vesicle in water in oil emulsion (v/w/o) (Yoshida et al., 1992; Hu et al., 2000). Cooling to room temperature forms vesicle in water in oil gel (v/w/o gel) (Yoshioka et al., 1992). The prepared v/w/o gel can entrap the hydrophilic active ingredients which are susceptible for enzymatic degradation such as proteins/proteinous drugs and also provide a controlled release pattern in drug delivery.

### 2.1.4. DEFORMABLE NIOSOMES

Elastic niosomes are prepared of nonionic surfactants, ethanol and water. They show superior to conventional niosomes due to their capability to increase penetration efficiency of a compound through intact skin by passing through pores in the stratum corneum, which are smaller than the vesicles (figure 3). The flexibility of their structure allows them to pass through pores that are less than one-tenth of these vesicles (Cevc, 1996; Cevc et al., 1996).

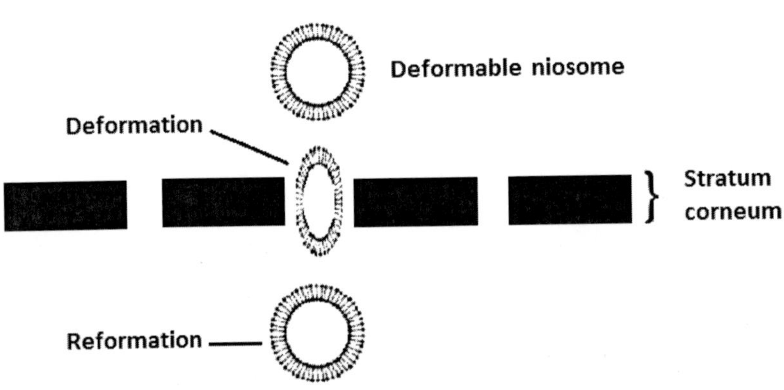


**Figure 3.** Mechanism of skin permeation of deformable niosome adapted from reference (Kumar et al., 2012)

## 2.2. ADVANTAGES OF NOISOME

The major advantages of niosomes can be mentioned as: i) niosomes are biodegradable, biocompatible, non-toxic and non-immunogenic (Azeem et al., 2009); ii) niosomes are able to encapsulate large amount of materials in a small volume of vesicles (Nasr et al., 2008); iii) niosomes have better patient adherence and satisfication and also better effectiveness than conventional oily formulations (Jain et al., 2006); iv) niosomes can entrap wide range of chemicals (hydrophilic, lipophilic and amphiphilic drugs) due to its unique structure (Raja Naresh et al., 1994); v) the characteristics of niosome such as shape, fluidity and size can be easily controlled by changing in structural composition and method of production (Bayindir et al., 2010); vi) niosomes can be prescribed via different administration routes such as oral, parenteral and topical, etc. with different dosage forms such as semisolids, powders, suspensions (Malhotra et al., 1994) and vii) due to chemical stability of structural composition, the storage of the niosome is easy (Jain et al., 2006). In spite of several above mentioned merits, niosomes show some disadvantages. The aqueous suspensions of niosomes may undergo fusion, aggregation, leaking of entrapped drugs, and hydrolysis of encapsulated drugs, which lead to limited shelf life. The methods of preparation of multilamellar vesicles such as extrusion, sonication, are time consuming and may require specialized equipments for processing (Khan et al., 2011)

## 2.3. APPLICATION OF NIOSOME

Niosomes have been successfully used in drug targeting to various organs such as skin (Agarwal et al., 2001), brain (Abdelkader et al., 2012), liver (Baillie et al., 1986; Lala et al., 2004), lung (Desai et al., 2002; Abd-Elbary et al., 2008) ocular systems (Pugeat et al., 1991; Abdelkader et al., 2012), tumor (Ruckmani et al., 2000; Shi et al., 2005) etc. Niosomes show a higher bioavailability than conventional dosage forms (Raja Naresh et al., 1994). Controlled and sustained release of drugs have been achieved by niosomes (Bayindir et al., 2010). Permeation of drugs through the skin has been enhanced by niosomes (Pardakhty et al., 2007). Noisome, itself improves the stratum corneum properties both by reducing transepidermal water loss and skin condition by increasing smoothness via reloading lost skin lipids (Firthouse et al.). Niosomes can be applied for drug protection from biological enzymes and acid thereby increasing the drug stability (Jain et al., 2006).

## 2.4. NIOSOMES IN COMPARISON WITH LIPOSOMES

Niosomes and liposomes have similar application in drug delivery but chemically differ in structure units. Niosomes constitute of non-ionic surfactant whereas liposomes comprise of phospholipids (Khan et al., 2011). They are functionally the same, have the same physical properties and act as amphiphilic vesicules. Both can be used in targeted and sustained drug delivery system. Property of both depends upon composition of the bilayer and methods of their preparation (Verma et al., 2012). Studies have also shown that the function of niosomes in vivo is similar to that of liposomes (Hofland et al., 1994). In spite of these comparable characteristics, niosomes offer several advantages over liposomes: intrinsic skin penetration enhancing properties, higher chemical stability and lower costs (Nasr et al., 2008). Both of the last features make the niosome more attractive for industrial manufacturing (Hu et al., 2000). Also, niosomes do not require special conditions such as low temperature or inert atmosphere during preparation and storage (Verma et al., 2012). Although the niosome shows better chemical stability, the physical instability during dispersion may be comparable to that of the liposome. Both niosomes and liposomes are at risk of aggregation, fusion, drug leakage, or hydrolysis of entrapped drugs during storage (Hu et al., 2000; Rahimpour et al., 2012).

# 3. MECHANISMS OF NIOSOMAL SKIN DELIVERY

Several mechanisms have been suggested to describe the ability of niosomes in transdermal and dermal drug delivery: i) niosomes diffuse from the stratum corneum layer of skin as a whole; ii) new smaller vesicles are formed in skin (re-formation of noisome vesicles). The water content of skin is crucial issue for interpreting and establishing this mechanism. Smaller diameter of lipid lamellar spaces of the stratum corneum than noisome vesicles makes this mechanism more meaningful (Sahin, 2007). iii) noisomes interact with stratum corneum with aggregation, fusion and adhesion to the cell surface which causes a high thermodynamic activity gradient of the drug at the vesicle-stratum corneum surface, which is the driving force for the penetration of lipophilic drugs across the stratum corneum (Ogiso et al., 1996). Scanning electron microscopy confirmed the fusion of niosome vesicles of estradiol on the surface of skin (Schreier et al., 1994) iv) niosomes may modify stratum corneum structure which makes the intercellular lipid barrier of stratum corneum looser and more permeable (Fang et al., 2001); v) non-ionic surfactant itself, the composing ingredient of niosome, acts as a permeation enhancer and might partly contribute to the improvement of drug permeation from niosomes (Javadzadeh et al., 2010). The type of surfactant plays an important role in modification of permeation using niosome vehicles. Niosomes fabricated from polyoxyethylene stearyl ether and existing in the gel state did not enhance estradiol permeation, and those prepared from polyoxyethylene lauryl ether and polyoxyethylene oleyl ether, both existing as liquid crystalline vesicles, considerably improved transport (Hofland et al., 1991).

## 4. TOXICITY OF NIOSOMES

Surfactants are suspected to show toxicity but there are virtually not enough research about toxicity of niosomes (Yadav et al., 2011). A study on the toxicity effect of surfactant type of niosomal formulations on human keratocytes showed that the ester type surfactants are less toxic than ether type due to enzymatic degradation of ester bounds (Hofland et al., 1991). Hofland et al. studied the toxicity of CxEOy surfactants via ciliotoxicity model on nasal mucosa (which is important for intranasal administration) and on human kerationocytes (which is important for the transdermal application of vesicles). The results showed that increase in alkyl chain length of surfactant causes a reduction in toxicity, while, increase in the polyoxyethylne chain length enhances ciliotoxicity. The study supposed that ciliotoxicity related to liquid state formation with increasing in polyoxyethylene chain length, while increase in alkyl chain length of surfactant leads to formation of gel which is more safe than liquid state (Hofland et al., 1992). In another study, vincristine, a potent anti-tumor agent, was loaded into niosomes and administered intravenously. Result showed a significant increase in vincristine anti-tumor activity in S-180 sarcoma and Erlich ascites mouse models followed by reduction of its side effect such as diarrhea, neurological toxicity and alopecia compared with free drug (Parthasarathi et al., 1994). Toxicity effect of niosomes should be considered according to the intended route of delivery. For example, hemocompatibility studies should be carried out when the niosomes are meant to be delivered by intravenous route to evaluate their toxic potential (Uchegbu et al., 1997). The first in vivo experiment on drug delivery by means of synthetic non-ionic surfactant vesicles were carried out by Azmin et al. and reported that no unfavorable effects were observed in the performed experiment (Azmin et al., 1985). Rogerson et al. reported in vivo experiment over 70 male BALB/C mice and stated that no fatalities were related to niosomes. The drug associated toxicity were also reduced (Rogerson et al., 1987). Niosomes which have been prepared with Bola-surfactants showed a certain and encouraging safety and tolerability both in vitro on human keratinocyte cells up to an incubation time of 72 h for the different concentrations studied (0.01-10 μM) and in vivo on human volunteers that showed no skin erythema when topically treated with the drug free Bola-niosome formulation (Paolino et al., 2007).

## 5. INDICATIONS FOR NIOSOMES AS DRUG CARRIERS IN DERMATOLOGY

Niosomes were formulated and patented for the dermatological purposes in 1975 for the first time and since then many of products were developed based on this technology and appeared in the market such as Lancome Noisome Plus as an anti-ageing formulation (Azeem et al., 2009). Recently, the topical delivery of certain drugs using niosome has been developed. Here, current attempts with a focus on clinical application were reviewed to prove the ability of niosomes as the superior topical carrier.

### 5.1. LOCAL ANESTHESIA

Dermatologists take benefit of topical anesthetics for decreasing pain relief prior to cutaneous procedures, pain associated with laser pulses, or soft tissue augmentation. Inefficient formulations of local anesthetics resulted in severe dermatitis, systemic toxicity, or inadequate local analgesia. Carafa et al. fabricated lidocaine and lidocaine hydrochloride-loaded non-ionic surfactant vesicles using Tween 20™ and cholesterol. The ability of drug to diffuse through a model lipophilic membrane (Silastic™) and through mouse skin were studied and compared with classical liposomes and Tween 20 micelles. Dicetylphosphate and N-cetylpyridinium chloride were also used to prepare negatively and positively charged vesicles, respectively to study the effect of vesicle charge on drug encapsulation efficiency. Diffusion experiments indicated that the flux of charged lidocaine (lidocaine hydrochloride) through Silastic™ membrane was possible only after the vesicle encapsulation. Permeation of lidocaine hydrochloride-loaded vesicles through mouse abdominal skin presented a higher flux and a shorter lag time with respect to classical liposome formulations, whereas lidocaine permeation rate was quite similar for niosomes and liposome formulations. Furthermore fluorescence quenching study showed that positive and negative charged vesicles had negligible entrapment efficiency of drug, at pH 5.5 compare with neutral vesicles (Tween 20 and cholesterol). The importance of non-ionic surfactant vesicles in dermal delivery of charged local anesthetics is concluded in this study (Carafa et al., 2002).

## 5.2. PSORIASIS

Psoriasis is a chronic inflammatory condition of the skin which may drastically undermined the patient quality of life. Psoriasis, a T-lymphocyte-mediated autoimmune disease of the dermis and epidermis, is characterized by leukocyte infiltration into the skin and localized deregulated skin growth, which leads to the development of scaling erythematous plaques (Dubey et al., 2007). Although psoriasis is rarely life-threatening, it causes an unpleasant appearance that makes the patients to miss their confidence and suffer from itching, painful and disfiguring skin lesions. Methotrexate, anthralin, corticosteroids, coal tar, vitamin D3 analogs, tacrolimus and retinoids are administered topically for psoriasis treatment (Su et al., 2008). Topical therapy is the commonly used in patients, even though the use of topical formulations based on conventional excipients shows some disadvantages that limit considerably their use in therapy (Puglia et al., 2012). With the use of niosomes as carrier for topical drug delivery, the possibility to improve efficacy and safety of the topical products has improved manifold. Dithranol, one of the key medicines in the topical treatment of psoriasis, has staining, burning, irritating and necrotizing effects on the normal and also the diseased skin. Entrapment of dithranol in niosomal and liposomal systems could be achieved after optimizing the various process and formulation variables. These systems presented size stability and improved drug permeation properties. Although the in vitro study using laca mice abdominal skin shows higher skin penetration for vesicular systems compared with the cream base but niosomal vesicular systems had three times less percutaneous permeation of dithranol compared with liposomal formulation (Agarwal et al., 2001). Methotrexate is an antifolate class of anti-neoplastic medicine which is commonly used in the psoriasis therapy. The systemic administration of this drug causes several side effects such as hepatic toxicity. Dermal delivery of methotrexate offers a valuable alternative way to reduce its adverse effects (Javadzadeh et al., 2011). The double-blind placebo-controlled study of methotrexate-loaded niosomal vesicles in chitosan gel on healthy human volunteers and psoriasis patients carried out and its efficacy compared with marketed methotrexate gel. The irritation and skin sensitivity of formulations were assessed via human repeated insult patch test (HRIPT). The HRIPT method did not yield any significant sensitization or irritation on healthy human volunteers. The severity of the lesions of psoriasis was assessed via Psoriasis Area Severity Index (PASI). The global score used to assess the outcome of therapy (on a scale of 0-5), where score of 5 indicates the worsening of lesion and score 0 indicates complete clearance of lesion. There was a three times reduction in PASI scores after 12 weeks of niosomal methotrexate gel. The results of study offer niosomal formulation of methotrexate for dermal treatment of psoriasis due to its better clinical efficacy, tolerability and patient compliance (Lakshmi et al., 2007). Urea is an emollient topically used for the non-surgical removal of dystrophic nails in cases of fungal infections for decades and used as a penetration enhancer for the topical corticosteroid treatment of hyperkeratotic psoriatic plaques (Draelos, 2008). Urea may increase ability of skin to retain water due to hygroscopic effect. The same group in another study encapsulated urea into niosomes and prepared a gel using chitosan polymer, to test the same on healthy human volunteers to check the irritation on the skin and to study its clinical effectives on psoriasis patients. Niosomes prepared using span 60 showed a better entrapment than other spans. Better diffusion of drug through the human skin and skin drug deposition were concluded from niosomal gel in comparison to plain gel. The niosomal urea gel and plain gel did not produce any irritation of the human skin. The gels were assessed on psoriasis patients with less than 25% severity of any types of psoriasis. The niosomal gel showed a significant decrease in the lesion ($p<0.05$) than plain urea gel. It is suggested that chitosan gel can be used as an adjuvant in the treatment of psoriasis due to antifungal and anti-inflammatory effect of chitosan that supported the action of urea (Lakshmi et al., 2011).

## 5.3. WHITENING EFFECT

The attractiveness of pigment-lightening cosmeceuticals comes from the desire to not only fade pigmentation but also to even lighten skin tone (Choi et al., 2006). N-acetyl glucosamine (NAG), which is an amino sugar that occurs widely in nature and essential component of dermal tissues, is well-known for its role as a precursor of hyaluronic acid, a key structural composition of skin. NAG shown to inhibit melanin production in melanocyte culture, thus has a potential to reduce hyperpigmentation by topical administration (Bissett et al., 2007). To improve NAG penetration into the skin Shatalebi et al. encapsulated it into niosomes and investigated its flux across excised rat skin using Franz diffusion cells. All formulations significantly enhanced the drug localization in the skin, as compared to NAG hydroalcoholic solution. Application of negatively charged dicetyl phosphate was suggested the reason for relatively high amount of entrapment of the very water soluble NAG. This study showed the potential of niosomes for improved NAG localization in the skin, as needed in hyperpigmentation disorders (Shatalebi et al., 2010). Ellagic acid, a polyphenol widely found in plants such as pomegranates, inhibits tyrosinase by its copper chelation. It may selectively inhibit melanin synthesis only in UV-activated melanocytes (Choi et al., 2006). A niosomal formulation of ellagic acid was developed from the mixture of Span 60 and Tween 60 for its dermal delivery. Skin distribution study revealed that the ellagic acid-loaded niosomes showed more efficient delivery of ellagic acid through human epidermis and dermis than ellagic acid solution. The results pointed out that the Span 60 and Tween 60 niosomes may be a potential carrier for dermal delivery of ellagic acid (Junyaprasert et al., 2011).

## 5.4. VITILIGO

Vitiligo is an acquired idiopathic, dermatological disorder described by well-circumscribed milky white macules in which melanocytes in the skin are damaged. Although vitiligo is not a life threatening issue but it might have an important negative impaction on the quality of life, even leading to attempted suicide in some cases (Nogueira et al., 2009; Bhawna et al., 2010). Application of novel dermal drug delivery systems can play a key role in vitiligo treatment because side-effects or poor efficacy of conventional topical dosage forms affect their utility and patient compliance (Bhawna et al., 2010). Human tyrosinase gene is responsible for the production of tyrosinase, an enzyme implicates in melanogenesis. The defect of tyrosinase gene is one of the reasons for depigmented skin or vitiligo (Zhang et al., 2005; Kingo et al., 2007). Manosroi et al. prepared elastic cationic niosomes (Tween 61/Cholesterol/ dimethyl dioctadecyl ammonium bromide at 1:1:0.5 molar ratio) for the effective dermal delivery of pMEL34 (tyrosinase encoding plasmid). Percutaneous absorption of formulation was investigated through exercised rat skin by Franz diffusion cells during 6 hours. The flux of pMEL34-loaded elastic niosomes was more than non-elastic niosomes in viable epidermis and dermis, while only pMEL34 loaded in elastic cationic noisome was observed in the receiver solution. By application of pMEL34-loaded elastic cationic niosomes in melanoma cell lines showed about four times higher tyrosinase gene expression than the free and the loaded plasmid in nonelastic niosomes means higher tyrosinase activity for efficient topical delivery in vitiligo therapy (Manosroi et al., 2010). In another study, luciferase plasmid (pLuc) was encapsulated in non-elastic and elastic cationic nanovesicles (niosomes and liposomes) and its transdermal absorption was investigated through rat skin follow by stratum corneum stripping or iontophoresis techniques. Free pLuc with or without the stratum corneum stripping and iontophoresis techniques and pLuc-loaded in nonelastic vesicles without the application techniques could not penetrate skin. Though, the elastic vesicles even without any application techniques can increase the transdermal absorption of pLuc. In case of elastic vesicles, the pLuc-loaded niosomes provided higher pLuc flux than that in liposomes. After 6 hours, pLuc encapsulated in nanovesicles with the iontophoresis application was still intact, but the free pLuc was degraded. Result of this study has showed the superior delivery of pLuc thorough skin by loading in niosomes, together with the application of iontophoresis, which can be used as a novel method to deliver genetic materials via dermal administration in gene therapy. Specifically, elastic cationic niosomes appeared to be a more promising approach since no additional equipment is required (Manosroi et al., 2009). Both mentioned studies demonstrated the potential application of elastic cationic niosomes as an efficient topical delivery for the purpose of gene therapy.

## 5.5. CUTANEOUS INFLAMMATION

### 5.5.1. NON - STEROIDAL ANTI-INFLAMMATORY DRUGS (NSAIDS)

Celecoxib, a selective COX–2 inhibitor and most commonly used drug in the treatment of arthritis was embedded in niosomal gel for the purpose of sustained and site-specific delivery. In vitro, ex-vivo and in vivo studies were carried out through albino rats to compare the efficiency of formulation with carbopol gel as control formulation. Niosomal gel showed 6.5 times higher drug deposition in deep skin layer and muscle compare with carbopol gel indicating better drug localization with niosomal gel. A significant reduction of rat paw edema was resulted after administration of niosomal formulation compared to that after application of conventional gel confirming better skin permeation and deposition of celecoxib from niosomes. The authors concluded that niosomal gel formulation has great potential for improving site specific delivery, skin accumulation and prolonging release of celecoxib (Kaur et al., 2007). Multilamellar liposomes and niosomes of aceclofenac, a potent analgesic, anti-pyretic and anti-inflammatory agent were prepared and a comparative study was done between them through evaluation of entrapment efficiency, particle size, shape, differential scanning calorimetry, in vitro drug release and 3 months stability study. Results proved that niosomes have better stability than liposomes. Both vesicular systems showed considerable sustained anti-inflammatory activity compared with the commercial product, however niosomes being superior to liposomes as clearly showed by both oedema rate and inhibition rate percentages assessed by the rat paw oedema technique (Nasr et al., 2008). Proniosomal formulation of gugulipid (anti-inflamatory agent) was fabricated and characterized through in vitro drug release study and invivo anti-inflammatory activity via carrageenan-induced rat hind-paw method. In vitro study of proniosomal gel throught semi-permeable membrane exhibit the initial faster release followed by slow sustained release of gugulipid for 8 h. Gugulipid incoporated proniosomal gel showed good anti-inflammatory activity but not as good as commercial product diclofenac (Voveran® Emulgel). The authors state that proniosome formulation improve anti-inflammatory activity of gugulipids comparable to topical NSAIDs (Goyal et al., 2011). A niosome based transdermal drug delivery of nimesulide was prepared by lipid film hydration technique using different nonionic surfactants, Tweens® and Spans® and optimized for highest percent drug entrapment. Formulations were extensively characterized and evaluated in-vitro performance followed by in-vivo evaluation in rats by carrageenan induced rat paw edema method. The results were compared with plain drug gel, niosomally entrapment drug in carbopol gel base and marketed formulation. The percentage of edema inhibition was the highest for niosomal nimesulide gel after 24 hours more than five and three times than plain drug gel and market formulation, respectively. The results of this research suggest that niosomal formulation can offer consistent and prolonged anti-inflammatory effect and may improve therapeutic index of the formulation and is also expected to minimize the side effect due to drug localization at the site of action (Shahiwala et al., 2002).

### 5.5.2. GLUCOCORTICOSTEROIDS

Topical corticosteroids are administered for the variety of dermatological disorders. Application of corticosteroid in proper carrier may help to prolonged action, subsequently less frequent administration and reduction of adverse effects. In a study, clobetasol propionate, a potent corticosteroid acts as an anti-inflammatory and anti-pruritic, was loaded in niosomal gel and its performance was compare with marketed gel and pure drug in term of in vitro drug release and in vivo pharmacodynamic studies. The results showed that the niosomal gel formulation provided a prolonged action due to the entrapment of clobetasol in vesicles (Lingan et al., 2011).

### 5.5.3. ANTIHISTAMINES

Hence antihistamines are frequently administered as first line treatment to reduce the symptoms of urticaria pigmentosa because histamine is the single most important mediator involved (Osvaldo et al., 2010). The conventional oral administration of hydroxyzine hydrochloride (an antihistamine) causes CNS sedation, dry mouth and tachycardia whereas topical use in the form of semisolid dosage forms would lead to systemic side effects (Elzainy et al., 2003). A modified proniosomal gel of hydroxyzine hydrochloride was prepared by coacervation phase separation technique with different combination of non-ionic surfactants (Tweens and Spans) with phospholipids. Statistical experimental design was applied to optimize the various formulation variables. The optimized formulations were evaluated in vitro, ex vivo permeation, skin deposition, skin irritation and stability studies. The three months stability at refrigeration temperature and quite high encapsulation efficiency (95%) and drug deposition in the stratum corneum in 24 h (90%) were found for optimized formulation. The results indicated that modified proniosomal formulations of hydroxyzine hydrochloride were appropriate for topical drug delivery system for the treatment of localized urticarial (Rita et al., 2012). This formulation potentially improves drug penetration into the stratum corneum and localizes the drug within the dermoepidermal layers which would offer prompt onset and prolonged duration of action due to maintenance of effective concentrations in the skin, while systemic serum concentrations would be low (Carafa et al., 1998; Kirjavainen et al., 1999; Elzainy et al., 2003). Chlorpheniramine maleate is one of the most commonly used antihistamines and topically administered for skin disorders such as sunburns, urticaria, angioedema, pruritus, and insect bites. The proniosomes containing Span 40/lecithin/cholestrol formulated by ethanol showed optimum stability, loading efficiency, and particle size and appropriate release kinetic for percutaneous delivery of chlorpheniramine maleate. Ease of preparation and use of proniosomes were introduced as the greatest advantages provided by these types of dosage forms (Varshosaz et al., 2005).

## 5.6. HAIR LOSS - ALOPECIA

The pilosebaceous unit including sebaceous gland, hair follicle and hair shaft has a unique biochemistry, metabolism and immunology. Targeted drug delivery may improve current therapeutic approaches to treat diseases of follicular origin (Weiner, 1998). In an increasing amount of topical studies, niosomes have been revealed to target drug delivery to the pilosebaceous unit. Androgenic alopecia (male pattern hair loss) is the most common reason of hair loss in men and characterized by the progressive hair thinning in genetically susceptible men (Jung et al., 2006). Semi-purified fraction of Oryza sativa contains the unsaturated fatty acids such as gamma-linolenic acid, linoleic acid and oleic acid have been proved to have anti-hair loss activity by inhibition of 5a-reductase type 1 (a key enzyme of androgenic alopecia) in DU-145 cell lines (Ruksiriwanich et al., 2011). Manosroi et al. prepared cationic niosomes (for higher stability) encapsulated with this extract and investigated physicochemical characteristics and transfollicular penetration of niosomes through porcine skin using follicular closing technique by Franz diffusion cells. The result of

this study confirmed efficient transfollicular delivery of unsaturated fatty acids using cationic niosomes as well as the advantage of low systemic effect than the neutral niosomes (Manosroi et al., 2012). Thai Lanna medicinal plants have been reported to improve hair growth and reduce hair loss owing to increase the blood circulation, anti-fungal, anti-bacterial, and anti-oxidation of the hair roots. But, the extracts of these plants are naturally not stable and are problematic to be absorbed through hair follicles. Niosomal formulation containing the Thai Lanna plant extracts, such as turmeric, chili, ginger and Tong-Pan-Chang extract incorporated in gel was fabricated and tested in 20 human volunteers (9 males and 11 females). Results showed a significant increase in hair density and a decrease in hair loss without any irritation in all subjects from the 8-week application ($p<0.01$) in non-heredity alopecia volunteers, with non-differences in male and female volunteers. This in vivo study confirms potential of niosomes carrier for topical application of Thai Lanna medicinal plants for anti-hair loss (Manosroi et al., 2008). The enzyme 5a-reductase, responsible for production of dihydrotestosterone from testosterone in hair follicles, which is supposed to be the reason of androgenetic alopecia, can be inhibited by finasteride. Finasteride shows several unwanted systemic adverse effects which will be reduced if it acts locally in the hair follicles

(Javadzadeh et al., 2010). Tabbakhian et al. studied dermal application of finasteride-containing vesicles (niosomes and liposomes) for increasing drug concentration at the pilosebaceous units, as compared with finasteride hydroalcoholic solution. Both in vitro permeation of 3H-finasteride through hamster flank skin and in vivo deposition studies in hamster ear demonstrated the potentials of liquid-state niosomes and liposomes for successful delivery of finasteride to the pilosebaceous units compared with hydroalcoholic solution while optimized niosomal formulation also showed higher targeting ration than liposomal vesicles (Tabbakhian et al., 2006). Minoxidil, the most commonly used medicine for the treatment of androgenic alopecia with unknown mechanism of action on hair follicles (Messenger et al., 2004) were encapsulated into noisome and liposome vesicles. The percutaneous absorption study was carried out in vitro using vertical diffusion Franz cells using human skin and the results compared with dissolved minoxidil in propylene glycol–water–ethanol solution as a control. Although penetration of niosomal minoxidil in epidermal and dermal layers was greater than control solution but lower than liposomal formulations. These differences suggested to be attributed to the smaller size and the greater potential targeting to skin and skin appendages of liposomal carriers, which enhanced globally the skin drug delivery. This work generally suggests that niosomes and liposomes have a proper potential for drug dermal targeting and could be considered as a reasonable and practicable therapeutic approach to skin diseases such as hair loss (Mura et al., 2007). In a another study the effects of niosomal minoxidil formulation on the drug penetration in hairless mouse skin were investigated by in vitro permeation experiments, and the results compared with control minoxidil hydroalcoholic solution and a leading commercial topical formulation "Minoxyl™" containing 5% minoxidil and 1% dexpentanol. The result of study showed niosomal formulations increased the percentage of dose accumulated in the skin (1.03±0.18 to 19.41±4.04%) compared with control and commercial formulations (0.48±0.17 and 0.11±0.03 %, respectively). Physical stability of niosomal formulations which was evaluated for three month at refrigerator temperature (2–8 °C) have shown a fairly high retention of minoxidil inside the vesicles (80%). The authors finally proposed that these niosomal formulations could be used as a feasible cargo carrier for the dermal delivery of minoxidil and promising approach in treatment alopecia (Balakrishnan et al., 2009). Recently minoxidil-loaded niosomes were prepared with series of surfactant and cholesterol in different molar ratio by ethanol injection method. Surfactant screening exhibited that only Span 20, Span 60 and Tween 20 with cholesterol have ability of nano size vesicle formation and Span 60 was shown to be a better surfactant for niosomal stable form with maximum entrapment efficiency (31.27±1.5 %) and minimal particle size (approx. 219 nm). The in vitro skin permeation and deposition study of minoxidil-loaded niosomal gel formulation prepared with 1:2 ratio of Span 60 and cholesterol showed significant improvement in skin accumulation (more than eightfold) as compared with plain minoxidil gel (17.21±3.2 and 2.26±1.3 %, respectively). Result of study demonstrates an increase in cholesterol concentration in niosome vesicles enhance minoxidil skin retention and effect on entrapment efficiency as well as size of niosomes to better cutaneous treatment. It was also concluded that the developed niosomal formulation could be a suitable option for cutaneous targeting of minoxidil (Mali et al., 2012).

## 5.7. ACNE

Acne is the most common skin disease of multifactorial origin with an incidence of 70 - 80% in adolescence. While topical therapy has an important role in acne treatment, side effects associated with several topical antiacne agents affect their efficacy and patient satisfaction. Niosomes, capable of great features for skin administration, can play an essential role in improving the dermal delivery of antiacne agents by increasing their topical localization with an associated reduction in their adverse effects (Maibach et al., 2005). Benzoyl peroxide is a macrolide antibiotic generally applied for the management of acne either alone or in combination with other antiacne agents. Dermal administration of benzoyl peroxide causes side effects such as skin redness, itching, irritation and edema which lead to discomfort and ignorance of therapy and outcomes in no profit or emergence of resistant to microorganisms. In a study, niosomal benzoyl peroxide incorporated into HPMC gel designed and optimized by partial factorial design. Ex vivo release study on human cadaver skin showed increase in drug skin retention, extended drug release and improved permeation of drug across the skin which in turn will reduce the toxicity of drug and enhance the therapeutic efficacy (Vyas et al., 2011). Gallidermin is mainly promising for the dermal and cosmetic treatment of acne in human medicines because of its greatly active against *Propionibacterium acnes* and treatment of multidrug resistant*Staphylococcus Aureus* strains, which is a snowballing problem especially in the hospitals (Kempf et al., 1999). Gallidermin has limited absorption through skin and chemical instability due to its large molecular structure and peptide nature, respectively (Manosroi et al., 2005). Anionic niosomal gallidermin composed of tween 61/cholesterol /dicetylphosphate prepared and antibacterial activity of formulations against *Propionibacterium acnes* and *Staphylococcus Aureus* assayed with macrodilution method to determine the minimal concentration of the sample necessary to inhibit or kill the microorganisms. Result of study demonstrates gallidermin loaded in niosomes offered lower antibacterial activity against tested microeorganisms compare with unloaded gallidermin due to the niosomes protecting role and making a sustained release of drug. Niosomal furmulation of gallidermin in gel showed more chemically stable at high temperatures and two fold higher cumulative amounts in viable epidermis and dermis of rat skin than aqueous solution of gallidermin. This study suggests that anionic niosomes of gallidermin can be considered as a superior topical antibacterial formulation because of chemical stability and high skin localization with no threat of systemic effect (Manosroi et al., 2010). Trans-retinoic acid or tretinoin, a vitamin A metabolite, is widely used in the topical treatment of various skin diseases such as acne, psoriasis and photoaging. But, high chemical instability and skin irritation strongly limited its administration for topical delivery (Ridolfi et al., 2011). Transdermal delivery of tretinoin-loaded niosomal and liposomal formulation was studied through the newborn pig skin using Franz diffusion cells and compared with commercial formulation (RetinA®). The effect of charge on the performance niosomes was studied by the preparation of niosomes with either stearylamine and dicetylphosphate as a positive and negative charge inducer, respectively. Small unilamellar negatively charged niosomal formulations saturated with tretinoin showed more upper cutaneous drug retention than both commercial and liposomal formulation. Result of this study demonstrates cutaneous delivery of tretinoin is powerfully affected by vesicle morphology, composition and thermodynamic activity of the drug (Manconi et al., 2006). The ability of niosomes as topical carriers capable of improving the stability of photosensitive drugs was studied by comparing the chemical stability of tretinoin in methanol and in vesicular suspensions exposed both to UV and artificial daylight conditions. Liposomes were also prepared and compared with niosomes. In order to evaluate the influence of vesicle structure on the photostability of tretinoin, tretinoin-loaded vesicles were prepared by the film hydration method, extrusion technique and sonication. Methanol dissolved tretinoin degraded immediately after UV irradiation while the loaded drug into vesicles showed a considerable reduction of the photodegradation process. The photoprotection provided by vesicles varied depending on the vesicle structure and composition. In addition, unilamellar vesicles showed a higher protection of tretinoin than the multilamellar ones. Unilamellar niosomes made from Brij®30 were the formulations with the highest protection of tretinoin (Manconi et al., 2003). In another study, the antiacne activity of the mixture of aromatic volatile oil extracted from Thai medicinal plants enhanced with encapsulating into nano sized niosomal vesicles (Manosroi et al., 2008). Slow penetration of drug through skin is the main disadvantage of transdermal route of delivery. An increase in the penetration rate has been achieved by transdermal delivery of erythromycin incorporated in niosomes for acne therapy (Jayaraman et al., 1996).

## 6. CONCLUSION

Niosomal drug delivery systems have been demonstrated to be promising controlled drug delivery systems for percutaneous administration. Niosomes also offer successful drug localization in skin which are relatively non-toxic and stable. This advantage of niosomes has the potential of strengthening the efficacy of the drug accompanying with reducing its adverse effects associated with drug systemic absorption. Drug-associated challenges such as physical and chemical instability is also can be protected by vesicular carriers. Niosomes appeared to be a well preferred drug delivery system over liposome as niosomes being stable and cost-effective. Hence, many topical drugs may be developed using niosomal systems. But there are still some challenges in this area. Although some new approaches have been developed to overcome the problem of drug loading, it is still remain to be addressed. The researchers should be more alert in the selection of suitable surfactant for noisome preparation due to this fact that the type of surfactant is the main parameter affecting the formation of the vesicles, their toxicity and stability.

## REFERENCES


1. A. Abd-Elbary, H. M. El-laithy, M. I. Tadros, 2008Sucrose stearate-based proniosome-derived niosomes for the nebulisable delivery of cromolyn sodium.Int J Pharm, 3571-21891980378-5173

2. H. Abdelkader, S. Ismail, A. Hussein, Z. Wu, R. Al-Kassas, R. G. Alany, 2012Conjunctival and corneal tolerability assessment of ocular naltrexone niosomes and their ingredients on the hen's egg chorioallantoic membrane and excised bovine cornea modelsInt J Pharm, 4321-21100378-5173

3. H. Abdelkader, Z. Wu, R. Al-Kassas, R. G. Alany, 2012Niosomes and discomes for ocular delivery of naltrexone hydrochloride: morphological, rheological, spreading properties and photo-protective effectsInt J Pharm, 4331-21421480378-5173

4. R. Agarwal, O. P. Katare, S. P. Vyas, 2001Preparation and in vitro evaluation of liposomal/niosomal delivery systems for antipsoriatic drug dithranolInt J Pharm, 228143520378-5173

5. D. Akhilesh, G. Hazel, J. V. Kamath, 2011Proniosomes- A propitious provesicular drug carrier International Journal of Pharmacy and Pharmaceutical Science Research, 13981032249-0337

6. A. Azeem, M. K. Anwer, S. Talegaonkar, 2009Niosomes in sustained and targeted drug delivery: some recent advancesJ Drug Target, 1796716890106-1186X.

7. M. N. Azmin, A. T. Florence, R. M. Handjani-Vila, 1985The effect of non-ionic surfactant vesicle (niosome) entrapment on the absorption and distribution of methotrexate in mice.J Pharm Pharmacol, 3742372420022-3573

8. A. J. Baillie, G. H. Coombs, T. F. Dolan, J. Laurie, 1986Non-ionic surfactant vesicles, niosomes, as a delivery system for the anti-leishmanial drug, sodium stibogluconate. J Pharm Pharmacol,3875025050022-3573

9. P. Balakrishnan, S. Shanmugam, W. S. Lee, W. M. Lee, J. O. Kim, D. H. Oh, D. D. Kim, J. S. Kim, B. K. Yoo, H. G. Choi,

2009Formulation and in vitro assessment of minoxidil niosomes for enhanced skin deliveryInt J Pharm, 3771180378-5173

10. B. W. Barry, 1991Lipid-Protein-Partitioning theory of skin penetration enhancementJ Control Release, 1532372480168-3659

11. Z. S. Bayindir, N. Yuksel, 2010Characterization of niosomes prepared with various nonionic surfactants for paclitaxel oral deliveryJ Pharm Sci, 994204920601520-6017

12. G. Bhawna, S. Abir, B. Amit, K. Om, 2010Topical treatment in vitiligo and the potential uses of new drug delivery systemsIndian J Dermatol Venereol Leprol, 760378-6323

13. D. L. Bissett, L. R. Robinson, P. S. Raleigh, K. Miyamoto, T. Hakozaki, J. Li, G. R. Kelm, 2007Reduction in the appearance of facial hyperpigmentation by topical N-acetyl glucosamine. J Cosmet Dermatol, 6120261473-2165

14. M. B. Brown, G. P. Martin, S. A. Jones, F. K. Akomeah, 2006Dermal and transdermal drug delivery systems: current and future prospectsDrug Deliv, 1331751871071-7544

15. M. Carafa, E. Santucci, F. Alhaique, T. Coviello, E. Murtas, F. Riccieri, G. Lucania, M. R. Torrisi, 1998Preparation and properties of new unilamellar non-ionic/ionic surfactant vesiclesInt J Pharm, 160151590378-5173

16. M. Carafa, E. Santucci, G. Lucania, 2002Lidocaine-loaded non-ionic surfactant vesicles: characterization and in vitro permeation studies.Int J Pharm, 231121320378-5173

17. G. Cevc, 1996Transfersomes, liposomes and other lipid suspensions on the skin: permeation enhancement, vesicle penetration, and transdermal drug delivery. Crit Rev Ther Drug Carrier Syst, 133-42570743-4863

18. G. Cevc, G. Blume, A. Schätzlein, D. Gebauer, A. Paul, 1996The skin: a pathway for systemic treatment with patches and lipid-based agent carriersAdv Drug Deliv Rev, 1833493780016-9409X.

19. C. M. Choi, D. S. Berson, 2006Cosmeceuticals. Semin Cutan Med Surg, 251631681085-5629

20. T. R. Desai, W. H. Finlay, 2002Nebulization of niosomal all-trans-retinoic acid: An inexpensive alternative to conventional liposomes.Int J Pharm, 24123113170378-5173

21. Z. D. Draelos, 2008New channels for old cosmeceuticals: aquaporin modulationJournal of cosmetic dermatology7283831473-2165

22. A. Dubey, P. Prabhu, J. Kamath, 2012Nano Structured lipid carriers: A Novel Topical drug delivery system. Int J PharmTech Res, 427057140000-0974

23. V. Dubey, D. Mishra, T. Dutta, M. Nahar, D. K. Saraf, N. K. Jain, 2007Dermal and transdermal delivery of an anti-psoriatic agent via ethanolic liposomesJ Control Release, 12321481540168-3659

24. A. A. W. Elzainy, X. Gu, F. E. R. Simons, K. J. Simons, 2003Hydroxyzine from topical phospholipid liposomal formulations: Evaluation of peripheral antihistaminic activity and systemic absorption in a rabbit model. The AAPS Journal, 544148

25. J. Y. Fang, C. T. Hong, W. T. Chiu, Y. Y. Wang, 2001Effect of liposomes and niosomes on skin permeation of enoxacin. Int J Pharm, 2191-261720000-0378

26. P. U. M. Firthouse, S. M. Halith, S. U. Wahab, M. Sirajudeen, S. K. Mohideen, 2011Formulation and evaluation of miconazole niosomesInt J PharmTech Res, 32101910220974-4304

27. M. Gašperlin, M. Gosenca, 2011Main approaches for delivering antioxidant vitamins through the skin to prevent skin ageingExpert Opin Drug Del, 879059191742-5247

28. T. Ghafourian, P. Zandasrar, H. Hamishekar, A. Nokhodchi, 2004The effect of penetration enhancers on drug delivery through skin: a QSAR studyJ Control Release, 9911131250168-3659

29. D. Gopinath, D. Ravi, B. R. Rao, S. S. Apte, D. Renuka, D. Rambhau, 2004Ascorbyl palmitate vesicles (Aspasomes): formation, characterization and applications.Int J Pharm, 2711-2951130378-5173

30. C. Goyal, M. Ahuja, S. K. Sharma, 2011Preparation and evaluation of anti-inflammatory activity of gugulipid-loaded proniosomal gel.Acta Pol Pharm, 6811471500001-6837

31. R. M. Handjani-Vila, A. Ribier, B. Rondot, G. Vanlerberghe, 1979Dispersions of lamellar phases of non-ionic lipids in cosmetic products.Int J Cosmetic Sci, 1303314

32. K. Higaki, K. Nakayama, T. Suyama, C. Amnuaikit, K. Ogawara, T. Kimura, 2005Enhancement of topical delivery of drugs via direct penetration by reducing blood flow rate in skin.Int J Pharm, 28822272330378-5173

33. H. Hofland, J. A. Bowuwstra, M. Ponec, H. E. Boddé, F. Spies, Verhoef. J. Coos, H. E. Junginger, 1991Interactions of non-ionic surfactant vesicles with cultured keratinocytes and human skin in vitro: a survey of toxicological aspects and ultrastructural changes in stratum corneumJ Control Release, 1611551670168-3659

34. H. E. J. Hofland, J. A. Bouwstra, F. Spies, H. E. Bodde, 1992Safety aspect of nonionic surfactant vesicles- a toxicity study related to the physicochemical characteristics of nonionic surfactants. J Pharm Pharmacol, 442872920022-3573

35. H. E. J. Hofland, R. van der Geest, H. E. Bodde, H. E. Junginger, J. A. Bouwstra, 1994Estradiol permeation from nonionic surfactant vesicles through human stratum corneum in vitroPharm Res, 1156596640000-0724

36. C. Hu, D. G. Rhodes, 2000Proniosomes: a novel drug carrier preparation.Int J Pharm 2061101220378-5173

37. C. P. Jain, S. P. Vyas, V. K. Dixit, 2006Niosomal system for delivery of rifampicin to lymphatics. Indian J Pharm Sci, 6855750025-0474X.

38. Y. Javadzadeh, H. Hamishehkar, 2011Enhancing percutaneous delivery of methotrexate using different types of surfactantsColloid Surface B, 8224224260927-7765

39. Y. Javadzadeh, J. Shokri, S. Hallaj-Nezhadi, H. Hamishehkar, A. Nokhodchi, 2010Enhancement of percutaneous absorption of Finasteride by cosolvents, cosurfactant and surfactantsPharm Dev Technol, 1566196251083-7450

40. S. C. Jayaraman, C. Ramachandran, N. Weiner, 1996Topical delivery of erythromycin from various formulations: An in vivo hairless mouse studyJ Pharm Sci, 8510108210841520-6017

41. S. Jung, N. Otberg, G. Thiede, H. Richter, W. Sterry, S. Panzner, J. Lademann, 2006Innovative liposomes as a transfollicular drug delivery system: penetration into porcine hair follicles.J Invest Dermatol, 1268172817320002-2202X.

42. V. B. Junyaprasert, P. Singhsa, J. Suksiriworapong, D. Chantasart, 2011Physicochemical properties and skin permeation of span 60/tween 60 niosomes of ellagic acid. Int J Pharm, Vol. doi:10.1016/j.ijpharm.2011.11.032,0000-037803785173

43. K. Kaur, S. Jain, B. Sapra, A. K. Tiwary, 2007Niosomal gel for site-specific sustained delivery of anti-arthritic drug: in vitro-in vivo evaluation.Curr Drug Deliv, 442762821567-2018

44. M. Kempf, U. Theobald, H. P. Fiedler, 1999Economic improvement of the fermentative production of gallidermin by Staphylococcus gallinarumBiotechnol lett, 2186636670141-5492

45. A. Khan, P. K. Sharma, S. Visht, R. Malviya, 2011Niosomes as colloidal drug delivery system: A review. Journal of Chronotherapy and Drug Delivery, 211521

46. K. Kingo, E. Aunin, M. Karelson, M. A. Philips, R. Rätsep, H. Silm, E. Vasar, U. Soomets, S. Kőks, 2007Gene expression analysis of melanocortin system in vitiligoJ Dermatol Sci, 4821131220923-1811

47. M. Kirjavainen, J. Mönkkönen, M. Saukkosaari, R. Valjakka-Koskela, J. Kiesvaara, A. Urtti, 1999Phospholipids affect stratum

corneum lipid bilayer fluidity and drug partitioning into the bilayers.J Control Release, 5822072140168-3659

48. G. P. Kumar, P. R. Rao, 2012Ultra deformable niosomes for improved transdermal drug delivery: The future scenario. Asian Journal of Pharmaceutical Sciences, 72961090974-2441

49. P. K. Lakshmi, S. Bhaskaran, 2011Phase II study of topical niosomal urea gel- an adjuvant in the treatment of psoriasis. International Journal of Pharmaceutical Sciences Review and Research, 71170000-0976X

50. P. K. Lakshmi, G. S. Devi, S. Bhaskaran, S. Sacchidanand, 2007Niosomal methotrexate gel in the treatment of localized psoriasis: Phase I and phase II studiesIndian J Dermatol Venereol Leprol, 7331570378-6323

51. S. Lala, S. Pramanick, S. Mukhopadhyay, S. Bandyopadhyay, M. K. Basu, 2004Harmine: Evaluation of its antileishmanial properties in various vesicular delivery systemsJ Drug Target, 1231651750106-1186X.

52. M. A. Lingan, A. A. H. Sathali, M. R. V. Kumar, A. Gokila, 2011Formulation and evaluation of topical drug delivery system containing clobetasol propionate niosomes. Sci Revs Chem Commun, 11717

53. H. I. Maibach, M. J. Choi, 2005Liposomes and niosomes as topical drug delivery systemsSkin Pharmacol Physiol, 182092191660-5527

54. M. Malhotra, N. K. Jain, 1994Niosomes as drug carriersInd Drugs, 3138186

55. N. Mali, S. Darandale, P. Vavia, 2012Niosomes as a vesicular carrier for topical administration of minoxidil: formulation and in vitro assessment. Drug Deliv Transl Res, 160219-0393X.

56. M. Manconi, C. Sinico, D. Valenti, F. Lai, A. M. Fadda, 2006Niosomes as carriers for tretinoin: III. A study into the in vitro cutaneous delivery of vesicle-incorporated tretinoin.Int J Pharm, 3111-211190378-5173

57. M. Manconi, D. Valenti, C. Sinico, F. Lai, G. Loy, A. M. Fadda, 2003Niosomes as carriers for tretinoin: II. Influence of vesicular incorporation on tretinoin photostability.Int J Pharm, 26022612720378-5173

58. A. Manosroi, P. Khanrin, W. Lohcharoenkal, R. G. Werner, F. Götz, W. Manosroi, J. Manosroi, 2010Transdermal absorption enhancement through rat skin of gallidermin loaded in niosomesInt J Pharm, 39213043100378-5173

59. A. Manosroi, N. Khositsuntiwong, F. Götz, R. G. Werner, J. Manosroi, 2009Transdermal enhancement through rat skin of luciferase plasmid DNA loaded in elastic nanovesiclesJ Liposome Res, 19291980898-2104

60. A. Manosroi, W. Ruksiriwanich, M. Abe, W. Manosroi, J. Manosroi, 2012Transfollicular enhancement of gel containing cationic niosomes loaded with unsaturated fatty acids in rice (Oryza sativa) bran semi-purified fractionEur J Pharm Biopharm, 8123033130939-6411

61. A. Manosroi, T. Sritapunya, P. Jainonthee, J. Manosroi, 2008Anti P. acne activity of cream containing aromatic volatile oil from Thai medicinal plants entrapped in niosomes for acne treatment.

62. A. Manosroi, P. Wongtrakul, J. Manosroi, U. Midorikawa, Y. Hanyu, M. Yuasa, F. Sugawara, H. Sakai, M. Abe, 2005The entrapment of kojic oleate in bilayer vesicles.Int J Pharm, 298113250378-5173

63. J. Manosroi, N. Khositsuntiwong, A. Manosroi, 2008Performance test of gel containing extracts from Thai Lanna medicinal plants entrapped in niosomes for hair loss treatment.

64. J. Manosroi, N. Khositsuntiwong, W. Manosroi, F. Götz, R. G. Werner, . A. Manosroi, 2010Enhancement of transdermal absorption, gene expression and stability of tyrosinase plasmid (pMEL34)-loaded elastic cationic niosomes: Potential application in vitiligo treatment. J Pharm Sci, 998353335411520-6017

65. A. Messenger, J. Rundegren, 2004Minoxidil: mechanisms of action on hair growthBrit J Dermatol, 15021861940007-0963

66. S. Mura, F. Pirot, M. Manconi, F. Falson, A. M. Fadda, 2007Liposomes and niosomes as potential carriers for dermal delivery of minoxidil.J Drug Target, 1521011080106-1186X.

67. M. Nasr, S. Mansour, N. D. Mortada, A. A. Elshamy, 2008Vesicular aceclofenac systems: A comparative study between liposomes and niosomesJ Microencapsul, 2574995120265-2048

68. L. S. Nogueira, P. C. Zancanaro, R. D. Azambuja, 2009[Vitiligo and emotions].An Bras Dermatol, 84141451806-4841

69. M. M. Nounou, L. K. El -Khordagui, N. A. Khalafallah, S. A. Khalil, 2008Liposomal formulation for dermal and transdermal drug delivery: past, present and futureRecent Pat Drug Deliv Formul, 219181872-2113

70. T. Ogiso, N. Niinaka, M. Iwaki, 1996Mechanism for enhancement effect of lipid disperse system on percutaneous absorptionJ Pharm Sci, 8557641520-6017

71. C. Osvaldo, A. F. Duarte, Q. Paula, A. Rosa, D. Luis, 2010Cutaneous mastocytosis: Two pediatric cases treated with topical pimecrolimus. Dermatol Online J, 16581087-2108

72. D. Paolino, R. Muzzalupo, A. Ricciardi, C. Celia, N. Picci, M. Fresta, 2007In vitro and in vivo evaluation of Bola-surfactant containing niosomes for transdermal deliveryBiomed Microdevices, 944214331387-2176

73. A. Pardakhty, J. Varshosaz, A. Roulholamini, 2007In vitro study of polyoxyethylene alkyl ether niosomes for delivery of insulinInt J Pharm, 3281301410378-5173

74. G. Parthasarathi, N. Udupa, P. Umadevi, G. K. Pillai, 1994Niosome encapsulated of vincristine sulfate: Improved anticancer activity with reduced toxicity in mice.J Drug Target, 221731820106-1186X.

75. S. Perrett, M. Golding, W. P. Williams, 1991A simple method for the preparation of liposomes for pharmaceutical application and characterization of liposomes.J Pharm Pharmacol, 431541612042-7158

76. M. Pugeat, M. H. Nicolas, H. Dechaud, M. Elmidani, 1991Combination of cyproterone acetate and natural estrogens in the treatment of hirsutism]. J Gynecol Obst Bior R, 20810570368-2315

77. C. Puglia, F. Bonina, 2012Lipid nanoparticles as novel delivery systems for cosmetics and dermal pharmaceuticalsExpert Opin Drug Del, 944294411742-5247

78. Y. Rahimpour, H. Hamishehkar, 2012Liposomes in cosmeceuticsExpert Opin Drug Del, 944434551742-5247

79. Naresh. R. A. Raja, G. K. Pillai, N. Udupa, G. Chandrashekar, 1994Antiinflammatory activity of niosome encapsulated diclofenac sodium in arthitic rats. Indian J Pharmacol, 2646480253-7613

80. R. Rajera, K. Nagpal, S. K. Singh, D. N. Mishra, 2011Niosomes: A controlled and novel drug delivery system. Bio Pharm Bull, 3479459530000-0918

81. D. M. Ridolfi, P. D. Marcato, G. Z. Justo, L. Cordi, D. Machado, N. Durán, 2011Chitosan-solid lipid nanoparticles as carriers for topical delivery of TretinoinColloid Surface B, 0927-7765

82. B. Rita, P. K. Lakshmi, 2012Preparation and evaluation of modified proniosomal gel for localised urticaria and optimisation by statistical method. Journal of Applied Pharmaceutical Science, 2038591

83. A. Rogerson, J. Cummings, A. T. Florence, 1987Adriamycin-loaded niosomes: drug entrapment, stability and release.J Microencapsul, 443213280265-2048

84. L. Rubio, C. Alonso, O. López, G. Rodríguez, L. Coderch, J. Notario, A. de la Maza, J. L. Parra, 2011Barrier function of intact and impaired skin: percutaneous penetration of caffeine and salicylic acid.Int J Dermatol, 5078818891365-4632

85. K. Ruckmani, B. Jayakar, S. K. Ghosal, 2000Nonionic surfactant vesicles (niosomes) of cytarabine hydrochloride for effective treatment of leukemias: Encapsulation, storage, and in vitro release.Drug Dev Ind Pharm, 2622172220000-0363

86. W. Ruksiriwanich, J. Manosroi, M. Abe, W. Manosroi, A. Manosroi, 2011alpha]-Reductase type 1 inhibition of Oryza sativa bran extract prepared by supercritical carbon dioxide fluid. J Supercrit Fluid, 0896-8446

87. N. O. Sahin, Niosomes as nanocarrier systems. Nanomaterials and nanosystems for biomedical applications20076781

88. A. A. H. Sathali, G. Rajalakshmi, 2010Evaluation of transdermal targeted niosomal drug delivery of terbinafine hydrochlorideInt J PharmTech Res, 23208120890974-4304

89. H. Schreier, J. Bouwstra, 1994Liposomes and niosomes as topical drug carriers: dermal and transdermal drug deliveryJ Control Release, 3011150168-3659

90. A. Shahiwala, A. Misra, 2002Studies in topical application of niosomally entrapped nimesulide.J Pharm Pharm Sci, 532201482-1826

91. M. A. Shatalebi, S. A. Mostafavi, A. Moghaddas, 2010Niosome as a drug carrier for topical delivery of N-acetyl glucosamineRes Pharm Sci, 521071735-5362

92. B. Shi, C. Fang, M. X. You, Y. Y. Pei, 2005Influence of PEG chain length on in vitro drug release and in vivo pharmacokinetics of hydroxycamptothecin (HCPT) loaded PEG-PHDCA niosomes. Chinese Pharmaceutical Journal, 402116431646

93. Y. H. Su, J. Y. Fang, 2008Drug delivery and formulations for the topical treatment of psoriasisExpert Opin Drug Del, 522352491742-5247

94. M. Tabbakhian, N. Tavakoli, M. R. Jaafari, S. Daneshamouz, 2006Enhancement of follicular delivery of finasteride by liposomes and niosomes:: 1. In vitro permeation and in vivo deposition studies using hamster flank and ear models. Int J Pharm, 3231-21100378-5173

95. I. F. Uchegbu, R. Duncan, 1997Niosomes containing N-(2-hydroxypropyl) methacrylamide copolymer-doxorubicin (PK1): effect of method of preparation and choice of surfactant on niosome characteristics and a preliminary study of body distribution. Int J Pharm, 15517170378-5173

96. J. Varshosaz, A. Pardakhty, S. Mohsen, H. Baharanchi, 2005Sorbitan monopalmitate-based proniosomes for transdermal delivery of chlorpheniramine maleateDrug Deliv, 12275821071-7544

97. V. V. Venuganti, O. P. Perumal, Nanosystems for dermal and transdermal drug deliveryIn: Pathak Y, Thassu D, editors. Drug delivery nanoparticles formulation and characterization. New York: Informa Healthcare USA, Inc; 2009126155

98. A. K. Verma, M. Bindal, 2012A review on niosomes: an ultimate controlled and novel drug delivery carrierInt J Nanoparticles 517387

99. J. Vyas, P. Vyas, D. Raval, P. Paghdar, 2090-6064

100. N. Weiner, 1998Targeted follicular delivery of macromolecules via liposomesInt J Pharm, 1621-229380378-5173

101. J. D. Yadav, P. R. Kulkarni, K. A. Vaidya, G. T. Shelke, 2011Niosomes: a review. J Pharm Res, 46326360974-6943

102. H. Yoshida, C. M. Lehr, W. Kok, H. E. Junginger, J. C. Verhoef, J. A. Bouwstra, 1992Niosomes for oral delivery of peptide drugsJ Control Release, 211-31451530168-3659

103. T. Yoshioka, M. Sternberg, M. Moody, A. T. Florence, 1992Niosomes from Span surfactants: Relations between structure and form. J Pharm Pharmacol, 44104410440022-3573

104. X. J. Zhang, J. J. Chen, J. B. Liu, 2005The genetic concept of vitiligo.J Dermatol Sci, 3931371460923-1811

# Chapter 2

# Dual Cross-Linked Carboxymethyl Sago Pulp-Gelatine Complex Coacervates for Sustained Drug Delivery

**Saravanan Muniyandy [1,*], Thenapakiam Sathasivam [1,†], Anand Kumar Veeramachineni [2,†] and Pushpamalar Janarthanan [2,†]**

[1]*School of Pharmacy, Monash University Malaysia, Jalan Lagoon Selatan, Bandar Sunway 47500, Selangor Darul Ehsan, Malaysia*

[2]*School of Science, Monash University Malaysia, Jalan Lagoon Selatan, Bandar Sunway 47500, Selangor Darul Ehsan, Malaysia*

## ABSTRACT

In the present work, we report for the first time the complex coacervation of carboxymethyl sago pulp (CMSP) with gelatine for sustained drug delivery. Toluene saturated with glutaraldehyde and aqueous aluminum chloride was employed as cross-linkers. Measurements of zeta potential confirm neutralization of two oppositely charged colloids due to complexation, which was further supported by infrared spectroscopy. The coacervates encapsulated a model drug ibuprofen and formed microcapsules with a loading of 29%–56% *w/w* and an entrapment efficiency of 85%–93% *w/w*. Fresh coacervates loaded with drug had an average diameter of 10.8 ± 1.93 μm ($n$ = 3 ± s.d.). The coacervates could encapsulate only the micronized form of ibuprofen in the absence of surfactant. Analysis through an optical microscope evidenced the encapsulation of the drug in wet spherical coacervates. Scanning electron microscopy revealed the non-spherical geometry and surface roughness of dried drug-loaded microcapsules. X-ray diffraction, differential scanning calorimetry and thermal analysis confirmed intact and crystalline ibuprofen in the coacervates. Gas chromatography indicated the absence of residual glutaraldehyde in the microcapsules. Dual cross-linked microcapsules exhibited a slower release than mono-cross-linked microcapsules and could sustain the drug release over the period of 6 h following Fickian diffusion.

**Keywords:** complex coacervation; ibuprofen; gelatine; carboxymethyl sago pulp; sustained release; microencapsulation

## 1. INTRODUCTION

One of the most crucial innovations in recent years is the conversion of plant waste into useful products. Sago palm (*Metroxylon sagu*) is found abundantly in Malaysia (particularly in Johor Bharu and Sarawak) and has a rich source of starch that serves as one of the most important food sources for communities across the globe. Carboxymethyl sago pulp (CMSP), a semisynthetic polymer, was synthesized from Malaysian sago biomass and characterized by Pushpamalar *et al.*, 2006 [1,2]. CMSP typically contains [3] sodium carboxymethyl hemicellulose (38%–40%) and sodium carboxymethyl alpha cellulose (23%–25%), along with lignin (28%–30%) and non-starch polysaccharides (3%–5%). Recently, CMSP bead was exploited for colon targeted drug delivery of 5-aminosalicylic acid [4]. These CMSP beads were prepared by ionotropic gelation followed by radiation cross-linking. This method yields larger particles and also need radiation facilities. In addition radiation cross-linking might not suit radiation sensitive materials. In contrast, complex coacervation does not require sophisticated equipment and can produce smaller particles. Hence, in the present work, complex coacervation of CMSP with gelatin is attempted for microencapsulation and sustained drug delivery.

Complex coacervation is one of the oldest and simplest methods [5] of encapsulating drugs for sustained drug delivery. The process is simple and does not require high temperatures or toxic solvents.

Hence, it is also employed in the encapsulation of delicate materials such as protein [6] and human cells [7]. Coacervation refers to a phase separation process, and complex coacervation involves the complexation between two oppositely charged colloids to yield a colloid-rich region that is used to coat the core (drug) particles. Anionic polysaccharides [8], such as acacia, pectin, alginate and carboxymethyl cellulose, were used with cationic protein molecules, such as gelatine, casein, albumin and chitosan, to produce a complex coacervation. The concentration of colloids, physicochemical properties of the drug being encapsulated, cross-linking agents and pH at which coacervation takes places are the most important parameters to obtain the final product [9]. Complex Coacervation also established using oppositely charged polyelectrolytes [10,11] as well as polypeptides [12]. Parameters such as salt concentration, chirality/hydrogen bonding and molecular weight also have a significant effect on complex coacervation [13,14]. Ibuprofen is a non-steroidal anti-inflammatory drug primarily used for relief of symptoms from arthritis, primary dysmenorrhea, fever, and as an analgesic, especially when an inflammatory component is part of the illness [15]. In conventional therapy, frequent administration of ibuprofen is required due to its short biological half-life (1.9 to 2.2 h), which may lead to fluctuation in plasma drug profile. Excessive use of ibuprofen has been related to an increase in hearing loss [16] and an elevated risk of myocardial infarction [17]. The short biological half-life and associated side effects make ibuprofen a suitable candidate for controlled-release formulation.

In the present investigation, ibuprofen is encapsulated in CMSP/gelatine complex coacervates using glutaraldehyde as the cross-linking agent. A few select formulations were also treated with aluminum chloride to sustain the release further. CMSP/gelatine coacervates were characterized by zeta-potential and Fourier-transform infrared spectroscopy (FT-IR) to confirm complex formation. Drug-loaded coacervates were evaluated for loading/entrapment efficiency, particle size/distribution, optical and field emission scanning electron microscopy (FE-SEM), differential scanning calorimetry (DSC), thermogravimetric analysis (TGA), X-ray diffraction (XRD), residual glutaraldehyde and *in vitro* release.

# 2. EXPERIMENTAL SECTION

## 2.1. Materials

Sago biomass was obtained from PPES Sago Industries Sendirian Berhad (Mukah, Dalat, Sarawak, Malaysia). Ibuprofen was purchased from Lianyungang Zhongyi International Trade Co. Ltd. (Lianyungang, China). Gelatine from porcine skin (Type A, 300 bloom strength) was obtained from Sigma-Aldrich (St. Louis, MO, USA). Glutaraldehyde (25% aqueous solution), aluminum chloride, sodium lauryl sulfate (SLS) and other chemicals used in this study were of analytical grade, obtained from HmbG chemicals and Bumi-Pharma Sdn. Bhd. (Balakong, Malaysia).

## 2.2. Preparation of Carboxymethyl Sago Pulp

Carboxymethyl sago pulp (CMSP) with a degree of substitution of 0.4, an intrinsic viscosity of 184 dL/g and a molecular weight of 76,000 g/mol was synthesized from sago biomass using the Williamson ether synthesis, as described in previous publications [1,2,3]. Briefly, 20 g of the sago waste was transferred into a 1000-mL Erlenmeyer flask and suspended in 640 mL of hot distilled water. Four milliliters of glacial acetic acid and 6 g of sodium chlorite were subsequently added. The mixture was later heated at 70 °C for 3 h and then filtered and washed with cold distilled water. The resulted white residue (sago pulp) was dried in the oven to its constant weight.

Five grams of the sago pulp was added into 100 mL of isopropanol and 10 mL of 30% sodium hydroxide. The mixture was stirred for an hour at 160 rpm in a thermo stated water bath with a horizontal shaker (Model SW22, Julabo, Germany). The carboxymethylation reaction was started by adding 3 g of sodium monocholoroacetate to the reaction mixture. Then, the stirring (160 rpm) was continued at 45 °C for 3 h. The mixture was filtered and suspended in 300 mL of methanol overnight and neutralized with glacial acetic acid. The mixture was filtered again and washed thoroughly with 150 mL of ethanol to remove undesirables and was dried in an oven at 60 °C.

## 2.3. Preparation of Micronized Ibuprofen

Micronization of ibuprofen native particles was performed using a modified version of the solvent/anti-solvent precipitation method reported previously [18]. Native ibuprofen was dissolved in isopropanol until saturation. The alcohol solution was added dropwise into 0.5% *w/v* sodium lauryl sulfate (SLS) and was homogenized using an IKA T25 Digital Ultra-Turrax (IKA, Wilmington, DE, USA) at 12,000 rpm for 3 min. Then, the resulting micronized ibuprofen (m-INN) suspension was collected by centrifugation at 15,300 rpm for 20 min and washed several times with distilled water to remove SLS. Finally, m-INN was oven-dried at 35 °C for 24 h and sieved through a 500-µm sieve. Dried m-INN particles were transferred to a glass vial and closed using a rubber cap before being stored in a desiccator.

## 2.4. Encapsulation of m-INN Using CMSP/Gelatine Complex Coacervation

As shown in Table 1, different batches of m-INN-loaded CMSP-gelatine microcapsules were formulated as follows. Aqueous solutions of 2% *w/v* CMSP and gelatine solutions were prepared separately by stirring at 300 rpm using a magnetic stirrer at 45 °C. The pH of the individual solution was adjusted to 5 using 10% *v/v* acetic acid. The required quantity of the m-INN was dispersed throughout the CMSP solution using ultrasonication (Hielscher UIP500hd, Teltow, Germany, 60% amplitude for 4 min). Then, an equal volume of gelatine solution was added and stirred at 300 rpm for 15 min. The pH was adjusted to 3.8 using 1% *v/v* acetic acid to induce complex coacervation. The coacervate was allowed to equilibrate by continuous stirring at 160 rpm, and the mixture was slowly cooled to reach room temperature. Microcapsules were cross-linked by slow addition of toluene saturated with glutaraldehyde (GST) and stirred for 3 h at 5 °C to harden the walls. Then, the cross-linking was quenched by adding 20 mL of 10% *w/v* sodium metabisulfite. The microcapsules were allowed to sediment, and the supernatant was discarded. The sediments were washed with 50 mL of 50%, 75%, and 99% *v/v*isopropyl alcohol and dried at room temperature for 24 h. To further cross-link with aluminum chloride ($AlCl_3$), new batches of A, D and, E were stirred with 200 mL of 5% *w/v* of $AlCl_3$ at 300 rpm for 15 min before washing with isopropanol. Similarly, unloaded coacervates were also prepared without the addition of the m-INN.

**Table 1.** Physicochemical parameters of m-INN loaded CMSP-gelatine microcapsules prepared by complex coacervation.

| Formulation Code | CMSP (g) | Gelatine (g) | m-INN (g) | GST (mL) | Drug Loading (%) ($n = 3 \pm$ s.d.) | | Entrapment Efficiency (%) ($n = 3 \pm$ s.d.) |
|---|---|---|---|---|---|---|---|
| | | | | | Theoretical | Experimental | |
| A | 2 | 2 | 2 | 10 | 33.33 | 29.54 ± 0.71 | 88.62 ± 2.15 |
| B | 2 | 2 | 4 | 10 | 50 | 44.72 ± 4.03 | 89.44 ± 8.06 |
| C | 2 | 2 | 6 | 10 | 60 | 56.09 ± 2.31 | 93.48 ± 3.85 |
| D | 2 | 2 | 2 | 20 | 33.3 | 28.22 ± 0.84 | 84.66 ± 2.53 |
| E | 2 | 2 | 2 | 30 | 33.3 | 30.07 ± 0.55 | 90.21 ± 1.66 |

## 2.5. Drug Loading and Entrapment Efficiency

Approximately 100 mg of samples were placed in 100 mL of 2 N NaOH and stirred for 24 h at room temperature. Then, the samples were filtered using Whatman filter paper, and the amount of ibuprofen was estimated at 264 nm [19] using a Shimadzu UV-visible spectrophotometer (UVmini-1240, Shimadzu, Kyoto, Japan). A known concentration of ibuprofen solution (2 N NaOH) premixed with unloaded coacervates was used as a reference standard. The theoretical percentage of drug loading (*TDL*) was calculated using the following equation.

$$TDL = (Weight\ of\ drug\ added / Weight\ of\ polymers\ and\ drug\ added) \times 100 \quad (1)$$

The percentage of drug entrapment efficiency (*DEE*) was calculated according to the following equation [20].

$$DEE = (Experimental\ drug\ loading / Theoretical\ drug\ loading\ (TDL)) \times 100 \quad (2)$$

## 2.6. Particle Size Analysis and Zeta Potential Measurement

Particle size analysis (Mastersizer 3000, Malvern, UK) was performed on fresh samples, and size distributions were plotted using the Mastersizer 3000 software. Size distribution of native ibuprofen, m-INN and CMSP/gelatine complex coacervates with and without m-INN were measured after 30 s of sonication. An average of three scans was used for size determination. The surface charges of 2% *w/v* CMSP and gelatine at pH 3.8, 5 and 7, along with complex coacervates at pH 3.8, were measured by a Zetasizer (Nano ZS90, Malvern, Worcestershire, UK) using a fold capillary cuvette (Folded Capillary Cell-DTS 1060, Malvern, Worcestershire, UK).

## 2.7. Fourier Transform Infrared Spectroscopy

The infrared spectrums of the samples were measured between 600 and 3800 $cm^{-1}$ in a Varian 640-IR FTIR spectrophotometer (Agilent Technologies, Santa Clara, CA, US) using an attenuated total reflection accessory.

## 2.8. Optical and Field Emission Scanning Electron Microscopy

An optical microscope (Olympus BX50, Tokyo, Japan) was used to obtain images of fresh coacervate and dried samples. A field emission scanning electron microscope (SU8010, Hitachi, Krefeld, Germany) was used to observe surface morphology and the shape of the dried microcapsules. The samples were fixed in stubs using double-faced copper adhesive tape and were coated with a thin layer of platinum using a Q150R S rotary-pumped sputter coating system (Quorum Technologies, East Sussex, UK) before being observed.

## 2.9. X-Ray Diffractometry

An X-ray diffraction apparatus (InXitu BTXII, Olympus, Waltham, MA, USA) was used to obtain the X-ray diffraction patterns of the samples. Each sample was ground to produce particles less than 75 μm in size and homogeneously mixed. Approximately 15 mg of each sample was loaded into the apparatus via the sample spinner assembly, and a 90-

min acquisition produced the diffractograms over a 2θ range. The analysis was performed with a cobalt target X-ray tube operating at 30 kV and 330 μA.

## 2.10. Differential Scanning Calorimetry

Differential scanning calorimetry (DSC) analyses were performed in a temperature range from 25 to 120 °C on a DSC 4000 (Perkin Elmer, Waltham, MA, USA). Approximately 5 mg of each respective sample was weighed and sealed into the aluminum pans. The heating rate was 5 °C/min, and the nitrogen flow rate was 20 mL/min.

## 2.11. Thermogravimetric Analysis

The thermal properties of samples were analyzed on a thermogravimetric analyzer (TGA Q50, TA Instruments, New Castle, DE, USA). Three milligrams of sample was heated at the rate of 25 °C/min up from 20–600 °C under constant nitrogen flow.

## 2.12. In Vitro Release

The *in vitro* release study was performed using 200 mL of phosphate buffer (pH 7.4), as the dissolution medium in a 250-mL flask [19]. The flasks were kept in a water bath shaker (100 rpm and 37.0 ± 0.5 °C) and microcapsules containing the equivalent of 100 mg of ibuprofen were added to the buffer. Five-milliliter aliquots were withdrawn from the flask at different intervals, and the same volume of the fresh phosphate buffer media was replaced. The amount of ibuprofen in the samples was measured at 264 nm using a spectrophotometer (UVmini-1240, Shimadzu, Kyoto, Japan).

## 2.13. Test for Residual Glutaraldehyde

Approximately 0.5 g of each sample was extracted with 10 mL of isopropyl alcohol by vigorous shaking for 24 h. The extract was filtered, and 0.5 μL of filtrate was injected into the chromatographic system column for glutaraldehyde determination [21]. The Clarus 580

GC gas chromatograph model (Perkin Elmer, Waltham, Massachusetts, USA) was equipped with a flame ionization detector and a carbowax column (Carbowax-20M, 10%, 3 m, 1/800, 80/100 meshes). Hydrogen at a flow-rate of 4 mL/min was employed as a carrier gas. The operating temperatures were as follows: detector, 200 °C; and oven, initial 50 °C with 2 min hold time and a ramp of 15 °C/min up to 200 °C.

# 3. RESULTS AND DISCUSSION

## 3.1. Complex Coacervation and m-INN Encapsulation

The pH at which coacervation occurs is a critical point in the encapsulation process by complex coacervation. The coacervates were produced when the pH was adjusted to 3.8 in the CMSP/gelatine mixture. At that point, gelatine has a maximum positive charge, and CMSP has a maximum negative charge. These charges induce complexation followed by phase separation. The attempt to encapsulate native ibuprofen particles failed because the particles were larger than the coacervates. The inclusion of a non-ionic surfactant (Tween 20) in the system was attempted during the coacervation to obtain spherical and less aggregated microcapsules. The presence of Tween 20 produced spherical and small size coacervates. It also formed a protective barrier between the drug particle and coacervate, thus preventing the coalescence of coacervates around the drug particles. To successfully coalesce the coacervates, the native ibuprofen particle size was reduced to produce m-INN. The CMSP-gelatine coacervates were then able to coalesce around the m-INN to form microcapsules only in the absence of surfactant.

As shown in Table 1, the DEE of the batches of microcapsules was 85%–93% *w/w*, indicating good encapsulation efficiency; however, some of the drug was lost during washing and recovery. At a higher drug to polymer ratio (Formulation B and C), the DEE was slightly high; this increase in DEE could be due to the development of multinucleate microcapsules prepared at higher theoretical loading. Normally, higher cross-linking would reduce drug loading due to the drug particles being pushed out of the microcapsules by the closer arrangement of the highly cross-linked polymeric network. In contrast, as seen in Table 1, the higher degree of cross-linking did not significantly change the drug loading. This discrepancy could be due to the poor solubility of ibuprofen at coacervation pH along with the formation of multinucleate microcapsules. In addition, a higher amount of cross-linking agent caused inter-particle cross-linking and produced larger aggregated particles. Glutaraldehyde and aluminum chloride were used as cross-linking agents. Glutaraldehyde and aluminum cross-linked the gelatine and carboxyl group of CMSP in the complex coacervates, respectively. Dual cross-linking might be more beneficial than mono to get prolonged release.

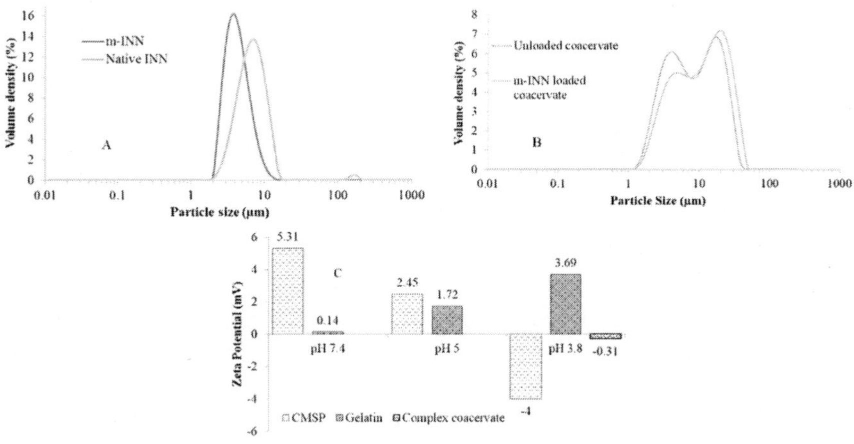


**Figure 1.** (**A**) Particle size distribution (log scale) of native and micronized ibuprofen (INN); (**B**) The size distribution (log scale) of unloaded and drug loaded coacervates; and (**C**) The zeta potential of CMSP, gelatine and complex coacervates.

### 3.2. Particle Size and Zeta Potential Analysis

The micronization of native ibuprofen resulted in size reduction as well as narrow size distribution, as indicated inFigure 1A. The size of the micronized particles was within the range of 1 to 20 µm, whereas the native ibuprofen particles were in the range of 1 to 200 µm. The average sizes of native ibuprofen and micronized ibuprofen particles were 8.88 ± 1.56 µm and 6.67 ± 1.21 µm, respectively ($n$ = 3 ± s.d.). As seen in Figure 1B, the size distribution of the freshly prepared unloaded and ibuprofen loaded complex coacervates is approximately the same. The size distribution of unloaded and 30%*w/w* drug loaded complex coacervate particles were in the range of 1–48 µm and 1–55 µm, respectively, with an average size of 8.25 ± 1.78 and 10.8 ± 1.93 µm, respectively (*n* =3 ± s.d.). As shown in Figure 1B, the drug loading did not affect the size or size distribution. Microcapsules with higher loading (45% and 56% *w/w*) have also produced similar size distributions. This result could be due to the narrow size distribution of the m-INN employed in the encapsulation process. The size distribution of dried microcapsules was discontinued due to particle aggregation, which was difficult to disperse in spite of ultrasonication. To validate the complexation between CMSP and gelatine, the zeta potential of individual colloids at different pH values as well as at the pH of coacervation was recorded and presented in Figure 1C. The zeta potential of CMSP was reduced from 5.31 to −4.00 mV with decreasing pH from 7.4 to 3.8. The initial higher zeta potential is due to the presence of excess sodium counter ions. The zeta potential decreased when pH was adjusted to 3.8 due to neutralization of counter ions and the ionization of carboxylic acid groups (pKa 3.8–4.2) in CMSP [4]. The zeta potential value of gelatine shifts from 0.14 to 3.69 mV with a decrease in pH. At pH 3.8, the net charges of CMSP and gelatine were −4 and 3.69 mV, respectively. The zeta potential of complex coacervates formed at pH 3.8 was −0.31 mV, indicating the presence of charge neutralization due to complexation. The small negative value indicates the presence of excess negative CMSP ions. The neutralization of the charges confirmed formation of a complex between the two colloids. Moreover, an excess of carboxyl groups allows further cross-linking with aluminum chloride.

### 3.3. Fourier Transform Infrared Spectroscopy Studies

The IR spectrum of CMSP showed a broad peak at 3326 $cm^{-1}$ due to the stretching vibration of the –OH group (Figure 2a). The peak at 2897 $cm^{-1}$ is due to C–H stretching vibrations. The presence of a strong absorption band at 1596 $cm^{-1}$confirms the presence of a –$COO^-$ group and acts as evidence of the carboxylation of sago pulp. The bands at 1417 and 1319 $cm^{-1}$ are for $CH_2$ scissors and OH bending vibrations, respectively. The broad bands from 1000 to 1200 $cm^{-1}$ were due to sugar ring absorption [2,22,23,24]. The FT-IR spectrum of gelatine (Figure 2b) shows characteristic peaks at 3297 $cm^{-1}$ due to O–H stretching vibrations. Peaks at 3080, 2963 and 2840 $cm^{-1}$ revealed the amino groups. Other notable peaks in gelatine were at 2963 $cm^{-1}$ (C–H stretching of alkenes), 2846 $cm^{-1}$ (C–H stretching of alkanes), 1637 $cm^{-1}$ (amide-I CO and CN stretching) and 1545 $cm^{-1}$ (amide-II). The peaks observed in gelatine at 1082 and 1017 $cm^{-1}$ are due to the C–O stretching of carboxylic acids and the C–N stretching of amines, respectively [25]. The CMSP has a free carboxyl group that imparts a negative charge to these molecules, whereas gelatine has a positive charge at acidic pH due to the presence of amino groups. Most of the peaks of coacervate resemble the gelatine spectrum. The weak peaks of the free amino group at 2840 $cm^{-1}$ in gelatine disappeared (Figure 2c) in the CMSP/gelatine complex coacervate. A characteristic peak for an amide group in the region of 800–600 $cm^{-1}$ appeared in the complex coacervate (out of the plane, –N–H wagging of primary and secondary amide) and confirmed the formation of the complex due to the reaction between the amino groups of gelatine and the carboxylic group of CMSP. The spectrum of complex coacervates resembles the gelatine-pectin coacervate reported by Saravanan and Rao, 2011 [9]. Moreover, a less intensive peak of a sugar ring appeared at 1040 $cm^{-1}$ in the complex coacervate and indicated the association of CMSP with gelatine. These observations along with zeta potential measurements confirm the complexation of CMSP and gelatine.

The FTIR spectrum of raw ibuprofen (Figure 2d) shows two characteristic bands of medium intensity at 2633 $cm^{-1}$ and 2731 $cm^{-1}$, corresponding to the stretching vibration of the cyclic dimerized hydroxyl groups. The bending –OH absorption at 1231 $cm^{-1}$ reveals free hydroxyl groups, and a peak at 1185 $cm^{-1}$ indicates C–O stretching vibrations. Characteristic peaks at 1710 and 2955 $cm^{-1}$ were observed for C=O and –OH stretching, respectively, for the carboxylic acid group [19] in the ibuprofen. The peaks at 1508, 1462 and 780 $cm^{-1}$ are associated with the vibration in the skeleton of benzene. The multiple spectral lines observed around 3100–2900 $cm^{-1}$ are attributed to C–H stretching vibrations [26]. These characteristic peaks of raw ibuprofen presented in the spectrum of the m-INN (Figure 2e), indicating the intact nature of ibuprofen after micronization. The FTIR spectrum of drug-loaded CMSP-gelatine

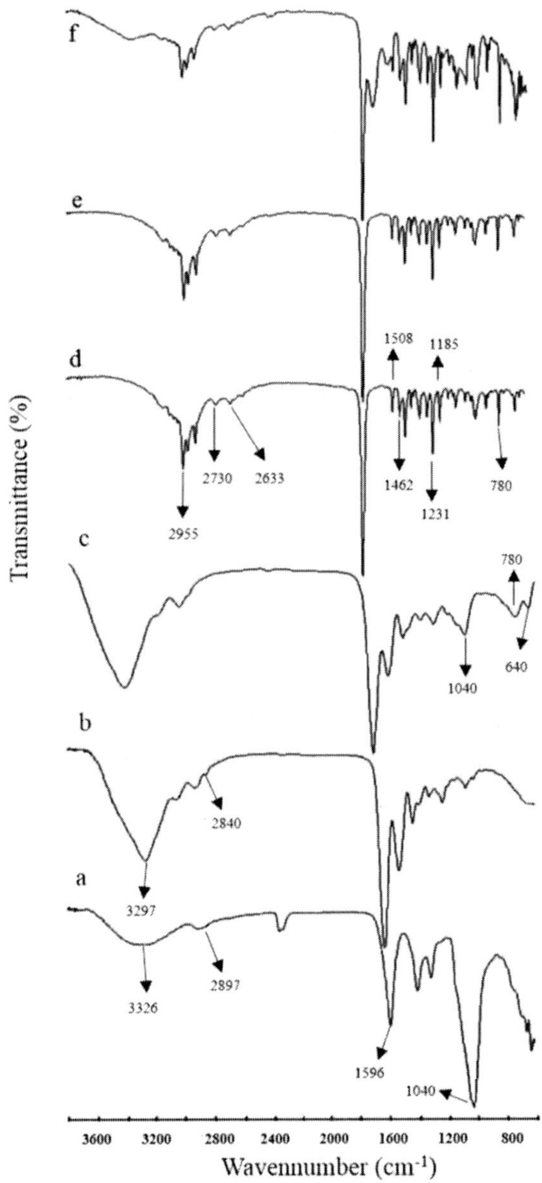


**Figure 2.** FT-IR spectrum of CMSP (a), gelatine (b), CMSP-gelatine complex coacervate (c), native ibuprofen (d), m-INN (e) and 45% m-INN loaded in CMSP-gelatine microcapsules (f).

coacervates (Figure 2f) showed the characteristic peaks of ibuprofen and confirmed successful encapsulation of the drug.

### 3.4. X-Ray Diffractometry

The X-ray diffraction (XRD) patterns of micronized ibuprofen (Figure 3a) showed numerous characteristic sharp and intense peaks at 2°, 16°, 18°, 20° and 22°, revealing a crystalline state of the drug [27]. The XRD of complex coacervates (Figure 3b) did not display any sharp peaks and suggests an amorphous state of the encapsulating material. The peaks of ibuprofen in the XRD of loaded microcapsules (Figure 3c) confirmed the crystalline form of the encapsulated drug. As drug loading increased, the peak intensities also increased (Figure 3c–e) proportionately.

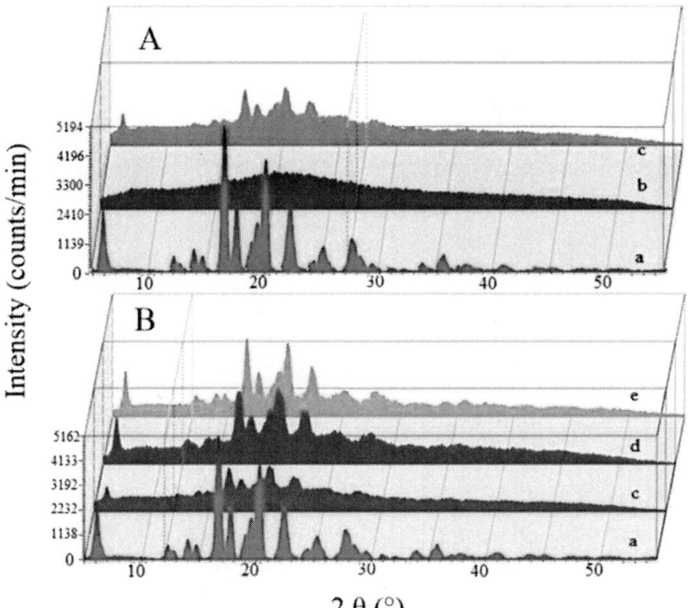


**Figure 3.** X-ray diffractograms of micronized ibuprofen (a), unloaded (b), 30 (c), 45 (d) and 56% *w/w* (e) m-INN-loaded complex coacervate. (**A**) shows crystalline nature of ibuprofen (a) and amorphous nature of unloaded coacervates (b); and (**B**) shows proportional increase in crystalline peak intensity with increasing ibuprofen content.

### 3.5. Differential Scanning Calorimetry

The DSC thermogram of CMSP-gelatine coacervates did not show any definite peaks and revealed its amorphous nature (Figure 4A(a)). The m-INN (Figure 4A(b)) and physical mixture (1:1:1 ratio) of m-INN/CMSP-gelatine (Figure 4A(c)) shows an endothermic peak at ibuprofen's melting point (71.8 °C), indicating the crystalline nature of the drug and absence of a drug-polymer interaction [19]. The drug-loaded coacervate showed a sharp endothermic peak at 72 °C, revealing the crystalline state of ibuprofen. The intensity of this peak proportionally increased (Figure 4B(d–f)) with drug loading. Along with XRD, DSC results confirm the crystalline nature of the intact ibuprofen within the microcapsules.

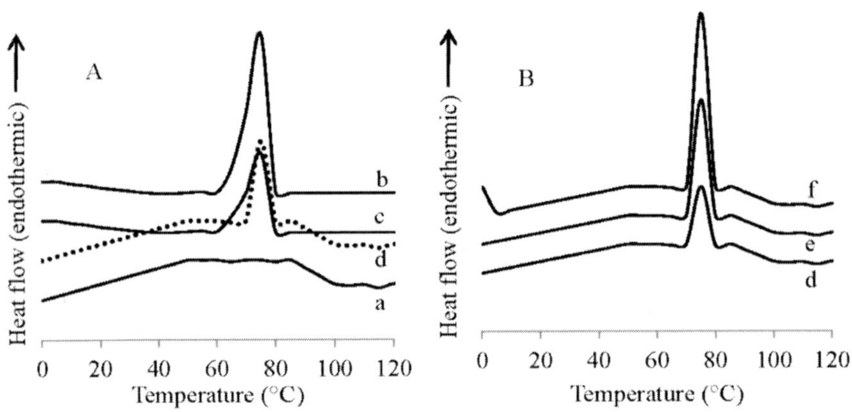


**Figure 4.** DSC thermogram of unloaded complex coacervate (a), m-INN (b), 1:1:1 physical mixture of CMSP: gelatine: m-INN (c), 30 (d), 45 (e) and 56% *w/w* (f) m-INN-loaded complex coacervate. (**A**) represents thermograms of unloaded coacervate (a), m-INN (b), 1:1:1 physical mixture of CMSP: gelatine: m-INN (c) and 30% *w/w* (d) loaded coacervate. (**B**) indicates influence of different drug loading in the intensity of crystalline peak.

### 3.6. Thermogravimetric Analysis

The TGA of CMSP, gelatine and the coacervates are shown in Figure 5a. CMSP has shown a weight loss of 20% at 100–275 °C; this loss in weight is due to loss of moisture. The thermal degradation of CMSP was observed at 275–300 °C, with a 60% weight loss at 600 °C.

Gelatine exhibited degradation over a temperature range of 200–400 °C with a net weight loss of 80%. The complex coacervates followed a similar trend as gelatine; however, a slightly slower degradation was observed between 225 and 300 °C due to complexation. Complex coacervate exhibits less degradation than gelatine and CMC in the range of 20–225 °C. The TGA curve of the m-INN (Figure 5b) shows two stages of degradation. The first stage ranges in temperature between 50 and 150 °C, with a weight loss of 10% that is probably due to absorbed moisture and melting. Later, a thermal degradation from 175 to 250 °C, with a weight loss of 100%, was observed that could be due to sublimation [28]. The TGA curve of the m-INN loaded coacervates showed the combination of the coacervate and drug. A relationship between drug loading and weight loss was observed in the TGA of the microcapsules. At 275 °C, an approximate weight loss of 40%, 50% and 60% were observed in microcapsules loaded with 30%, 45% and 56% *w*/*w* of the m-INN, respectively. The different decreasing slopes of the TGA curves of various drug-loading amounts indicate that no interaction between the coacervates and the drug is present. Ibuprofen was completely removed during the heating process due to sublimation and thus showed 100% weight loss. However, CMSP and gelatin left residual ashes after degradation and hence showed a residual weight at higher temperatures.

## 3.7. Optical Microscopy and FESEM

Photomicrograph (Figure 6a) show native ibuprofen with larger particles. Coacervates unable to encapsulate the native drug particles in the presence of surfactant are shown in Figure 6b. Pictures of micronized ibuprofen and freshly prepared unloaded coacervate are shown in Figure 6c,d, respectively. A picture of coacervate (Figure 6d) reveals the spherical to oval-shaped coacervate formed during phase separation. The incorporation of the m-INN in the newly prepared coacervates is shown in Figure 6e,f. Though the freshly prepared microcapsules appeared to be spherical, the dried one was irregular in shape, as evidenced by FESEM. The irregular shape might be due to

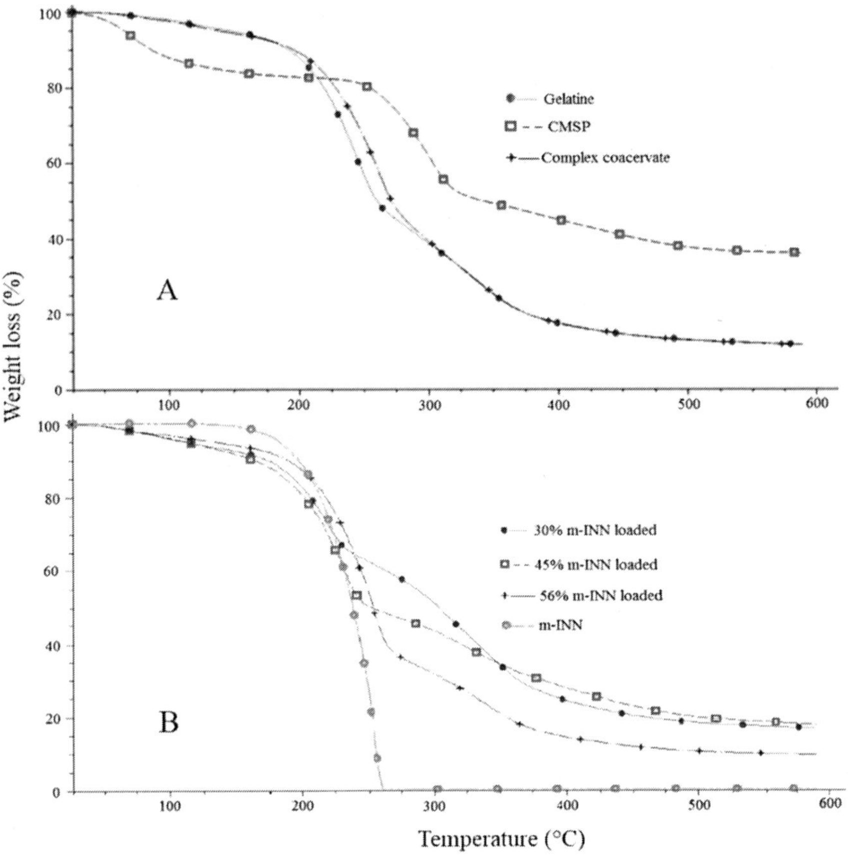


**Figure 5.** (**A**) TGA of gelatine, CMSP and unloaded complex coacervates; and (**B**) TGA of micronized ibuprofen, 30, 45 and 56% *w/w* drug loaded microcapsules.

the dehydration of the coacervates, which produces a membrane around the drug particles to form microcapsules. FESEM pictures of the microcapsules (Figure S1) are provided in the supplementary document. The surface of the unloaded microcapsule (Figure S1A,B) was smoother than the drug-loaded microcapsule (Figure S1C,D). Crystals of ibuprofen are seen on the surface of drug-loaded microcapsules (Figure S1F).

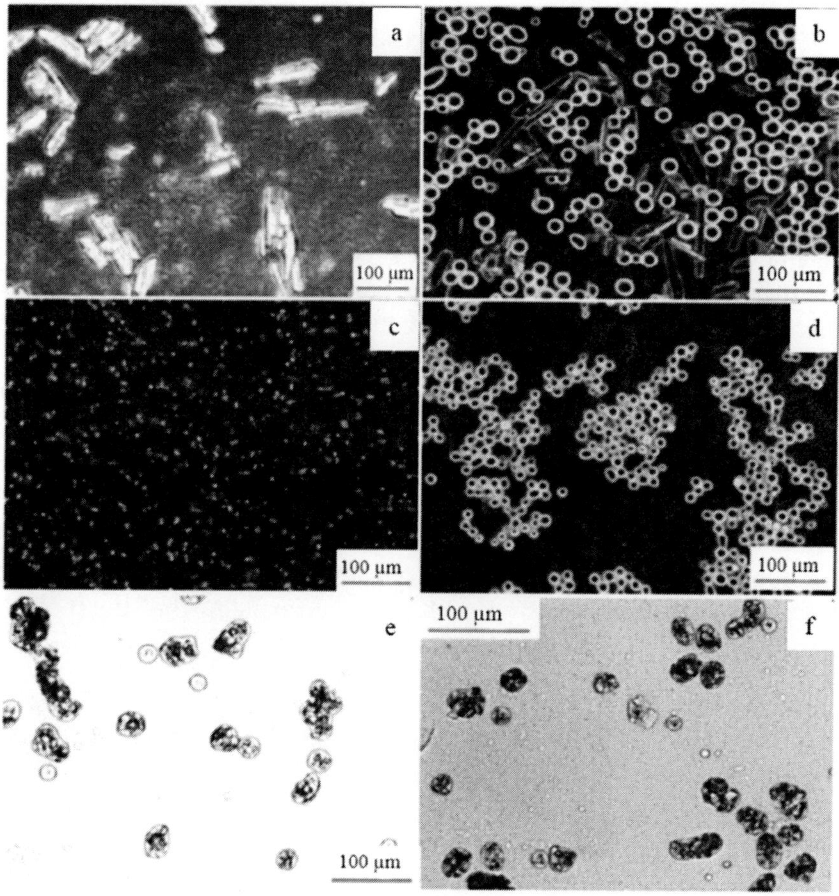


**Figure 6.** Photomicrographs showing native ibuprofen (**a**) that is not encapsulated by the coacervate (**b**) in presence of surfactant; Micronized ibuprofen (**c**) when added to coacervates without surfactant (**d**) successfully encapsulated by the coacervates (**e**,**f**).

### 3.8. In Vitro Drug Release

The release profiles of ibuprofen from CMSP-gelatine microcapsules are shown in Figure 7. Crosslinking with glutaraldehyde played an important role in hardening and making a compact capsule wall. A decrease in release rate was observed as the concentration of GST increases from 10 to 30 mL (Figure 7A). As shown in Figure 7A, the addition of $AlCl_3$resulted in much slower release of the drug from the

GST cross-linked microcapsules. The CMSP-gelatine microcapsules loaded with 30% drug and cross-linked with GST/$AlCl_3$ could sustain the release up to 6 h. This sustained release could be due to an increase in extent of cross-linking in the microcapsule wall by the interaction of $AlCl_3$ with CMSP. As indicated inFigure 1, the coacervate has a negative charge due to the excess carboxyl group, which may interact with $AlCl_3$ to provide further cross-linking. A burst release of the drug was observed in all formulations (Figure 7), and the extent of this effect was less in the samples with higher cross-linking. This burst release could be due to surface drugs or poorly encapsulated drug. As shown in Figure 7, the burst release varied from 38% to 60% depending on drug loading and the level of cross-linking. The relative dimensions of wall thickness and the extent of cross-linking in the microcapsules account for the size of the initial burst release [29]. At higher drug loading amounts, the drug may present very near to the surface of the microcapsules due to a smaller wall thickness or poorly encapsulated drug, both of which may explain the burst effect [29,30,31].

As shown in Table 1, the microcapsules were prepared with increasing quantities of drug with the same quantity of coacervates. The coacervates loaded with a higher amount of drug would encapsulate the entire drug resulting in a relatively thinner capsule wall [32] than that of the microcapsules loaded with lower drug amounts. This results in a faster diffusion of the drug in highly loaded microcapsules and a less sustained effect [20]. As shown in Figure 7b, 56% of the loaded microcapsules could sustain release for only 90 min. In contrast, formulations with lower drug loading showed a better sustained effect due to relatively thick wall formation because of higher coacervate content with respect to the drug. Devi *et al.* [33] (2012) reported a similar observation in gelatine-sodium alginate complex coacervate loaded with a different level of olive oil.

### 3.9. Release Kinetics

Data obtained from *in vitro* release studies were fitted to various kinetic equations [19,34]. The kinetic models used are zero order, first order and the Higuchi equation. The following plots were made: $Q_t$ *vs.* $t$ (zero order); log $(Q_0 - Q_t)$ *vs.* $t$ (first-order); $Q_t$ *vs.* the square root of $t$ (Higuchi), where $Q_t$ is the amount of m-INN released at time $t$ and $Q_0$ is the initial amount of drug in microcapsules. Furthermore, to determine the mechanism of drug release, the first 60% drug release was fitted to the Korsmeyer-Peppas model.

$$M_t/M_\alpha = kt^n \tag{3}$$

$M_t/M_\alpha$ is the fraction of drug released at time $t$, $k$ is rate constant and $n$ is the release exponent. The $n$ value is used to characterize different release mechanisms. Higher correlation was observed in first order and Higuchi ($R \geq 0.90$) than in the zero order ($R \leq 0.76$). The highest correlation was observed in the Korsmeyer-Peppas model with an $R$ value above 0.95. The value of the release exponent $n$ was found to be less than 0.39, suggesting Fickian diffusion. All of these parameters indicate that the drug release followed first order kinetics and was regulated by diffusion rather than swelling. Individual values of each formulation are included in the supplementary document (Tables S1 and S2) that is available in the online version of this article.

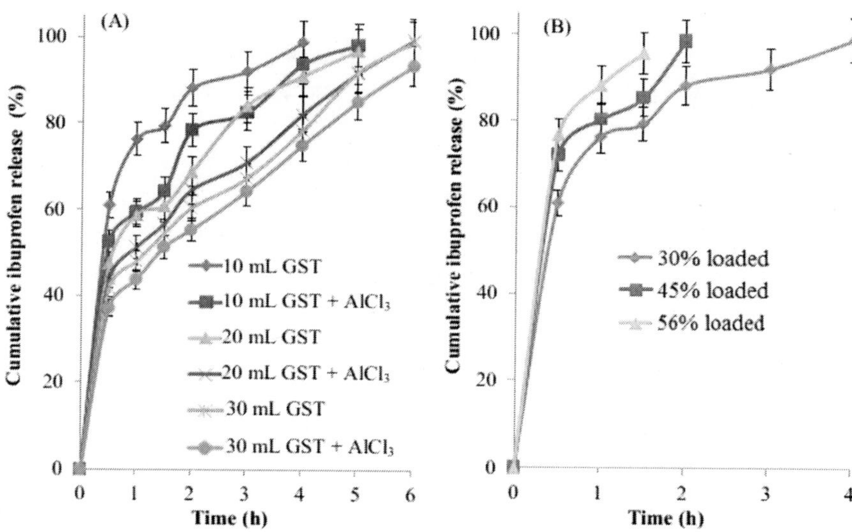


**Figure 7.** Influence of various cross-linking parameters (**A**) on the release profile of 30% m-INN loaded microcapsules, in which each point represents an average of three determinations; and the influence of m-INN loading on the release profile (**B**) of GST cross-linked microcapsules ($n$ = 3).

As shown in Figure 7, the effect of aluminum chloride on sustain release was higher in 10-mL GST cross-linked coacervates than 20- and 30-mL GST cross-linked coacervates. This result shows that the effect of GST cross-linking is dominant at its higher concentration. Addition of aluminum chloride sustained 10%–20%, 5%–15%, 5%–8% *w/w* of ibuprofen release from 10, 20, 30 mL GST cross-linked coacervates, respectively. Because the coacervates were highly cross-linked at high GST levels, aluminum chloride was unable to penetrate the coacervate for further cross-linking.

### 3.10. Residual Glutaraldehyde

Because glutaraldehyde is known for toxicity, the microcapsules must be free from residual glutaraldehyde, which could cause irritation and inflammation [21]. The American Congress of Government Industrial Hygienists [35] lowered their limit to 0.05 ppm. United States Pharmacopeia classifies toluene as a class 2 residual solvent and its presence should be less than 890 ppm. Gas chromatography analysis qualitatively confirms the absence of residual glutaraldehyde and toluene in the microcapsules. A representative gas chromatogram in the supplementary document (Figure S2) shows peaks of isopropanol, toluene and glutaraldehyde in the physical mixture of these substances. The peaks of toluene and glutaraldehyde were absent in the chromatogram of formulations, suggesting the absence of these materials. The toluene might have removed while washing with isopropanol as well as during drying. The quenching agent sodium metabisulfite, used during the recovery process, effectively removed the unreacted glutaraldehyde from the microcapsules. We have also reported similar observation in a previous publication [21].

## 4. CONCLUSIONS

The present work reports a new complex coacervation microcapsule based on CMSP-gelatine for sustained drug delivery. The $AlCl_3$ further sustained the drug release from glutaraldehyde cross-linked coacervates. The dual cross-linking could be optimized to obtain the required drug release profile, which was found to be diffusion controlled. The same method could encapsulate biological material, as a less harsh environment is used in the manufacturing process. Because CMSP is obtained from waste biomass of Malaysian sago industries, its synthesis and application in the microencapsulation process will reduce environmental pollution and sustain a green environment.

## ACKNOWLEDGMENTS

The synthesis of CMSP from sago biomass was funded by the Ministry of Higher Education through Exploratory Research grant (ERGS) (ERGS/1/2012/TK04/MUSM/03/1). The remaining work supported by a seed grant (BCHH-SS-6-02-2010) obtained from Monash University, Malaysia. APC of this manuscript was supported by School of Pharmacy, Monash, Malaysia.

## AUTHOR CONTRIBUTIONS

Pushpamalar Janarthanan has contributed to the synthesis and the characterization of CMSP from Sago biomass; Thenapakiam Sathasivam has conducted all the experiments and analyzed the results; Anand Kumar Veeramachineni contributed to the characterization of the microcapsules; and Saravanan Muniyandy has written the manuscript and contributed in the development and characterization of complex coacervates.

## CONFLICTS OF INTEREST

The authors declare no conflict of interest.

## REFERENCES

1. Pushpamalar, V.; Langford, S.; Ahmad, M.; Lim, Y. Optimization of reaction conditions for preparing carboxymethyl cellulose from sago waste. Carbohydr. Polym. 2006, 64, 312–318.

2. Pushpamalar, V.; Langford, S.; Ahmad, M.; Hashim, K.; Lim, Y. Absorption characterization of Ca2+, Na+, and K+ on irradiation cross-linked carboxymethyl sago pulp hydrogel. J. Appl. Polym. Sci. 2013, 128, 1828–1833.

3. Pushpamalar, V. Preparation and Characterisation of Carboxymethyl Cellulose and Carboxymethyl Cellulose Hydrogels from Sago Waste; Monash University: Clayton, Australia, 2010.

4. Thenapakiam, S.; Kumar, D.G.; Pushpamalar, J.; Saravanan, M. Aluminium and radiation cross-linked carboxymethyl sago pulp beads for colon targeted delivery. Carbohydr. Polym. 2013, 94, 356–363.

5. Deasy, P.B. Microencapsulation and Related Drug Processes; Marcel Dekker Inc.: New York, NY, USA, 1984.

6. Polk, A.; Amsden, B.; de Yao, K.; Peng, T.; Goosen, M. Controlled release of albumin from chitosan—Alginate microcapsules. J. Pharm. Sci. 1994, 83, 178–185.

7. Wen, S.; Alexander, H.; Inchikel, A.; Stevenson, W.T. Microcapsules through polymer complexation: Part 3: Encapsulation and culture of human burkitt lymphoma cells in vitro. Biomaterials 1995, 16, 325–335.

8. De Kruif, C.G.; Weinbreck, F.; de Vries, R. Complex coacervation of proteins and anionic polysaccharides. Curr. Opin. Colloid Interface Sci. 2004, 9, 340–349.

9. Saravanan, M.; Rao, K.P. Pectin–gelatin and alginate–gelatin complex coacervation for controlled drug delivery: Influence of anionic polysaccharides and drugs being encapsulated on physicochemical properties of microcapsules.Carbohydr. Polym. 2010, 80, 808–816.

10. Harada, A.; Kataoka, K. Formation of polyion complex micelles in an aqueous milieu from a pair of oppositely-charged block copolymers with poly(ethy1ene glycol) segments. Macromolecules 1995, 28, 5294–5299.

11. Harada, A.; Kataoka, K. Pronounced activity of enzymes through the incorporation into the core of polyion complex micelles made from charged block copolymers. J. Control. Release 2001, 72, 85–91.

12. Black, K.A.; Priftis, D.; Perry, S.L.; Yip, J.; Byun, W.Y.; Tirrell, M. Protein encapsulation via polypeptide complex coacervation. ACS Macro Lett. 2014, 3, 1088–1091.

13. Perry, S.L.; Li, Y.; Priftis, D.; Leon, L.; Tirrell, M. The effect of salt on the complex coacervation of vinyl polyelectrolytes. Polymers 2014, 6, 1756–1772.

14. Chollakup, R.; Beck, J.B.; Dirnberger, K.; Tirrell, M.; Eisenbach, C.D. Polyelectrolyte molecular weight and salt effects on the phase behavior and coacervation of aqueous solutions of poly(acrylic acid) sodium salt and poly(allylamine) hydrochloride. Macromolecules 2013, 46, 2376–2390.

15. Wong, R.C.; Kang, S.; Heezen, J.L.; Voorhees, J.J.; Ellis, C.N. Oral ibuprofen and tetracycline for the treatment of acne vulgaris. J. Am. Acad. Dermatol. 1984, 11, 1076–1081.

16. Curhan, S.G.; Eavey, R.; Shargorodsky, J.; Curhan, G.C. Analgesic use and the risk of hearing loss in men. Am. J. Med.2010, 123, 231–237.

17. Hippisley-Cox, J.; Coupland, C. Risk of myocardial infarction in patients taking cyclo-oxygenase-2 inhibitors or conventional non-steroidal anti-inflammatory drugs: Population based nested case-control analysis. BMJ 2005, 330, 1366.

18. Mansouri, M.; Pouretedal, H.R.; Vosoughi, V. Preparation and characterization of Ibuprofen nanoparticles by using solvent/antisolvent precipitation. Open Conf. Proc. J. 2011, 2, 88–94.

19. Saravanan, M.; Bhaskar, K.; Rao, G.S.; Dhanaraju, M. Ibuprofen-loaded ethylcellulose/polystyrene microspheres: An approach to get prolonged drug release with reduced burst effect and low ethylcellulose content. J. Microencapsul.2003, 20, 289–302.

20. Boppana, R.; Kulkarni, R.V.; Mutalik, S.S.; Setty, C.M.; Sa, B. Interpenetrating network hydrogel beads of carboxymethylcellulose and egg albumin for controlled release of lipid lowering drug. J. Microencapsul. 2010, 27, 337–344.

21. Saravanan, M.; Bhaskar, K.; Maharajan, G.; Pillai, K.S. Development of gelatin microspheres loaded with diclofenac sodium for intra-articular administration. J. Drug Target. 2011, 19, 96–103.

22. Barbucci, R.; Magnani, A.; Consumi, M. Swelling behavior of carboxymethylcellulose hydrogels in relation to cross-linking, pH, and charge density. Macromolecules 2000, 33, 7475–7480.

23. Charpentier-Valenza, D.; Merle, L.; Mocanu, G.; Picton, L.; Muller, G. Rheological properties of hydrophobically modified carboxymethylcelluloses. Carbohydr. Polym. 2005, 60, 87–94.

24. Wang, M.; Xu, L.; Hu, H.; Zhai, M.; Peng, J.; Nho, Y.; Li, J.; Wei, G. Radiation synthesis of PVP/CMC hydrogels as wound dressing. Nucl. Instrum. Methods. Phys. Res. Section B 2007, 265, 385–389.

25. Muyonga, J.; Cole, C.; Duodu, K. Fourier transform infrared (FTIR) spectroscopic study of acid soluble collagen and gelatin from skins and bones of young and adult Nile perch (Lates niloticus). Food Chem. 2004, 86, 325–332.

26. Garrigues, S.; Gallignani, M.; de la Guardia, M. FIA-FT-IR determination of ibuprofen in pharmaceuticals. Talanta1993, 40, 89–93.

27. Han, X.; Ghoroi, C.; To, D.; Chen, Y.; Davé, R. Simultaneous micronization and surface modification for improvement of flow and dissolution of drug particles. Int. J. Pharm. 2011, 415, 185–195.

28. Garnero, C.; Aloisio, C.; Longhi, M. Ibuprofen-maltodextrin interaction: Study of enantiomeric recognition and complex characterization. Pharmacol. Pharm. 2013, 4, 18.

29. Huang, X.; Brazel, C.S. On the importance and mechanisms of burst release in matrix-controlled drug delivery systems. J. Control. Release 2001, 73, 121–136.

30. Batycky, R.P.; Hanes, J.; Langer, R.; Edwards, D.A. A theoretical model of erosion and macromolecular drug release from biodegrading microspheres. J. Pharm. Sci. 1997, 86, 1464–1477.

31. Brazel, C.S.; Peppas, N.A. Mechanisms of solute and drug transport in relaxing, swellable, hydrophilic glassy polymers. Polymer 1999, 40, 3383–3398.

32. Hedayati, R.; Jahanshahi, M.; Attar, H. Fabrication and characterization of albumin-acacia nanoparticles based on complex coacervation as potent nanocarrier. J. Chem. Technol. Biotechnol. 2012, 87, 1401–1408.

33. Devi, N.; Hazarika, D.; Deka, C.; Kakati, D. Study of complex coacervation of gelatin A and sodium alginate for microencapsulation of olive oil. J. Macromol. Sci. Part A 2012, 49, 936–945.

34. Costa, P.; Lobo, J.M.S. Modeling and comparison of dissolution profiles. Eur. J. Pharm. Sci. 2001, 13, 123–133.

35. Smilanick, J.L.; Sorenson, D.; Verduzco, G.; Ames, Z.R.; Mansour, M. Evaluation of disinfectants forcitrus packinghouses. Citrograph 2011, 49, 50–55.

# Chapter 3

# Nanoemulsion: an advanced mode of drug delivery system

**Manjit Jaiswal, Rupesh Dudhe, and P. K. Sharma**

*Department of Pharmacy, School of Medical and Allied Sciences, Galgotias University, G. B. Nagar, Uttar Pradesh, India*

## ABSTRACT

An advanced mode of drug delivery system has been developed to overcome the major drawbacks associated with conventional drug delivery systems. This review gives a detailed idea about a nanoemulsion system. Nanoemulsions are nano-sized emulsions, which are manufactured for improving the delivery of active pharmaceutical ingredients. These are the thermodynamically stable isotropic system in which two immiscible liquids are mixed to form a single phase by means of an emulsifying agent, i.e., surfactant and co-surfactant. The droplet size of nanoemulsion falls typically in the range 20–200 nm. The main difference between emulsion and nanoemulsion lies in the size and shape of particles dispersed in the continuous phase. In this review, the attention is focused to give a basic idea about its formulation, method of preparation, characterization techniques, evaluation parameters, and various applications of nanoemulsion.

**Keywords:** Nanoemulsion, Drug delivery, Emulgents, High-pressure, homogenization

## INTRODUCTION

Nanoemulsions are a colloidal particulate system in the submicron size range acting as carriers of drug molecules. Their size varies from 10 to 1,000 nm. These carriers are solid spheres and their surface is amorphous and lipophilic with a negative charge. Magnetic nanoparticles can be used to enhance site specificity. As a drug delivery system they enhance the therapeutic efficacy of the drug and minimize adverse effect and toxic reactions. Major application includes treatment of infection of the reticuloendothelial system (RES), enzyme replacement therapy in the liver, treatment of cancer, and vaccination. An emulsion is a biphasic system in which one phase is intimately dispersed in the other phase in the form of minute droplets ranging in diameter from 0.1 to 100 μm. It is a thermodynamically unstable system, which can be stabilized by the presence of an emulsifying agent (emulgent or emulsifier). The dispersed phase is also known as internal phase or the discontinuous phase while the outer phase is called dispersion medium, external phase or continuous phase. The emulsifying agent is also known as intermediate or interphase. The term 'nanoemulsion' also refers to a miniemulsion which is fine oil/water or water/oil dispersion stabilized by an interfacial film of surfactant molecule having droplet size range 20–600 nm. Because of small size, nanoemulsions are transparent. There are three types of nanoemulsion which can be formed: (a) oil in water nanoemulsion in which oil is dispersed in the continuous aqueous phase, (b) water in oil nanoemulsion in which water droplets are dispersed in continuous oil phase, and (c) bi-continuous nanoemulsions.

## ADVANTAGES OF NANOEMULSION

a. It may be used as substitute for liposomes and vesicles (Bouchemal et al. 2004a, b).

b. It improves the bioavailability of drug (Kim et al. 2001; Wagner et al. 1996).

c. It is non-toxic and non-irritant in nature.

d. It has improved physical stability.

e. Nanoemulsions have small-sized droplets having greater surface area providing greater absorption.

f. It can be formulated in variety of formulations such as foams, creams, liquids, and sprays.

g. It provides better uptake of oil-soluble supplements in cell culture technology.

h. It helps to solubilize lipophilic drug.

i. Helpful in taste masking.

j. Less amount of energy is required.

k.

## Components of nanoemulsion

The main components of nanoemulsion are oil, emulsifying agents, and aqueous phases (Gasco et al. 1991; Kriwet and Müller-Goymann 1995; Trotta 1999). Oils can be of any type like castor oil, corn oil, coconut oil, evening primrose oil, linseed oil, mineral oil, olive oil, peanut oil, etc. A mixture of oil and water may yield a crude temporary emulsion, which upon standing, will separate in two distinct phases due to the coalescence of the dispersed globules. Emulgents or emulsifying agents can impart stability to such systems. Emulgents are broadly classified as surfactants like spans and tweens, hydrophilic colloids such as acacia and finely divided solids, e.g., bentonite and veegum. An emulgent, in addition to its emulsifying properties, should be nontoxic and its taste, odour and chemical stability should be compatible with the product. Some of the desirable properties of an emulgent are: (1) it should be able to reduce the surface tension to below 10 dynes/cm, (2) it should be adsorbed rapidly around dispersed phase globule to form a complete and coherent film to prevent coalescence, (3) it should help in building up an adequate zeta potential and viscosity in the system so as to impart optimum stability, and (4) it should be effective in a fairly low concentration. Emulgents form monomolecular, multimolecular or particulate films around the dispersed globules (Sharma and Jain 1985).

## Monomolecular films

Surfactant type of emulgents stabilizes a nanoemulsion by forming a monolayer of adsorbed molecules or ions at the interface reducing interfacial tension. In modern day practice, combination of emulgents is preferred over single emulgent. The combination consists of a predominantly hydrophilic emulgent in the aqueous phase and a hydrophobic agent in the oily phase to form a complex film at the interface.

## Multimolecular films

Hydrated lyophilic colloids form multimolecular films around globules of dispersed oil. Hydrated colloids do not cause any appreciable lowering of surface tension and their ability to form strong, coherent multimolecular films. Their tendency to increase the viscosity of the continuous phase enhances the stability of emulsion.

## Solid particulate films

The emulgents forming particulate films are small solid particles that are wetted to some degree by both aqueous and non-aqueous liquid phases. They are concentrated at the interface where they produce a film around the dispersed globules thus preventing coalescence.

## Formulation aspects and method of preparation of nanoemulsion

Formulation of nanoemulsion includes active drug, additive and emulsifier. The various methods for the preparation of nanoemulsion include two methods: (a) high-energy emulsification and (b) low-energy emulsification. The high-energy emulsification method includes high-energy stirring, ultrasonic emulsification, high-pressure homogenization, microfluidization, and membrane emulsification (Tiwari and Amiji 2006; Perdiguer et al.1997; Banker et al. 2002). The low-energy emulsification method includes phase inversion temperature, emulsion inversion point, and spontaneous emulsification

(Ahuja et al. 2008). Using a combined method, which includes the high-energy and low-energy emulsification, it is possible to prepare reverse nanoemulsion in a highly viscous system.

### Ultrasonic emulsification

Ultrasonic emulsification is very efficient in reducing droplet size. In ultrasonic emulsification, the energy is provided through sonotrodes called as sonicator probe. It contains piezoelectric quartz crystal which can expand and contract in response to alternating electric voltage. As the tip of sonicator contacts the liquid, it produces mechanical vibration and cavitation occurs. Cavitation is the formation and collapse of vapour cavities in liquid. Thus, ultrasound can be directly used to produce emulsion; it is mainly used in laboratories where emulsion droplet size as low as 0.2 micrometer can be obtained.

### High-pressure homogenization

The preparation of nanoemulsion requires high-pressure homogenization. This technique makes use of high-pressure homogenizer/piston homogenizer to produce nanoemulsion of extremely low particle size (up to 1 nm) (Asua 2002; Anton et al. 2008).

### Microfluidization

Microfluidization is a patented mixing technology, which makes use of a device called microfluidizer. This device uses high pressure which forces the drug product through the interaction chamber resulting in a very fine particle of submicron range. The process is repeated several times to obtain a desired particle size to produce uniform nanoemulsion.

### Phase inversion temperature

This method involves change in phase by applying a higher temperature to a microemulsion (El-Aasser et al. 1986; Pouton 1997).

## Spontaneous emulsification

It involves three steps: (a) preparation of homogeneous organic solution consisting of oil and lipophilic surfactant in water miscible solvent and hydrophilic surfactant, (b) the organic phase is injected in aqueous phase under continuous magnetic stirring, o/w emulsion is formed, and (c) the aqueous phase is removed by evaporation under reduced pressure (Solans et al. 2005; Tadros et al. 2004).

## Factors to be considered during preparation of nanoemulsion

1. Surfactant must be selected carefully such that an ultralow interfacial tension may be achieved which is a primary requirement to produce nanoemulsion.
2. Concentration of surfactant must be high enough to stabilize the microdroplets to produce nanoemulsion.
3. The surfactant must be flexible or fluid enough to promote the formation of nanoemulsion.

## Characterization of nanoemulsion

A stable nanoemulsion is characterized by the absence of the internal phase, absence of creaming, absence of deterioration by microorganisms, and maintenance of elegance in respect of appearance, colour, odour and consistency (Sharma and Jain 1985). Hence the instability of emulsion can be classified as follows:

## Flocculation and creaming

Flocculation consists of the joining together of globules to form large clumps or floccules, which rise or settle in the emulsion more rapidly than the individual globules. The rising up or settling down of dispersed globules to give a concentrated layer is known as creaming. Thus flocculation leads to creaming.

### Cracking

Cracking of an emulsion refers to separation of the dispersed phase as a layer. Whereas a creamed emulsion may be reconstituted by shaking or agitation, a cracked emulsion cannot be corrected. Cracking represents permanent instability. Cracking of the emulsion may be due to: (1) addition of an emulgent of opposite nature, (2) decomposition or precipitation of emulgent, (3) addition of a common solvent in which both oily and aqueous phases are miscible, (4) extremes of temperature, (5) microorganisms, (6) creaming.

### Miscellaneous instability

Emulsions may deteriorate if stored under extremely high or low temperature or in the presence of light. Hence emulsions are usually packed in air-tight, coloured containers and stored at moderate temperature.

### Phase inversion

It is the change in the type of emulsion from o/w to w/o and vice versa. It is the physical process. Phase inversion may be brought about by varying the phase volume ratio, addition of electrolytes, and temperature changes.

## Evaluation parameters of nanoemulsion

### Droplet size analysis

Droplet size analysis of nanoemulsion is measured by a diffusion method using a light-scattering, particle size-analyzer counter, LS 230. It is also measured by correlation spectroscopy that analyzes the fluctuation in scattering of light due to Brownian motion. Droplet size analysis of nanoemulsion can also be performed by transmission electron microscopy (TEM) (Bouchemal et al. 2004a, b; Alka et al. 2007; Farhan et al. 2008).

### Viscosity determination

The viscosity of nanoemulsion is measured by using Brookfield-type rotary viscometer at different shear rates at different temperatures.

### Dilution test

Dilution of a nanoemulsion either with oil or with water can reveal this type. The test is based on the fact that more of the continuous phase can be added into a nanoemulsion without causing the problem of its stability. Thus, an o/w nanoemulsion can be diluted with water and a w/o nanoemulsion can be diluted with oil.

### Drug content

Preweighed nanoemulsion is extracted by dissolving in a suitable solvent, extract is analyzed by spectrophotometer or HPLC against standard solution of drug (Singh and Vingkar 2008; Chen et al. 2008).

### Polydispersity

It indicates the uniformity of droplet size in nanoemulsion. The higher the value of polydispersity, lower will be uniformity of droplet size of nanoemulsion. It can be defined as the ratio of standard deviation to mean droplet size. It is measured by a spectrophotometer.

### Dye test

If a water-soluble dye is added in an o/w nanoemulsion the nanoemulsion takes up the colour uniformly. Conversely, if the emulsion is w/o type and the dye being soluble in water, the emulsion takes up the colour only in the dispersed phase and the emulsion is not uniformly coloured. This can be revealed immediately by microscopic examination of the emulsion.

### Refractive index

Refractive index of nanoemulsion is measured by Abbes refractometer.

### pH

The pH of nanoemulsion can be measured by pH meter.

### Zeta potential

Zeta potential is measured by an instrument known as Zeta PALS. It is used to measure the charge on the surface of droplet in nanoemulsion (Erol and Hans-Hubert 2005).

### Fluorescence test

Many oils exhibit fluorescence when exposed to UV light. When a w/o nanoemulsion is exposed to a fluorescence light under a microscope, the entire field fluoresces. If the fluorescence is spotty, the nanoemulsion of o/w type.

### Percentage transmittance

Percentage transmittance of nanoemulsion is measured by a UV-visible spectrophotometer.

### Conductance measurement

The conductance of nanoemulsion is measured by a conductometer. In this test a pair of electrodes connected to a lamp and an electric source is dipped into an emulsion. If the emulsion is o/w type, water conducts the current and lamp gets lit due to passage of current between the electrodes. The lamp does not glow when the emulsion is w/o: oil being in external phase does not conduct the current.

### Filter paper test

This test is based on the fact that an o/w nanoemulsion will spread out rapidly when dropped onto filter paper. In contrast, a w/o nanoemulsion will migrate only slowly. This method should not be used for highly viscous creams (Sharma and Jain 1985).

## CONCLUSION

Nanoemulsions are widely used in pharmaceutical systems. Nanoemulsion formulation offers several advantages such as delivery of drugs, biological or diagnostic agents. The most important application of nanoemulsion is for masking the disagreeable taste of oily liquids.

Nanoemulsion may also protect the drugs, which are susceptible to hydrolysis and oxidation. Nowadays, nanoemulsions are used for targeted drug delivery of various anticancer drugs, photo sensitizers or therapeutic agents. Nanoemulsion can also provide prolonged action of the medicaments. Overall all nanoemulsion formulation may be considered as effective, safe and with increased bioavailability. It is expected that further research and development will be carried out in the future regarding nanoemulsion.

## CONFLICT OF INTEREST

The authors hereby want to declare that there is no conflict of interest whatsoever in this publication.

## REFERENCES


1. Ahuja A, Ali J, Baboota S, Faisal MS, Shakeell F, Shafiq S. Stability evaluation of Celecoxib nanoemulsion containing Tween 80. Thai J Pharm Sci. 2008;32:4–9.

2. Alka AJA, Baboota S, Shakeel F, Shafiq S. Design development and evaluation of novel nanoemulsion formulations for transdermal potential of Celecoxib. Acta Pharm.2007;57:315–332.

3. Anton N, Benoit JP, Saulnier P. Design and production of nanoparticles formulated from nano-emulsion templates-a review. J Control Release. 2008;128:185–199.

4. Asua JM. Miniemulsion polymerization. Prog Polym Sci. 2002;27:1283–1346.

5. Banker GS, Lieberman HA, Rieger MM. Pharmaceutical dosage forms. Disperse Syst Marcel Dekker. 2002;2(3):339–340.

6. Bouchemal K, Briancon S, Fessi H, Perrier E. Nano-emulsion formulation using spontaneous emulsification: solvent, oil and surfactant optimization. Int J Pharm.2004;280:242.

7. Bouchemal K, Briancon S, Fessi H, Perrier E. Nano-emulsion formulation using spontaneous emulsification: solvent, oil and surfactant optimization. Int J Pharm.2004;280:243.

8. Chen H, Du D, Mao CMD, Wan J, Xu H, Yang X. Hydrogel-thickened nanoemulsion system for topical delivery of lipophilic drugs. Int J Pharm. 2008;353:272.

9. El-Aasser MS, Lack CD, Vanderhoff JW, Fowkes FM. Miniemulsification process-different form of spontaneous emulsification. Coll Surf. 1986;29:103–118.

10. Erol Y, Hans-Hubert B. Design of a phytosphingosine-containing, positively-charged nanoemulsion as a colloidal carrier system for dermal application of ceramides. Eur J Pharm Biopharm. 2005;60:93.

11. Farhan AJ, Mushir A, Faiyaz S, Cushman T, Roop KK, Sheikh S. Investigation of nanoemulsion system for transdermal delivery of domperidone: ex-vivo and in vivo studies. Curr Nanosci. 2008;4(4):381–390.

12. Gasco MR, Gallarate M, Pattarino F. In vitro permeation of azelaic acid from viscosized microemulsions. Int J Pharm. 1991;69:193–196.

13. Kim CK, Cho YJ, Gao ZG. Preparation and evaluation of biphenyl dimethyl dicarboxylate microemulsions for oral delivery. J Control Release. 2001;70:149–155.

14. Kriwet K, Müller-Goymann C. Diclofenac release from phospholipid drug systems and permeation through excised human stratum corneum. Int J Pharm. 1995;125:231–242.

15. Perdiguer AC, Dachs FJG, Carreras N, Valdivia (1997) Nanoemulsion of the oil water type, useful as an ophthalmic vehicle and process for the preparation thereof Assignee: Laboratorios Cusi, S.A. (Barcelona, ES)

16. Pouton CW. Formulation of selfemulsifying drug delivery systems. Adv Drug Deliv Rev.1997;25:47–58.

17. Sharma SN, Jain NK (1985) A text book of professional pharmacy. Vallabh Prakashan, 1st edn, p 201

18. Singh KK, Vingkar SK. Formulation, antimalarial activity and biodistribution of oral lipid nanoemulsion of primaquine. Int J Pharm. 2008;347:138.

19. Solans C, Izquierdo P, Nolla J, Azemar N, Garcia-Celma MJ. Nanoemulsions. Curr Opin Coll Interface Sci. 2005;10:102–110.

20. Tadros T, Izquierdo P, Esquena J, Solans C. Formation and stability of nano-emulsions.Adv Coll Interface Sci. 2004;108:303–318.

21. Tiwari SB, Amiji MM (2006) Nanoemulsion formulations for tumor-targeted delivery. Nanotech Cancer Therapy. Taylor and Francis Group Editors, pp 723–739

22. Trotta M. Influence of phase transformation on indomethacin release from microemulsions.J Control Release. 1999;60:399–405.

23. Wagner JG, Gerrard ES, Kaiser DG. The effect of the dosage form on serum levels of indoxole. Clin Pharmacol Ther. 1996;7:610–619.

# Chapter 4

# Colloidal Microgels in Drug Delivery Applications

**Serguei V. Vinogradov***

*Center for Drug Delivery and Nanomedicine and Department of Pharmaceutical Sciences, University of Nebraska Medical Center, Omaha*

## ABSTRACT

Colloidal microgels have recently received attention as environmentally responsive systems and now are increasingly used in applications as carriers for therapeutic drugs and diagnostic agents. Synthetic microgels consist of a crosslinked polymer network that provides a depot for loaded drugs, protection against environmental hazards and template for post-synthetic modification or vectorization of the drug carriers. The aim of this manuscript is to review recent attempts to develop new microgel formulations for oral drug delivery, to design metal-containing microgels for diagnostic and therapeutic applications, and to advance approaches including the systemic administration of microgels. Novel nanogel drug delivery systems developed in the authors' laboratory are discussed in details including aspects of their synthesis, vectorization and recent applications for encapsulation of low molecular weight drugs or formulation of biological macromolecules. The findings reviewed here are encouraging for further development of the nanogels as intelligent drug carriers with such features as targeted delivery and triggered drug release.

# APPLICATIONS OF MICROGELS

Microscopic particles of hydrogels (microgels) are presently under intense investigation for drug delivery and controlled release of bioactive molecules. Hydrogels can be defined as cross-linked or interwoven polymeric networks, which absorb and retain large amounts of water. The water content in a hydrogel and crosslinking density can determine the drug transfer in and out of the gel. Microgels can be classified as neutral, anionic or cationic. Electrostatic repulsion of charged groups dispersed in the microgel will result in additional swelling of the elastic polymer network in aqueous media. Interactions with protonated network can be restricted by the pore size that biomolecules having net charge opposite to that of the microgel will accumulate only on the microgel surface without diffusion into the internal volume. Nevertheless, encapsulating of biomolecules, for example, plasmid DNA, into the flexible polymer network of microgels can provide another opportunity for encapsulation and protection of biomolecules. Complementary hydrophobic, hydrogen or coordination bonding may significantly affect release of a drug from a hydrogel. Hydrogels have the unique property of undergoing abrupt volume changes in response to environmental factors, such as temperature, ionic strength and pH [1]. Thus, controlled release of a drug depends on properties of the drug and polymer design of the microgel. Many new applications of microgels for drug delivery have been proposed and experimentally evaluated during the last few years [2,3].

## Mucoadhesive microgels

Microgels composed of mucoadhesive polymers may be used to design new types of carriers for oral and non-oral drug delivery [4,5,6]. Understanding of the surface interactions between hydrophilic polymer surfaces and mucins could lead to improved adhesion. Alternatively, decoration of a microgel surface with tethers of linear or block copolymers containing anionic or thiolated moieties could provide interpenetration and anchoring within the mucus. Encapsulation of anticancer drug bleomycin in microgels was only possible during the microgel synthesis - via UV-initiated radical polymerization from metacrylic acid and ethylene glycol. When taken orally, these microgels were shown to preferentially release the drug at higher pH levels, such as in the small intestine [7]. This type of hydrogels could be promising carriers in attempts to expand the number of chemotherapeutics capable of being administered orally. A novel oral drug delivery system (DDS) based on polymer microgels of polyacrylic acid (PAA) and Pluronics has been recently discussed [8]. Nine Pluronic® copolymers ranging in nominal molecular weight and poly(propylene oxide) (PPO) and poly(ethylene oxide) (PEO) content were grafted to PAA with or without the use of a crosslinker, ethylene glycol dimethacrylate (EGDMA). The hydrogel elasticity increased with the PPO content in the copolymers, as well as in the presence of EGDMA. It was demonstrated that PAA bonded to the longest Pluronic® copolymers resulted in copolymeric gels with strongest mucoadhesive properties. An approach including thiomers in the design of a microparticulate delivery system for peptide drugs was recently developed [9]. Cysteine-modified PAA polymers were able to form disulfide bonds and intermolecular crosslinks with mucus material that significantly (14-fold) improved mucoadhesive properties of the thiolated microgels compared to particles comprising unmodified PAA.

## Metal-containing nanocarriers

Metal-containing microgels have been recently developed and tested in a wide range of therapeutic and diagnostic applications including magnetic, photoactive or quantum dot nanogels [10,11,12]. The major approach employed polymer microgels as templates for the synthesis of metal nanoparticles impregnated into the polymer network. In the field of diagnosis, magnetic resonance imaging was one of the first and most developed applications of metal nanoparticles. Very new biosensors based on the optical properties of colloidal gold and fluorescent nanocrystals, called quantum dots, seem to be ready to be implemented in both diagnosis and *in situ* medical imaging [13,14]. For therapeutic applications, the metal-containing microgels could aid in treatment by delivering and releasing drugs in a controlled manner. Magnetically guided carriers or thermal responsive matrices, in which drug release is triggered by the heating of metal nanoparticles have provided effective examples of drug delivery applications, while more recently efforts to develop metal-containing vectors for transfection and vaccination have been multiplied. Microgel templates were particularly useful in the synthesis of polymer nanoparticles heavily loaded with monodisperse superparamagnetic iron(III) oxide. One of the most interesting challenges for the future could be the use of metal-containing nanoparticles for an innovative, effective and selective physical treatment of solid tumors via targeted intracellular hyperthermia.

## Systemic drug delivery

Finally, hydrophilic and biocompatible microgels could provide a unique mode for targeted delivery of encapsulated drugs via blood circulation. In this paper, several recent examples of microgel polymeric carriers with an effective diameter <100 nm (nanogels) will be discussed. For earlier reviews on nanogels developed in our laboratory for systemic delivery of different classes of drugs, see [15]. Biological and pharmaceutical applications of microgels and structurally similar PEGylated nanoparticles have been recently comprehensively reviewed [16,17].

Nanocarriers are smaller than typical blood cells, such as erythrocytes or lymphocytes (ca. 7–10 μm). After intravenous injection, they can freely float in the bloodstream into the smallest vessels and capillaries and achieve site- or tissue-specific delivery by exploiting physiological clearance mechanisms. Release of the drug then occurs after uptake of the nanocarriers inside the cells of the targeted tissue. Unfortunately, most particulate DDSs are eliminated by the reticuloendothelial system (RES) within minutes after intravenous injection. These particles accumulate in the macrophages of liver and spleen by phagocytosis. Uptake of nanocarriers is caused by the adsorption of blood proteins to the particle surface. These proteins, such as immunoglobulins or components of the complement system are well-known opsonins promoting phagocytosis. To achieve long circulation time in blood and localization in non-RES tissues, surface modifications of nanocarriers using PEO polymers have been used extensively. In particular, nanocarriers with PEO polymer loops on their surface demonstrated a better protection from protein binding (opsonisation) and avoidance of RES than PEO chains in brush conformation because, compared to PEO polymer loops, the PEO brush was too soft for efficient shielding [18,19].

## Polymeric nanogels

Microgels can be rendered sensitive to physiological conditions. A responsive drug release system is recognized as one of the most important technologies necessary for an intelligent drug delivery. It must be able to regulate drug release in response to external chemical, physical, or biological stimuli. Biocompatible PAA was commonly incorporated in hydrogels to introduce pH sensitivity. The PAA-based microgels can protect protein or other sensitive drugs against digestion by proteolytic/nucleolytic enzymes in the stomach, due to their low swelling ratio at a low pH. However, when the hydrogels pass through the GI tract they swell due to ionization of carboxylic acid groups at higher pH and become able to release drug from the polymer network. A novel type of nanosized polymeric microgel (nanogels) consisting of a crosslinked polymer network of polyionic segments, such as polyethylenimine (PEI) or PAA, and neutral segments, such as polyethylene glycol (PEG) or Pluronic®, was recently developed in our laboratory [20,21]. Some applications of these nanogels for drug delivery have been later demonstrated [15]. This structure offered many advanced features as a DDS including simplicity of formulation, exceptional dispersion stability, and storage in the freeze-dried form, to name a few. Freeze-dried nanogels can be stored at ambient temperature and easily resuspended in aqueous media forming particulate dispersions with the hydrodynamic diameter of 120–350 nm. Initially, cationic nanogels were designed for encapsulation of therapeutic antisense oligonucleotides (SODN). These polyanionic compounds could be loaded into nanogels by simply mixing the nanogel dispersion with SODN solution in aqueous media. Polyionic complexes of negatively charged SODN with protonated PEI backbone of nanogels formed spontaneously in a matter of minutes and this process was accompanied by a significant compaction of the nanogel network leading to an 8–10-fold volume reduction [22]. While swelling degree of nanogels depended on the number of crosslinks in polymer network (or PEG/PEI molar ratio), an average 100% reduction in diameter was observed in nanogels loaded with oppositely charged drugs. We have found that the minimal number of six crosslinks per PEI molecule was required to obtain nanogels with desirable mechanical properties. At this PEG/PEI molar ratio homologous macrogels demonstrated the highest swelling degree in the range of 30–40-fold [23]. Drug loading capacity of nanogels was as high as 30% of their dry weight. Thus, even compacted drug-loaded nanogel particles will retain water in a quantity about 2/3 of their weight in swollen form, which added significantly to the dispersion stability of nanogels.

## SYNTHESIS OF NANOGELS

Chemical crosslinking is a highly versatile method of creating polymeric microgels with large pore sizes [24]. Crosslinks have to be present in a hydrogel in order to prevent dissolution of the hydrophilic polymer chains in aqueous media. Since it is advantageous for drug delivery applications that hydrogels be biodegradable, labile bonds are frequently introduced into the gels [25]. These bonds can be present either in the polymer backbone or in the crosslinks used to prepare the gel. In cationic nanogels, PEI and PEG polymer chains were crosslinked via urethane bonds, usually considered as stable links. However, due to the presence of highly protonated PEI, hydrolysis of these bonds was significantly accelerated, and the polymer network of nanogels could rapidly degrade in aqueous solution at the physiological pH during a period of about two weeks.

According to the previously described method, synthesis of nanogels was conducted in a dichloromethane (dichloroethane)-in-water emulsion, followed by evaporation of the solvent *in vacuo* and maturation of the nanogel network in aqueous solution [22]. This procedure was convenient, except it used organic solvents, a vacuum evaporation step, and produced particles with a wide size distribution. Another synthetic approach was recently employed to obtain nanogels using a simple procedure and without organic solvents. The general outline of the method is illustrated in Fig. (1). Initially, a Pluronic® block copolymer, both ends of which were activated by 1,1′-carbonyldiimidazole (A), was dissolved in water at concentration above its critical micellization concentration and thoroughly stirred so that a micellar solution had formed (B). A diluted aqueous solution of PEI was then added dropwise to the micellar solution and stirred overnight. During this procedure a covalently linked cationic polymer layer was formed on the Pluronic® micelles (C). The last step of the one-pot procedure consisted of the efficient crosslinking of the PEI layer by carbonylimidazole-activated PEG molecules to produce nanogels with narrow size distribution covered with PEO loops (D). Purification of nanogels from all reactants could be achieved in one dialysis step and after that products were lyophilized. Using this procedure, nanogels based on Pluronic® P85/PEG and F127/PEG have been obtained with final yields of 55 and 70% by weight and an average hydrodynamic diameter of 100 and 180 nm, respectively. A similar approach based on micellar properties of Pluronic® block copolymers was recently used in the synthesis of Pluronic®-PAA crosslinked micelles [26].

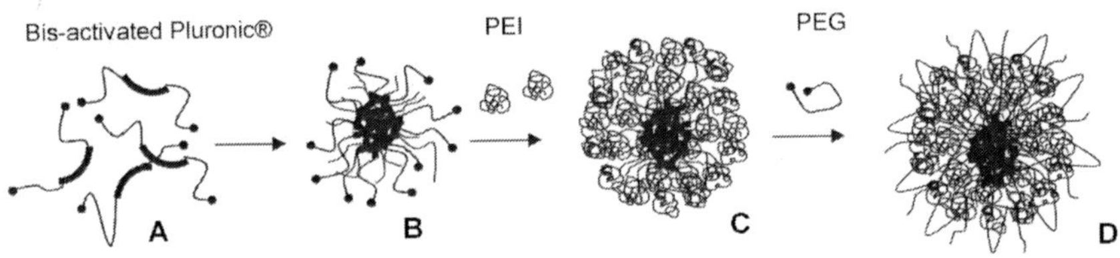


**Figure 1.** Scheme of nanogel synthesis using micellar approach. The carbonyldiimidazole-activated Pluronic® (A) formed micelles in aqueous solution (B) that were sequentially covered by a layer of branched PEI molecules (C) and crosslinked using carbonyldiimidazole-activated ...

To probe the structure of PEI-based nanogels, we have recently tagged them with heavy metals such as copper(II) that form coordination complexes with amino groups of PEI [23]. Copper (II) formed stable blue complexes with nanogels having absorbance at 280 nm. These complexes retained all drug-binding properties and did not affect particle size of nanogels. These tagged nanogels could be studied by transmission electron microscopy (TEM) as illustrated in Fig.(2). Initially, nanogels obtained by the emulsification-evaporation method showed particles with a well-developed surface and snowflake-like (PEG-cl-PEI) (Fig.2A) or sponge-like (Pluronic® P85-cl-PEI) (Fig.2C) structures. The white area were characteristic for locations of the PEG segments and grey area - for locations of the copper(II)-bound PEI segments. Drug-loading (ATP) has resulted in a compaction of nanogels into much smaller particles having only their dark cores visible (Fig.2B and Fig.2D). The neutral polymer envelope surrounding drug-PEI complexes was not observable at these conditions. In the case of nanogels obtained by the micellar approach, another type of structure was frequently detected

(Fig.2E and Fig.2F). These donut-like structures could reflect an existence of a neutral hydrophobic Pluronic micellar core surrounded by a well-contrasted PEI layer.

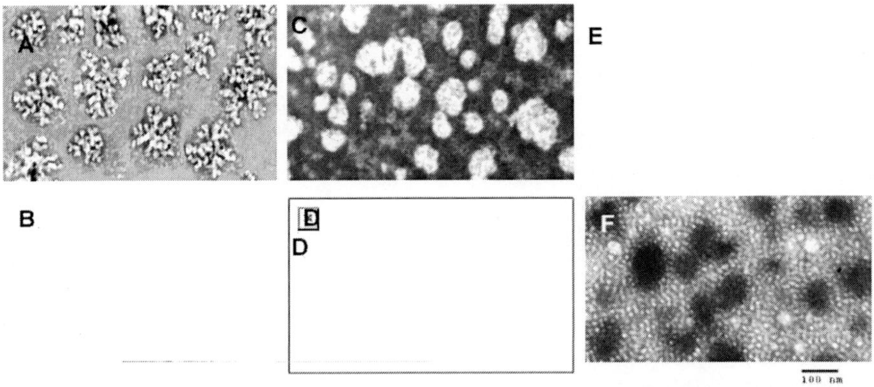


**Figure 2.**TEM pictures of nanogels: (A) PEG-*cl*-PEI, (B) ATP-loaded PEG-*cl*-PEI, (C) Pluronic® P85-*cl*-PEI, (D) ATP-loaded Pluronic® P85-*cl*-PEI, (E) Pluronic® F127-*cl*-PEI and (F) ATP-loaded Pluronic® F127-*c*l-PEI (the latter nanogel **...**

## VECTORIZATION OF NANOGELS

Targeted DDS could be compared to microscopic pills delivered directly to the disease-affected site (organs, tumors or cancer metastases). The most effective method is to inject/infuse dispersion of submicron-sized drug-loaded particles into the blood stream. Floating nanoparticles, which are able to reach even smaller capillaries, would consequently accumulate in the sites where specific receptors are present to bind nanogel-targeting ligands. However, this strategy has posed various problems before developers of these DDS. These problems are very similar to those encountered by viruses soon after propagation in the blood. First, nanocarriers can interact with serum proteins forming complexes (opsonisation) or aggregates (agglutination). Next, the RES consisting mostly of macrophages is directed against the particles, and the complexes with serum proteins are efficiently seized from the circulation. Finally, nonspecific clearance of nanocarriers through kidney glomerules is observed in many circumstances [27]. Therefore, major requirements for an adequate systemic DDS include reducing the level of the carrier's interaction with serum proteins, extended circulation time and small size, efficiently restricting them from renal clearance. All these requirements have once been met by PEG-covered (stealth) liposomes with the sizes between 100 and 200 nm [28]. Comparing nanogels with stealth liposomes, one can see many common properties. However, preliminary data on the *in vivo* properties of nanogels have shown that nanogels have a shorter plasma half-life than stealth liposomes, although both particles have longer half-lives than previously described nanoparticles. Nanogels can be additionally optimized for prolonged blood circulation in terms of size and PEG coverage, factors extensively studied previously for other cationic micellar systems [29,30,31]. A similar task of covering polymetacrylate microgels with tethered PEG chains possessing carboxylic groups was performed efficiently by using a α-vinylbenzyl-ω-carboxy-PEG in the emulsion polymerization procedure [32].

In previous research, we described biotinylated nanogels that could be vectorized via (strepta)avidin by biotinylated ligands (transferrin or insulin). Using these ligands, a significant increase of the blood-brain barrier (BBB) permeability for these SODN-loaded carriers was recently observed in the BBMEC monolayers, a cellular model of the BBB; transferrin and biotin were nearly equal in potency [33]. Although this system has demonstrated the targeting efficacy of nanogels, complications associated with slow aggregation of the nanogel-avidin constructs made the search for alternative targeting approaches a first priority. Recently, we have developed three novel methods for introduction of covalently linked targeting ligands in the nanogel structure. They included:

A. Attachment of folate moieties via water-soluble carbodiimide (Fig.3A). A simple modification of 1–5% of primary amino groups in nanogels with folic acid was performed using 1-ethyl-3-(3-dimethylaminopropyl)carbodiimide (EDC) in aqueous media. To reduce problems associated with folate availability for corresponding cellular receptors, several authors recommended insertion of polymer linker between the folate moiety and drug carrier [34,35]. Recently obtained polymetacrylate microgels modified with folate demonstrated an increased and selective cellular uptake in cancer cell lines overexpressing folate receptors [36].

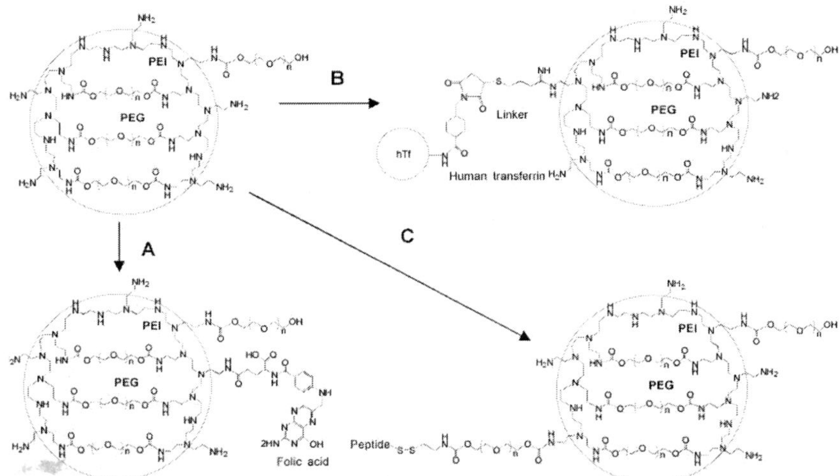


Figure 3. Scheme of the nanogel vectorization with targeting ligands. (A): Reaction of nanogel with folic acid and water-soluble carbodiimide (EDC) in aqueous medium, (B): Modification of (i) human transferrin (hTf) with a bifunctional reagent (SMCC), (ii) nanogel **...**

B. Modification with human transferrin (hTf) - a tumor-specific receptor target protein Fig.(3B). In this method, an amino group in the hTf protein is first reacted with a bifunctional reagent, sulfosuccinimidyl 4-(N-meleimidomethyl)-cyclohexane-1-carboxylate (SMCC), to obtain a maleimide derivative of hTf. Second, thiol groups are introduced into nanogels by reaction with 2-iminothiolane (Trout's reagent). Finally, reaction between maleimide-hTf and thiol-nanogels yields hTf-nanogels with 4–12 hTf molecules per particle. Because of the protein size, most of hTf molecules are located on the surface of nanogels and allows for easy access to cellular transferrin receptors. Additionally, this procedure has also been applied to cancer-specific mAbs.

C. Introduction of protein/peptide ligands through a disulfide bridge using a PEG linker Fig.(3). First, a mono-N-acetylcystamine-PEG linker was prepared, activated by 1,1'-carbonyldiimidazole, and conjugated to a nanogel. Next, groups on the proteins/peptides were activated to form thiol-specific derivatives. These reactions included activation of amino groups with N-succinimidyl 3-(2-pyridyldithio)-propionate (SPDP), and thiol groups with 2, 2'-dipyridyldisulfide. Lastly, nanogels were treated with dithiothreitol (DTT), followed by thiol-specific protein/peptide derivatives to yield peptide-modified nanogels. Several short homing peptides and PSMA-specific mAbs have been conjugated to nanogels using this synthetic approach (data will be published elsewhere).

## DRUG DELIVERY OF SMALL MOLECULAR THERAPEUTICS

A significant progress was achieved in recent years in application of nanogels as DDS for small biologically active molecules. By contrast to SODN, these molecules usually contain only small number of ionic groups, which are able to interact with nanogels. It was evident that only ionic interactions between drug and nanogels could not provide complex stability at physiological conditions. Only if another force, like hydrophobic interactions between drug molecules, stabilized the complexes, could nanogels carry these small molecules. Initially, we successfully encapsulated retinoic acid into nanogels and obtained stable dispersions of the solubilized drug [37]. Retinoic acid was known to provide an anticancer effect and this formulation would be of interest for application in complex drug therapies [38]. Recently, a similar formulation of valproic acid (VA) in nanogels was prepared and studied in the cellular model of the BBB, BBMEC monolayers (Fig.4A). At the same low concentrations of tritium-labeled VA and VA-nanogel formulation, a more than 70% increase in the transcellular transport was observed when encapsulated drug was applied on the apical side of BBMEC monolayers. At chosen nanogel concentration no change in monolayer integrity was observed, therefore this effect could be explained only by a successful transcytosis of drug-loaded nanogels. We have already reported an increased transport of nanogels across BBMEC monolayers and an enhanced *in vivo* accumulation of the DDS in the brain [33]. Transfer of VA across the BBB was shown to be quite effective by means of a membrane-located carboxylic acid transporter (MCT1). However, at higher concentrations of VA in the blood, this transporter soon becomes saturated, and therapeutic doses in the brain do not accumulate [39,40]. Importantly, nanogel transport is evidently independent of this transporter; therefore, we could expect a significant amount of VA delivered to the brain using a nanogel formulation.

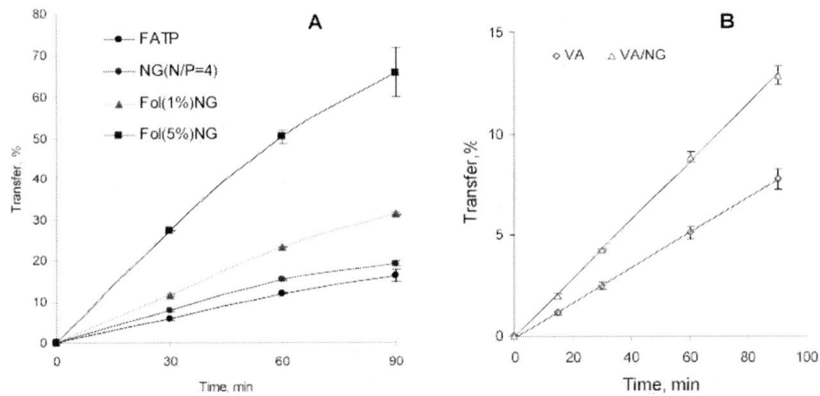


**Figure 4.** Study of drug delivery using drug-nanogel (NG) formulations in cellular models of the gastrointestinal tract (Caco-2) and of the blood-brain barrier (BBMEC): (A) Fludarabine 5′-triphosphate (FATP)/Caco-2 cells, and (B) valproic acid (VA)/BBMEC. ...

An anti-leishmaniasis drug, arjunglucoside I, was recently incorporated into nanogels composed of cross-linked random copolymers of N-isopropylacrylamide and N-vinyl pyrrolidone [41]. This formulation showed a two-fold enhanced therapeutic efficacy against parasites compared to free drug and a similar activity compared to the poly(lactic acid) (PLA) nanoparticles. Both DDS were found effective in reducing hepatotoxicity and nephrotoxicity of the drug to nearly the same extent. Similarly, PAA-Pluronic® microgels efficiently delivered encapsulated an anticancer drug doxorubicin overcoming the MDR-related efflux of this drug [42]. This type of microgels also demonstrated a low toxicity in cellular model of the gastrointestinal (GI) tract.

Another recently developed application of nanogels is delivery of nucleoside analogs. These anticancer drugs usually undergo complex transformation following administration to become an active compound. These drugs are first phosphorylated into nucleoside 5′-phosphates by intracellular nucleoside kinases. This initial phosphorylation is a critical step in anticancer treatment [43]. Further activation steps include formation of nucleoside 5′-diphosphates, conversion of ribonucleotides into deoxyribonucleotides by nucleoside reductases, and synthesis of nucleoside analog 5′-triphosphates (NTPs), which terminate cellular transcription and DNA replication events [44]. Previously, many of prospective nucleoside analogs were discarded in earlier preclinical studies, or withdrawn later from clinical studies, because their intracellular conversion into NTPs was insufficient in the acceptable dosage range. Thus, direct delivery of NTPs into cancer cells would be a promising strategy. Additionally, it can broaden considerably the choice of available efficient anticancer drugs. To test this hypothetical strategy, we prepared and studied nanogel formulations of cytotoxic NTPs. Several nucleoside analogs (Fludarabine, AZT and Cytarabine) were converted into NTPs and complexed with cationic nanogels. The cytotoxicity of these formulations tested in various cancer cell lines was about two orders of magnitude higher than that of the original drugs (Fig.5). This cytotoxic effect is independent of any an additional cytotoxicity of nanogels because similar ATP-nanogel complexes were shown to exhibit markedly lower cytotoxicity levels at higher concentrations. Besides, these complexes could be stored in dry form at 4°C without any trace of NTP decomposition at least for one year. Additionally, nanogels could deliver intact NTPs injected in the blood, providing sufficient protection of encapsulated drugs against phosphatases. As a proof of principle, folate-vectorized nanogels have shown clear advantages as a DDS for a fludarabine 5′-triphosphate in transport experiments using Caco-2 cell monolayers, a cellular model of GI tract (Fig.4B).

The mechanism of drug release from NTP-nanogel formulations is not yet fully understood. Evidently, a considerable amount of the drug was released in 5′-monophosphorylated form, which easily formed and dissociated from nanogels at the physiological conditions. However, a significant part (up to 50%) of the formulated drug could be untied only as the result of substitution of the bound NTP by competitive cellular (poly)anions. Previously, we suggested a mechanism of such substitution by interaction of nanogel network with phospholipids of

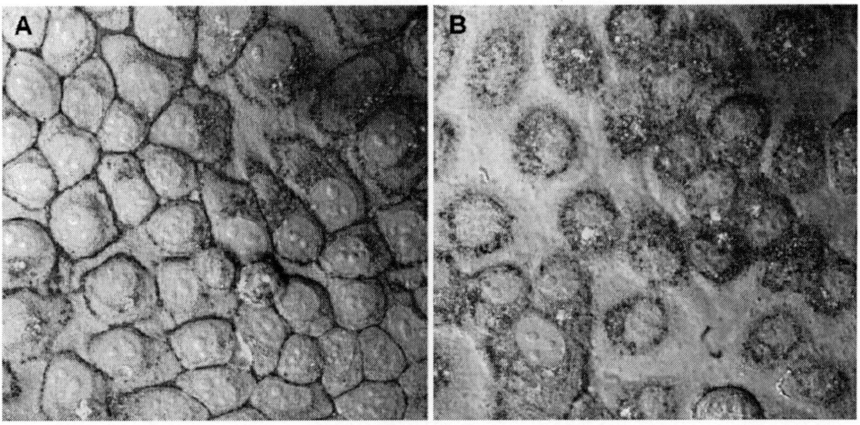


**Figure 5.** Trafficking of drug-loaded nanogel in human breast carcinoma MCF-7 cells. (A) 30 min, and (B) 60 min- treatment with ATP-BODIPY FL (green) encapsulated into Rhodamine-labeled nanogel (PEG-cl-PEI).

the cellular membrane [15]. In the following experiment we traced the intracellular fate of rhodamine-labeled nanogels loaded with a fluorescein-labeled ATP (Fig.6). Initial accumulation of red nanogels on the cellular membrane was evident in these micrographs. This process was accompanied with a fast release of the green drug into cytosol. At a later time point, most of the drug-loaded nanogels, as well as membrane-bound unloaded nanogels, were taken inside by endocytosis (yellow dots), and accumulated in endosomes. However, the process of drug release continued inside the cells and a clearly higher level of green fluorescence was now observed in cytosol. This result was interpreted as an indication of the membrane-triggered drug release mechanism involved in the cellular dissociation of NTP-nanogel complexes. Additional studies should be performed to evaluate criteria that determine the relative importance of this mechanism in drug release from nanogel-based DDS.

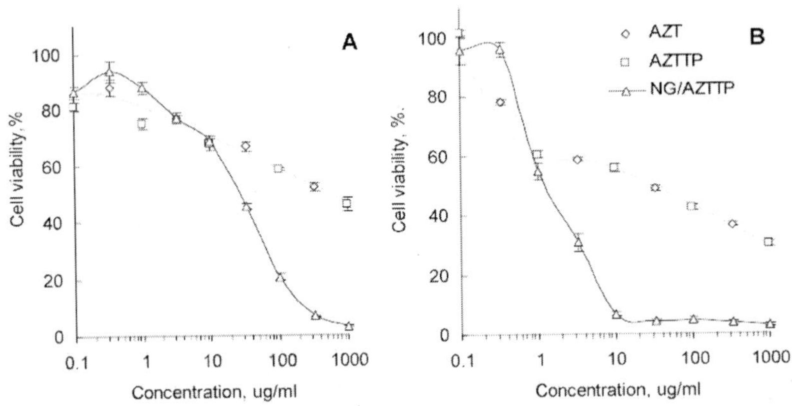


**Figure 6.** Cytotoxicity of 3′-azido-3′-deoxythymidine 5′-triphosphate (AZTTP) and its nanogel (PEG-*cl*-PEI) formulation in human breast carcinoma MCF-7 (A) and MDA-MB-231 (B) cells.

## DELIVERY OF MACROMOLECULAR THERAPEUTICS

One of the most important features of a swollen nanogel particle with low number of crosslinks is the flexibility of its macroporous network in aqueous medium. Charged nanogel network can accommodate biomolecules penetrating the pores or form a kind of polymeric envelope surrounding larger biomolecules. Problems associated with the encapsulation of macromolecular drugs into microgels were critically reviewed recently [45]. One recent application of cationic nanogels is encapsulation of plasmid DNA (pDNA) for non-viral gene therapy or DNA vaccination. Our preliminary studies have demonstrated efficacy of nanogels for transfection of various cancer cells, although the observed level of transgene expression was significantly lower than that obtained with other transfection reagents, such as Lipofectine, Superfect, ExGene 500 or PEI 25kDa in the range of N/P ratios between 3 and 15. We first suggested an explanation related to the low surface charge of nanogels compared to those mostly highly cationic compounds. Since this charge was not increased significantly at high N/P ratios (>15), we did not expect an increase in transfection efficacy of pDNA-nanogel formulations at higher N/P ratio. However, we have found that transfection rose dramatically when N/P ratio reached to 25–30. This clearly meant a formation of some optimal complex between pDNA and nanogel network, confirmed also by dynamic light scattering data when size of the complexes stabilized at the lowest value for complexes prepared at N/P ratios ~ 25–30 (Fig.7A). We have calculated that at this N/P ratio an average swollen nanogel particle formed complex with only one molecule of supercoiled plasmid DNA. Thus, only at N/P ratio ≥ 25 could we obtain a population of pDNA-loaded nanogels with the smallest size, because at lower N/P ratios many nanogel particles had to accommodate two or more pDNAs molecules. This could also result in reduced stability of pDNA against nucleases, inactivation of the loaded pDNA and low levels of transfection (Fig.7B). Because the size of pDNA was estimated as about 110 nm from electron microscopy data, nanogel with an average diameter 150 nm could play the role of a soft pillow wrapping around anionic DNA strands. Additional modification of nanogels with human transferrin has helped to radically increase the transfection efficacy to the levels observed among the best known transfection reagents in the presence of serum (Fig.8A). Further optimization of the nanogel-based transfection system could be achieved by using efficient excipients or post-synthetic chemical derivatization. As an example, the partial complexation of pDNA with fish protamine (PA) before encapsulation into nanogels was shown to markedly increase expression level of transgene in human prostate carcinoma cells (Fig.8A). We hypothesized that a nuclear-localization signal sequence presented in PA, along with an additional nuclease protection of the PA-complexed pDNA in cytosol after release from nanogels, could increase chances for intact pDNA to reach the nucleus.

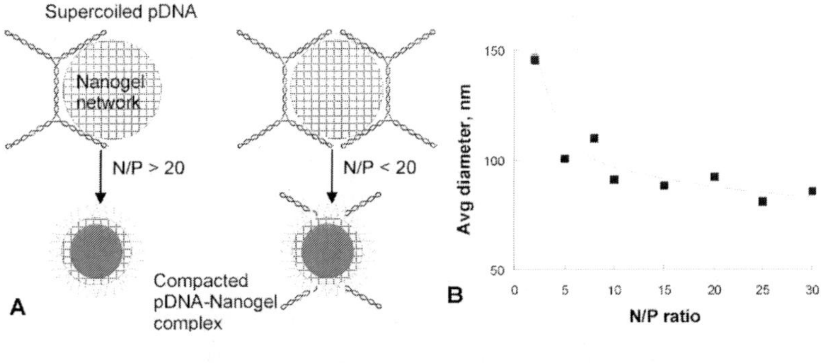


**Figure 7.** Formation of nanogel complexes with plasmid DNA (pDNA). (A) Schematic view of optimal (N/P>25) and non-optimal (N/P<25) formulations of pDNA with nanogels. (B) Size of the compacted pDNA-nanogel formulations as a function of N/P ratio ...

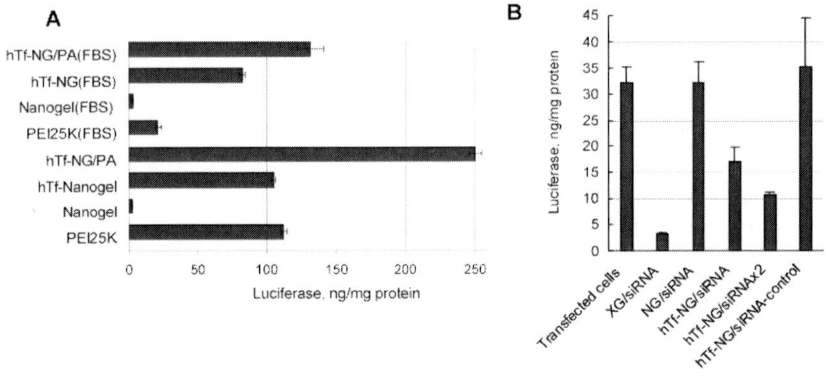


**Figure 8.** Transfection of human prostate carcinoma PC-3 cells with (A) luciferase-encoding pDNA in different nanogel formulations, and (B) siRNA-nanogel complexes for a suppression of the luciferase expression in transiently transfected PC-3 cells.

Vectorized nanogels could also be considered also as a prospective DDS for the novel class of potent gene inhibitors, small interfering RNAs (siRNAs). These double-stranded RNAs with a molecular mass less than 15kDa were able to penetrate into the large pores of nanogels and form polyionic complexes. We compared transfection efficacy of nanogels with commercial X-treme Gene reagent (La Roche) in prostate carcinoma PC-3 cell line and demonstrated the same level of inhibition (70–90%) in both cases at low concentrations of siRNA encapsulated in hTf-labeled nanogels (Fig.8B). This effect was sequence-specific, because no decrease in luciferase expression was detected in the case of nonspecific siRNA-loaded nanogels. We have previously confirmed nucleolytic protection of nanogel-loaded ASO. In the formulations with siRNA, not only was protection of RNA structure against degradation achieved, but also delivery of active double-stranded molecules of siRNAs into the cytosol of transfected cancer cells was also demonstrated. By contrast, another cationic carrier, modified polyacrylate microgel, which is among the most biocompatible and smallest particulate DDSs produced by reverse emulsion polymerization, was not capable of increased delivery of the biologically active free SODN into cytosol of treated cells [46].

## CONCLUSIONS AND FUTURE PROSPECTS

Polymer microgels and nanogels as drug delivery vehicles have a unique set of properties that ideally fit conditions of drug transport via systemic routes of administration. They could be useful for the encapsulation of delicate compounds with low- or high molecular weights, significantly prolonging their activity in biological environments. Chemical engineering would further advance this drug delivery system by optimizing the properties of the nanogel carriers. Nanogels could be vector-driven carriers with high differential organs distribution ratios. Various mechanisms of drug release could be utilized by using microgels, from biodegradation to a stimuli-triggered release. Metal-microgel constructs could also provide additional ways to control drug release trace drug accumulation in targeted organs or provide new modalities of radioactive/cytotoxic cell treatment. Various fields of applications of these drug carriers are now extensively probed and moving closer to clinical practice.

## ACKNOWLEDGMENTS

Financial support was provided from the NIH grants (CA102791 and NS050660). Michael Jacobsen's help in preparation of this manuscript is greatly appreciated.

## REFERENCES

1. Kaneko YS, K.; Okano, T. Temperature-responsive hydrogels as intelligent materials. In: Biorelated Polymers and Gels: Academic Press, 1998. pp. 29–66.

2. Kashyap N, Kumar N, Kumar MN. Hydrogels for pharmaceutical and biomedical applications. Crit Rev Ther Drug Carrier Syst. 2005;22 (2):107–49.

3. Peppas NA, Wood KM, Blanchette JO. Hydrogels for oral delivery of therapeutic proteins. Expert Opin Biol Ther. 2004;4 (6):881–7.

4. Chowdary KP, Rao YS. Mucoadhesive microspheres for controlled drug delivery. Biol Pharm Bull.2004;27 (11):1717–24.

5. Alpar HO, Somavarapu S, Atuah KN, Bramwell VW. Biodegradable mucoadhesive particulates for nasal and pulmonary antigen and DNA delivery. Adv Drug Deliv Rev. 2005;57 (3):411–30.

6. Peppas NA, Huang Y. Nanoscale technology of mucoadhesive interactions. Adv Drug Deliv Rev.2004;56 (11):1675–87.

7. Blanchette J, Peppas NA. Oral Chemotherapeutic Delivery: Design and Cellular Response. Annals of biomedical engineering. 2005;33 (2):142–9.

8. Bromberg L, Temchenko M, Alakhov V, Hatton TA. Bioadhesive properties and rheology of polyether-modified poly(acrylic acid) hydrogels. Int J Pharm. 2004;282 (1–2):45–60.

9. Krauland AH, Bernkop-Schnurch A. Thiomers: development and in vitro evaluation of a peroral microparticulate peptide delivery system. Eur J Pharm Biopharm. 2004;57 (2):181–7.

10. Zhang J, Xu S, Kumacheva E. Polymer microgels: reactors for semiconductor, metal, and magnetic nanoparticles. J Am Chem Soc. 2004;126 (25):7908–14.

11. Sonvico F, Dubernet C, Colombo P, Couvreur P. Metallic colloid nanotechnology, applications in diagnosis and therapeutics. Curr Pharm Des. 2005;11 (16):2095–105.

12. Arya H, Kaul Z, Wadhwa R, Taira K, Hirano T, Kaul SC. Quantum dots in bio-imaging: Revolution by the small. Biochem Biophys Res Commun. 2005;329 (4):1173–7.

13. Hasegawa U, Nomura SM, Kaul SC, Hirano T, Akiyoshi K. Nanogel-quantum dot hybrid nanoparticles for live cell imaging. Biochem Biophys Res Commun. 2005;331 (4):917–21.

14. Medintz IL, Uyeda HT, Goldman ER, Mattoussi H. Quantum dot bioconjugates for imaging, labelling and sensing. Nat Mater. 2005;4 (6):435–46.

15. Vinogradov SV, Bronich TK, Kabanov AV. Nanosized cationic hydrogels for drug delivery: preparation, properties and interactions with cells. Adv Drug Deliv Rev. 2002;54 (1):135–47.

16. Hoffman AS. Hydrogels for biomedical applications. Adv Drug Deliv Rev. 2002;54 (1):3–12.

17. Otsuka H, Nagasaki Y, Kataoka K. PEGylated nanoparticles for biological and pharmaceutical applications. Adv Drug Deliv Rev. 2003;55 (3):403–19.

18. De Jaeghere F, Allemann E, Feijen J, Kissel T, Doelker E, Gurny R. Cellular uptake of PEO surface-modified nanoparticles: evaluation of nanoparticles made of PLA:PEO diblock and triblock copolymers. J Drug Target. 2000;8 (3):143–53.

19. Oupicky D, Ogris M, Howard KA, Dash PR, Ulbrich K, Seymour LW. Importance of lateral and steric stabilization of polyelectrolyte gene delivery vectors for extended systemic circulation. Mol Ther. 2002;5(4):463–72.

20. Kabanov AV, Vinogradov SV, Alakhov YV. Nanogel networks and biological agent compositions. US Patent 6,333,051, 2001, Dec 25.

21. Kabanov AV, Vinogradov SV. Nanogel networks including polyion polymer fragments and biological agent compositions. US Patent 6,696,089, 2004, Febr 24.

22. Vinogradov S, Batrakova E, Kabanov A. Poly(ethylene glycol)-polyethylenimine NanoGel particles: novel drug delivery systems for antisense oligonucleotides. Colloids and Surfaces B: Biointerfaces. 1999;16(4):291–304.

23. Vinogradov SV, Zeman AD, Batrakova EV, Kabanov AV. Polyplex Nanogel formulations for drug delivery of cytotoxic nucleoside analogs. J Controlled Release 2005;xx:xxx-xxx.

24. Hennink WE, van Nostrum CF. Novel crosslinking methods to design hydrogels. Adv Drug Deliv Rev.2002;54 (1):13–36.

25. Park H, Temenoff JS, Holland TA, Tabata Y, Mikos AG. Delivery of TGF-beta1 and chondrocytes via injectable, biodegradable

hydrogels for cartilage tissue engineering applications. Biomaterials 2005.

26. Bromberg L, Temchenko M, Alakhov V, Hatton TA. Kinetics of swelling of polyether-modified poly(acrylic acid) microgels with permanent and degradable cross-links. Langmuir. 2005;21 (4):1590–8.

27. Mao HQ, Roy K, Troung-Le VL, Janes KA, Lin KY, Wang Y, August JT, Leong KW. Chitosan-DNA nanoparticles as gene carriers: synthesis, characterization and transfection efficiency. J Control Release.2001;70 (3):399–421.

28. Moghimi SM, Szebeni J. Stealth liposomes and long circulating nanoparticles: critical issues in pharmacokinetics, opsonization and protein-binding properties. Prog Lipid Res. 2003;42 (6):463–78.

29. Oupicky D, Ogris M, Seymour LW. Development of long-circulating polyelectrolyte complexes for systemic delivery of genes. J Drug Target. 2002;10 (2):93–8.

30. Ogris M, Wagner E. Targeting tumors with non-viral gene delivery systems. Drug Discov Today. 2002;7(8):479–85.

31. Torchilin VP, Lukyanov AN, Gao Z, Papahadjopoulos-Sternberg B. Immunomicelles: targeted pharmaceutical carriers for poorly soluble drugs. Proc Natl Acad Sci U S A. 2003;100 (10):6039–44.

32. Hayashi H, Iijima M, Kataoka K, Nagasaki Y. pH-Sensitive Nanogel Possessing Reactive PEG Tethered Chains on the Surface. Macromolecules. 2005;37 (14):5389–96.

33. Vinogradov SV, Batrakova EV, Kabanov AV. Nanogels for oligonucleotide delivery to the brain.Bioconjug Chem. 2004;15 (1):50–60. [PMC free article]

34. Leamon CP, Cooper SR, Hardee GE. Folate-liposome-mediated antisense oligodeoxynucleotide targeting to cancer cells: evaluation in vitro and in vivo. Bioconjug Chem. 2003;14 (4):738–47.

35. Shiokawa T, Hattori Y, Kawano K, Ohguchi Y, Kawakami H, Toma K, Maitani Y. Effect of polyethylene glycol linker chain length of folate-linked microemulsions loading aclacinomycin A on targeting ability and antitumor effect in vitro and in vivo. Clin Cancer Res. 2005;11 (5):2018–25.

36. Nayak S, Lee H, Chmielewski J, Lyon LA. Folate-mediated cell targeting and cytotoxicity using thermoresponsive microgels. J Am Chem Soc. 2004;126 (33):10258–9.

37. Bronich TV, Vinogradov SV, Kabanov AV. Interaction of nanosized copolymer networks with oppositely charged amphiphilic molecules. NanoLetters. 2001;1 (10):535–40.

38. Soprano DR, Qin P, Soprano KJ. Retinoic acid receptors and cancers. Annu Rev Nutr. 2004;24:201–21.

39. Bolanos JP, Medina JM. Effect of valproate on the metabolism of the central nervous system. Life Sci.1997;60 (22):1933–42.

40. Fisher RS, Ho J. Potential new methods for antiepileptic drug delivery. CNS Drugs. 2002;16 (9):579–93.

41. Tyagi R, Lala S, Verma AK, Nandy AK, Mahato SB, Maitra A, Basu MK. Targeted delivery of arjunglucoside I using surface hydrophilic and hydrophobic nanocarriers to combat experimental leishmaniasis. Journal of Drug Targeting. 2005;13 (3):161–71.

42. Bromberg L, Alakhov V. Effects of polyether-modified poly(acrylic acid) microgels on doxorubicin transport in human intestinal epithelial Caco-2 cell layers. Journal of Controlled Release. 2003;88 (1):11–22.

43. Hatse S, De Clercq E, Balzarini J. Role of antimetabolites of purine and pyrimidine nucleotide metabolism in tumor cell differentiation. Biochem Pharmacol. 1999;58 (4):539–55.

44. Galmarini CM, Mackey JR, Dumontet C. Nucleoside analogues and nucleobases in cancer treatment.Lancet Oncol. 2002;3 (7):415–24.

45. Varde NK, Pack DW. Microspheres for controlled release drug delivery. Expert Opinion on Biological Therapy. 2004;4 (1):35–51.

46. McAllister K, Sazani P, Adam M, Cho MJ, Rubinstein M, Samulski RJ, DeSimone JM. Polymeric nanogels produced via inverse microemulsion polymerization as potential gene and antisense delivery agents.J Am Chem Soc. 2002;124 (51):15198–207.

# Chapter 5

# Rapid Detection and Identification of Overdose Drugs in Saliva by Surface-Enhanced Raman Scattering Using Fused Gold Colloids

**Stuart Farquharson [*], Chetan Shende, Atanu Sengupta, Hermes Huang and Frank Inscore**

*Real-Time Analyzers, Inc., Middletown, CT 06457, USA*

## ABSTRACT

The number of drug-related emergency room visits in the United States doubled from 2004 to 2009 to 4.6 million. Consequently there is a critical need to rapidly identify the offending drug(s), so that the appropriate medical care can be administered. In an effort to meet this need we have been investigating the ability of surface-enhanced Raman spectroscopy (SERS) to detect and identify numerous drugs in saliva at ng/mL concentrations within 10 minutes. Identification is provided by matching measured spectra to a SERS library comprised of over 150 different drugs, each of which possess a unique spectrum. Trace detection is provided by fused gold colloids trapped within a porous glass matrix that generate SERS. Speed is provided by a syringe-driven sample system that uses a solid-phase extraction capillary combined with a SERS-active capillary in series. Spectral collection is provided by a portable Raman analyzer. Here we describe successful measurement of representative illicit, prescribed, and over-the-counter drugs by SERS, and 50 ng/mL cocaine in saliva as part of a focused study.

**Keywords:** drug analysis; illicit drugs; drug overdose; SERS; Raman spectroscopy; emergency room

## 1. INTRODUCTION

In 2009 the number of drug-related emergency room (ER) visits in the United States reached 4.6 million, nearly double the 2.4 million visits in 2004 [1]. Of these visits, 2.1 million were attributed to illicit drugs and 2.3 million to pharmaceutical drugs. Access to prescription drugs over the internet has certainly added to the increase in the latter. Cocaine and heroin represent the largest portion of illicit drugs at 43 and 22%, respectively, followed by methamphetamine, PCP, MDMA (known as ecstasy), and LSD. Pharmaceutical drugs include prescription and over-the-counter drugs (OTC), leading prescription drugs being oxycodone, hydrocodone and diazepam at 14.1, 8.4, 2.4%, respectively, and leading OTC drugs being acetaminophen and ibuprofen at 4.8, 2.7%, respectively. Overdose represents a significant challenge to ER personnel, since it can result in a variety of symptoms [2], confusing diagnosis. For example, cocaine may cause myocardial infarction, hypothermia, seizures, hallucinations, and/or arrhythmias [3]. Acetaminophen overdose symptoms include abdominal pain, convulsions and sweating [4]. Physical assessment of these patients is insufficient, especially in the case of acetaminophen, as most patients are over 65 and have existing health issues. Currently, a two step approach is used to determine drug abuse and overdose: screening and verification [3,5]. Screening devices, such as immunoassay kits, provide drug identification, but they are subject to a number of interferences [6,7]. This leads to a high incidence of false positives. Therefore, sophisticated instruments, such as gas chromatographs coupled with mass spectrometers, are used to verify drug identification, as well as provide quantification [8]. Unfortunately, these analyses, performed in the clinical laboratory, usually take in excess of an hour to perform [9], delaying patient diagnosis and selection of appropriate medical care.

Consequently, there is a need for a device capable of correctly identifying overdose drugs in ER patients at relevant concentrations,*i.e.*, above a threshold, without false positives or negatives, in just a few minutes. Ideally, the device would be portable, easy to use, and relatively non-invasive so that patients can be tested as they enter the ER, or in an ambulance prior to arrival. The last requirement can be best met using saliva as the sample medium [10]. This is a reasonable approach since drugs are represented in saliva at concentrations similar to blood plasma (e.g., cocaine at 0.6–0.8 mcg/mL [11-13] acetaminophen at 10–50 mcg/mL [14]), saliva is 99.5% water making it easy to chemically analyze [15], and simple saliva collectors are available [16].

In an effort to develop such a device, and take advantage of saliva as a sample source, we have been investigating the potential of surface-enhanced Raman spectroscopy (SERS) to both identify and quantify drugs and their metabolites in this body fluid [17,18]. This approach is based on the extreme sensitivity of SERS demonstrated by the detection of single molecules [19,20], the ability to measure very small samples (0.1 mL), and the ability to identify molecular structures of drugs through the rich vibrational information provided by Raman spectroscopy [21].

Towards this goal, we have developed and patented a method to immobilize fused silver and gold colloids in a porous glass matrix in glass capillaries to produce a SERS-active sampling device [22-24]. In contrast to most SERS substrates, the sample does not have to be dried to achieve enhancement [25], but can be drawn into the capillary and measured immediately. Furthermore, the capillary format allows the incorporation of chromatographic materials to aid in the separation of the drugs from saliva. Here we describe the use of a solid-phase extraction (SPE) capillary in combination with a SERS-active capillary to detect and identify cocaine, PCP, diazepam, and acetaminophen in saliva using a portable Raman analyzer suitable for emergency room diagnosis of overdose patients.

## 2. EXPERIMENTAL SECTION

All drugs were obtained from Cerilliant (Austin, TX) as 1 mg/mL in methanol or acetonitrile forensic samples (Figure 1, Table 1). The

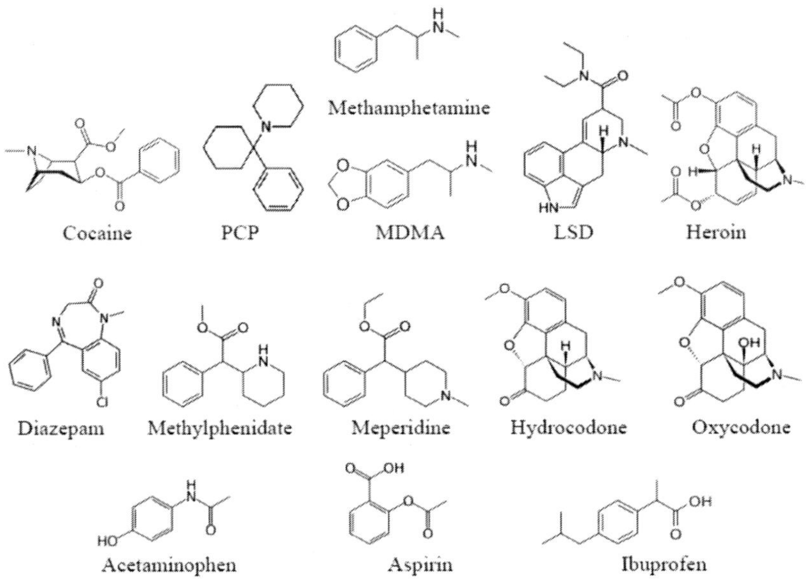


**Figure 1.** Chemical structures for the drugs presented in this study.

chemicals and solvents used to prepare the sol-gels were obtained at their purest commercially available grade from Sigma-Aldrich (Milwaukee, WI) and used as received. The SPE material was obtained from United Chemical Technology (Bristol, PA). The fused gold colloid sol-gels were prepared according to previous published procedures [26,27], by mixing a gold chloride salt ($HAuCl_4$•$3H_2O$) with tetramethyl orthosilicate in methanol. The SERS capillaries were prepared by drawing 20 μL of the gold colloid-doped sol-gels into 10 cm long, 1-mm diameter glass capillaries to produce ~1 cm plugs. After sol-gel formation, the incorporated ions were reduced with dilute sodium borohydride forming fused colloids. This was followed by a water wash to remove residual reducing agent.

Solid-phase extraction packed capillaries (also 1-mm diameter glass) were prepared by first drawing ~5 mcL of methyltrimethoxysilane (MTMS) into one end of a glass capillary by syringe to form a porous sol-gel frit as a support for the SPE material. Secondly, ~100 mcL of a 20 mg/mL SPE/ethanol slurry was drawn into the capillary to form an ~5 cm plug. And thirdly, a second 5 mcL of MTMS was drawn into the

**Table 1.** Drugs measured to build a spectral library. Drugs presented in this study are in bold type. Metabolites are italicized.

| | | | |
|---|---|---|---|
| *11-nor-Ä$^9$-THC-9-COOH* | **Cocaine HCl** | Lactose | Penacillamine |
| *11-OH-Ä$^9$-THC* | Codeine | l-amphetamine | Phenacetin |
| *6-acetylcodeine* | d-amphetamine (Dexedrine) | l-ephedrine HCl | Phenethylamine |
| *6-acetylmorphine* | Ä$^9$-THC | Levamisole (Ergamisol) | Phenobarbital |
| **Acetaminophen** | Dextromethorphan | Lidocaine (lignocaine) | Phentermine |
| Acetylcholine chloride | **Diazepam (Valium)** | Lorazepam (Ativan) | Phenylephrine |
| **Acetylsalicylic acid (aspirin)** | Dimenhydrinate (Dramamine) | **LSD** | Phenylpropanolamine HCl |
| Alfentanil HCl | Diphenhydramine | Mannitol | *PMA HCl* |
| Alprazolam (Xanax) | dl-amphetamine | MDA | *PMMA HCl* |
| Amifostin | dl-ethylamphetamine | MDEA | Pregabalin (Lyrica) |
| Aminorex | **dl-methamphetamine** | **MDMA** | Prilocaine |
| Amitriptyline (Elavil) | d-methamphetamine | MDPV | Procaine (novacaine) |
| Amobarbital (Amytal) | Dopamine HCl | **Meperidine (Demerol)** | Promethazine |
| Amyl nitrite | Doxylamine succinate | Mephedrone HCl | Propranolol HCl |
| Atropine | d-propoxyphene (Darvocet) | Mescaline | Proxymetacaine |
| Benzocaine | Duloxetine (Cymbalta) | Methadone | Pseudoephedrine |
| *Benzoylecgonine* | *Ecgonine methyl ester* | Methaqualone (Quaalude) | Psilocin |
| Benzylpiperazine | *EDDP perchlorate* | Methcathinone | Quetiapine fumarate (Seroquel) |
| Buprenorphine | *EMDP HCl* | Methicillin | Quinine |
| Bupropion | Erythromycin | Methylone HCl | Risperidone (Risperidol) |
| Caffeine | Estazolam | **Methylphenidate (Ritalin)** | Salicylic acid |
| Cannabidiol | Etomidate | Midazolam (Dormicum) | Scopolamine |
| *Cannabinol* | Excedrin pill | *Morphine glucuronide* | Serotonin HCl |
| Carbamazepine | Fenfluramine (Fen-Phen) | Morphine | Sertraline HCl (Zoloft) |
| Carisoprodol | Fentanyl | Naltrexone HCl | Sildenafil citrate (Viagra) |
| Celecoxib (Celebrex) | Flunitrazepam (Rohypnol) | Naproxen | Sodium pentothal |
| Chloral hydrate | Fluoxetine HCl (Prozac) | *n-desmethyltramadol HCl* | Strychnine |
| Chloramphenicol | Flurazepam (Dalmane) | Nicotine | Sulfadoxine |
| Chlordiazepoxide (Librium) | Haloperidol (Haldol) | *Norcocaine HCl* | Temazepam (Restoril) |
| Chlorpheniramine | **Heroin** | *Norcodeine* | Tetracaine (amethocaine) |
| Chlorpromazine HCl (Thorazine) | Hydrochlorothiazide | Nordiazepam | Tetracycline |
| Ciprofloxacin | **Hydrocodone** | Olanzapine | *Theophylline* |
| cis-Tramadol HCl | Hydromorphone (Dilaudid) | Oxazepam | Trazodone |
| Citalopram HBr | Ibogaine | *Oxazepam glucuronide* | Triazolam (Halcion) |
| Clonazepam (Klonopin) | **Ibuprofen** | **Oxycodone (Oxycotin)** | Vancomycin |
| Clonazipine | Inositol | Oxymorphone | Zaleplon (Sonata) |
| *Cocaethylene* | Isoniazide | *Paraxanthine* | Zolpidem tartrate (Ambien) |
| Cocaine base | Ketamine | **PCP** | Zopiclone (Lunesta stereoisomer) |

capillary to secure the SPE material. The SPE capillary was preconditioned by sequentially flowing 1 mL each of methanol, water and 10 mM acetic acid. Each experiment was performed by drawing the test sample through the SPE capillary, then washing the capillary to remove any interferents, and just prior to the final elution step, the SERS capillary was attached to the SPE capillary so that the extracted drugs could be eluted directly into the SERS capillary.

Saliva used in preparing artificial samples was collected using oral swabs (Medimpex United Inc, Bensalem, PA) from consenting employees at Real-Time Analyzers, Inc. (RTA, Middletown, CT). The foam head attached to a syringe plunger was placed into the person's mouth for approximately one minute to let sufficient saliva collect in the foam. The swab was then placed into the plastic syringe barrel, and pressed to expel the saliva into a vial. Approximately 1 mL of saliva was collected in 1 minute by this process.

The drug-doped saliva samples were prepared in plastic centrifuge tubes by adding a small amount of aqueous drug at the required concentration into the saliva and uniformly mixed by gently vortexing the sample for 10 seconds. For example, 10 mcL of a 5 mcg/mL aqueous cocaine was added to 0.990 mL of saliva to yield a 1 mL 50 ng/mL cocaine-doped saliva sample. The samples were allowed to equilibrate for 0.5 hours at room temperature. Samples were measured within 1 hour of saliva collection. Approximate concentrations were verified by gas chromatography (Shimadzu, model 17A).

A searchable surface-enhanced Raman spectra library was prepared by measuring all of the drugs using a Fourier transform Raman spectrometer (RTA, model RamanPro) that provided 100 to 3350 $cm^{-1}$ spectral coverage with constant 8 $cm^{-1}$ resolution. The SERS-active capillaries were fixed horizontally to an XY positioning stage (Conix Research, Springfield, OR) mounted above a fiber optic probe. The probe delivered 75 mW of 785 nm laser excitation to the capillary and collected the 180° scattered radiation. A pure cocaine sample was prepared by drying a forensic sample on a glass slide. The Raman spectrum of this residue was measured using 300 mW of 785 nm laser power and a 5 minute acquisition time. Further instrument details have been published [21]. To demonstrate ER measurement capability, the drug-doped saliva samples were also measured using a 5 lb, battery operated, hand-held Raman analyzer (RTA, model SERS-ID, Figure 2). The SERS capillaries were fixed horizontally in the sample compartment of the portable analyzer, which delivered 45 mW of 785 nm excitation laser to the capillary and collected the 180° scattered radiation. In the case of all the spectra presented here, three capillaries were measured and the average spectrum reported.

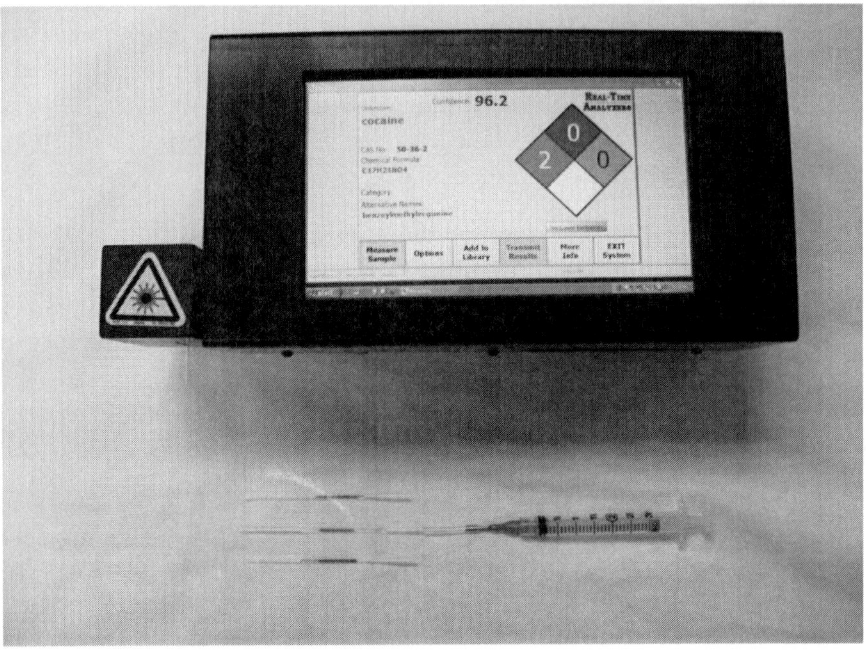


**Figure 2.** Photographs of surface-enhanced Raman spectroscopy (SERS)-ID and SERS-active capillaries.

## 3. RESULTS AND DISCUSSION

One hundred and fifty drugs; illicit, prescription, over-the-counter, and in many cases their primary metabolites, were measured by SERS using fused gold colloids immobilized within a sol-gel matrix contained in glass capillaries. The gold colloids enhanced the Raman scattering for virtually all of the drugs tested, with some barbiturates as the primary exception. In many cases the normal Raman spectra were also measured to verify spectral integrity as well as to estimate surface enhancement factors (EF). This is shown for cocaine, the primary drug of concern (Figure 3) [1]. The Raman spectrum of cocaine is dominated by peaks at 872, 999, 1026, 1273, 1597, and 1716 $cm^{-1}$, which have been assigned to a tropine ring stretch, the symmetric and asymmetric phenyl ring breathing modes, the C-phenyl stretch, the trigonal phenyl ring breathing mode, and the ester carbonyl stretch [28,29]. There are clear changes in relative intensity

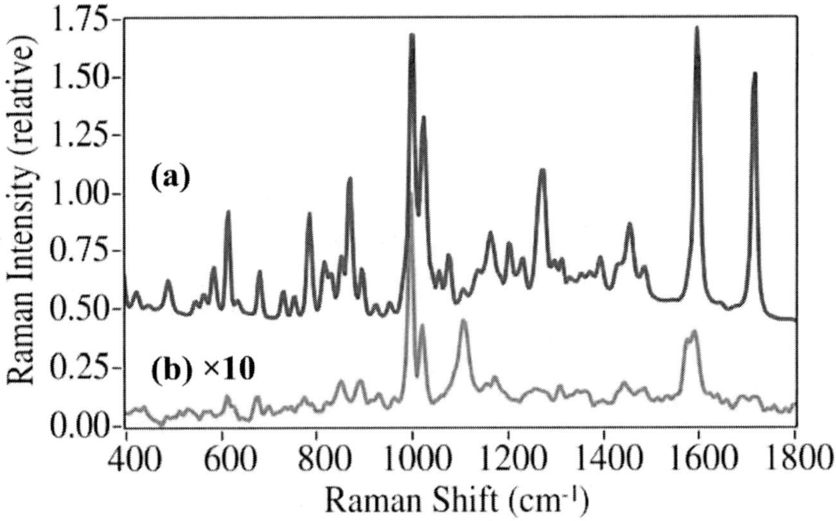


**Figure 3.** Comparison of **(a)** Raman spectroscopy (RS) of pure cocaine on a glass slide to **(b)**SERS for 100 ng/mL (100 ppb) cocaine in water (as cocaine•HCl) using a fused gold colloid-doped sol-gel in a 1 mm capillary. Conditions: **(a)** 300 mW of 785 nm, 5 minute acquisition,**(b)** 75 mW of 785 nm excitation, 1 minute acquisition; both at 8 $cm^{-1}$ resolution. The SERS spectral intensity has been multiplied by 10 so that features are evident, and offset for clarity.

and frequency for these modes in the SER spectra due to the extent with which each vibrational mode interacts with the gold surface and the plasmon field [17]. Notably, the symmetric mode at 999 $cm^{-1}$ is enhanced the most, the asymmetric mode shifts to 1018 $cm^{-1}$, a new unassigned peak appears at 1107 $cm^{-1}$, the trigonal mode looses relative intensity as its splits into a 1578 and 1593 $cm^{-1}$ doublet, and the carbonyl stretch is virtually absent. An enhancement factor of 3.1 $\times$ $10^6$ was determined based on the relative concentrations, intensities of the 999 $cm^{-1}$ peak, and laser powers for the two spectra (EF = [1 g/mL/100 ng/mL] × [0.1 I/1.3 I] × [300 mW/75 mW]). EFs were typically between $10^5$ and 5 × $10^6$ for the drugs presented in this paper.

In addition to cocaine, this study focused on the illicit, prescription and OTC drugs that most often result in ER visits [1]. The additional illicit drugs included PCP (1-(1-phenylcyclohexyl) piperidine), dl-

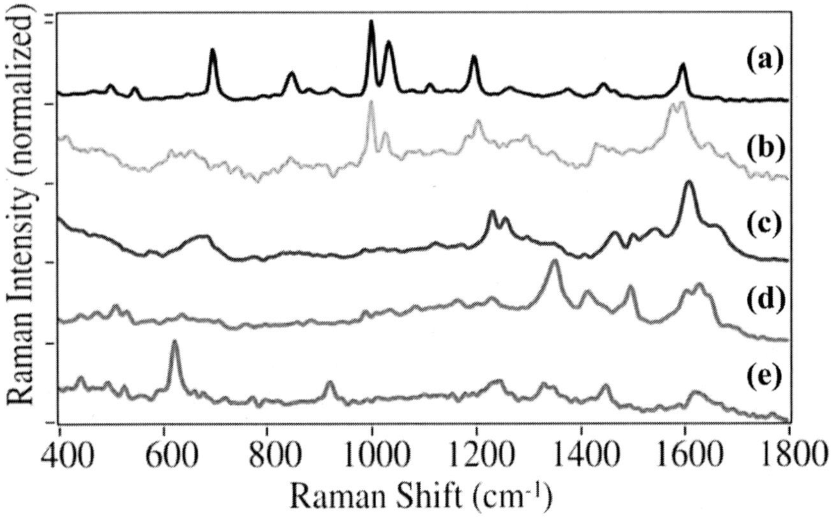


**Figure 4.** SERS of illicit drugs: **(a)** 1-(1-phenylcyclohexyl) piperidine (PCP), **(b)**methamphetamine, **(c)** 3,4-methylenedioxymethamphetamine (MDMA), **(d)** lysergic acid diethylamide (LSD), and **(e)** heroin. Conditions as in Figure 3(b), except at 0.1 mg/mL. Ordered to show spectral similarity. Intensities normalized and offset for clarity.

methamphetamine, MDMA (3,4-methylenedioxymethamphetamine), LSD (lysergic acid diethylamide), and heroin (diacetylmorphine). Each drug produces a unique SERS spectrum that can be used for identification (Figure 4). While the spectra for cocaine, PCP, and methamphetamine are dominated by the phenyl stretching modes at 999, ~1030 and ~1595 $cm^{-1}$, they each have unique peaks: 1107 $cm^{-1}$ for cocaine, 702 and 849 $cm^{-1}$ due to the cyclohexane and piperidine ring modes for PCP, respectively, and 1578 $cm^{-1}$ phenyl mode for methamphetamine [30,31]. The phenyl modes are absent as expected for MDMA, LSD, and heroine [32]. MDMA has a unique doublet at 1233 and 1258 $cm^{-1}$ due to the dioxole ring and a C-N stretching mode, LSD at 1350 $cm^{-1}$ also due to a ring or C-N stretching mode, and heroin at 624 and 921 $cm^{-1}$ due to ring modes.

The SERS spectra were measured for prescription drugs with the following active ingredient (Figure 5): diazepam (Valium®), methylphenidate (Ritalin®), meperidine (Demerol®), hydrocodone (Vicodin®), and oxycodone (Oxycotin®). Identifying unique peaks for these drugs is more difficult than the illicit drugs due to their structural similarity. Once again the phenyl modes are present at ~1000, 1030, and 1595 $cm^{-1}$ for diazepam, methylphenidate, and meperidine, but as expected, not for hydrocodone and oxycodone. A number of unique peaks appear between 600 and 700 $cm^{-1}$, as well as at 833 and 941 $cm^{-1}$ for diazepam, all attributed to aromatic ring deformation modes, except the 833 $cm^{-1}$ peak, which is attributed to the diazapine ring [33]. Although methylphenidate and meperidine have nearly identical structures, the piperidine ring of the former appears to interact with the gold through the amine resulting in two peaks at 849 and 903 $cm^{-1}$. The spectra of hydrocodone and oxycodone are very similar with C=C ring modes at 1293 and ~1605 $cm^{-1}$. The former has a unique doublet at 664 and 675 $cm^{-1}$, which is attributed to ring modes as was done for heroin, while the latter has a unique peak at 1505 $cm^{-1}$ that has been attributed to a scissoring mode of the methyl group [34].

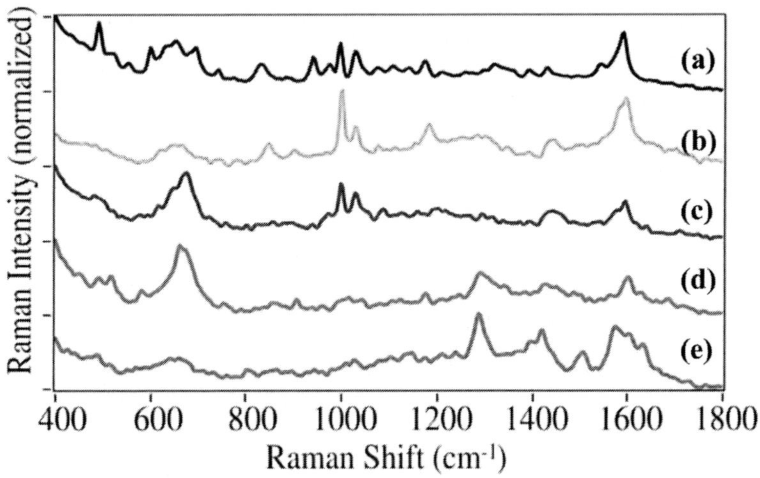


**Figure 5.** SERS of prescription drugs: **(a)** diazepam (Valium®), **(b)** methylphenidate (Ritalin®), **(c)** meperidine (Demerol®), **(d)** hydrocodone (Vicodin®), and **(e)** oxycodone (Oxycotin®). Conditions as in Figure 4. Ordered to show spectral similarity. Intensities normalized and offset for clarity.

The OTC drugs included acetaminophen, aspirin (acetylsalicylic acid), and ibuprofen. While acetaminophen and ibuprofen have been implicated in numerous overdose cases (often unintentionally), aspirin has been included in this study as it is often taken with many of the other drugs. Again, each drug has unique peaks suitable for identification. For acetaminophen this includes the 1165, 1555, and 1647 $cm^{-1}$ phenol, C=C ring, and amide stretches, respectively (Figure 6). For aspirin this includes numerous unassigned peaks between 500 and 900 $cm^{-1}$, the 1080 $cm^{-1}$ ortho-substituted ring mode, and the 1655 $cm^{-1}$ ester mode. For ibuprofen a COOH bending mode appears at 1439 $cm^{-1}$. Aspirin and ibuprofen also have COOH stretching modes at 1597 and 1582 $cm^{-1}$, respectively.

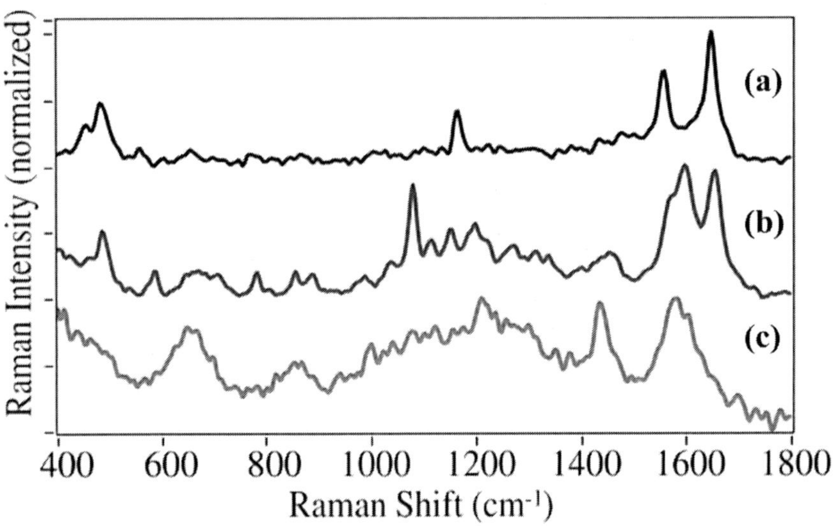


**Figure 6.** SERS of OTC drugs: **(a)** acetaminophen, **(b)** aspirin, and **(c)** ibuprofen. Conditions as in Figure 4. Intensities normalized and offset for clarity.

While the traditional method of identifying unique peaks can be used to identify drugs as described above, a more reliable method is to compare the entire spectrum to a library of previously recorded spectra for identification. This not only eliminates the tedium of identifying peaks, but also allows the identification process to be automated. Four algorithms, Absolute Value, Least Squares, Euclidean Distance, and Correlation, were examined for this purpose [35]. In essence the first two algorithms subtract the measured spectrum from each library spectrum, such that an exact match would equal zero, while the second two algorithms divide the measured spectrum by each library spectrum, such that an exact match would equal one. However, the latter two algorithms subtract the results from one to conform to the first two algorithms. In all cases, the results are reported as the Hit Quality Index (HQI) where a perfect match and complete mismatch (no peaks in common) would result in HQIs of 0 and 1, respectively. Here the spectra were pretreated by restricting the spectral region from 400 to 1800 $cm^{-1}$ and setting the baseline intensity to zero and the most intense peak to one. The Correlation algorithm proved best, and the results are shown for a measurement of oxycodone as an unknown compared to the 152 drug spectral library (Table 1, Figure 7). Even though this drug has the least unique SERS spectrum presented here, it is easily identified as the best match with an HQI score of 0.073, and hydrocodone, the next best match, has an HQI score of 0.734, clearly a mismatch (Table 2). The success of this method is very similar to a previous study of 309 pharmaceuticals by Raman spectroscopy [36].

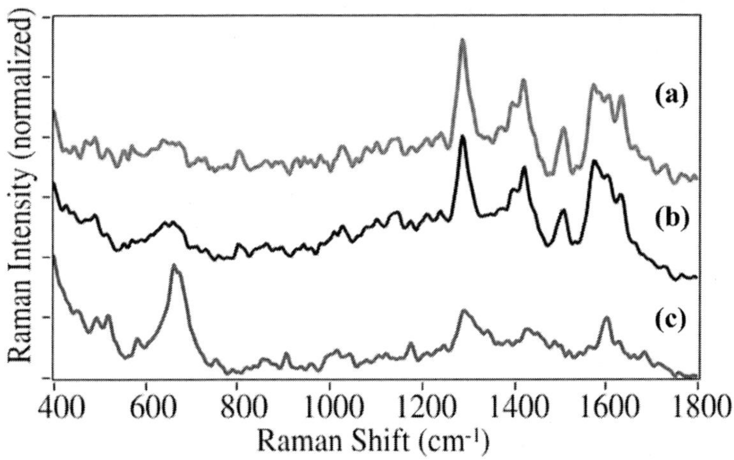


**Figure 7.** SERS of **(a)** oxycodone as an unknown, **(b)** oxycodone in the spectral library, and**(c)** hydrocodone as the second best match in the spectral library. The Hit Quality Index (HQI) scores were **(b)** 0.073 and **(c)** 0.734, indicating **(a)** as the best match. Conditions as inFigure 4.

**Table 2.** Spectral search and match results for drugs in saliva (except oxycodone in water).

| Unknown | Oxycodone (0.1 mg/mL water) | | Cocaine (50 ng/mL) | | PCP (1 mcg/mL) | | Diazepam (1 mcg/mL) | | Acetaminophen (10 mcg/mL) | |
|---|---|---|---|---|---|---|---|---|---|---|
| Rank | HQI | Chemical | HQI | Chemical | HQI | Chemical | HQI | Chemical | HQI | Chemical |
| 1 | 0.073 | Oxycodone | 0.287 | Cocaine | 0.019 | PCP | 0.022 | Diazepam | 0.276 | Acetaminophen |
| 2 | 0.734 | Hydrocodone | 0.348 | Ethyl-benzoyl-ecgonine | 0.315 | Fentanyl | 0.317 | Tema-zepam | 0.639 | Sulfadoxine |
| 3 | 0.800 | Trazadone | 0.349 | Benzoyl-ecgonine | 0.325 | EMDP* | 0.328 | Nor-diazepam | 0.704 | Serotonin |

* EMDP is 2-Ethyl-5-methyl-3,3-diphenylpyrroline.

Previous measurements of saliva samples artificially doped with cocaine demonstrated a measured limit of 250 mcg/mL [17]. This is not surprising since salivary mucins (a class of high molecular weight glycosylated proteins) can physically and in some cases chemically bind the drugs so that they are unavailable for enhancement at the metal colloid surfaces [37,38]. Furthermore, the highly viscous nature of these mucins can clog the sol-gel pores, as well as block the metal surface. In an effort to make the drugs available for SERS, a simple method suitable to the ER was developed to break-up the mucins and release the drugs from proteins using acetic acid, and to separate the drugs for analysis using solid-phase extraction. As part of this method development, SPE capillary columns were prepared using 1-mm glass capillaries to match, and be used in-line with, the SERS-active capillaries. The SPE material chosen consisted of silica particles functionalized with octyl groups and benzyl sulfonic acid groups, as this material has been successfully used to separate numerous drugs, including cocaine from biological fluids [39]. The final method consisted of the following steps. 1) A 1 mL saliva sample (500 mcL of saliva plus 500 mcL of 10 mM acetic acid) was drawn through a 1 micron filter into a SPE capillary column, depositing the drug and passing some of the saliva components. 2) 1 mL each of 10 mM acetic acid, methanol and water were drawn through the SPE capillary column removing any residual saliva components. 3) A 20 mcL 2% ammonium hydroxide in acetonitrile solution was drawn through the SPE capillary column into a SERS capillary, extracting the drug from the SPE, and depositing it on the fused gold colloid-doped sol-gel. 4) The SERS capillary was placed in the sample compartment of the portable Raman analyzer and measured. The entire process took less than 10 minutes for each sample.

Using this procedure, a series of saliva samples doped with cocaine, PCP, diazepam, and acetaminophen were prepared beginning at 1 mg/mL, then diluted by factors of 10 to 1 mcg/mL and measured. In the case of cocaine, the dilution was continued to 10 ng/mL. While cocaine, PCP and diazepam produced consistent SERS at 1 mcg/mL and above, acetaminophen was sporadic at this concentration, but consistent at 10 mcg/mL and above (Figure 8).

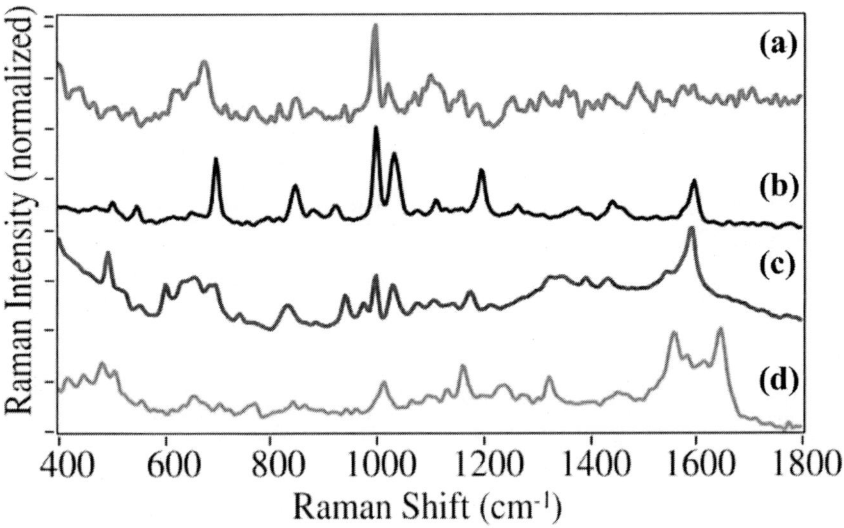


**Figure 8.** SERS of **(a)** 50 ng/mL cocaine, **(b)** 1 mcg/mL PCP, **(c)** 1 mcg/mL diazepam, and**(d)** 10 mcg/mL acetaminophen extracted from saliva. Conditions as in Figure 4, except at indicated concentrations.

In the case of cocaine, for which the above method was optimized, it was consistently detected at 50 ng/mL and higher, and sporadically at 10 ng/mL. These sensitivities demonstrated for cocaine and acetaminophen are sufficient to detect typical overdose saliva concentrations of ~0.6–0.8 and 10–50 mcg/mL for these drugs, respectively [13,14]. It should be noted that the analyzer does not have to quantify the drugs, but it does need to have sufficient sensitivity to detect and subsequently identify them. The ability of the analyzer and the developed method to perform this task is shown in Figure 9 for cocaine at 50 ng/mL, the reproducible limit of detection. The measured sample was compared to the 152 drug spectral library, and as can be seen, the best match is the library spectrum of cocaine. However, the HQI score is relatively high due to the lower signal-to-noise ratio, and the scores for the next best matches were close at 0.348 and 0.349 for ethylbenzoylecgonine and benzoylecgonine, both metabolites of cocaine with near identical structures (Table 2). The former is formed in the presence of alcohol in the body by replacing the methyl group of the methyl ester with an ethyl group. The latter is formed as part of the metabolic breakdown of cocaine by replacing the methyl group of the methyl ester with a hydrogen. As mentioned above for cocaine, the ester modes are very weak in the SERS spectra, and consequently, the spectra are very similar. Considerably better results were obtained for PCP, diazepam, and acetaminophen, albeit at higher concentrations (Table 2). In all cases the HQI score of the second best match was considerably higher (worse) than the first.

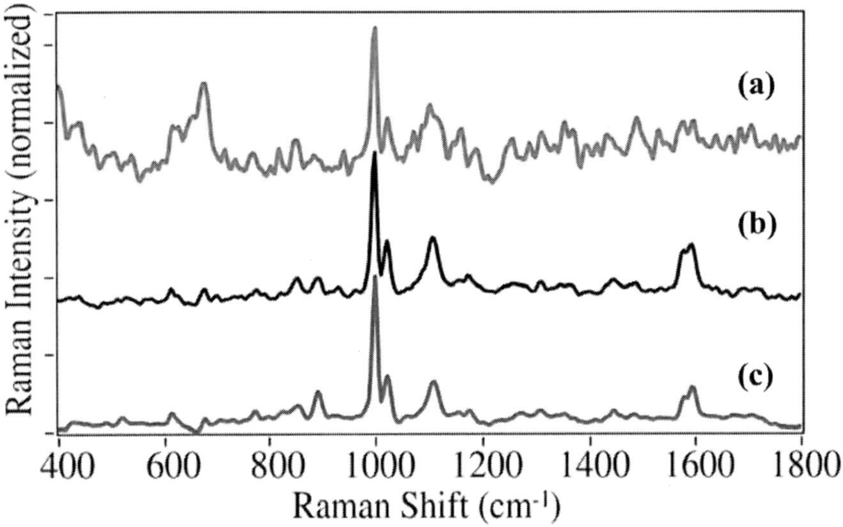


**Figure 9.** SERS of **(a)** 50 ng/mL cocaine in saliva as an unknown, **(b)** 0.1 mg/mL cocaine in the spectral library, and **(c)** ethylbenzoylecgonine as the second best match in the spectral library. The HQI scores were **(b)** 0.287 and **(c)** 0.348. Conditions as in Figure 4, except at indicated concentrations.

# 4. CONCLUSIONS

Surface-enhanced Raman spectra of 152 drugs and metabolites were successfully collected using fused gold colloids immobilized in a porous glass matrix contained in glass capillaries. Spectra are shown for a series of illicit, prescription, and OTC drugs. A method was successfully developed to measure such drugs in saliva by combining a solid-phase extraction capillary to separate the drugs from saliva with the SERS-active capillary. The method allowed the detection and identification of 50 ng/mL cocaine, 1 mcg/mL PCP, 1 mcg/mL diazepam, and 10 mcg/mL acetaminophen in saliva using a 152 spectral library and a search and match software program. The entire analysis, from sample collection to positive identification was performed in less than 10 minutes. The cocaine measurement represents a vast improvement compared to a previously reported SERS measurement of cocaine in saliva; the measurement was 5000-times better [17]. Future work will develop the capillaries into a lab-on-a-chip as part of a sample kit to be used by ambulance and emergency room personnel in conjunction with a hand-held Raman analyzer.

# ACKNOWLEDGMENTS

The authors are grateful for the support of Sarah Lamping and Helen Turner of the UK Home Office Centre for Applied Science and Technology, as well as the National Institute of Health (Grant Number 1R43CA94457-01) and the National Science Foundation (Grant Number DMI-0215819).

# CONFLICT OF INTEREST

The authors declare no conflict of interest.

## REFERENCES AND NOTES

1. Highlights of the 2009 Drug Abuse Warning Network (DAWN) findings on drug-related emergency department visits. The DAWN Report; Center for Behavioral Health Statistics and Quality, Substance Abuse and Mental Health Services Administration: Rockville, MD, USA, 28 December 2010. Available online http://dawninfo.samhsa.gov (accessed on 26 April 2011).

2. Jatlow, P. Cocaine: Analysis, Pharmacokinetics, and Metabolic Disposition. Yale J. Biol. Med. 1988, 61, 105–113.

3. Rainey, P.M.; Schonfeld, D.J. Toxicology, Monitoring of Drug Therapy, and Testing for Substance Abuse. In The Yale University School of Medicine Patient's Guide to Medical Tests; Zaret, B.L., Jatlow, P.I., Katz, L.D., Eds.; Houghton-Mifflin Co: New York, NY, USA, 1997; pp. 587–596.

4. Burgess, S. FDA limits acetaminophen in prescription combination products; requires liver toxicity warnings. U.S. Food and Drug Administration: Silver Spring, MD, USA, 13 January 2011. Available online http://www.fda.gov/NewsEvents/Newsroom/PressAnnouncements/ucm239894.htm (accessed on 26 April 2011).

5. Bates, D.W.; Soldin, S.J.; Rainey, P.M.; Miceli, J.N. Strategies for Physician Education and Therapeutic Drug Monitoring.Clin. Chem. 1998, 44, 401–407.

6. Ammann, H.; Vinet, B. Accuracy, Precision, and Interferences of Three Modified EMIT Procedures for Determining Serum Phenobarbital, Urine Morphine, and Urine Cocaine Metabolite with a Cobas-Fara. Clin. Chem. 1991, 37, 2139–2141.

7. Rainey, P.M.; Rogers, K.E.; Roberts, W.L. Metabolite and Matrix Interference in Phenytoin Immunoassays. Clin. Chem. 1996,42, 1645–1653.

8. Rainey, P.M.; Jatlow, P. Advances in Therapeutic Drug Monitoring. In Advances in Pathology and Laboratory Medicine; Weinstein, R.S., Ed.; Mosby: St. Louis, MO, USA, 1993; Volume 6, pp. 185–206.

9. Puopolo, P.R.; Chamberlin, P.; Flood, J.G. Detection and Confirmation of Cocaine and Cocaethylene in Serum Emergency Toxicology Specimens. Clin. Chem. 1992, 38, 1838–1842.

10. Crouch, D.; Day, J.; Baudys, J.; Fatah, A. Evaluation of Saliva/Oral Fluid as an Alternate Drug Testing Specimen.; Report Number 605-03; National Institute of Justice: Rockville, MD, USA; July; 2004.

11. Van Dyke, C.; Ungerer, J.; Jatlow, P.; Barash, P.G.; Byck, R. Oral cocaine plasma concentrations and central effects. Science1978, 200, 211–213.

12. Jenkins, A.J.; Oyler, J.M.; Cone, E.J. Comparison of heroin and cocaine concentrations in saliva with concentrations in blood and plasma. J. Anal. Toxicol. 1995, 19, 359–374.

13. Musshoff, F.; Madea, B. Cocaine and Benzoylecgonine Concentrations in Fluorinated Plasma Samples of Drivers Under Suspicion of Driving Under Influence. Forensic Sci. Int. 2010, 200, 67–72.

14. Sanaka, M.; Kuyama, Y.; Nishinakagawa, S.; Mineshita, S. Use of salivary acetaminophen concentration to assess gastric emptying rate of liquids. J. Gastroenterol. 2000, 35, 429–433.

15. Chamberlain, J. The Analysis of Drugs in Biological Fluids, 2nd ed.; CRC Press: Boca Raton, FL, USA, 1995.

16. For example, Medimpex United Inc. (Bensalem, PA).

17. Shende, C.; Inscore, F.; Gift, A.; Maksymiuk, P.; Farquharson, S. Ten-minute analysis of drugs and metabolites in saliva by surface-enhanced Raman spectroscopy. P. Soc. Photo-Opt. Instrum. Eng. 2005, 6007, 165–171.

18. Farquharson, S.; Shende, C.; Inscore, F.; Maksymiuk, P.; Gift, A. Analysis of 5-fluorouracil in saliva using surface-enhanced Raman spectroscopy. J. Raman Spectrosc. 2005, 36, 208–212.

19. Kneipp, K.; Wang, Y.; Dasari, R.R.; Feld, M.S. Approach to Single-Molecule Detection Using Surface-Enhanced Resonance Raman Scattering (SERRS). Appl. Spectrosc. 1995, 49, 780–784.

20. Nie, S.; Emory, S.R. Probing Single Molecules and Single Nanoparticles by Surface-Enhanced Raman Scattering. Science1997, 275, 1102–1106.

21. Farquharson, S.; Gift, A.; Shende, C.; Inscore, F.; Ordway, B.; Farquharson, C.; Murran, J. Surface-enhanced Raman Spectral Measurements of 5-Fluorouracil in Saliva. Molecules 2008, 13, 2608–2627.

22. Farquharson, S.; Lee, Y.H.; Nelson, C. Material for SERS and SERS sensors and method for preparing the same. U.S. Patent 6,623,977, 3 September 2003.

23. Farquharson, S.; Maksymiuk, P. Simultaneous chemical separation and surface-enhanced Raman spectral detection using metal-doped sol-gels. U.S. Patent 6,943,032, 13 September 2005.

24. Farquharson, S.; Maksymiuk, P. Separation and Plural-point surface-enhanced Raman spectral detection using metal-doped sol-gels. U.S. Patent 6,943,031, 13 September 2005.

25. Turner, H.; Lamping, S. Commercial SERS Substrates for a Roadside Screening Device for Drugs in Oral Fluids. Proceedings of the Joint Meeting of the International Council on Alcohol, Drugs and Traffic Safety and The International Association of Forensic Toxicologists, Seattle, WA, USA, 24 August, 2007.

26. Farquharson, S.; Gift, A.D.; Inscore, F.E.; Shende, C.S. SERS Method for Rapid Pharmacokinetic Analysis of Drugs in Saliva. U.S. Patent 7,393,691, 1 July 2008.

27. Farquharson, S.; Gift, A.D.; Maksymiuk, P.; Inscore, F. Rapid dipicolinic acid extraction from Bacillus spores detected by surface-enhanced Raman spectroscopy. Appl. Spectrosc. 2004, 58, 351–354.

28. Angel, S.M.; Carter, J.C.; Stratis, D.N.; Marquardt, B.J.; Brewer, W.E. Some new uses for filtered fiber-optic Raman probes:in situ drug identification and in situ and remote Raman imaging. J. Raman Spectrosc. 1999, 30, 795–805.

29. Carter, J.C.; Brewer, W.E.; Angel, S.M. Raman spectroscopy for the in situ identification of cocaine and selected adulterants.Appl. Spectrosc. 2000, 54, 1876–1881.

30. Tsuchihashi, H.; Katagi, M.; Nishikawa, M.; Tatsuno, M.; Nishioka, H.; Nara, A.; Nishio, E.; Petty, C. Determination of Methamphetamine and Its Related Compounds Using Fourier Transform Raman Spectroscopy. Appl. Spectrosc. 1997, 51, 1796–1799.

31. Sägmüllera, B.; Schwarzeb, B.; Brehmc, G.; Trachtac, G.; Schneide, S. Identification of illicit drugs by a combination of liquid chromatography and surface-enhanced Raman scattering spectroscopy. J. Mol Struct. 2003, 661-662, 279–290.

32. Hodges, C.M.; Hendra1, P.J.; Willis, H.A.; Farley, T. Fourier transform Raman spectroscopy of illicit drugs. J. Raman Spectrosc. 1989, 20, 745–749.

33. Neville, G.A.; Shurvell, H.F. Fourier transform Raman and infrared vibrational study of diazepam and four closely related 1,4-benzodiazepines. J. Raman Spectrosc. 1990, 21, 9–19.

34. Rana, V.; Cañamares, M.V.; Kubic, T.; Leona, M.; Lombardi, J.R. Surface-enhanced Raman Spectroscopy for Trace Identification of Controlled Substances: Morphine, Codeine, and Hydrocodone. J. Forensic Sci. 2011, 56, 200–207.

35. Gemperline, P. Practical Guide to Chemometrics, 2nd ed.; Taylor & Francis Group CRC Press: Boca Raton, FL, USA, 2006.

36. McCreery, R.; Horn, A.; Spencer, J.; Jefferson, E. Noninvasive Identification of Materials inside USP Vials with Raman Spectroscopy and a Raman Spectral Library. J. Pharm. Sci. 1998, 87, 1–8.

37. Kaliszan, R.; Nasal, A.; Turowski, M. Binding site for basic drugs on a1-acid glycoprotein as revealed by chemometric analysis of biochromatographic data. Biomed. Chromatogr. 1995, 9, 211–215.

38. Kala, J.; Pang, W.; Zubaidah, H.; Hashim, O. Proteomic Analysis of Whole Human Saliva Detects Different Altered Secretions of Seven Proteins in Heavy Cigarette Smokers Compared to Non-smokers. Int. J. Mol. Sci. 2010, 11, 4488–4505.

39. Badawi, N.; Simonsen, K.; Steentoft, A.; Bernhoft, I.; Linnet, K. Simultaneous Screening and Quantification of 29 Drugs of Abuse in Oral Fluid by Solid-Phase Extraction and Ultraperformance LC-MS/MS. Clin. Chem. 2009, 55, 2004–2018.

# Chapter 6

# Structural Versatility of Bicellar Systems and Their Possibilities as Colloidal Carriers

**Barbosa-Barros Lucyanna [1], Rodríguez Gelen [2], Cócera Merce [2], Rubio Laia [2], López-Iglesias Carmen [3], de la Maza Alfons [2] and López Olga [2,*]**

[1]*Departament de Fisicoquímica, Facultat de Farmàcia, Universitat de Barcelona, 08028 Barcelona, Spain*

[2]*Departament de Tecnologia Química i de Tensioactius, Institut de Química Avançada de Catalunya (I.Q.A.C.), Consejo Superior de Investigaciones Científicas (C.S.I.C.), C/Jordi Girona 18-26, 08034 Barcelona, Spain*

[3]*Centres Científics i Tecnològics, Universitat de Barcelona, Parc Científic de Barcelona, C/Josep Samitier 1-5, 08028 Barcelona, Spain*

## ABSTRACT

Bicellar systems are lipid nanostructures formed by long- and short-chained phospholipids dispersed in aqueous solution. The morphological transitions of bicellar aggregates due to temperature, composition and time variations have been revised in this work. To this end, two bicellar systems have been considered; one formed by dimyristoyl-phosphatidylcholine (DMPC) and dihexanoyl- phosphatidylcholine (DHPC) and another formed by dipalmitoyl-phosphatidylcholine (DPPC) and DHPC. The relationship between the magnetic alignment, the morphology of the aggregates and the phase transition temperature ($T_m$) of lipids is discussed. In general terms, the non-alignable samples present rounded objects at temperature below the $T_m$. Above this temperature, an increase of viscosity is followed by the formation of large elongated aggregates. Alignable samples presented discoidal objects below the $T_m$. The best alignment was achieved above this temperature with large areas of lamellar stacked bilayers and some multilamellar vesicles. The effect of the inclusion of ceramides with different chain lengths in the structure of bicelles is also revised in the present article. A number of physical techniques show that the bicellar structures are affected by both the concentration and the type of ceramide. Systems are able to incorporate 10% mol of ceramides that probably are organized forming domains. The addition of 20% mol of ceramides promotes destabilization of bicelles, promoting the formation of mixed systems that include large structures. Bicellar systems have demonstrated to be morphologically stable with time, able to encapsulate different actives and to induce specific effects on the skin. These facts make bicellar systems good candidates as colloidal carriers for dermal delivery. However, water dilution induces structural changes and formation of vesicular structures in the systems; stabilization strategies have been been explored in recent works and are also updated here.

**Keywords:** bicellar systems; bicelles; ceramides; nanostructures; colloids; freeze fracture electron microscopy; phospholipids; skin; stratum corneum; transition temperature

## 1. INTRODUCTION

Bicelles are lipid nanostructures formed by a long and a short chain phospholipid dispersed in aqueous solution [1,2]. These aggregates have been used as membrane models for nuclear magnetic resonance (NMR) structural studies of membrane biomolecules [3]. Depending on the composition and the long/short chain phospholipid molar ratio ($q$), these structures may display a bilayered discoidal morphology alignable in magnetic fields at temperatures above the long chain phospholipid phase transition ($T_m$). The total lipid concentration of bicelles is also an important factor, since the dilution of these aggregates promotes important morphological transitions [4]. The disks formed by the combination of the dimyristoyl phosphatidylcholine (DMPC) constituting the flat bilayer, plus the dihexanoyl phosphatidylcholine (DHPC) stabilizing the rim of the structures have been the most applied systems for these kind of studies [5-7]. Some works have shown the morphology and phase diagram of DMPC/DHPC bicelles to be very complex. In general, it is accepted that bicelles for which the long chain to short chain phospholipid molar ratio is between 2.8 and 6.5 will spontaneously align in a magnetic field, such that the bilayer plane is parallel to the magnetic field. The short chain amphiphile (DHPC) plays a slightly different role in such aligned aggregates; in most cases, DHPC-rich torroidal defects are believed to be scattered throughout an extended bilayer resembling a perforated lamellar morphology [8,9]. The DHPC-rich defects lend sufficient mobility to the overall aggregate that spontaneous alignment can occur.

One of the aims of this review is to understand the morphology and phase behavior of bicelles over a wide range of temperatures and compositions. This is interesting considering that bicelles are able to mimic particular types of cell membranes [10-14]. The formation of bicelles with different phospholipids as well as the inclusion of cholesterol, ceramides (Cer), cardiolipin and polyethylene glycol (PEG) lipids in the systems has been also recently reported [15-19]. Thus, bicelles are replacing lipid based liposomes and surfactant based micellar systems as models to study membrane proteins.

Bicelles exhibit an intermediate morphology between lipid vesicles and the classical mixed micelles, combining some of the attractive properties of both of these model membrane systems. Like micelles, bicelles are non-compartmentalized, optically transparent, and effectively mono-disperse. Consequently, it is much easier to achieve homogeneous mixing in bicelles than in lipid vesicles. On the other hand, bicelles, in contrast with the classical mixed micelles, have not surfactants in their structure and maintain some key bilayer properties that are absent in the latter systems [20]. Although both liposomes and micelles have often been used in skin treatment [21,22] their application to date has been extensively debated. In fact, the large size of liposomes makes its penetration in the skin difficult, and micelles usually promote skin irritation due to their surfactant composition. In this field, the bicellar systems seems to offer advantages over liposomes because of its dimensions (diameters in the range of 10–50 nm and thickness about 4–6 nm [1]), small enough for passing through the stratum corneum SC lipid lamellae; and over micelles due to its bilayered structure and exclusively lipid composition [23,24].

This revision includes studies of the morphological transformations of specific bicellar systems due to the changes in the composition, temperature and time after preparation. Two bicellar systems have been revised; a classic one formed by dimyristoyl phosphatidylcholine (DMPC) and dihexanoyl phosphatidylcholine (DHPC) and another formed by DPPC dipalmitoyl phosphatidylcholine and also by the DHPC. Besides, the influence of different Cer in these systems has also been described. In general, the alignment of the systems has been studied using $^{31}$P-NMR. The characterization of the structural changes produced in bicelles by effect of different factors is focused, combining different techniques such as: small-angle X-ray scattering (SAXS); dynamic light scattering (DLS) and freeze fracture electron microscopy high-pressure freezing (FFEM-HPF).

Taking into account the specific characteristics of bicelles and their high versatility, the use of these lipid nanostructured systems as colloidal carrier should be considered.

# 2. DMPC/DHPC BICELLAR SYSTEMS

## 2.1. Relationship between the Changes in the Physico-Chemical Characteristics of Bicelles and the Temperature

The classical description of bicelles as discoidal objects formed by a DMPC bilayer closed in the edges by DHPC molecules has been well accepted for non-aligned samples below their main phase transition temperature ($T_m$). However, the description above the $T_m$ was in the past extensively discussed, where the magnetically alignable phase was thought to be formed by shaped-disks [1-4,25].

In the last years diverse studies have shown the morphology and phase diagram of DMPC/DHPC bicelles to be very complex and under some debate [26-29]. Nieh and co-workers proposed a model for bicelles with and without lanthanide cations ($Ln^{3+}$), which is commented on in the following paragraph [9,27].

At temperatures below the $T_{m,}$ of the DMPC, the resulting bicelles were shaped disks [9]. As the temperature rose from the gel to liquid crystalline phase in the presence of $Ln^{3+}$ the bicelles fused together in an end-to-end manner to form lamellar sheets with perforated holes that were lined with DHPC. Further temperature increase caused phase separation with the formation of DHPC-rich mixed micelles and DMPC-rich oriented lamellae, and the DHPC-rich mixed micelles became incorporated into the oriented bilayers at even higher temperatures [30]. In the absence of $Ln^{3+}$, bicelles were disk-shaped in the gel phase, and chiral nematic in the liquid crystalline phase, which were described as wormlike micelles, and at higher temperatures were multilamellar vesicles [27]. Additionally, recent studies have demonstrated that inclusion of small amount of charged lipids eliminated the appearance of the worm-like or ribbon phase [31] Hereafter, the use of the term bicelle in most studies refers only to the sample composition and not to the disk-shaped morphology. A comparative study of alignable and non-alignable bicelles associated to the temperature changes of the system could be helpful to clarify the morphological transitions involved in this process.

Our group has recently published studies [32,33], in which high pressure freeze fixation and freeze fracture electron microscopy techniques [34,35] were combined with the $^{31}$P-NMR to correlate the magnetic alignment of DMPC/DHPC bicelles, morphological transitions and the changes in the temperature of the system. Two lipid molar ratios ($q$ = 2 and $q$ = 3.5) were investigated. Direct observations showed that $q$ = 2 bicelles (S-q2) were very fluid and transparent at 20 °C, but as the temperature rose, the sample became viscous with a gel-like appearance maintaining the transparency until 60 °C. When q was 3.5 (S-q3.5) the system became fluid and transparent only at temperatures below DMPC $T_m$, (around 24 °C) [36]. At 25 °C the sample became viscous, at 30 °C it was viscous and slightly milky and from 40 °C to 60 °C was milky and fluid.

Bicelle alignment was studied using $^{31}$P-NMR technique. Figure 1 shows the spectra for (S-q2) and (S-q3.5) bicelles in a temperature range from 20 to 60 °C [32]. The reference peak is shown at 0 ppm. The spectra of the S-q2 (Panel A) showed isotropic behavior at all temperatures. At 20 °C the spectrum was a doublet near −1 ppm reflecting the slightly different environments of the DMPC sites (bilayer) and DHPC sites (rim) on the bicelle structure [37]. At 25 °C, these peaks overlapped. The single peak slightly shifted downfield with increasing temperature until 60 °C, showing a characteristic behavior of non-alignable phospholipid mixtures [38,39].

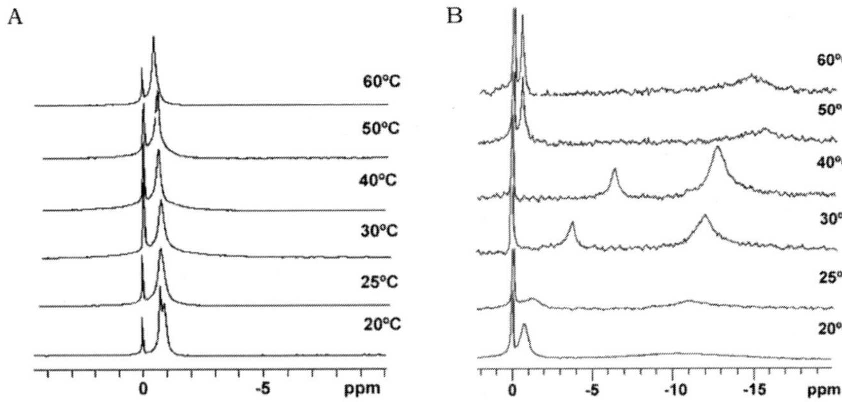


**Figure 1.** $^{31}P$ NMR spectra under $^{1}H$ decoupling as a function of temperature of the S-q2 system (left column) and the S-q3.5 system (right column). The temperature is indicated in the figure and was increased smoothly starting from 15 °C with equilibration times of 15 min between different temperatures—the reference resonance at 0 ppm arises from 85% phosphoric acid. Water content in both systems was 80%.

The spectra of S-q3.5 (Figure 1, Panel B) presented considerable variations depending on the temperature. At 20 °C a single resonance peak was shown at −0.77 ppm and a broad protuberance was seen around −10 ppm, suggesting that the sample had some orientation with respect to the magnetic field. The presence of two well differentiated resonances in bicellar samples has been reported by Gaemers and Bax as a result of the alignment occurring with the bilayer normal oriented perpendicular to the magnetic field [40]. The high-field resonance would correspond to DMPC oriented bilayers and the low-field resonance to DHPC forming disks or hole edges [6]. Just above the DMPC Tm, at 25 °C, the spectrum showed two broad resonances at −1.19 and −10.82 ppm. From this temperature, the observed resonances move towards the right and the lines became more intense, indicating an improvement of the magnetic alignment that reaches a maximum at 40 °C. The integration of the high and low-field peaks gave a relative intensity of 3.3. This value was close to the q ratio of this sample 3.5, confirming that the downfield peak corresponded to the DHPC and the upfield to the DMPC. The gradual upfield shift of DMPC peak reflected an increase of the bilayer order with respect to the magnetic field and the upfield shift of the DHPC peak was related to the increasing presence of DHPC in the DMPC bilayer. That is, the rise of temperature promoted the miscibility of the DHPC molecules in the DMPC bilayer that resulted in the migration of the DHPC molecules from the edges of the bicelles to the bilayer area. Hence, the absence of enough DHPC molecules to fill the bicelle edges led to the fusion of bilayers, which increased the bicellar diameters and improved the alignment until a certain point. From 50 °C the sample orientation was lost and a typical isotropic low field peak around −0.54 ppm and a broad protuberance around −15 ppm were present. According to Triba and co-workers [37] this change on the spectra was characteristic of a phase transition from bicellar aggregates to bigger structures with slow motion. To elucidate the morphological characteristics of these bicellar systems electron microscopy experiments were performed. To this end, alignable (S-q3.5) and non-alignable (S-q2) samples, below the DMPC $T_m$ and above this temperature were analyzed. Bicelles were high pressure frozen (HPF) at −150 °C from sample temperature of 20 °C and 40 °C. These temperatures were chosen to compare the morphology of these alignable and non-alignable samples, to further correlate with the corresponding $^{31}$P-NMR data.

The HPF method was developed to allow for the freezing of hydrated material from a defined state [35]. The great advantage of this method is the non-requirement of sample pre-treatments, which frequently leads to the formation of artefacts. The freeze fracture replicas were visualized mainly by a cryo-SEM technique [33]. Replica cleaning for TEM is tedious and sometimes difficult, large replicas tend to disintegrate during cleaning and the field of view is restricted by the grid bars. These problems are circumvented by cryo-SEM [41], in which no replica cleaning is requested. In SEM, the sample does not have to be transparent to the electron beam, and bulk samples can be analyzed. Using the combination of HPF and cryo-SEM, samples difficult to clean for the TEM were imaged and large areas were investigated. All investigated samples were free of visible ice crystal artefacts. The cryo-SEM images for S-q2 and S-q3.5 samples are shown in Figures 2and 3, respectively.

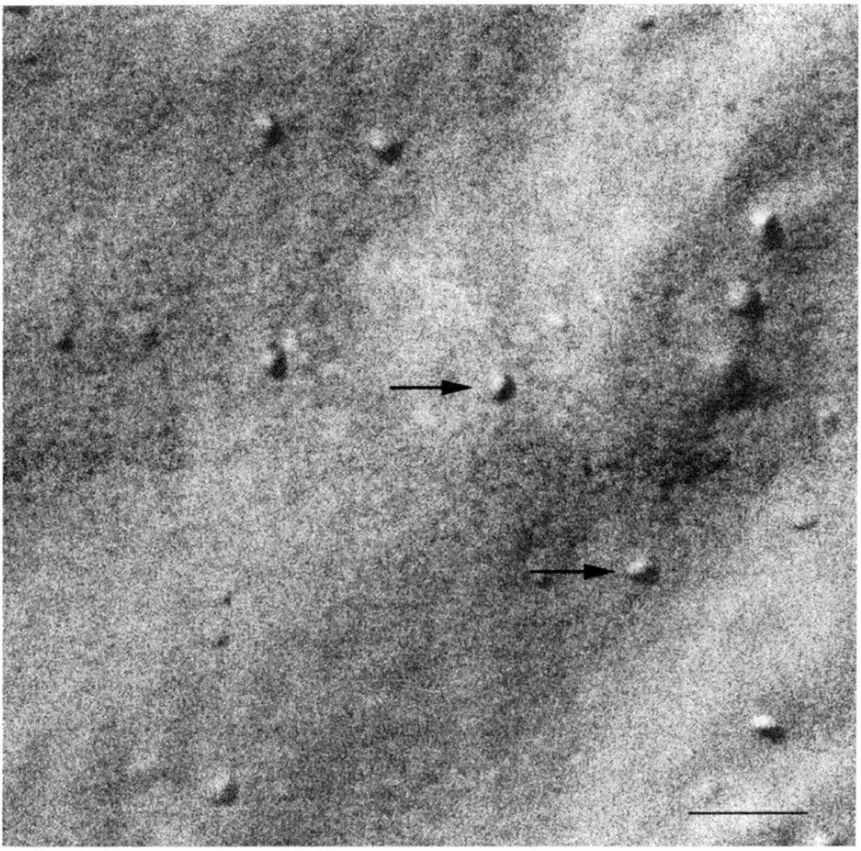

**Figure 2.** Electron micrograph of the S-q2 system at 20 °C. The arrows indicate the small bicelles of about 20 nm. Bar = 100 nm.

**Figure 3.** Electron micrograph of the S-q3.5 system at 20 °C. The arrows denote disks viewed face-on and the arrow heads denote disks viewed edge-on. Bar = 50 nm.

At 20 °C, temperature below $T_m$, small aggregates were visualized in both cases (Figures 2 and 3). Figure 2 shows small rounded aggregates with diameters around 20 nm (arrows). In Figure 3 the aggregate diameters of S-q3.5 were about 40 nm (slightly larger than those of S-q2), being also visualized a discoidal structure shape. Two different zones in the discoidal structures are observed. The arrows indicate aggregates with face-on and the arrow heads point to aggregates with edges-on.

Comparison of these images with the corresponding $^{31}$P-NMR spectra, revealed a relation between the aggregate structure and its magnetic orientation. The rounded shape aggregates of the S-q2 image did not allow for magnetic alignment, whereas the two well differentiated areas of the disks visualized in the S-q3.5 micrograph accounted for the onset of orientation detected in Figure 1B by the presence of the two separated resonances.

At temperature of 40 °C large aggregates were observed for both in the S-q2 and the S-q3.5 systems. Figure 4 shows an image for S-q2 system with elongated aggregates with about 2000 nm. Similar results have been reported by vam Dam and co-workers for DMPC/DHPC systems at $q$ = 2, low concentrated samples ($c_L$ = 3%) at temperatures of 36 °C and 46 °C using a cryo-TEM technique [42].

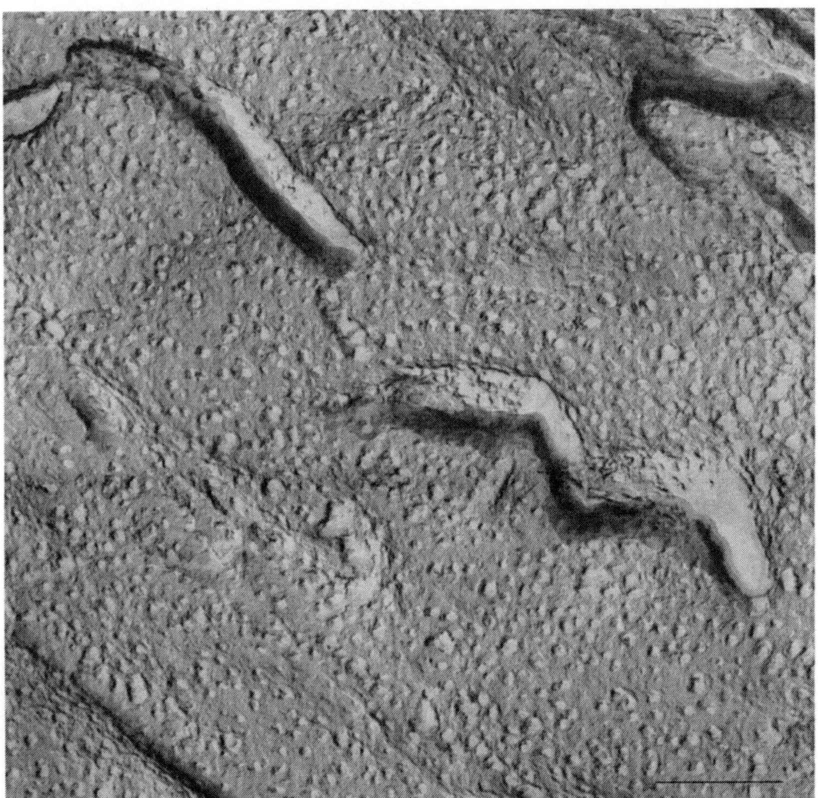

**Figure 4.** Electron micrograph image of the S-q2 system at 40 °C showing isolated elongated aggregates. Bar = 1.00 μm.

In Figure 5 a cryo-SEM image of the sample S-q3.5 at 40 °C is displayed in which extended areas of stacked lamellar sheets (arrows) were visualized. The presence of multilamellar vesicles was also detected.

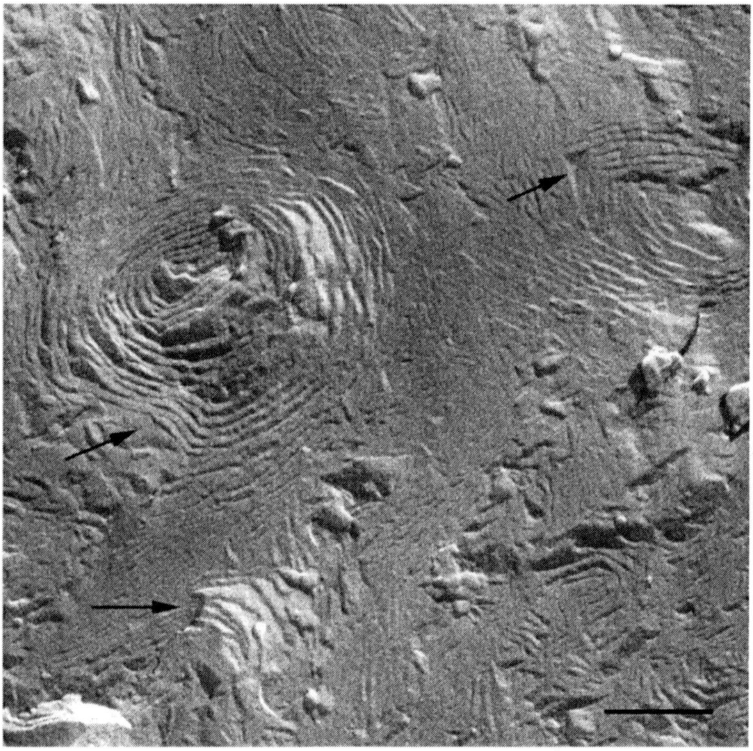

**Figure 5.** Electron micrograph image of the S-q3.5 system at 40 °C showing stacked bilayer sheets (arrows). Bar = 500 nm.

Figure 6 depicts a detail of one of these multilamellar vesicles with a size around 1000 nm. The large structures observed in these micrographs accounts for the milky appearance of this sample. This lamellar phase probably represents the most ordered phase of this sample since the best alignment in $^{31}$P-NMR experiments was obtained at this temperature.

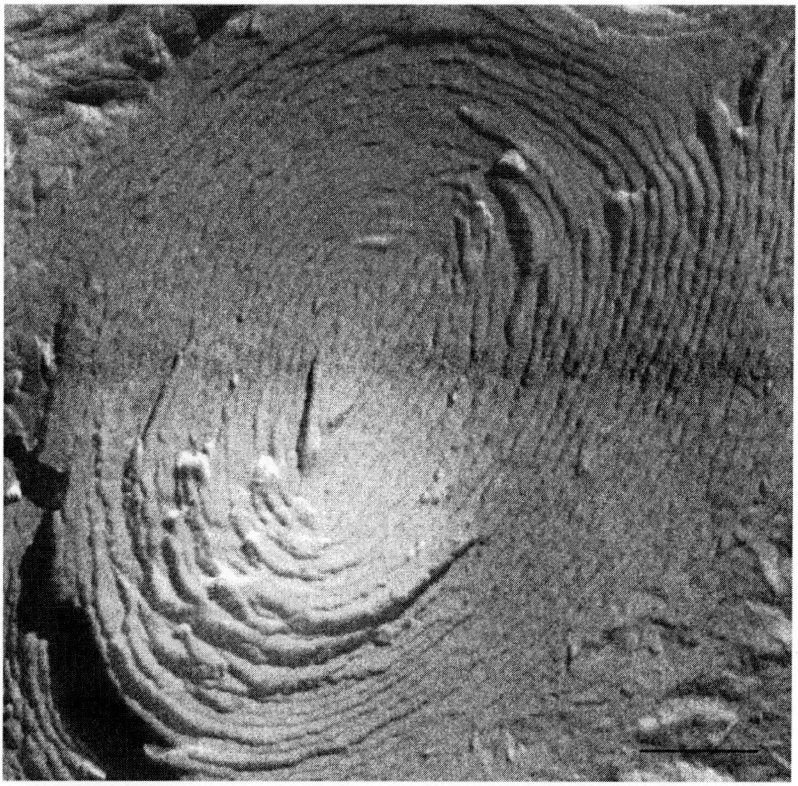

**Figure 6.** Electron micrograph showing a multilamellar vesicle present in the S-q3.5 system at 40 °C. Bar = 250 nm.

The current discussion about the morphology of the DMPC/DHPC aligned aggregates may be summarized in two hypotheses. Both coincide in the morphological transitions of the aggregates from disks to elongated micelles, perforated lamellar sheets and mixed multilamellar vesicles. Also, both hypotheses take into account the initial increase of sample viscosity and the subsequent drop in this viscosity caused by the continuous increase of temperature. Nevertheless, they diverge on the morphology of the structures when sample shows magnetic alignment. One of the theories defends that elongated aggregates correspond to the morphology of the magnetic aligned phase and are present when the sample viscosity increases [43]. The other, claims that the perforated lamellar sheets corresponded to the morphology of the magnetic aligned phase. The formation of these lamellar structures would take place when the sample viscosity drops and the sample appearance is milky [5,6]. Moreover, in a deep $^{31}$P-NMR study Triba and co-workers [37] admitted the compatibility of both elongated and perforated lamellar structures with the NMR aligned spectra, although they did not disprove the discoidal structure as possible in the aligned phase.

The results obtained by our group combining HPF, FFEM and $^{31}$P-NMR techniques [32] are in accordance with some points of the mentioned theories. In the experiments with the sample S-q2 we observed the increase of sample viscosity when the sample was heated. The cryo-SEM images of this sample at 40 °C showed elongated structures, as described by Harroun [43] (Figure. 4). Nevertheless, this sample did not align in magnetic fields (Figure 1A). At this q ratio, the proximity of the DMPC and DHPC molecules in the elongated structures formed at 40 °C as well as in the spherical objects formed at 20 °C did not allow for an anisotropic environment. Hence, the two phosphorus signals in $^{31}$P-NMR overlap and a single resonance is seen. In this way, although the increase of sample viscosity can be attributed to the formation of elongated aggregates, these structures did not correspond to the morphology of the magnetic aligned phase.

On the other hand, evidence of the morphology of aligned aggregates was obtained by the analysis of the S-q3.5 micrographs. This sample also presented an increase of the viscosity when the temperature raised, but when the best alignment was detected (40 °C), the sample had a milky appearance. The cryo-SEM micrographs at this temperature (Figures 5 and 6) showed areas plenty of stacked bilayer sheets and some multilamellar liposomes. The closing up of the bilayer sheets in vesicles is the result of a spontaneous process probably caused by the reduction of the energetic cost of bending by the effect of temperature. The existence of a mixed system accounts for the broad peaks obtained in the spectrum at 40 °C. The multilamellar vesicles probably interfere in the perfect alignment of the structures which would produce narrow resonance peaks. In any case, the segregation of DMPC and DHPC in the S-q3.5 aggregates accounts for the orientation of this system in the magnetic field. Even below $T_m$, the discoidal shape of these aggregates (Figure 3) caused the onset of orientation reflected in the appearance of the broad resonance at −10 ppm in the NMR spectra at 20 °C (Figure 1B**)**. The improvement of the alignment of this sample was observed with the increase of temperature reaching a maximum at 40 °C, temperature at which stacked lamellar sheets were mainly observed. From 50 °C, the lost magnetic alignment and the resonance signal at −15 ppm probably indicated the complete closing up of the aligned bilayer sheets into isotropic vesicles. From these data it may be assumed that the combination of NMR and HPF, FFEM techniques was appropriated to evaluate the relation between the magnetic alignment and the morphology of the two bicellar systems revised.

As for the isotropy of the non-alignable sample S-q2, morphological evolutions from spherical to elongated aggregates were reported, verifying that despite of their growth, these elongated aggregates were not able to orient in magnetic fields. As for S-q3.5 these samples presented anisotropy for magnetic orientation even below $T_m$, given that the morphology of the aggregates allows distinct phosphorus environments. As the temperature increased the sample achieved best alignment, and the morphology of the aggregates evolved from disks to lamellae. At the temperature of the best magnetic alignment, the aggregates were formed by stacked bilayer sheets and multilamellar liposomes. The present data could be very useful to modulate the alignment of systems in magnetic fields and therefore to optimize the use of bicellar systems as membrane mimics.

## 2.2. Stability of Bicelles against the Time

The temporal stability of these aggregates has been analyzed using $^{31}$P-NMR, FFEM, HPF, Small-Angle X-ray Scattering (SAXS) [44-46], and Dynamic Light Scattering (DLS) techniques.

Figure 7 shows the $^{31}$P-NMR spectra for bicelles 24 h (7A) and 14 days (7B) after preparation [47]. A doublet was observed with peaks around −0.754 and −0.927 ppm (7A) and −0.764 and −0.935 ppm (7B) respectively, in addition to the reference peak sited at 0.000 ppm. As aforementioned, this spectral appearance has been previously reported by Triba and co-workers for small disks in rapid rotation [37]. The reproducibility of the bicelles characteristic resonances after 24 h and 14 days indicated a good structural stability of the sample at least for 2 weeks.

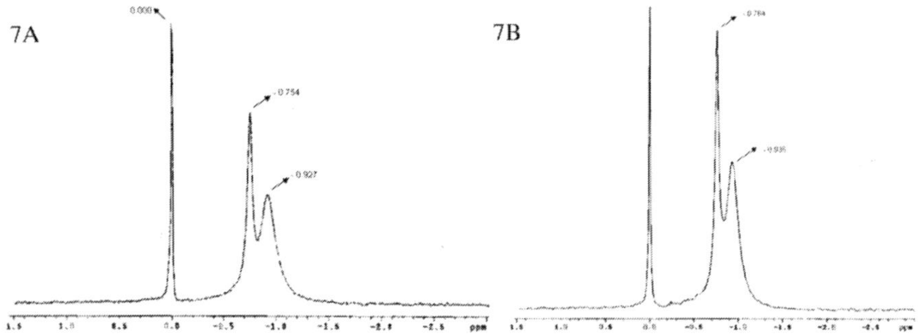


**Figure 7.** P NMR spectra spectra at 20 °C for DMP/DHPC bicelles ($q$ = 2 and 80% water content) 24 h **(A)** and 14 days **(B)** after preparation.

Figure 8 plots the SAXS curve of bicelles 24 h after preparation [47]. The fact that no differences were detected between this scattering curve and that obtained 14 days after preparation (data not shown), also corroborates the stability of the system. The lamellar repeated distance "d" was estimated from the analysis of the peak by the Bragg's law and was attributed to the bilayer thickness in a similar way that studies with liposomes and other bilayer models [48]. A repeat distance value *of d* = 4.5 nm was obtained in both spectra (24 h and 14 days after preparation), indicating that no alteration in the bilayer occurred during the 14 days of experiment.

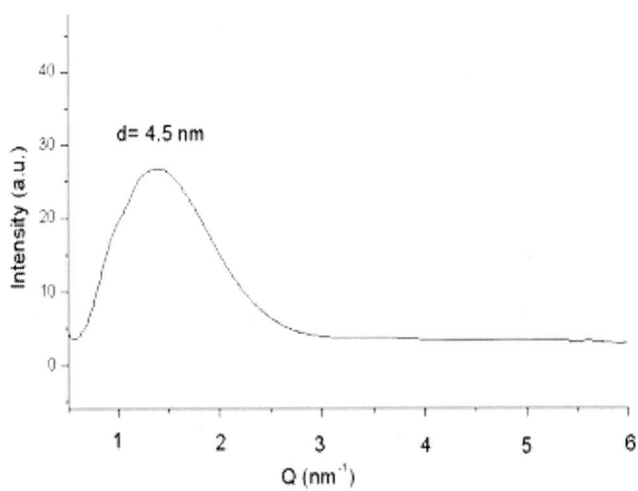


**Figure 8.** Small angle X-ray scattering (SAXS) curve at 20 °C of bicelles ($q$ = 2, 80% water content) 24 h after preparation.

The size distributions curves obtained by DLS exhibited a monomodal distribution with a hydrodynamic diameter (HD) of 15.9 nm and a polydispersity index (PI) of 0.211, 24 h after preparation [47]. Values for the same sample 14 days after preparation resulted very similar: (HD = 16.3 nm and PI = 0.303). The HD obtained by DLS is that of a hypothetical hard sphere that diffuses with the same speed as the particle under experiment. As the bicelles present a flat appearance, the values of particle size obtained may be considered as an estimation of the structure's dimension. The particle size values obtained showed quite good agreement with the structure sizes visualized by SEM. Figure 9 shows SEM micrograph of the S-q2 bicelles at 20 °C, 14 days after preparation. The arrows indicate the small rounded bicelles of about 20nm (Bar = 100 nm) similar to those shown in a SEM micrograph of bicelles S-q2 after preparation also at 20 °C (Figure 2). Similar structures have been reported by other authors using other electron microscopy techniques [32,34,36,49,50].

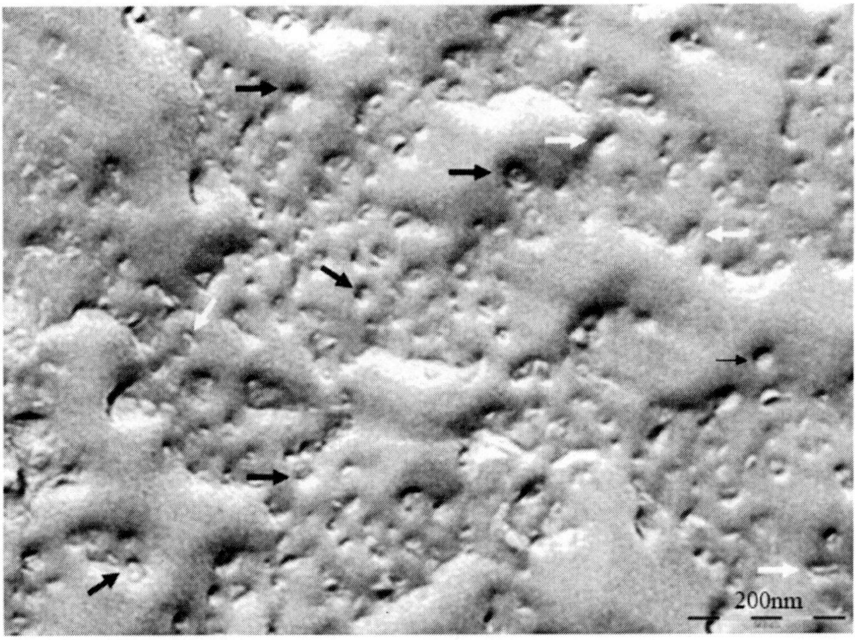


**Figure 9.** Electron micrograph of DMPC/DHPC $q$ = 2 bicelles. The image depicts a zone full of bicelles. Black arrows denote disks viewed face-on and white arrows denote disks viewed edge-on.

In resume, the physicochemical characterization of the bicellar system S-q2 indicated structural stability at least for 14 days after preparation.

## 3. DPPC/DHPC BICELLAR SYSTEMS

In the preceding section we revised some specific physico-chemical properties of the conventional DMPC/DHPC bicelles at different conditions. In the present section bicelles formed by 1,2-dipalmitoyl-sn-glycero-3-phosphocholine (DPPC) and the conventional DHPC have been updated. Furthermore, in these systems the q ratio has been also adjusted to 3.5 in order to diminish the concentration of DHPC and total lipid concentration (CL) was adjusted to 20%. Some reasons are considered to introduce these changes. One reason is based on the difference in the $T_m$ values (24.1 °C for DMPC and 41.5 °C for DPPC and [51,52]) despite the increase of only two carbons the long-chained lipid (from 14 to 16). This fact results in significantly different polarities above and below their $T_m$ [53]. Furthermore although bicelles formed by both lipids exhibit similar dynamical behavior, the DPPC lipid acyl chain displayed a somewhat lower degree of mobility evidenced by higher generalized order parameters throughout the acyl chain [54]. On the other hand, thinking in the application of bicellar systems as colloidal carriers the preservation of the shape and size of bicelles would be a requirement. Hence, it is necessary that Tm of lipids building bicelles exhibit higher values than the experimental temperature (for *in vivo*application about 37 °C). The increase in the q value to 3.5 (diminution in the relative proportion of DHPC) was chosen in order to diminish the surfactant character of the lipid mixture thus making the model more appropriate for *in vivo* studies.

In the present section we revised the dimensions and morphology of DPPC/DHPC bicelles and the bicelle-vesicle transition that takes place by the effect of dilution. A dilution of the systems would be desirable for purposes of the use of bicelles as colloidal delivery systems. The physico-chemical characteristics of this new bicellar system have been characterized using $^{31}$PNMR, SAXS, DLS, and FFEM techniques.

### 3.1. Dimensions and Morphology of the DPPC/DHPC Bicellar Systems

The characterization of the DPPC/DHPC bicelles is in general performed following the same methodology and techniques as those used to characterize the DMPC/DHPC bicelles (section 2.1.) [32,55]. Applying the form factor squared of the simplified Gaussian model to SAXS a bilayer thickness value ($d_B$ = 5.4 nm) was obtained [32,55]. The size distribution curve obtained by DLS shows a HD value of 11.3 nm and a PI of 0.072. This particle size provides a relative measurement of the structure dimensions. Therefore, this data should be interpreted taking into consideration also the electron microscopy images, in which a direct visualization of the bicellar structures is obtained. Figure 10 shows a cryo-SEM image at 37 °C, in which small discoidal aggregates of about 15 nm in diameter were observed. In this image, the face (black arrows) and the edges (white arrows) of the disks are visualized. As a consequence, this result shows quite good agreement with the DLS data despite the different resolution of each technique.

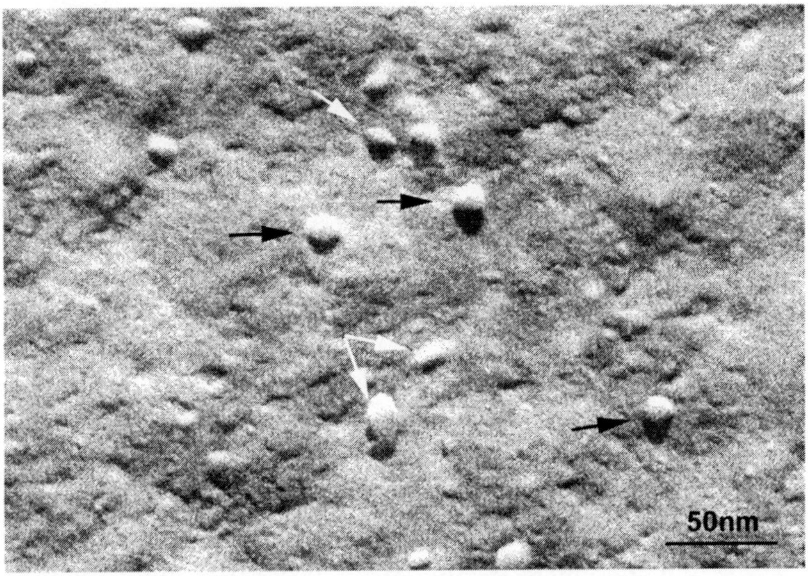


**Figure 10.** Micrograph of DPPC/DHPC bicelles at 37 °C. The black arrows denote the disks in face-on disposition and the white arrows correspond to the disks in edge-on.

### 3.2. Bicelle to Vesicle Transition States Obtained by Dilution

To monitor the effect of dilution on the structure of the bicelles, 2 mL of a bicelle sample ($q$ = 3.5, and lipid concentration of 20%) was sequentially diluted with de-ionized water in seven steps (D1-D7) to obtain concentrations from 5% to 0.07%. Twenty-four hours after the dilutions, the HD and PI of each diluted sample were measured by DLS at 37 °C. An overview of this process is plotted in Figure 11.

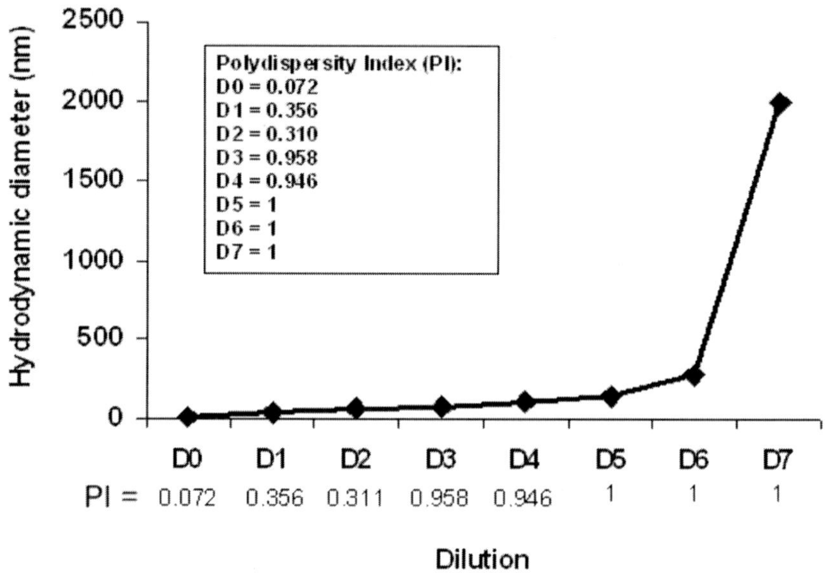


**Figure 11.** Evolution of the average particle size of the DPPC/DHPC bicelles with $q$ = 3.5 by the effect of dilution as measured by DLS. The polydispersity indices are shown in the inset.

The DLS curves of the diluted samples showed that the HDs of the structures increase upon dilution from values of about 11.3 nm (assigned to bicelle disks) to large size aggregates bigger than 1 μm.

For better understanding of the results, aside from the evolution of the average particle sizes, a detailed analysis of the scattering intensity was performed. The particle sizes obtained were separated in three groups: P1 included particle sizes in the range 10–100 nm, P2 included intermediate particle sizes ranging from 101 to 500 nm, and P3 included particle size values >500 nm. The HDs and the percents of light scattered of each group area plotted separately as a function of the sequential sample dilution in Figure 12. It is noteworthy that the intensity for small bicelles (P1) diminished with dilution, whereas the HD increased (Panel A). Intermediate aggregates (P2 in panel B) were present from the first dilution on and display a maximum of intensity and size at D3. From D4, the intensity of these aggregates diminishes and bigger structures are detected (P3 in panel C), coexisting with P1 and P2 until D6. The high PI values (shown in Figure 11 from D3 onward) are explained by the high variety of aggregates present in these samples.

It is noteworthy that the percent of the intensity curves does not represent the percentage of the structures present in the systems. In DLS, the HD is calculated from the intensity of the scattered light and gives information about the different particles present in the sample. From the Rayleigh approximation follows that the intensity is proportional to $d^6$ (d is the particle diameter); thus, the contribution of the light scattered from small particles is relatively small when compared to that of large particles that scatter much more light. Hence, the intensity curves obtained indicate the appearance of bigger aggregates by dilution but do not accurately quantify them. In general, the percent intensity of these structures and their HD increase in each dilution (Figure 12).

The coexistence of these big aggregates with the small bicelles is detected until the last dilution performed (D7). In order to investigate the morphology of these systems, the diluted bicellar solutions were analyzed by microscopy. A representative cryo-SEM image of the sample D5 is shown in Figure 13. This image reveals the presence of vesicles of about 200–500 nm (black arrows) together with small bicelles (white arrows). Comparing this micrograph to that of the original system (Figure 10), the increase of structures size and the variety of bigger aggregates in the sample are noteworthy. This result is fully consistent with DLS data corroborating the transition of bicelles from disks to vesicles by the effect of dilution. This transition took place by progressive steps that implied the coexistence of different aggregate structures in the medium.

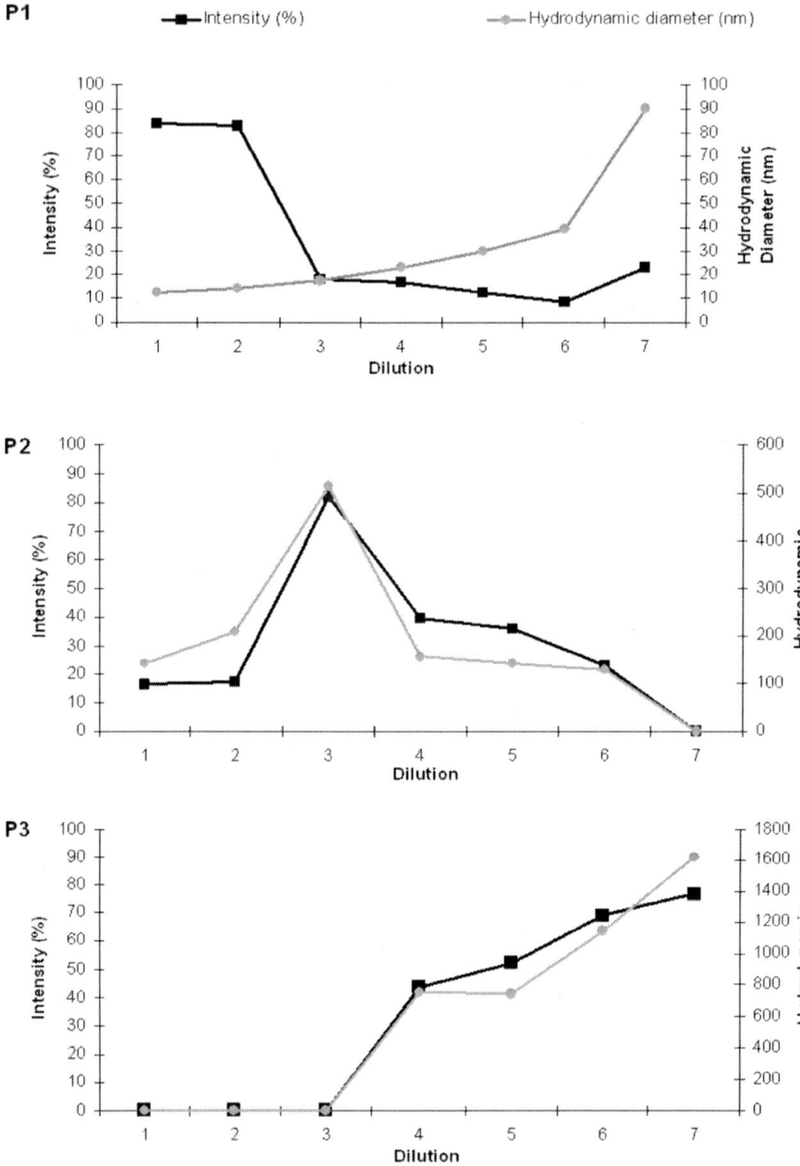


**Figure 12.** Evolution of the DLS scattered intensity and hydrodynamic diameter of the DPPC/DHPC bicelles upon dilution. P1 denotes the evolution of particles with sizes in the range of 10–100 nm (**A**). P2 denotes intermediate sized particles with diameters around 100–500 nm (**B**) and P3 indicates the bigger particles >500 nm (**C**).

**Figure 13.** Micrograph of the diluted DPPC/DHPC bicelles (D5) at 37 °C. The black arrows denote vesicle structures of about 200–500 nm and the white arrows point to bicellar structures.

In general terms, although the classical bicelle model formed by DMPC and DHPC has been successfully used, another bicelle systems made up of lipids with different acyl chains, backbones, or headgroups have offered alternatives for different studies [12,16,56-58]. As aforementioned, the DPPC is one of the most studied lipids for bilayer models due to its longer acyl chains, and the bilayer thickness [59] and has the additional advantage of having a higher value of $T_m$ [60-62].

The phase transitions that occurred at $T_m$ involve morphological changes in the bicellar structures, that is, from disks to cylindrical micelles to perforated lamellar sheets and mixed multilamellar vesicles [43,63]. Then, a system of small size at physiological temperature that could be use, for instance, for *in vivo* applications would be the DPPC/DHPC $q$ = 3.5 bicelles. At 37 °C, below the DPPC $T_m$, these structures have dimensions of about 15 nm in diameter and 5.4 nm in thickness. These values are consistent with previously reported data of DPPC bilayer thickness [64,65] and bicellar disk dimensions [5,66]

The passage of these small bicelles through some tissues as skin SC seems reasonable, considering that this region is formed by lipid lamellae with narrow interlamellar spaces (between 6 and 10 nm) Coderch 2002 [67]. In fact, the interaction of these systems with SC has been reported and although tracking the presence of the bicellar disks in the tissue was not possible, interestingly, vesicles and lamellar-like structures were observed in the lipid intercellular areas of the tissue after treatment with bicellar systems. These structures were probably the result of a structural rearrangement of bicelles inside the cutaneous SC [55].

DLS and FFEM analyses of the bicellar diluted samples demonstrated the tendency of the bicellar aggregates to grow and form vesicles by the effect of dilution (Figures 12 and 13). It is noteworthy that the phase transitions the bicelles underwent due to the variation of lipid concentration, temperature, and phospholipids molar ratio [68] are very similar to those involved in the reconstitution of the surfactant-lipid micellar systems [69-71]. The transformation of these structures in vesicles was largely discussed in a number of works [72-75]. In earlier studies, we investigated kinetics aspects of this process [76]. A model for the micelle-to-vesicle transition proposed by Leng and co-workers described the rapid formation of disk-like aggregates and their growth and closure to form vesicles [77]. This model took into account line tension dominating bending energy. Certainly, the resemblance of surfactant-lipid micelles and phospholipid bicelles justifies their similar behavior. DHPC solubilizes the DPPC bilayer forming the bicellar structures in a similar way that a surfactant solubilizes lipid vesicles forming micelles. In addition, the high water solubility of DHPC accounts for the structural changes the bicelles underwent. When DHPC is removed from the bicelles upon dilution ($q$ increases), the bilayers tend to fuse and the bicellar diameter increases. Morphological changes in the bicelle structure then take place. When sufficient DHPC is removed from the bicelles, the precipitation of large aggregates is visible, that is, phase separation occurs [78].

From these findings, the presence of vesicles in the skin stratum corneum was attributed to a structural transition process from bicelles to vesicles occurring inside of this tissue. The solution used to treat the skin was composed of bicelles with dimensions suitable for stratum corneum penetration. Inside this tissue, bicelles probably transformed in vesicles following a process analogous to that observed in the DLS experiment with diluted bicellar solutions. A similar phenomenon was reported by our group applying octyl glucoside and phosphatidylcholine mixed micelles (OG/PC) in the SC [79]. In this investigation, was demonstrated that liposomes were solubilized by OG and the resulting mixed micelles penetrated through the skin and then were reconstituted in vesicles by effect of the hydration gradient of the tissue.

# 4. EFFECT OF THE INCLUSION OF CERAMIDES IN BICELLES

## 4.1. Type of Ceramides

The incorporation of two types of Cer in the system DMPC/DHPC $q$ = 2, one with alkyl chain of 14 carbons (Cer14) and another with 24 carbon alkyl chain (Cer24) has been reported [19,33]. Both Cer caused structural changes in bicelar systems. The low miscibility between Cer and phospholipids and also the ceramide ability to aggregate to form domains in the bilayer of bicelles was checked [80,81]. In this sense, the technique of $^{31}$P-NMR has been very useful to confirm the inclusion of Cer in bicellar systems. This inclusion was noted considering changes caused by Cer in the phosphorus spectra from bicelles. Cer14 has proven to be less miscible in bicelles than Cer24, causing a slight influence on the phosphorus signal in the spectra. On the other hand, the inclusion of Cer24 led to a clear differentiation of the phosphorus signal in the spectra, indicating the increased incorporation into systems (Figure 14). Cers have no phosphorus atoms and so do not contribute to the $^{31}$P NMR signal, but only indirectly through their effects on the phase/mobility/domain state of the phospholipids.

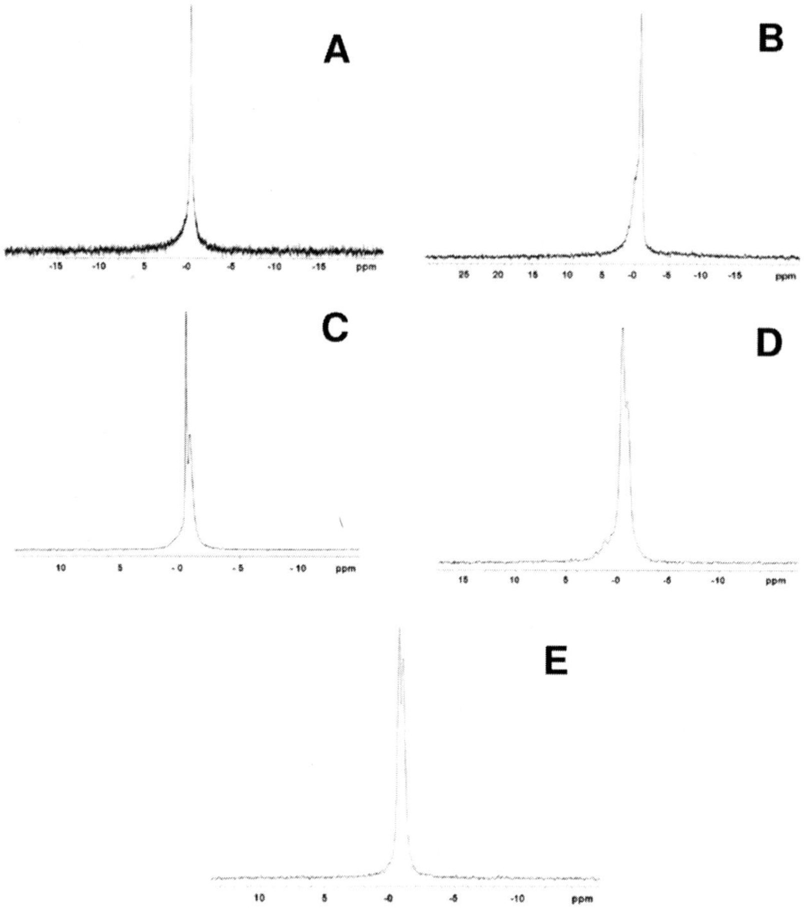


**Figure 14.** $^{31}$P-NMR spectra at 20 °C of the systems formed by DMPC/DHPC *q* = 2 **(A)**, DMPC/DHPC *q* = 2 + 10% mol C14-Cer **(B)**, DMPC/DHPC *q* = 2 + 10% mol C24-Cer **(C)**, DMPC/DHPC *q* = 2 + 20% mol C14-Cer **(D)** and DMPC/DHPC *q* = 2 + 20% mol C24-Cer**(E)**. Spectra were referenced to 85% phosphoric acid.

The domains formed by Cer in bicellar systems were detected by SAXS (Figure 15). In the spectra several peaks associated with different spacing values (d) were observed. These spaces were attributed to the width of the lipid bilayers of the bicelles [19]. The spacing value for the initial system DMPC/ DHPC (d = 4.5–4.8 nm) was detected in all spectra. In addition to this value, in systems including Cer two values of d, around 5.2–5.4 and 6.2–6.7 nm were obtained. These spacings have been published as related to the formation of different types of ceramide-rich domains that would modify the thickness of the bilayer [80,81].

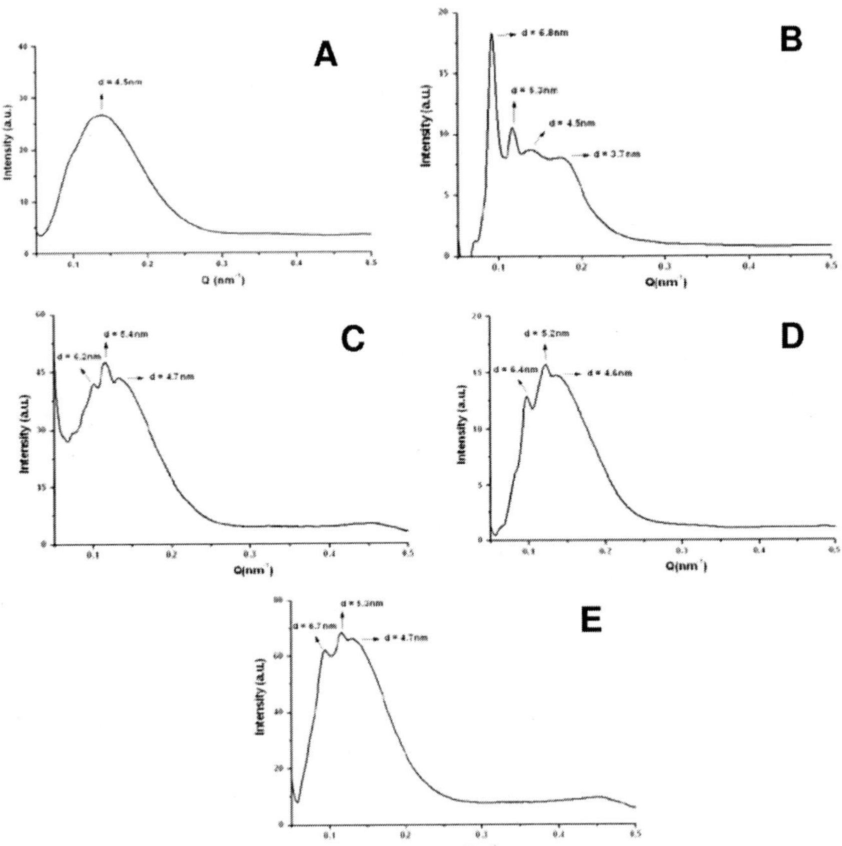


**Figure 15.** SAXS profiles at 20 °C of the systems formed by DMPC/DHPC $q$ = 2 **(A)**, DMPC/DHPC $q$ = 2 + 10% mol C14-Cer **(B)**, DMPC/DHPC $q$ = 2 + 10% mol C24-Cer **(C)**, DMPC/DHPC $q$ = 2 + 20% mol C14-Cer **(D)** and DMPC/DHPC $q$ = 2 + 20% mol C24-Cer**(E)**.

In the case of the system formed with Cer14, a fourth peak with a value of $d$ = 3.7 nm was detected. This value could correspond to non-lamellar structures composed of ceramide, suggesting that this lipid, due to its lower miscibility, probably had not been fully incorporated in the bicelles and it had been segregated. In fact DLS showed a great polydispersity in systems formed with Cer14. Images of this system obtained by FFEM showed rounded aggregates sizing about 15–20 nm and elongated aggregates of approximately 40 nm. This indicated a reorganization of the system with respect to that without Cer, which showed a single type of structure. The Cer14 may have been included in the system irregularly causing the DHPC displacement in some aggregates, thereby increasing the molar ratio (*q*) of these aggregates. This event was reflected in the increased size structures [33]. The displaced DHPC probably settled in the aggregate without Cer, decreasing the molar ratio (*q*) of these aggregates that consequently resulted even smaller than those present in the original system. In fact, the average particle size obtained by DLS for DMPC/DHPC/Cer14 system was about 15 nm, that is, a lower value than that reported for the initial system (about 16 nm) and also lower than the size obtained for DMPC/DHPC/Cer24 system (approx. 19 nm). This system including Cer24 showed homogeneous structures, with particle size slightly larger than the initial system without Cer, indicating that the Cer24 had been incorporated into bicelles [19,33].

## 4.2. Concentration of Ceramides

In order to determine the effect of increasing concentration of Cer on bicelles, systems including 10 and 20% mol of Cer have been studied. At room temperature, we observed that the system could incorporate up to 10% mol of Cer. The inclusion of 20 mol% of this lipid resulted in a destabilization of the structures with the formation of mixed bicelles and vesicles. It has been reported that this destabilization could be observed visually, given that the systems went from transparent to translucent [19]. The membrane destabilization effect of Cer on vesicles has been reported [80,82]. This effect has been ascribed to the high intrinsic curvature of Cer, which gives rise to lateral phase separations [83,84].

An investigation to determine the influence of temperature on bicellar systems with Cer24 has been carried out. This study, conducted at temperature below (20 °C) and above (40 °C) the $T_m$ of DMPC (24 °C) and using more sensitive techniques revealed the presence of new structures in the systems [33,83]. In the systems formed with 10% mol of Cer at 20 °C, small bicelles sizing 20 nm and elongated structures twisted at several points were detected (Figure 16).

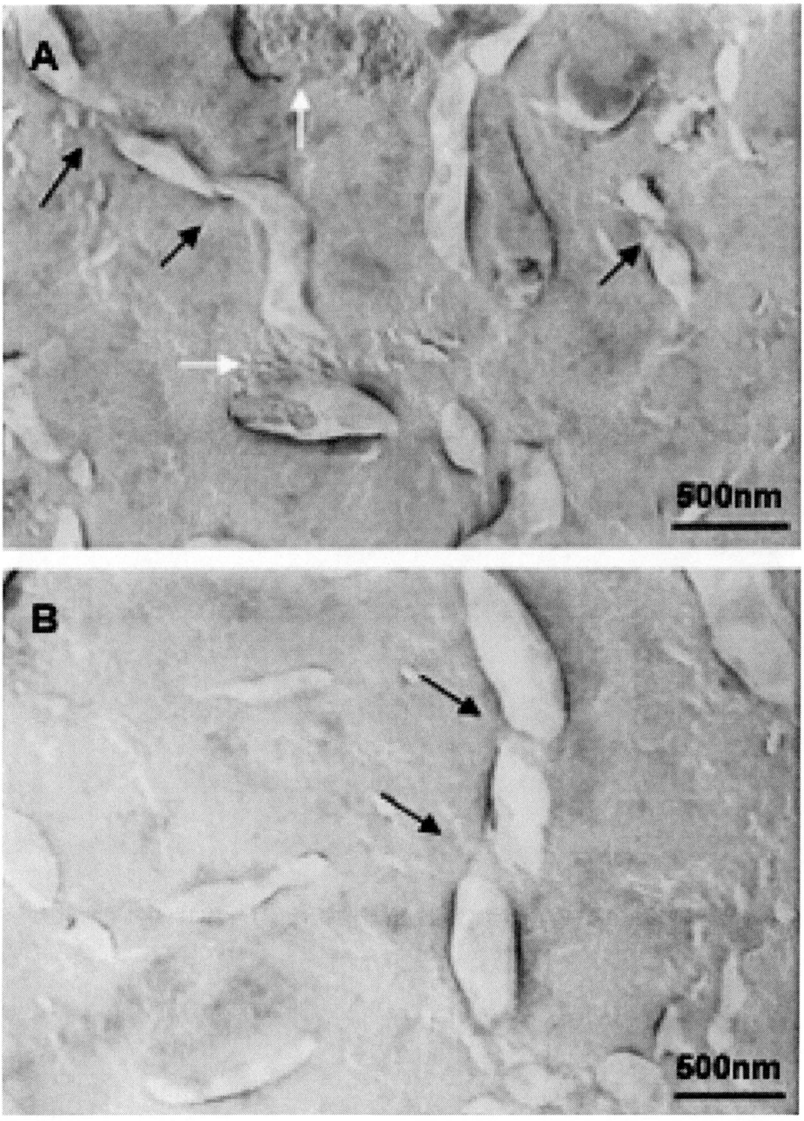


**Figure 16.** Micrographs of bicellar sample containing Cer at 20 °C. Two different regions of the same sample. Black arrows indicate the twisted zones along the elongated aggregates. The white arrows in image A show the presence of small bicelles in the range of 20–50 nm.

The folded or twisted areas are probably ceramide-rich domains and could be related with the different SAXS peaks showed in Figure 15. Moreover, due to this negative curvature Cer would not pack parallel to their nearest neighbors but rather with a twist angle, which should promote incurvations on the DMPC bilayer. In connection with this, López-Monteroet *al.* [85,86] described irregularities in phospholipid membranes as a consequence of asymmetric distribution of Cer between outer and inner monolayers. In those works, asymmetry was induced by the presence of Cer in the external leaflet of giant unilamellar vesicles. In bicellar systems containing Cer, the asymmetry between both leaflets is probable due to the formation of ceramide rich domains. Then, bicelles could twist to relax the surface tension generated by the lipid asymmetry in a similar way to how López-Montero *et al.* described [85]. Increasing the temperature to 40 °C led to the formation of large aggregates, which showed long branches that may have been formed from the folded and/or twisted areas (Figure 17). Such growth would be favored by the movement of DHPC in these areas.

It is interesting to note that the structures with 10% Cer formed at 25 °C, that is, above the $T_m$ of DMPC did not show large structures as might be expected of systems in fluid liquid crystal state. The structures found in this system were similar to those found in gel-state systems that are observed in different works [32,33,47,87]. This is explained by the fact that Cer induce the gel phase in DMPC systems [81,88], which extends the temperature range in which these systems would be in the gel phase.

It is also curious that systems at 20 °C presented greater structural diversity than systems at 25 °C [19,33]. This fact could be explained based on the sensitivity of the techniques used in these two experiments. The particle sizes of the systems studied at 20 °C and 40 °C were measured with a Nanosizer Nano ZS. This is an appropriate tool to study bicellar systems due to its ability to measure concentrated samples without dilution. The 4700c Malvern apparatus used to measure the samples at 25 °C in a previous work [19] is more suitable for diluted samples. In addition, the HPF used for samples at 20 °C and 40 °C [33] is also advantageous to the fixation by propane

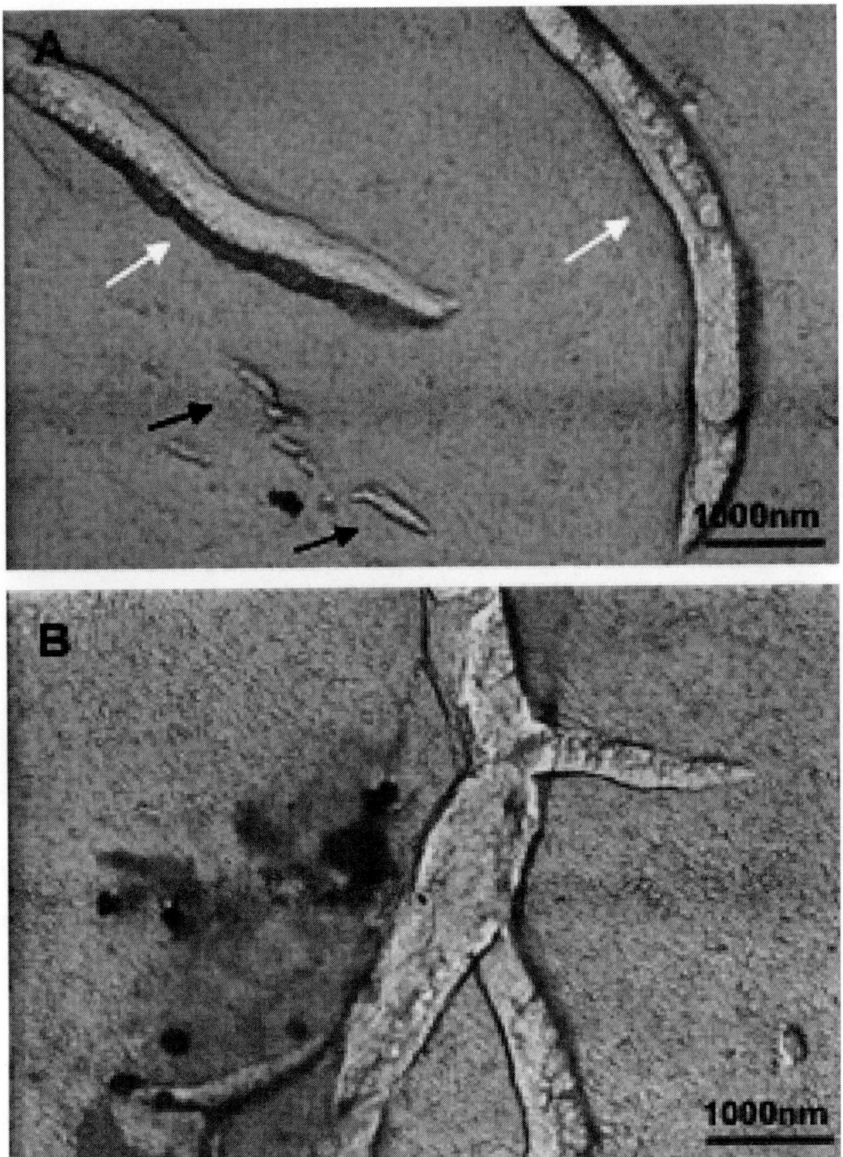


**Figure 17.** Micrographs of bicellar sample containing Cer at 40 °C. A) and B) represent two different regions of the same sample. In image A the arrows indicate the tubular objects with about 500 nm (black arrows) and 4000 nm (white arrows).

immersion used in the experiment at 25 °C [19]. Although none of the cryofixation methods used in the mentioned articles involves chemical treatment or dilution of samples, HPF is especially appropriate because the samples are frozen under optimal conditions of temperature and pressure, and changes in the structure of systems are avoiding. Thus, the implementation of high pressure fixation and use of Nanosizer with samples at 20 °C and 40 °C provided higher quality measures and, therefore, higher structural diversity could be detected in the samples.

In the systems formed with 20% mol of Cer, structures of various sizes and shapes were observed at all temperatures studied. The temperature increase, inducing the transition from gel phase to the fluid liquid crystal phase, promoted formation of multilamellar liposome and tubular structures coexisting with small bicelles. At this concentration, Cer are not incorporated completely in the systems and this fact cause destabilization of the systems.

## 5. NEW STRATEGIES BASED ON BICELLAR SYSTEMS

Bicelles constitute very promising systems for different applications. This review shows that such systems exhibit intelligent properties, since they respond to external stimuli. Its versatility, the ability to modulate its structure, organization and their lipid bilayer offer great advantages over other bilayer systems. Besides, some works have demonstrated that these systems are adequate to penetrate the skin and to reinforce the structure lipid system (DPPC / DHPC $q$ = 3.5) or to enhance the permeability of this tissue (DMPC / DHPC $q$ = 2) [47,55,87].

Structural characterization of bicelles has revealed interesting aspects about the behavior of these systems and about the different effect induced by inclusion of skin lipids, such as ceramide. In this way, the utility of bicelles as membrane model to study skin lipids could be considered in future research.

With regard to the use of bicellar systems as vehicles for skin delivery, the entrapping ability of bicelles is being evaluated [89]. Systems containing Cer and dichlofenac diethylamine have been analyzed by DLS and Cryo-TEM [89]. Systems including lipophilic compounds were

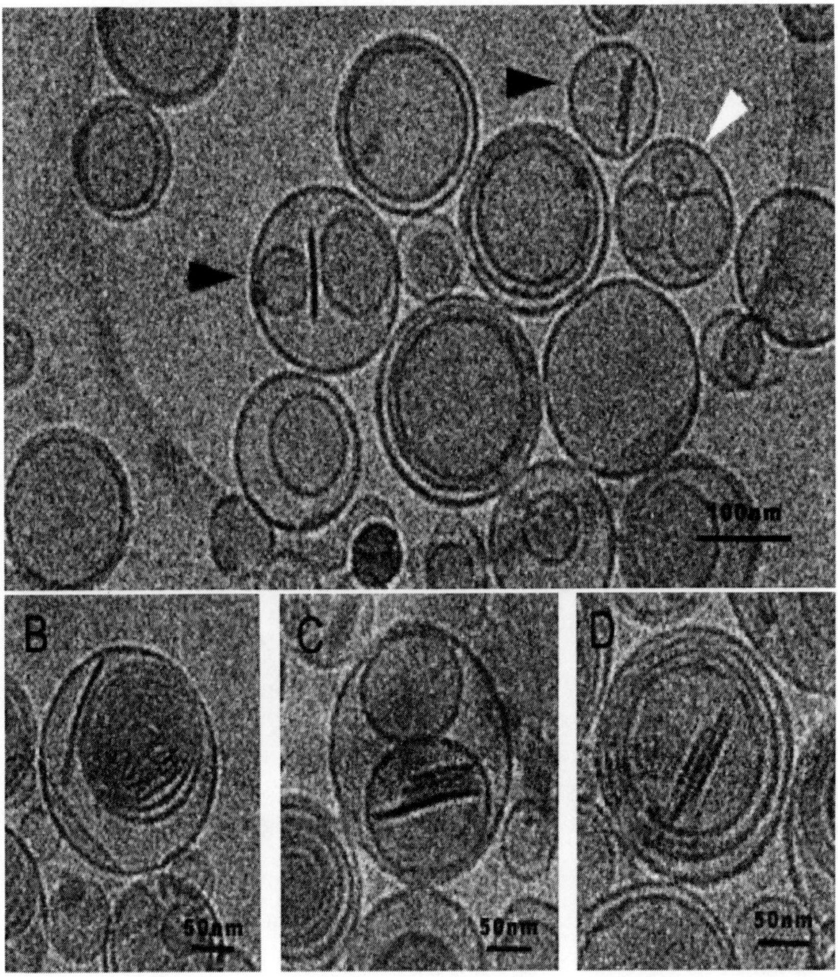


**Figure 18.** Cryo-TEM images of a sample containing bicosomes. **(A)** High variability of vesicles is observed: empty vesicles (black arrows); oligolamellar structures (white arrowheads) and multilamellar vesicles (white arrows); vesicles with bicelles inside (black arrowheads). **(B)** Multilamellar vesicles. **(C)** Stacked bicelles inside vesicles. **(D)**Stacked bicelles inside multilamellar vesicles.

found to be larger than the initial systems, suggesting that these actives may be incorporated in the bilayers of the bicellar structures. On the other hand, the inclusion of hydrophilic actives caused a reduction in size and a rounding of bicellar structures. This fact could be explained by the surfactant nature of the hydrophilic compounds includes, which have more affinity for incorporation into the edges of the bicelles, decreasing the molar ratio of the systems, a fact that would cause the decrease in the size of the aggregates.

Although the characteristic of bicelles to change structurally and morphologically depending on the environmental conditions allows for its use in different areas, this property may limit its application in environments where these conditions are variable. Bicelles can be considered good carriers for the skin. However, their application as carriers for administration through the systemic route, where the water content is high, would represent a challenge, as well as its simple addition to vehicles with higher water content. At diluted conditions bicelles properties would be lost and the systems would present variable morphologies and effects.

In order to address this limitation, Rodriguez *et al.* have recently proposed a strategy to preserve the discoidal morphology of bicelles for its use in high water content environments. This strategy consists in the preparation of new structures also formed by phospholipids, the so-called bicosomes that would protect bicelles from dilution, preserving the aggregates until the target tissue is achieved [90]. Cryo-TEM images of bicosomes are shown in Figure 18.

Other methods have been used to stabilize the morphology of discoidal bilayers, such as using bicelles with charged amphiphiles [91] or disks formed by mixtures containing polyethylene glycol-lipid conjugates [92]. However, with the use of PEG-lipids, the properties of bicelles related to structural versatility, such as the enhancer effect of the permeability on some physiological barriers, could be lost.

## 6. CONCLUSION

All in all, bicellar systems are emerging as a fascinating, morphologically versatile lipid nanostructure that open up new possibilities of study and applications owing to their size, shape and modulable structure. These bicellar systems could be useful as membrane mimics for studies in which Cer are involved. Differences in cer structure and concentration give rise to diverse effects on bicelles. The systems are able to incorporate 10% mol of Cer, which is probably organized in domains along the bilayer. The addition of 20% mol promotes destabilization of the discoidal bicelles, resulting in the formation of mixed systems with bigger structures. Results presented prove that it is possible to create a model membrane made up of bicelles including Cer. Additionally, the absence of surfactant in their exclusively lipid composition, and the possibility of including different actives, makes these systems a good candidate as colloidal carriers. Moreover, the systems *per se* are able to induce specific effects on the skin and the possibility of this being addressed for other tissues appears to pose another interesting option for the near future.

## ACKNOWLEDGMENTS

This work was supported by funds from CICYT (CTQ 2010-16964) and from Generalitat de Catalunya (2009 SGR 1212). M. Cócera is funded by the JAE-DOC program from CSIC (co-funded by FSE).

## REFERENCES

1. Sanders, C.R.; Schwonek, J.P. Characterization of magnetically orientable bilayers in mixtures of dihexanoylphosphatidylcholine and dimyristoylphosphatidylcholine by solid-state NMR. Biochemistry 1992, 31, 8898–8905.

2. Sanders, C.R. Visiting order on membrane proteins by using nanotechnology. Proc. Natl. Acad. Sci. USA 2007, 104, 6502–6503.

3. Whiles, J.A.; Deems, R.; Vold, R.R.; Dennis, E.A. Bicelles in structure–function studies of membrane-associated proteins. Bioorg. Chem. 2002, 30, 431–442.

4. Bolze, J.; Fujisawa, T.; Nagao, T.; Norisada, K.; Saitô, H.; Naito, A. Small angle X-ray scattering and 31P NMR studies on the phase behavior of phospholipid bilayered mixed micelles. Chem. Phys. Lett. 2000, 329, 215–220.

5. Ottiger, M.; Bax, A. Characterization of magnetically oriented phospholipid micelles for measurement of dipolar couplings in macromolecules. J. Biomol. NMR 1998, 12, 361–372.

6. van Dam, L.; Karlsson, G.; Edwards, K. Morphology of magnetically aligning DMPC/DHPC aggregates-perforated sheets, not disks. Langmuir 2006, 22, 3280–3285.

7. Park, S.H.; Loudet, C.; Marassi, F.M.; Dufoure, E.J.; Opella, S.J. Solid-state NMR spectroscopy of a membrane protein in biphenyl phospholipid bicelles with the bilayer normal parallel to the magnetic field. J. Magn. Reson. 2008, 193, 133–138.

8. Katsaras, J.H.T.A.; Pencer, J.; Nieh, M.-P. "Bicellar" lipid mixtures as used in biochemical and biophysical studies.Naturwissenschaften 2005, 92, 355–366.

9. Nieh, M.P.; Glinka, C.J.; Krueger, S.; Prosser, R.S.; Katsaras, J. SANS study of the structural phases of magnetically alignable lanthanide-doped phospholipid mixtures. Langmuir 2001, 17, 2629–2638.

10. Nieh, M.P.; Raghunathan, V.A.; Glinka, C.J.; Harroun, T.A.; Katsaras, J. Structural phase behaviour og high-concentration alignable biomimetic bicelle mixtures. Macromol. Symp. 2004, 219, 135–145.

11. Nieh, M.P.; Raghunathan, V.A.; Kline, S.R.; Harroun, T.A.; Huang, C.Y.; Pencer, J.; Katsaras, J. Spontaneously formed unilamellar vesicles with path-dependent size distribution. Langmuir 2005, 21, 6656–6661.

12. Aussenac, F.; Lavigne, B.; Dufourc, E.J. Toward bicelle stability with ether-linked phospholipids: temperature, composition, and hydration diagrams by 2H and 31P solid-state NMR. Langmuir 2005, 21, 7129–7135.

13. Aussenac, F.; Laguerre, M.; Schmitter, J.M.; Dufourc, E.J. Detailed structure and dynamics of bicelle phospholipids using selectively deuterated labels H-2 NMR and molecular mechanics study. Langmuir 2003, 19, 10468–10479.

14. Prosser, R.S.; Evanics, F.; Kitevski, J.L.; Al-Abdul-Wahid, M.S. Current applications of bicelles in NMR studies of membrane-associated amphiphiles and proteins. Biochemistry 2006, 45, 8453–8465.

15. Soong, R.; Macdonald, P.M. Lateral diffusion of PEG-Lipid in magnetically aligned bicelles measured using stimulated echo pulsed field gradient 1H NMR. Biophys. J. 2005, 88, 255–268.

16. Struppe, J.; Whiles, J.A.; Vold, R.R. Acidic phospholipid bicelles: a versatile model membrane system. Biophys. J. 2000,78, 281–289.

17. Marcotte, I.; Dufourc, E.J.; Quellet, M.; Auger, M. Interaction of the neuropeptide met-enkephalin with zwitterionic and negatively charged bicelles as viewed by 31P and 2H solid-state NMR. Biophys. J. 2003, 85, 328–339.

18. Lu, J.-X.; Caporini, M.A.; Lorigan, G.A. The effects of cholesterol on magnetically aligned phospholipid bilayers: a solid-state NMR and EPR spectroscopy study. J. Magn. Reson. 2004, 168, 18–30.

19. Barbosa-Barros, L.; de la Maza, A.; López-Iglesias, C.; López, O. Ceramide effects in the bicelle structure. Colloid. Surf. A 2008, 317, 576–584.

20. Sanders, C.R.; Prosser, R.S. Bicelles: a model membrane system for all seasons? Structure 1998, 6, 1227–1234.

21. Dubey, V.; Mishra, D.; Dutta, T.; Nahar, M.; Saraf, D.K.; Jain, N.K. Dermal and transdermal delivery of an anti-psoriatic agent via ethanolic liposomes. J. Control. Release 2007, 123, 148–154.

22. Sheu, M.T.; Chen, S.Y.; Ho, H.O. Influence of micelle solubilization by tocopheryl polyethylene glycol succinate (TPGS) on solubility enhancement and percutaneous penetration of estradiol. J. Control. Release 2003, 88, 355–368.

23. Benson, H.A. Transdermal drug delivery: penetration enhancement techniques. Curr. Drug Deliv. 2005, 2, 23–33.

24. Kartono, F.; Maibach, H.I. Irritants in combination with a synergistic or additive effect on the skin response: an overview of tandem irritation studies. Contact Dermatitis 2006, 54, 303–312.

25. Cardon, T.B.; Dave, P.C.; Lorigan, G.A. Magnetically aligned phospholipid bilayers with large q ratios stabilize magnetic alignment with high order in the gel and L(alpha) phases. Langmuir 2005, 21, 4291–4298.

26. Rowe, B.A.; Neal, S.L. Fluorescence probe study of bicelles structure as a function of temperature: developing a practical bicelles structure model. Langmuir 2003, 19, 2039–2048.

27. Nieh, M.P.; Raghunathan, V.A.; Glinka, C.J.; Harroun, T.A.; Pabst, G.; Katsaras, J. Magnetically alignable phase of phospholipid "bicelle" mixtures is a chiral nematic made up of wormlike micelles. Langmuir 2004, 20, 7893–7897.

28. Wang, H.; Nieh, M.P.; Hobbie, E.K.; Glinka, C.J.; Katsaras, J. Kinetic pathway of the bilayered-micelle to perforated-lamellae transition. Phys. Rev. E 2003, 67, 060902.

29. Faham, S.; Bowie, J.U. Bicelle crystallization: a new method for crystallizing membrane proteins yields a monomeric bacteriorhodopsin structure. J. Mol. Biol. 2002, 316, 1–6.

30. Prosser, R.S.; Hwang, J.S.; Vold, R.R. Magnetically aligned phospholipid bilayers with positive ordering: a new model membrane system. Biophys. J. 1998, 74, 2405–2418.

31. Mahabir, S.; Wan, W.; Katsaras, J.; Nieh, M.P. Effects of charge density and thermal history on the morphologies of spontaneously formed unilamellar vesicles. J. Phys. Chem. B 2010, 114, 5729–5735.

32. Barbosa-Barros, L.; de la Maza, A.; Walther, P.; Linares, A.M.; Feliz, M.; Estelrich, J.; López, O. Use of high-pressure freeze fixation and freeze fracture electron microscopy to study the influence of the phospholipid molar ratio in the morphology and alignment of bicelles. J. Microsc. 2009, 233, 35–41.

33. Barbosa-Barros, L.; de la Maza, A.; Walther, P.; Estelrich, J.; López, O. Morphological effects of ceramide on DMPC/DHPC bicelles. J. Microsc. 2008, 230, 16–26.

34. Walther, P. Recent progress in freeze-fracturing of high-pressure frozen samples. J. Microsc. 2003, 212, 34–43.

35. Walther, P.; Ziegler, A. Freeze substitution of high-pressure frozen samples: the visibility of biological membranes is improved when the substitution medium contains water. J. Microsc. 2002, 208, 3–10.

36. Sternin, E.; Nizza, D.; Gawrisch, K. Temperature dependence of DMPC/DHPC mixing in a bicellar solution and its structural implications. Langmuir 2001, 17, 2610–2616.

37. Triba, M.N.; Warschawski, D.E.; Deveaux, P.F. Reinvestigation by phosphorus NMR of lipid distribution of bicelles.Biophys. J. 2005, 88, 1887–1901.

38. Sanders, C.R.; Hare, B.J.; Howard, K.P.; Prestegard, J.H. Magnetically oriented phospholipid micelles as a tool for the study of membrane associated molecules. Prog. Nucl. Magn. Reson. Spectros. 1994, 26, 421–444.

39. Vold, R.R.; Prosser, R.S. Magnetically oriented phospholipid bilayered micelles for structural studies of polypeptides. Does the ideal bicelles exist? J. Magn. Reson. B 1996, 113, 267–271.

40. Gaemers, S.; Bax, A. Morphology of three lyotropic liquid crystalline biological NMR media studied by translational diffusion anisotropy. J. Am. Chem. Soc. 2001, 123, 12343–12352.

41. Echlin, P. Low-Temperature Microscopy and Analysis; Springer: New York, NY, USA, 1992.

42. van Dam, L.; Karlsson, G.; Edwards, K. Direct observation and characterization of DMPC/DHPC aggregates under conditions relevant for biological solution NMR. Biochim. Biophys. Acta 2004, 1664, 241–256.

43. Harroun, T.A.; Koslowsky, M.; Nieh, M.P.; de Lannoy, C.F.; Raghunathan, V.A.; Katsaras, J. Comprehensive examination of mesophases formed by DMPC and DHPC mixtures. Langmuir 2005, 21, 5356–5361.

44. Plaza, M.; Tadros, T.F.; Solans, C.; Pons, R. Characterization of Microemulsions Formed in a Water/ABA Block Copolymer [Poly(hydroxystearic acid)-Poly(ethylene oxide)-Poly(hydroxystearic acid)]/1,2-Hexanediol/Isopropyl Myristate System. Langmuir 2002, 18, 5673–5680.

45. Pabst, G.; Koschuch, R.; Pozo-Navas, B.; Rappolt, M.; Lohner, K.; Laggner, P. Structural analysis of weakly ordered membrane stacks. J. Appl. Cryst. 2003, 36, 1378–1388.

46. Pabst, G. Global properties of biomimetic membranes: Perspectives on molecular features. Biophys. Rev. Lett. 2006, 1, 57–84.

47. Barbosa-Barros, L.; Barba, C.; Cócera, M.; Coderch, L.; López-Iglesias, C.; de la Maza, A.; López, O. Effect of bicellar systems on skin properties. Int. J. Pharm. 2008, 352, 263–272.

48. Singh, M.; Ghosh, S.; Shannon, R. A direct method of beam-height correction in small-angle x-ray scattering. J. Appl. Cryst. 1993, 26, 787–794.

49. Glover, K.J.; Whiles, J.A.; Wu, G.; Yu, N.; Deems, R.; Struppe, J.O.; Stark, R.E.; Komives, E.A.; Vold, R.R. Structural evaluation of phospholipid bicelles for solution-state studies of membrane-associated biomolecules. Biophys. J. 2001,81, 2163–2171.

50. Arnold, A.; Labrot, T.; Oda, R.; Dufourc, E.J. Cation modulation of bicelle size and magnetic alignment as revealed by solid-state NMR and electron microscopy. Biophys. J. 2002, 83, 2667–2680.

51. Vist, M.R.; Davis, J.H. Phase equilibria of cholesterol/dipalmitoylphosphatidylcholine mixtures: 2H nuclear magnetic resonance and differential scanning calorimetry. Biochemistry 1990, 29, 451–464.

52. Almeida, P.F.; Vaz, W.L.; Thompson, T.E. Lateral diffusion in the liquid phases of dimyristoylphosphatidylcholine/cholesterol

lipid bilayers: a free volume analysis. Biochemistry 1992, 31, 6739–6747.

53. Wohl, C.J.; Helms, M.A.; Chung, J.O.; Kuciauskas, D. Phospholipid bilayer free volume analysis employing the thermal ring-closing reaction of merocyanine molecular switches. J. Phys. Chem. B 2006, 110, 22796–22803.

54. Lind, J.; Nordin, J.; Maler, L. Lipid dynamics in fast-tumbling bicelles with varying bilayer thickness: effect of model transmembrane peptides. Biochim. Biophys. Acta 2008, 1778, 2526–2534.

55. Barbosa-Barros, L.; de la Maza, A.; Estelrich, J.; Linares, A.M.; Feliz, M.; Walther, P.; Pons, R.; López, O. Penetration and growth of DPPC/DHPC bicelles inside the stratum corneum of the skin. Langmuir 2008, 24, 5700–5706.

56. Ottiger, M.; Bax, A. Bicelle-based liquid crystals for NMR-measurement of dipolar couplings at acidic and basic pH values. J. Biomol. NMR 1999, 13, 187–191.

57. Cavagnero, S.; Dyson, H.J.; Wright, P.E. Improved low pH bicelle system for orienting macromolecules over a wide temperature range. J. Biomol. NMR 1999, 13, 387–391.

58. Whiles, J.A.; Glover, K.J.; Vold, R.R.; Komives, E.A. Methods for studying transmembrane peptides in bicelles: consequences of hydrophobic mismatch and peptide sequence. J. Magn. Reson. 2002, 158, 149–156.

59. Tiburu, E.K.; Moton, D.M.; Lorigan, G.A. Development of magnetically aligned phospholipid bilayers in mixtures of palmitoylstearoylphosphatidylcholine and dihexanoylphosphatidylcholine by solid-state NMR spectroscopy.Biochim. Biophys. Acta 2001, 1512, 206–214.

60. Lewis, R.N.; Mak, N.; McElhaney, R.N. A differential scanning calorimetric study of the thermotropic phase behavior of model membranes composed of phosphatidylcholines containing linear saturated fatty acyl chains. Biochemistry1987, 26, 6118–6126.

61. Laughlin, R.G.; Munyon, R.L.; Fu, Y.-C.; Fehl, A.J. Physical Science of the Dioctadecyldimethylammonium Chloride-Water System. 1. Equilibrium Phase Behavior. J. Phys. Chem. 1990, 94, 2546–2552.

62. Marsh, D. CRC Handbook of Lipid Bilayers; CRC Press: Boca Raton, FL, USA, 1990.

63. Park, S.H.; De Angelis, A.A.; Nevzorov, A.A.; Wu, C.H.; Opella, S.J. Three-dimensional structure of the transmembrane domain of Vpu from HIV-1 in aligned phospholipid bicelles. Biophys. J. 2006, 91, 3032–3042.

64. Nagle, J.F.; Tristram-Nagle, S. Structure of lipid bilayers. Biochim. Biophys. Acta 2000, 1469, 159–195.

65. Luchette, P.A.; Vetman, T.N.; Prosser, R.S.; Hancock, R.E.; Nieh, M.P.; Glinka, C.J.; Krueger, S.; Katsaras, J. Morphology of fast-tumbling bicelles: a small angle neutron scattering and NMR study. Biochim. Biophys. Acta 2001,1513, 83–94.

66. Uhrikova, D.; Rybar, P.; Hianik, T.; Balgavy, P. Component volumes of unsaturated phosphatidylcholines in fluid bilayers: a densitometric study. Chem. Phys. Lipids 2007, 145, 97–105.

67. Coderch, L.; Lopez, O.; de la Maza, A.; Parra, J.L. Ceramides and skin function. Am. J. Clin. Dermatol. 2003, 4, 107–129.

68. Barbosa-Barros, L.; de la Maza, A.; Estelrich, J.; Linares, A.M.; Feliz, M.; López, O. Characterization of bicellar as a function of temperature and lipid alkyl-chain length. Biophys. J. 2007, 92, 234a.

69. Pinaki, R.M.; Blume, A. Temperature-Induced Micelle-Vesicle Transitions in DMPC-SDS and DMPC-DTAB Mixtures Studied by Calorimetry and Dynamic Light Scattering. J. Phys. Chem. B 2002, 106, 10753–10763.

70. Lopez, O.; Cocera, M.; Wehrli, E.; Parra, J.L.; de la Maza, A. Solubilization of liposomes by sodium dodecyl sulfate: new mechanism based on the direct formation of mixed micelles. Arch. Biochem. Biophys. 1999, 367, 153–160.

71. Lopez, O.; de la Maza, A.; Coderch, L.; Lopez-Iglesias, C.; Wehrli, E.; Parra, J.L. Direct formation of mixed micelles in the solubilization of phospholipid liposomes by Triton X-100. FEBS Lett. 1998, 426, 314–318.

72. Goltsov, A.N.; Barsukov, L.I. Synergetics of the Membrane Self-Assembly: A Micelle-to-Vesicle Transition. J. Biol. Phys. 2000, 26, 27–41.

73. Kashiwagi, H.; Ueno, M. Mechanism of micelle-vesicle transformation and control of vesicular sizes and properties.Yakugaku Zasshi 2008, 128, 669–680.

74. Dwiecki, K.; Gornas, P.; Wilk, A.; Nogala-Kalucka, M.; Polewski, K. Spectroscopic studies of D-alpha-tocopherol concentration-induced transformation in egg phosphatidylcholine vesicles. Cell. Mol. Biol. Lett. 2007, 12, 51–69.

75. Almgren, M. Mixed micelles and other structures in the solubilization of bilayer lipid membranes by surfactants.Biochim. Biophys. Acta 2000, 1508, 146–163.

76. López, O.; Cócera, M.; Coderch, L.; Parra, J.L.; Barsukov, L.I.; De la Maza, A. Octyl Glucoside-Mediated Solubilization and Reconstitution of Liposomes: Structural and Kinetic Aspects. J. Phys. Chem. B 2001, 105, 9879–9886.

77. Leng, J.; Egelhaaf, S.U.; Cates, M.E. Kinetics of the micelle-to-vesicle transition: aqueous lecithin-bile salt mixtures.Biophys. J. 2003, 85, 1624–1646.

78. Struppe, J.; Vold, R.R. Dilute bicellar solutions for structural NMR work. J. Magn. Reson. 1998, 135, 541–546.

79. López, O.; Cócera, M.; López-Iglesias, C.; Walter, P.; Coderch, L.; Parra, J.L.; de la Maza, A. Reconstitution of liposomes inside the intercellular lipid domain of the stratum corneum. Langmuir 2002, 18, 7002–7008.

80. Veiga, M.P.; Arrondo, J.L.; Goni, F.M.; Alonso, A. Ceramides in phospholipid membranes: effects on bilayer stability and transition to nonlamellar phases. Biophys. J. 1999, 76, 342–350.

81. Holopainen, J.M.; Lehtonen, J.Y.; Kinnunen, P.K. Lipid microdomains in dimyristoylphosphatidylcholine-ceramide liposomes. Chem. Phys. Lipids 1997, 88, 1–13.

82. Huang, H.W.; Goldberg, E.M.; Zidovetzki, R. Ceramides modulate protein kinase C activity and perturb the structure of Phosphatidylcholine/Phosphatidylserine bilayers. Biophys. J. 1999, 77, 1489–1497.

83. Hsueh, Y.W.; Giles, R.; Kitson, N.; Thewalt, J. The effect of ceramide on phosphatidylcholine membranes: a deuterium NMR study. Biophys. J. 2002, 82, 3089–3095.

84. Garidel, P.; Hauser, G.; Förster, G.; Blume, A.; Rapp, G. Aggregation behaviour of ceramide class 3 lipids. Hasilab Annu. Rep. 2003, 1009–1010.

85. Lopez-Montero, I.; Rodriguez, N.; Cribier, S.; Pohl, A.; Velez, M.; Devaux, P.F. Rapid transbilayer movement of ceramides in phospholipid vesicles and in human erythrocytes. J. Biol. Chem. 2005, 280, 25811–25819.

86. Lopez-Montero, I.; Velez, M.; Devaux, P.F. Surface tension induced by sphingomyelin to ceramide conversion in lipid membranes. Biochim. Biophys. Acta 2007, 1768, 553–561.

87. Barbosa-Barros, L.; Barba, C.; Rodríguez, G.; Cócera, M.; Coderch, L.; López-Iglesias, C.; de la Maza, A.; López, O. Lipid nanostructures: self-assembly and effect on skin properties. Mol. Pharm. 2009, 6, 1237–1245.

88. Holopainen, J.M.; Lemmich, J.; Richter, F.; Mouritsen, O.G.; Rapp, G.; Kinnunen, P.K. Dimyristoylphosphatidylcholine/C16:0-ceramide binary liposomes studied by differential scanning calorimetry and wide- and small-angle x-ray scattering. Biophys. J. 2000, 78, 2459–2469.

89. Rubio, L.; Alonso, C.; Rodriguez, G.; Barbosa-Barros, L.; Coderch, L.; De la Maza, A.; Parra, J.L.; Lopez, O. Bicellar systems for in vitro percutaneous absorption of diclofenac. Int. J. Pharm. 2010, 386, 108–113.

90. Rodriguez, G.; Soria, G.; Coll, E.; Rubio, L.; Barbosa-Barros, L.; Lopez-Iglesias, C.; Planas, A.M.; Estelrich, J.; de la Maza, A.; Lopez, O. Bicosomes: bicelles in dilute systems. Biophys. J. 2010, 99, 480–488.

91. Losonczi, J.A.; Prestegard, J.H. Improved dilute bicelle solutions for high-resolution NMR of biological macromolecules. J. Biomol. NMR 1998, 12, 447–451.

92. Johnsson, M.; Edwards, K. Liposomes, disks, and spherical micelles: aggregate structure in mixtures of gel phase phosphatidylcholines and poly(ethylene glycol)-phospholipids. Biophys. J. 2003, 85, 3839–3847.

# Chapter 7

## Etodolac Containing Topical Niosomal Gel: Formulation Development and Evaluation

**Gyati Shilakari Asthana, Abhay Asthana, Davinder Singh, and Parveen Kumar Sharma**

*Department of Pharmaceutics, M. M. College of Pharmacy, Maharishi Markandeshwar University, Mullana, Ambala, Haryana 133207, India*

### ABSTRACT

The present study aimed to investigate the delivery potential of Etodolac (ETD) containing topical niosomal gel. Niosomal formulations were prepared by thin film hydration method at various ratios of cholesterol and Span 60 and were evaluated with respect to particle size, shape, entrapment efficiency, and in vitrocharacteristics. Dicetyl phosphate (DCP) was also added in the niosomal formulation. Mean particle size of niosomal formulation was found to be in the range of 2 µm to 4 µm. Niosomal formulation $N_2$ (1 : 1) ratio of cholesterol and surfactant displayed good entrapment efficiency (96.72%). TEM analyses showed that niosomal formulation was spherical in shape. Niosomal formulation ($N_2$) displayed high percentage of drug release after 24 h (94.91) at (1 : 1) ratio of cholesterol : surfactant. Further selected niosomal formulation was used to formulate topical gel and was characterized with respect to its various parameters such as pH, viscosity, spreadability, ex vivo study, and in vivo potential permeation. Ex vivo study showed that niosomal gel possessed better skin permeation study than the plain topical gel.

Further in vivo study revealed good inhibition of inflammation in case of topical niosomal gel than plain gel and niosomal formulation. The present study suggested that topical niosomal gel formulations provide sustained and prolonged delivery of drug.

# 1. INTRODUCTION

Etodolac (ETD) is a nonsteroidal anti-inflammatory drug (NSAID) of selective COX-2 inhibitor class used for osteoarthritis and rheumatoid arthritis. Its therapeutic effects are due to its ability to inhibit prostaglandin synthesis ("as discussed by Inoue et al. [1]"). Prostaglandins are the chemicals which are responsible for pain and the fever and tenderness that occur with inflammation. It possesses poor solubility and also undergoes extensive first pass metabolism that could be the reason of its low bioavailability. Its terminal half life is 7 hrs and hence frequent dosing is required. Thus, to avoid aforementioned issues of ETD, it is desirable to encapsulate the drug in the vesicular system to prolong the existence of the drug in systemic circulation and perhaps increase the bioavailability. Continuous oral use of ETD causes serious gastrointestinal disturbance such as ulcer, stomach, or intestinal bleeding and chest pain which can be fatal. To avoid such problem there are other alternatives like coating of polymer that avoid release of drug molecule in gastrointestinal tract (GIT). Another approach to overcome such problem is changing the route of drug administration, namely, buccal route, topical route, nasal route, transdermal route, and so forth. Topical route is most preferable as easy to apply and provide high level of patient satisfaction. Transdermal route also avoid first pass metabolism associated with conventional route of drug administration. It also provides easy elimination of drug in case of toxicity and reduced fluctuation in plasma drug concentration level and thus decreased side effect. Various novel drug delivery technologies have been applied. Various novel delivery technologies including ethosomes ("as discussed by Chintala and Padmapreetha [2]"), microsphere ("as discussed by Kumar et al. [3]"), thermogels for rectal delivery ("as discussed by Barakat [4]"), and hydrophilic gel ("as discussed by Tas et al. [5]") have been reported for delivery of Etodolac.

Topical drug delivery means the application of drug to skin for localized effect. The skin is one of the most widespread and freely available structures of the human body. Skin of an average adult body covers a surface approximately 2 $m^2$ and receives about one-third of the blood circulating through the body ("as discussed by Sharma et al. [6]"). It acts as a regulator in retaining the body heat, plays a part in regulation of blood pressure, and protects against the penetration of ultraviolet rays. Dermal drug delivery has number of advantages like longer duration of action, dosing flexibility, reduced side effects, uniform plasma levels, high patient compliance, and so forth but it has some disadvantages like possibility of local irritation effect, erythema, itching, and low permeability of drugs in the stratum corneum ("as discussed by Bhowmik et al. [7]"). Stratum corneum is outermost and top layer of epidermis which is impermeable to water and behaves like tough flexible membrane. It contains dead keratinized cells called corneocytes. For the permeation of drug to this barrier many technologies and systems have been investigated and one of the most promising techniques is the vesicular carrier for drug delivery through the skin.

Novel drug delivery carriers have great potential for dermal delivery. The lipidic and nonlipidic vesicular systems like liposome, transfersome, ethosome, and niosome are used to overcome the problem associated with topical conventional formulation. Drug delivery system using novel vesicular carrier, such as liposome or niosome, has distinct advantages over microspheres, nanoparticles, and other carriers in terms of better entrapment of drugs (payload characteristics), target site specificity, and handling premature drug release (burst effect). In 1985, niosomes were studied as an alternative to liposome because they offer some benefits over liposome such as being more stable, nontoxic, and economic due to low cost of nonionic surfactant as compared to phospholipids which are prone to oxidation. Incorporation of surfactants within niosomes may also enhance the efficacy of the drug, possibly by facilitating its uptake by the target cells. Niosomes are biodegradable, biocompatible, relatively nontoxic, and an alternative of liposome. They can be utilized in the delivery of wide variety of drugs as it has capability to entrap hydrophilic, lipophilic, and amphiphilic drugs. For transdermal route of administration NSAIDs, hormone, antibacterial, and antifungal drugs are most preferably used.

The objectives of the present study were to develop ETD loaded niosomal gel for transdermal delivery and to provide prolonged and sustained release of drug, so that required dose is decreased, and to avoid GI side effect and first pass hepatic metabolism.

# 2. MATERIALS AND METHODS

## 2.1. Materials

Etodolac (ETD) was received as gift sample from IPCA Laboratories Ltd., Mumbai. Chloroform, acetone, potassium dihydrogen orthophosphate, sodium chloride, sodium hydroxide, methanol, Disodium hydrogen phosphate, and dialysis membrane were obtained from Himedia. Cholesterol, dicetyl phosphate (DCP), and Span 60 were taken from Sigma-Aldrich.

## 2.2. Preparation of Niosomal Formulation

In the present study, niosomal formulations were prepared by thin film hydration technique as reported earlier with slight modifications ("as discussed by Balakrishnan et al. [8]") by using various ratios of Span 60 and cholesterol as shown in Table 1. DCP (5 mg) was added in the formulation to keep the niosomal formulation stable for long period of time. Accurately weighted quantities of surfactants and cholesterol were taken to give the desired ratio and were dissolved in 10 mL chloroform in a round bottom flask and DCP was added to the above mixture. Then accurately weighed amount of drug was added into the solvent. The solvent was evaporated in a rotary flash evaporator under a vacuum of 20 inches of Hg at a temperature of 60°C at 120 rpm until a smooth, dry lipid film was obtained. Then film was hydrated with 10 mL of phosphate buffer saline (PBS) pH 7.4 for 3 hr at 60 ± 2°C with shaking on a water bath. The niosomal suspension was kept at 2–8°C for 24 hr. Developed niosomal formulation was evaluated with respect to particle size, shape, entrapment efficiency, and in vitro drug release profile.

**Table 1**. Composition of niosomal formulations at various ratios of cholesterol : Span 60.

| Sr. number | Formulation codes | Drug : cholesterol : Span 60 (molar ratio) | Dicetyl phosphate (DCP) (mg) |
|---|---|---|---|
| 1 | $N_1$ | 1 : 0.5 : 1 | 5.0 |
| 2 | $N_2$ | 1 : 1 : 1 | 5.0 |
| 3 | $N_3$ | 1 : 1.5 : 1 | 5.0 |
| 4 | $N_4$ | 1 : 1 : 0.5 | 5.0 |
| 5 | $N_5$ | 1 : 1 : 1.5 | 5.0 |

# 3. EVALUATION OF NIOSOMAL FORMULATION

Niosomes formulations were characterized with respect to shape, particle size distribution, entrapment efficiency, and in vitro release studies.

## 3.1. Particle Shape and Morphology

Shape and morphology of niosomal formulations were determined by optical microscopy and Transmission Electron Microscopy (TEM) and result were shown in Figures 1 and 2.

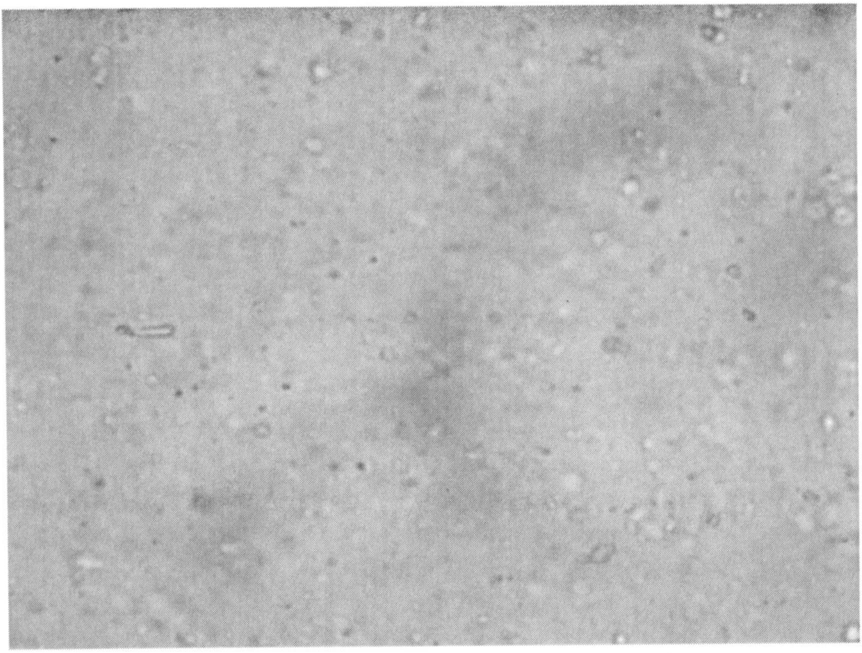

**Figure 1.** Optical microscopy of niosomal formulation at 45x.

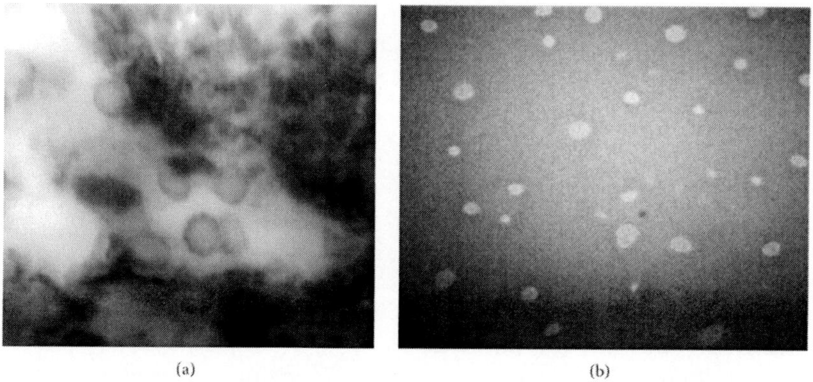


**Figure 2.** TEM image of $N_2$ formulation at (a) 60,000x and (b) 18,000x.

### 3.2. Particle Size

The particle size of the niosomal suspension was determined by optical microscopy. A drop of niosomal suspension was placed on a glass slide. A cover slip was placed over the niosomes suspension and evaluated the average vesicle size by an ordinary optical microscope using a precalibrated ocular eye piece micrometer ("as discussed by Firthouse et al. [9]").

### 3.3. Entrapment Efficiency

Entrapment efficiency of niosomal formulations was determined by centrifugation method. 10 mL niosomal suspension was poured into a stopper test tube and centrifuged by using cooling centrifuge at 10,000 rpm maintained at 4°C for 90 minutes and then filtered by using Whatman filter paper to obtain clear fraction. The clear fraction was used for the determination of free drug by using UV spectrophotometer at 278 nm ("as discussed by Sathali and Sangeetha [10]"). The encapsulation efficiency was calculated using the formula

$$\text{Entrapment Efficiency (\%)} = \left[ \frac{(C_t - C_f)}{C_t} \times 100 \right], \tag{1}$$

where is concentration of total drug and is concentration of unentrapped drug.

### 3.4. In Vitro Release Studies

In vitro release studies of niosomes suspension were carried out by dialysis bag method ("as discussed by Sathali and Rajalakshmi [11]"). A dialysis sac was washed and kept in distilled water for soaking. The vesicle suspension was pipetted into a bag made up of tubing and sealed followed by placing the dialysis bag into a beaker containing 500 mL of PBS pH 7.4. The beaker was placed over magnetic stirrer (50 rpm) and the temperature was maintained at 37°C ± 0.5°C. Samples were withdrawn at predetermined time intervals. Sink condition was maintained throughout the experiment by replacing the withdrawing sample with fresh medium. Samples were diluted and analysed for drug content by using UV/visible spectrophotometer at 278 nm ("as discussed by Sathali and Rajalakshmi [11]").

### 3.5. Formulation and Evaluation of Gels

Gel base was prepared by dispersing 1% w/w Carbopol 940 in distilled water and then was allowed to swell for 1 hour. After that glycerin was added to the dispersion with continuous homogenization. The pH was adjusted by triethanolamine ("as discussed by Solanki et al. [12]").

### 3.6. Preparation of Plain Topical Gel

Plain gel was prepared by adding drug (2% w/w) in 1% w/w Carbopol 940 base for the comparison with niosomal gel ($N_2G$).

### 3.7. Preparation of Niosomal Gel

The measured volume of $N_2$ niosomal formulation was centrifuged by using cooling centrifuge for 90 mins at 4°C and 12,000 rpm. The semisolid mass of niosomes was separated from supernatant and mixed in the 1% Carbopol gel base by using electric homogenizer ("as discussed by Solanki et al. [12]").

### 3.8. Evaluation of Topical Gel

The niosomal gel and plain topical ETD gel were characterized with respect to pH, viscosity, spreadability, andex vivo permeation studies.

### 3.9. pH Measurements

The pH of the gel formulations was delivered by using digital pH meter. Before measurement pH meter was calibrated and readings were taken by dipping the glass rod into the gel formulations ("as discussed by Jain et al. [13]").

### 3.10. Viscosity Measurement

The viscosity of gel formulations was determined by Brookfield viscometer. 25.0 g gel was taken in beaker and spindle number 4 was rotated at 50 rpm and viscosity of the sample was determined ("as discussed by Jain et al. [13]").

### 3.11. Spreadability

The spreadability of gel formulations was determined by using spreadability apparatus. 1.0 g of gel sample was placed on the lower slide and upper slide was placed on the top of the sample ("as discussed by Jain et al. [13]"). The spreadability was determined by the formula

$$S = \frac{m \times l}{t}, \tag{2}$$

where is spreadability, is weight tied to upper slide, is length travel by upper slide, and is time.

### 3.12. Ex Vivo Permeation Studies

The ex vivo permeation studies of plain topical gel and niosomal gel were carried out with Franz diffusion (FD) cell using dehaired rat skin followed by hydration for 30 minutes in PBS pH 7.4 at room temperature to remove the extraneous debris and leachable enzymes. Then excised skin was placed between donor and receptor compartments of the FD cell. Gel was placed in donor compartment and PBS pH 7.4 was taken in receptor compartments as media. Temperature of cell was maintained at 37°C ± 0.5°C. The assembly was kept on magnetic stirrer and samples were withdrawn at time intervals of 1, 2, 3, 4, 6, 8, 12, and 24 h and replaced with equal volume of fresh media. Samples were analyzed by UV spectrophotometer at 278 nm and cumulative % of drug release was calculated ("as discussed by Srikanth et al. [14]").

### 3.13. Stability Studies

Niosomal formulation was selected on the basis of entrapment efficiency and in vitro release studies. Stability studies were assessed by keeping $N_2$ niosomal suspension and niosomal gel in sealed glass vials and storing them in two different storage conditions, that is, refrigeration temperature and room temperature for a period of 30 days. The samples were withdrawn at different time intervals over a period of one month and the residual content was determined spectrophotometrically ("as discussed by Arora et al. [15]").

### 3.14. In Vivo Studies

White Albino rats of either sex weighing between 180 and 200 g were selected for study. The approval of the Institutional Animal Ethical Committee CPCEA No. MMCP/IAEC/12/8 was obtained before starting the study. The animals were divided into four groups, each consisting of six rats. Groups II, III, and IV were subjected to topical gel of ETD drug, niosomal formulation, and topical niosomal gel formulation, respectively, whereas Group I was treated as control. Anti-inflammatory activities of the drug by developed formulations were determined by using paw edema method on the basis of the inhibition of the volume of the hind paw edema induced by phlogistic agent. For present study 1% w/v carrageenan solution in 0.9% w/v was used as phlogistic agent.

## 3.15. Anti-Inflammatory Activity

The animals were fasted overnight and all groups were treated by applying the formulations containing drug equivalent to 20 mg/kg body weight on the left paw of the rats, with respective gels. The area of application was covered with bandages and it was left in place for 3 hrs. The dressing was then removed and the gel remaining on the surface was wiped off with cotton. The animals were then injected with 0.1 mL of 1% w/v of carrageenan solution in plantar region of left hind paw and the paw volume was measured after 1 hr, 2 hr, 3 hr, 4 hr, 5 hr, and 6 hr and 8 hr, using modified or specially designed assembly which works on the Archimedes principle. The right paw served as a reference of noninflamed paw for comparison. The percentage difference between right and left paw volumes was taken as percent edema produced ("as discussed by Shinde and Kanojiya [16]"). The percent edema produced with test samples was subtracted from percent edema produced in control group to obtain percent edema inhibition by respective groups. Percent inhibition of edema is directly proportional to the anti-inflammatory activity.

# 4. RESULT AND DISCUSSION

## 4.1. Evaluation of Niosomal Formulation

Developed niosomal formulations were characterized with respect to particle size, shape, entrapment efficiency, and in vitro drug release profile.

### 4.1.1. Shape and Morphology

Shape and morphology of niosomal formulations were determined by optical microscopy. It was clearly observed from Figure 1 that niosomes are spherical in shape.

### 4.1.2. Transmission Electron Microscopy (TEM)

Morphological characteristics of niosomal formulations were further confirmed by TEM analysis. TEM photomicrograph of ($N_2$) niosomal formulation at 60,000x and 18,000x magnification revealed the spherical shape of niosomes. Further it was observed from the TEM images that niosomes are hollow vesicular structure.

#### 4.1.3. Particle Size

Particle size of niosomal formulation at different ratio of cholesterol and surfactant was shown in Figure 3. Mean particle size of the niosomal formulation was found to be in the range of 2 µm to 4 µm. It was clearly depicted from Figure 3 that particle size of niosomal formulations was increased on increasing the cholesterol content. Cholesterol content provides strength to the nonpolar tail of nonionic surfactant. At low cholesterol content, it is to be expected that the cholesterol and nonionic surfactant are in close packing with increasing curvature and reducing size. As the cholesterol content increases, it would reduce the content of surfactants and also increased the hydrophobicity of bilayer membrane thus increasing vesicles radius in a way to establish more thermodynamic stable form. Rigid structure of bilayer membrane due to cholesterol content also provides resistance to reduce size due to sonication and results in vesicles with bigger size.

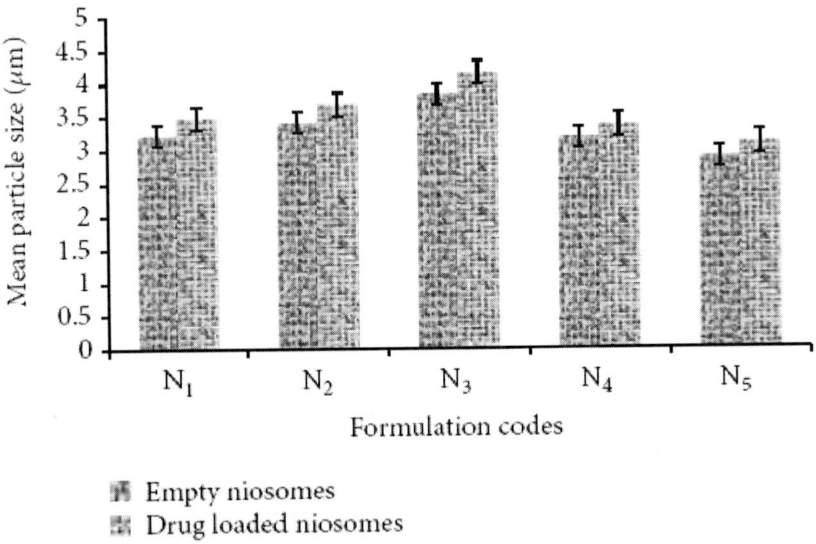


**Figure 3:** Particle size of niosomes containing Span 60.

#### 4.1.4. Entrapment Efficiency

Entrapment efficiency of various niosomal formulations was determined at different ratio of cholesterol and surfactant by centrifugation method and result was shown in Figure 4. It was clearly depicted from the data shown in Figure 4 that entrapment efficiency of the niosomal formulation was increased on increasing the cholesterol ratio from 0.5 to 1 whereas on further increase in cholesterol ratio from 1 to 1.5 the entrapment efficiency was decreased. There could be two factors for such result: first, with increase of cholesterol ratio, hydrophobicity and stability of bilayers vesicles increase and permeability decreases which may lead to efficiently trapping the hydrophobic drug into bilayers as the vesicles formed. Secondly higher amount of cholesterol may compete with the drug for packing space within the bilayer, hence excluding the drug as the amphiphiles assembled into drugs ("as discussed by Balakrishnan et al. [8]").

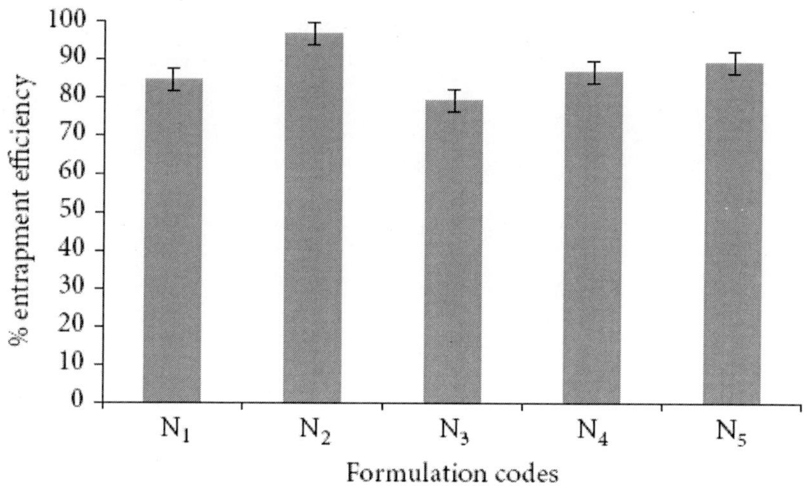


**Figure 4:** Entrapment efficiencies of various niosomal formulations containing Span 60.

Entrapment efficiency of niosomes was also influenced by varying the amount of surfactant. As the amount of surfactant in niosomal formulation increased, the decrease in leakage of drug results in enhancement of entrapment efficiency ("as discussed by Salih et al. [17]").

#### 4.1.5. In Vitro Studies

In vitro studies of niosomal formulations were carried out in PBS pH 7.4 by dialysis method on magnetic stirrer and results were shown in Figure 5 (see Table of Supplementary Material available online athttp://dx.doi.org/10.1155/2016/9324567). It was observed from the data that in vitro drug release of niosomal formulation was sharply increased up to 24 hr. It was found that $N_2$ formulation displayed maximum drug release that is 94.91% after 24 hr at 1 : 1 ratio of cholesterol to surfactant. Amount of surfactant varied in niosomal formulation affects the release profile of drug. As the ratio of surfactant increases from 1 : 1 to 1 : 1.5 (cholesterol : surfactant), the drug release from niosomal vesicles was decreased. This could be due to the fact that the increase in surfactant ratio acts as depot and reduces leakage of drug from niosomes to dissolution media ("as discussed by Salih et al. [17]").

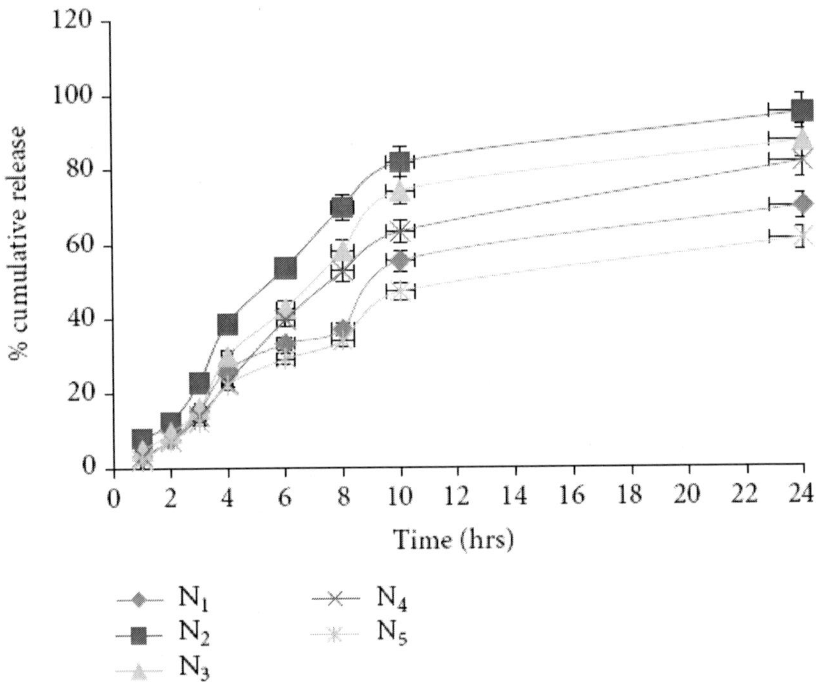


**Figure 5.** In vitro release profile of niosomal formulations.

On the basis of the above result it was found that $N_2$ possesses highest entrapment efficiency and in vitro release profile; thus it was selected for further study.

### 4.1.6. Characterization of Niosomal Gel Formulations

(1) Physical Examination. Gels were examined for physical appearance and results of the physical examination of the gel were shown in Table 2.

**Table 2:** Physical examination and other characteristics of plain and niosomal gel formulation.

| Sr. number | Formulation codes | Color | Homogeneity | Texture | pH | Viscosity (cps) | Spreadability (gm·cm/sec) |
|---|---|---|---|---|---|---|---|
| 1 | $N_2G$ | White | Homogenous | Smooth | 6.70 ± 0.05 | 6831 ± 9.47 | 18.25 ± 1.24 |
| 2 | Plain gel | White | Homogenous | Smooth | 6.60 ± 0.08 | 6502 ± 8.51 | 13.71 ± 0.83 |

Plain gel and niosomal gel formulations were white in color, were homogenous, and had smooth texture.

(2) pH Measurement. pH of the niosomal gel and plain gel as shown in Table 2 lied in the normal pH range of skin to avoid any risk of irritation upon the application to the skin.

(3) Viscosity Measurements. The viscosities of the gel formulations are optimum as they provide good in vitrorelease of drug through the gel and results were shown in Table 2.

(4) Spreadability. Spreadability of the plain gel and niosomal gel formulation were found to be better as compared to plain gel as shown in Table 2 and Figure 6. This could be because of loose gel matrix of gel due to presence of vesicles.

**Figure 6.** Spreadability studies.

(5) Ex Vivo Studies. The ex vivo skin permeation study of niosomal gel and plain gel was carried out with Franz diffusion cell using abdominal skin of male Albino rat by using PBS (pH 7.4) as quality media.

It was displayed from the data as shown in Figure 7 that from drug release 15.28% of drug release was reported from ETD topical gel after 1 hr and drug release was significantly increased from 15.28% to 97.57% up to 8 hrs; thereafter only 1.91% of drug was released in next 4 hrs, whereas in case of topical niosomal gel only 8.13% of drug release was observed after 1 hr and continuous and appreciable increase in cumulative drug releases was reported up to 24 hrs. After 24 hrs only 81.73% of drug release was recorded. These results show that the slow and sustained release of drug through the rat skin for prolonged period of time was obtained in case of niosomal gel formulation as compared to plain gel to ETD. Faster release of the ETD from the plain gel may be due to free drug being present in gel structure as compared to niosomal gel in which drug was entrapped into niosomal vesicular structure. In case of niosomal gel, drug permeated due to either the fusion of the niosomes with the intercellular lipid of the stratum corneum, direct transfer of drug from niosomes to the skin, or the penetration enhancement effect of the nonionic surfactant of niosomes ("as discussed by Shilpa and Vijay [18]").

(6) Stability Studies. Stability studies were carried out by keeping $N_2$ formulation and niosomal gel formulation ($N_2G$) for one month at different storage conditions. At different time points, sample was withdrawn and percent residual content was determined by UV spectrophotometer and results were shown in Figure 8.

It was observed from the results slight reduction in residual drug content at room temperature, whereas, in case of refrigerated temperature, no significant change was observed in residual content. Thus developed niosomal formulation was found to be stable at the end of the study on storage condition.

(7) In Vivo Studies. In vivo anti-inflammatory activity was determined by using carrageenan induced rat paw edema method. The percentage inhibition of edema was calculated from different formulations and results were shown in Figure 9 and Table of Supplementary Material.

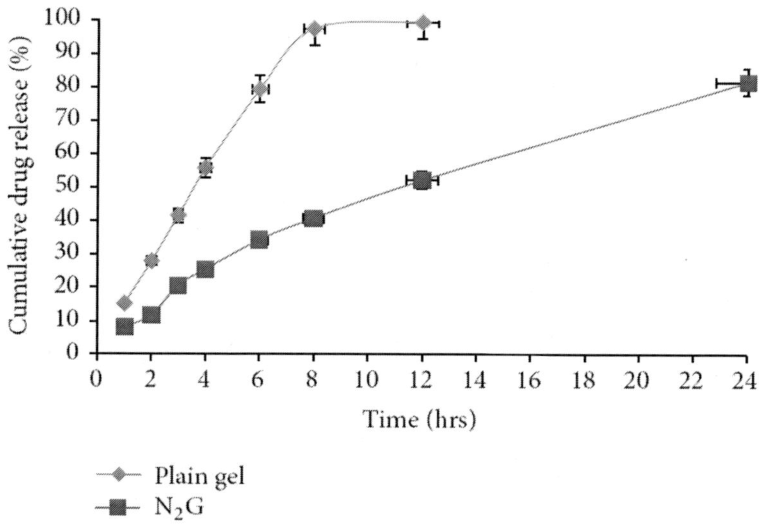


**Figure 7:** Comparative ex vivo permeation study of gel formulations.

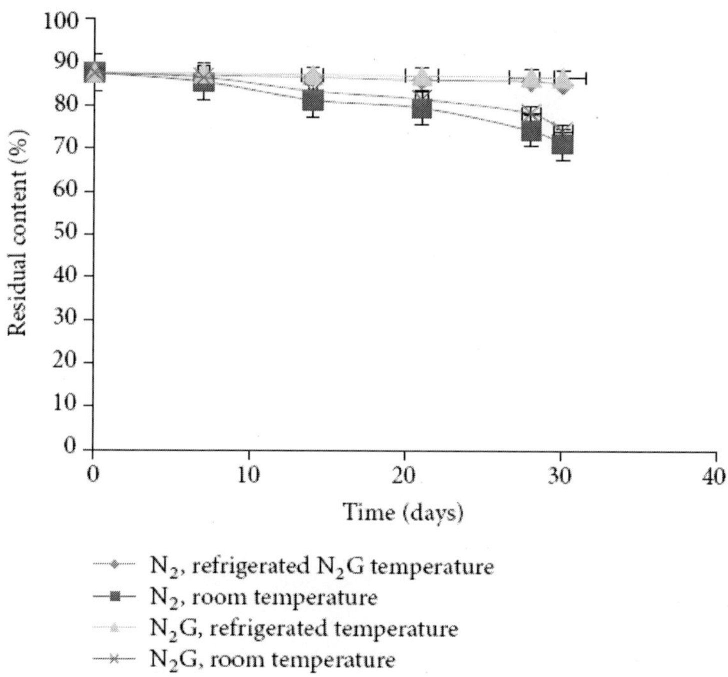


**Figure 8.** Stability studies of $N_2$ and $N_2G$ formulation at different storage conditions.

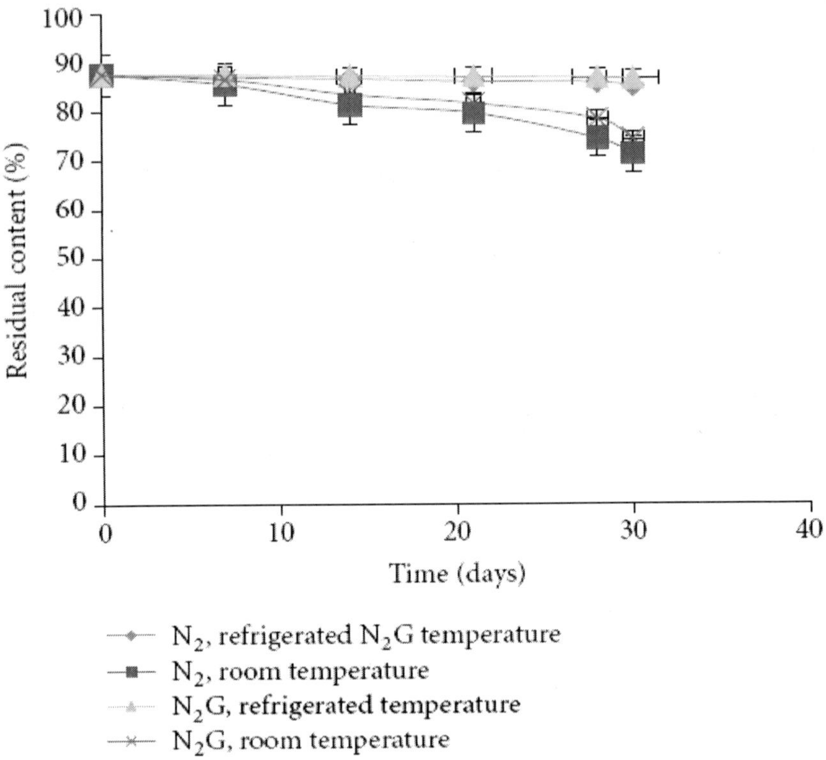


**Figure 9.** Comparative in vivo percentage edema inhibition.

Maximum% edema inhibition was observed with niosomal gel formulation as compared to the niosome suspension and plain gel after 8 hrs. Although the difference observed is narrow at end point, however, improvement is consistent at all time points, which presents the significance of outcome. According to both ex vivo and in vivo studies $N_2G$ gel showed the better permeation and effectiveness as compared to other formulations. This may be due to efficient hydration of thin film and more total amount of drug entrapped.

## 5. CONCLUSION

Niosomal formulation was successfully prepared by thin film hydration technique using different ratios of cholesterol and surfactant (Span 60) and dicetyl phosphate (DCP). It was found that niosomal formulation $N_2$having cholesterol : surfactant ratio (1 : 1) showed better entrapment efficiency and in vitro release profile. Selected niosomal formulation was further incorporated in Carbopol gel base to prepare niosomal gel. Both niosomal formulation and niosomal gel were found to be stable at different storage conditions. Niosomal gel was prepared, exhibiting better skin permeation study when compared with plain gel. Further inhibitions in inflammation by developed niosomal gel were also found maximum when compared to plain gel and niosomal formulation. The result of present research work reveals that niosomal gel formulation could be the better choice for delivery of wide verities of drug for transdermal administration.

## COMPETING INTERESTS

The authors declare that there is no conflict of interests regarding the publication of this paper.

## ACKNOWLEDGMENTS

The authors are highly thankful to IPCA Laboratory, Mumbai, for providing the gift sample of Etodolac and also thankful to Panjab University for providing TEM facility and MM University Mullana for giving the facility to carry out this research work.

## REFERENCES

1. N. Inoue, M. Nogawa, S. Ito, K. Tajima, S. Kume, and T. Kyoi, "The enantiomers of etodolac, a racemic anti-inflammatory agent, play different roles in efficacy and gastrointestinal safety," Biological and Pharmaceutical Bulletin, vol. 34, no. 5, pp. 655–659, 2011.

2. P. K. Chintala and J. Padmapreetha, "Formulation and in-vitro evaluation of gel containing ethosomes entrapped with etodolac," International Journal of Pharmaceutical Science and Research, vol. 5, no. 2, pp. 630–635, 2014.

3. SS. Kumar, K. Masilamani, SS. Srinivas, and V. Ravichandiran, "Formulation and Physico-Chemical Evaluation of Ethylcellulose Microspheres Containing Etodolac," in International Conference on Biotechnology and Pharmaceutical Sciences, pp. 372–375, 2011.

4. N. S. Barakat, "In vitro and in vivo characteristics of a thermogelling rectal delivery system of etodolac,"APPS Pharmaceutical Science and Technology, vol. 10, no. 3, pp. 724–731, 2009.

5. Tas, Y. Ozkan, A. Okyar, and A. Savaser, "In vitro and ex vivo permeation studies of etodolac from hydrophilic gels and effect of terpenes as enhancers," Drug Delivery, vol. 14, no. 7, pp. 453–459, 2007.

6. 6. N. Sharma, G. Agarwal, A. C. Rana, Z. A. Bhat, and D. Kumar, "A review: transdermal drug delivery system: a tool for novel drug delivery system," International Journal of Drug Development and Research, vol. 3, no. 3, pp. 70–84, 2011.

7. 7. D. Bhowmik, M. Chiranjib Chandira, B. Jayakar, and K. P. Sampath, "Recent advances in transdermal drug delivery system," International Journal of Pharmaceutical Technology, vol. 2, no. 1, pp. 68–77, 2010.

8. P. Balakrishnan, S. Shanmugam, W. S. Lee, et al., "Formulation and in vitro assessment of minoxidil niosomes for enhanced skin delivery," International Journal of Pharmaceutics, vol. 377, no. 1-2, pp. 1–8, 2009.

9. 9. P. U. M. Firthouse, S. M. Halith, S. U. Wahab, M. Sirajudeen, and S. K. Mohideen, "Formulation and evaluation of miconazole niosomes," International Journal of PharmTech Research, vol. 3, no. 2, pp. 1019–1022, 2011.

10. 10. A. A. H. Sathali and T. Sangeetha, "Formulation and evaluation of ocular niosomal in situ gel of levofloxacin hemihydrates," Journal of Pharmacy Research, vol. 4, pp. 4331–4337, 2011.

11. 11. A. A. H. Sathali and G. Rajalakshmi, "Evaluation of transdermal targeted niosomal drug delivery of terbinafine

hydrochloride," International Journal of PharmTech Research, vol. 2, no. 3, pp. 2081–2089, 2010.

12. 12. A. B. Solanki, J. R. Parikh, R. H. Parikh, and M. R. Patel, "Evaluation of different compositions of niosomes to optimize aceclofenac transdermal delivery," Asian Journal of Pharmaceutical Sciences, vol. 5, no. 3, pp. 87–95, 2010.

13. 13. A. Jain, P. Deveda, and N. Vyas, "Development of antifungal emulsion based gel for topical fungal infections," International Journal of Pharmaceutical Research and Development, vol. 2, pp. 18–25, 2011.

14. 14. K. Srikanth, M. Nappinnai, V. R. M. Gupta, and J. Suribabu, "Niosomes: a prominent tool for transdermal drug delivery," Research Journal of Pharmaceutical, Biological and Chemical Sciences, vol. 1, no. 2, pp. 308–316, 2010.

15. 15. S. Arora, B. Prashar, H. Dhamija, A. Chandel, and V. Thakur, "Niosomes: the unique vesicular drug carriers," Journal of Drug Delivery & Therapeutics, vol. 2, no. 1, pp. 96–101, 2012.

16. 16. U. A. Shinde and S. S. Kanojiya, "Serratiopeptidase niosomal gel with potential in topical delivery,"Journal of Pharmaceutics, vol. 2014, Article ID 382959, 9 pages, 2014.

17. 17. O. S. Salih, L. H. Samein, and W. K. Ali, "Formulation and in vitro evaluation of rosuvastatin calcium niosomes," International Journal of Pharmacy and Pharmaceutical Sciences, vol. 5, no. 4, pp. 525–535, 2013.

18. 18. D. J. Shilpa and K. P. Vijay, "Formulation, development and evaluation of niosomal drug delivery system for clindamycin phosphate," Pharma Science Monitor, vol. 5, no. 2, pp. 256–274, 2014.

# Chapter 8

# Formulation and Evaluation of Optimized Oxybenzone Microsponge Gel for Topical Delivery

**Atmaram P. Pawar, Aditya P. Gholap, Ashwin B. Kuchekar, C. Bothiraja, andAshwin J. Mali**

*Department of Pharmaceutics, Bharati Vidyapeeth University, Poona College of Pharmacy, Erandwane, Maharashtra 411038, India*

## ABSTRACT

Background. Oxybenzone, a broad spectrum sunscreen agent widely used in the form of lotion and cream, has been reported to cause skin irritation, dermatitis, and systemic absorption. Aim. The objective of the present study was to formulate oxybenzone loaded microsponge gel for enhanced sun protection factor with reduced toxicity. Material and Method. Microsponge for topical delivery of oxybenzone was successfully prepared by quasiemulsion solvent diffusion method. The effects of ethyl cellulose and dichloromethane were optimized by the $3^2$ factorial design. The optimized microsponges were dispersed into the hydrogel and further evaluated.Results. The microsponges were spherical with pore size in the range of 0.10–0.22 μm. The optimized formulation possesses the particle size and entrapment efficiency of 72 ± 0.77 μm and 96.9 ± 0.52%, respectively. The microsponge gel showed the controlled release and was nonirritant to the rat skin. In creep recovery test it had shown highest recovery indicating elasticity. The controlled release of oxybenzone from microsponge and barrier effect of gel result in prolonged retention of oxybenzone with reduced permeation activity. Conclusion. Evaluation study revealed remarkable and enhanced topical retention of oxybenzone for prolonged period of time. It also showed the enhanced sun protection factor compared to the marketed preparation with reduced irritation and toxicity.

## 1. INTRODUCTION

For topical application of active agents various novel carrier systems were explored till date in the form of microparticles, nanoparticles, liposomes and cochleates, and so forth. Food and Drug Administration (FDA) has approved wide range of products like Retin-A, Carac cream, MicroPeel Plus, and oil control lotion due to improved efficacy and safety compared to the conventional topical drug delivery systems. Typically, such products form a highly concentrated layer of active ingredients on the skin which results in skin irritation and toxicity [1–4].

At present, the need of an exclusive delivery system has been required for the topically active sunscreen agents. Microsponge is sponge-like porous polymeric system in the range of 10–25 μm with extended release of drug. It offers increased payload of drug and stability with reduced irritation, mutagenicity, allergenicity, and side effects for the topical applications. Due to these undue advantages, in the current era of topical products, microsponge has got wide acceptance. Microsponge for topical route has been reported for the controlled release of benzyl peroxide, mupirocin, retinoid, and 5-fluorouracil which reported minimal penetration through dermis, less drug accumulation, and irritation without sacrificing the efficacy of drug [5–7].

The ultraviolet (UV) rays responsible for sunburns increase the risk of basal cell carcinoma and malignant melanoma. These harmful UV radiations may be blocked by either absorption, reflection, or scattering of rays. The various actives were reported to avoid the exposure to harmful UV radiations. Based on the protective action, UV rays blocking agents are broadly divided into physical agents like zinc oxide and titanium dioxide and chemical agents like benzyl cinnamate and cinnamate derivatives, p-aminobenzoic acid, butyl methoxy dibenzoyl methane, and related compounds [8].

Oxybenzone is broad spectrum sunscreen agent widely used in the form of lotion and cream. It acts by absorbing entire UV-B radiations (280–320 nm) and mimics the energy conservation of law. The present oxybenzone loaded sunscreen formulations have been reported to cause skin irritation, photo allergic contact dermatitis, and systemic absorption [9, 10]. Therefore, it was hypothesized that controlled release of oxybenzone from microsponge offers a sophisticated way to increase the light absorbance capacity with reduced side effects and toxicity. This may be responsible for increasing the sun protection factor (SPF) of the formulation.

This is the first attempt to investigate the feasibility of oxybenzone loaded microsponge gel for enhanced sunscreening efficiency with reduced skin irritation and toxicity. The objective of the present study was to formulate oxybenzone loaded ethyl cellulose (EC) microsponge by quasiemulsion solvent diffusion method by $3^2$ factorial design. The optimized formulation was evaluated for physiochemical characterization, percentage yield, particle size, percent entrapment efficiency (%EE), drug release, surface topography, and differential scanning calorimetry (DSC). The optimized microsponge was incorporated into hydroxy propyl methyl cellulose (HPMC-K4M) gel. Further, prepared gel was evaluated for rheological characterization, skin irritation, minimal erythemal dose (MED), and sun protection factor (SPF) determination.

## 2. MATERIALS AND METHODS

Oxybenzone was provided by Nulife Pharmaceuticals Ltd., Pune, as a gift sample. Ethyl cellulose-N10, hydroxy propyl methyl cellulose, was gifted by Emcure Pharmaceuticals Pvt. Ltd. Polyvinyl alcohol, dichloromethane, and methanol were purchased from Emerck (India) Ltd., Mumbai.

### 2.1. Preparation of Oxybenzone Loaded Microsponge

All the microsponge formulations were prepared using quasiemulsion solvent diffusion method. Required amount of oxybenzone (0.1% w/v) and EC (0.1–0.3% w/v) were dissolved in dichloromethane (DCM) (3–

5 mL). The DCM solution was gradually added in 25 mL of aqueous solution of poly vinyl alcohol (PVA) (0.1% w/v) at room temperature with continuous magnetic stirring. Then the final mixture was filtered to separate formed microsponges and dried in the vacuum drier for 24 h.

## 2.2. Optimization of Formulation

A prior knowledge and understanding of the process variables under investigation led to preliminary experiments. Based on this preliminary data (not shown), the $3^2$ factorial design was adopted to optimize the amount of EC and DCM as the independent variables. The particle size, percent drug entrapped, and the drug release were considered as dependent variables. The response surface graphs of the obtained results were also plotted. The coded and actual values are given in Table 1. The obtained data was analyzed by the results observed from the multiple regression analysis using Design Expert 8.0.6.1 software (Stat-Ease Inc., USA).

**Table 1.** Factorial design and characterization of experimental formulations.

| Formulations (EC, DCM) (mg, mL) | % EE ± SD | % DC ± SD | % production yield | Particle size $d$ (0.9) $\mu$m ± SD | % DR ± SD |
|---|---|---|---|---|---|
| M1 (100, 3) | 92.3 ± 0.12 | 67.12 ± 0.42 | 50.14 ± 0.28 | 496 ± 0.12 | 20.08 ± 0.02 |
| M2 (100, 5) | 93.7 ± 0.22 | 70.00 ± 0.56 | 59.76 ± 0.10 | 619 ± 0.02 | 21.08 ± 0.82 |
| M3 (100, 7) | 98.6 ± 0.14 | 73.54 ± 0.82 | 73.54 ± 0.16 | 146 ± 0.32 | 22.28 ± 0.72 |
| M4 (200, 3) | 90.1 ± 0.21 | 44.26 ± 0.42 | 44.10 ± 0.14 | 347 ± 0.42 | 12.19 ± 0.42 |
| M5 (200, 5) | 96.3 ± 0.56 | 67.54 ± 0.32 | 67.76 ± 0.72 | 224 ± 0.52 | 12.88 ± 0.32 |
| M6 (200, 7) | 98.5 ± 0.72 | 54.28 ± 0.22 | 55.22 ± 0.32 | 105 ± 0.62 | 13.74 ± 0.42 |
| M7 (300, 3) | 95.3 ± 0.92 | 65.33 ± 0.29 | 65.11 ± 0.42 | 272 ± 0.02 | 12.23 ± 0.02 |
| M8 (300, 5) | 96.7 ± 0.62 | 42.02 ± 0.12 | 42.78 ± 0.62 | 119 ± 0.28 | 12.94 ± 0.11 |
| M9 (300, 7) | 96.9 ± 0.52 | 77.87 ± 0.92 | 77.56 ± 0.20 | 072 ± 0.77 | 13.76 ± 0.10 |

The following equation was obtained:

$$Y = \beta_o + \beta_1 X_1 + \beta_2 X_2 + \beta_{11} X_1 X_1 + \beta_{22} X_2 X_2 + \beta_{12} X_1 X_2, \qquad (1)$$

where is the measured response, is the levels of independent factors, and is the regression coefficient.

$X_1$ and $X_2$ indicate the amount of EC and DCM.

The optimized microsponge formulation was incorporated in 3% w/w HPMC base to obtain the gels.

## 2.3. Characterization of Optimized Oxybenzone Loaded Microsponge

### 2.3.1. Determination of Production Yield

Percentage yield is determined by calculating the initial weight of raw materials and the weight of microsponge. Percentage yield was calculated by using the following formula:

$$\text{Percentage yield} = \frac{\text{Practical yield}}{\text{Theoretical yield}} \times 100. \tag{2}$$

### 2.3.2. Microsponge Size Measurement

The mean particle size of the microsponge dispersion was determined by polarising microscope (model number E600POL). The scale was used which was numbered from one to ten microns, each unit corresponding to one micron.

### 2.3.3. Percentage Entrapment Efficiency Analysis

For the analysis of entrapped oxybenzone, microsponge was dispersed in methanol to release the entrapped drug. The unentrapped oxybenzone was separated from the microsponge by centrifugation. For this, the dispersion was transferred into Eppendorf tube and centrifuged at 20,000 rpm for 1 hr at 4°C. The free drug remained in supernatant while entrapped drug was retained in the pellet. The supernatant, with subsequent dilution and filtration, was then analyzed for drug concentration spectrophotometrically at 287 nm. The percent entrapment efficiency (%EE) was calculated as the following equation:

$$\%\mathrm{EE} = \frac{\text{Amount of drug entrapped in the microsponge}}{\text{Total amount of drug used}} \times 100. \tag{3}$$

#### 2.3.4. Drug Release Studies

To know the rate and extent of drug release from microsponge, dissolution of oxybenzone loaded microsponge was studied using USP dissolution test apparatus (USP XXIII). Accurately weighed samples of microsponge equivalent to 25 mg of oxybenzone were placed in 900 mL of phosphate buffer pH 7.4 and were subjected for dissolution with a paddle speed of 150 rpm at 37 ± 0.5°C. Aliquots (5 mL) were withdrawn at 5 min initially and then at hourly intervals up to 8 hours and assayed spectrophotometrically at 287 nm. The percentage of drug released at various time intervals was calculated and plotted against time [11, 12].

#### 2.3.5. Scanning Electron Microscopy (SEM)

Surface topography of the selected optimized formulation was characterised using scanning electron microscopy (SEM). Freshly prepared microsponge samples were mounted on the aluminium stub and coated with gold-palladium layer by autofine coater (Joel, JFC, Tokyo, Japan) and analyzed with a scanning electron microscope (Joel, JSM-6360, Tokyo, Japan) operated at a 10 kV acceleration.

#### 2.3.6. Differential Scanning Calorimetry (DSC)

DSC studies were carried out using Mettler-Toledo DSC 821e instrument equipped with an intercooler (Mettler-Toledo, Switzerland). Indium and zinc standards were used to calibrate the DSC temperature and enthalpy scale. The samples were hermetically sealed in aluminium crucibles and heated at a constant rate of 10°C/min over a temperature range of 25–300°C. Inert atmosphere was maintained by purging nitrogen gas at flow rate of 50 mL/min.

### 2.3.7. Rheological Characterization

Rheological measurements of the microsponge loaded gel and blank gel were performed using a controlled stress rheometer (Viscotech Rheometer, Rheological Instruments AB, Lund, Sweden). Data analysis was done with stress rheological basic software, version 5.0. A cone and plate geometry was used with 25 mm diameter and cone of 1.0° [13]. Fresh sample was used for test and all measurements were carried out in triplicate at 25°C and at 37°C.

### 2.3.8. Creep Recovery Test

In creep recovery, samples were subjected to a fixed stress from LVR for 100 s and then allowed to recover. The creep compliance, , was recorded against time.

### 2.3.9. Skin Irritation Test

Skin irritation test of optimized oxybenzone loaded microsponge gel (M9) was compared with the marketed and placebo gel. The present study was employed in the three groups of rats () to evaluate skin irritation. They were kept carefully following an acclimation period of 7 days to ensure their suitability for the study. Test animals were kept within a limited-access rodent facility with environmental conditions set to a temperature of 25 ± 2°C, a humidity of 60–90% RH, and a 12-h light/12-h dark cycle. Animals were provided ad labium access to a commercial rat diet and drinking water was supplied to each cage. The area on the back of each rat was shaved prior to the experiment. The first group of the rat was applied with microsponge gel and the second group was applied with commercial sunscreen lotion. The remaining group of rats was considered as a control group.

The 0.5 g of each test product was placed on each area (25 × 25 mm) for 30 minutes. Finally treated skin area of rats was washed off by tap water. Scoring of the erythema was performed at 24 and 72 hours and both the treated and controlled sites were covered and wrapped by cotton bandage. Reactions on skin were measured after 24 hr and 72 hr in form of erythema. The mean erythemal scores were recorded (ranging from 0 to 4) according to Draize scale [14]. The responses of all the formulations applied on rat skin surface were evaluated and primary irritation index (PII) was calculated and matched with response category as shown in Table 3. The score of primary irritation was calculated for each rat. Scores for erythema at 24 and 72 hours were summed and divided by the number of the observations for the treated sites [15].

### 2.3.10. Determination of Minimal Erythemal Dose (MED)

The study was performed using Wistar rat model. This model is suitable for the study because of the photochemical changes taking place in rat skin after UV exposure. Before conducting actual SPF testing, a study was carried out to determine MED with respect to time of unprotected skin and protected skin of Wistar rat. This was carried out on total of nine rats. They were divided into three different groups each comprising three rats and maintained separately. A solar simulator high pressure mercury vapour lamp (Osram Ultra Vitalex of 300 w) was used as a UV light source. First group of rats was kept directly under the solar simulator lamp and was sampled after every one minute. The rats in the second and third group were applied with marketed sunscreen lotion and oxybenzone loaded microsponge gel, respectively, and the same sampling procedure was followed. The presence of reddening (erythema) of skin was noted after 3 hr of completion of study.

### 2.3.11. SPF Testing

The in vivo analysis was performed to study the effectiveness of the optimized formulation (M9) in comparison to the marketed formulation. All studies were approved by the institutional animal ethics committee of Poona College of Pharmacy (1703/PO/c/13/CPCSEA), Pune, India, and were conducted under the provisions of the approved protocol. According to the personal care product council (PCPC), formerly Cosmetics, Toiletries and Fragrance Association (CTFA) and European Cosmetic Toiletry and Perfumery Association (COLIPA), SPF determination protocol, the amount of sunscreen formulation to be applied should be 2 mg/cm$^2$ [16] and the same was used in present study. The SPF was determined by using the following formula:

$$SPF = \frac{MED\,(PS)}{MED\,(US)}.$$

MED (PS) = minimal erythemal dose of protected skin; MED (US) = minimal erythemal dose of unprotected skin.

# 3. RESULTS AND DISCUSSION

## 3.1. Preparation of Oxybenzone Loaded Microsponge

During the preliminary study, concentration of EC and DCM which would produce nonaggregating, nonregimenting, and porous microsponge dispersion was determined. The predicted concentration of EC and DCM was decisive in the preparation and stabilization of microsponge. EC was added to provide structural integrity and PVA was added as an emulsifying agent. The concentration of DCM showed influence on EE and porosity. The preliminary data suggested that the concentration of PVA required was 100 mg. This was kept constant. Altering the concentration of EC and DCM caused pronounced effect on microsponge dispersion.

## 3.2. Optimization of Independent Variables of Microsponge Formulation

The concentration of PVA and oxybenzone was kept constant. The effects of EC and DCM on the microsponge size, entrapment efficiency, and in vitro release were analyzed.

## 3.3. Characterization of Oxybenzone Loaded Microsponge

### 3.3.1. Effect of Variables on Microsponge Size

The size of the microsponge ranges from 72 ± 0.77 to 619 ± 0.02 μm which has been shown in Table 1. The most important parameter which needs to be monitored during microsponge preparation for its best performance was the size of microsponge. Thus for the effective topical application, the selected method should result in optimum size range and homogeneous microsponges. In the present study, quasiemulsion solvent diffusion method was found to produce uniform microsponge. The obtained microsponge has narrow size of distribution. It was observed that the relative amount of EC and DCM was found to play an important role in determining size of microsponge which was found to be in the range of 100–600 μm. The multiple regression analysis for the mean particle size of factorial batches revealed the good fit () as shown in (5). The effect of both independent variables on the size of the particle was given by the following equation:

According to (5) and Figure 1(a), indicates negative effect on particle size which may be due to increase in concentration of EC that leads to an increase in the intramolecular cohesive forces. These forces may be reduced due to the surfactant property of the PVA which further leads to increase in the microsponge size [16]. However, the interaction term is positive supporting the fact that increase in polymer concentration leads to increase in the viscosity of the internal phase; thus bigger globules are formed during emulsification leading to an increase in mean particle sizes.

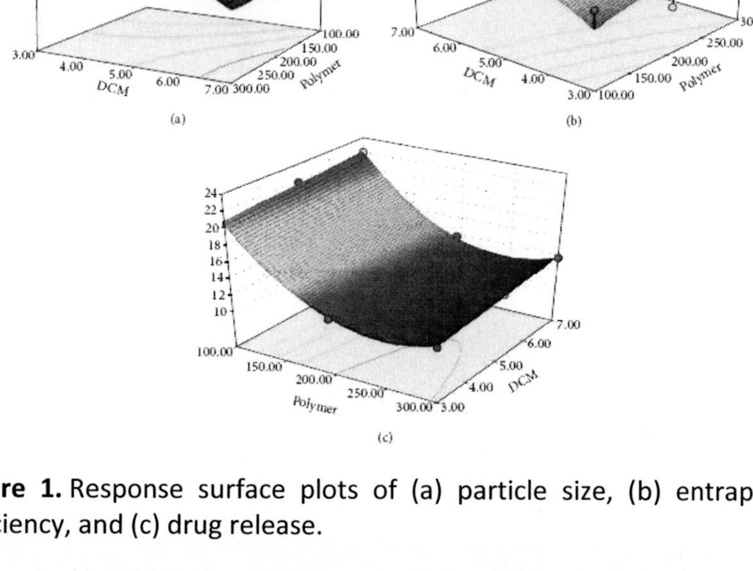


**Figure 1.** Response surface plots of (a) particle size, (b) entrapment efficiency, and (c) drug release.

The negative value of indicates that an increase in DCM concentration reduces the particle size. When the dispersed phase with lower viscosity (batch M9 contains 7 mL DCM) was poured into the continuous phase, the globules of the formed emulsion could be subdivided into smaller particles [1, 17, 18].

The interaction term is negative supporting the fact that increase in DCM concentration leads to decrease in the viscosity of the internal phase; thus smaller globules are formed of the emulsion leading to a decrease in mean particle sizes. The interaction terms , that is, combined effect of concentration of EC and DCM, have a positive influence on particle size. This may be because of increase in the viscosity of internal phase with polymer concentration where the globules of formed emulsion can hardly be subdivided into smaller particles [19, 20].

### 3.3.2. Effect of Variables on Entrapment Efficiency

It is general observation that increase in the polymer ratio increases the EE. The reason for increase in EE with high polymer ratios is reduced diffusion rate of drug solution from concentrated polymeric solutions into external phase. This provides more time for the droplet formation and may improve the yield of microsponge and entrapment efficiency. The equation was generated by fitting the observed coefficient in (1) as follows:

$$Y2 = 95.29 + 1.03X_1 + 2.33X_2 + 0.12X_1X_1$$

$$- 0.47X_2X_2 - 0.55X_1X_2,$$

$$R^2 = 0.75.$$

According to results of EE as shown in (6) and Figure 1(b), the higher drug concentration was obtained at the higher polymer ratios which was above 95% as shown in Table 1. When DCM diffuses out, nearly all of the dispersed phase is converted to solid microsponge particles.

The positive value of indicates highest drug EE in the microsponge. This can be explained by the fact that the amount of drug per unit of polymer was greater than other microsponge formulations. The reduced diffusion rate of DCM from the concentrated solution results in more time for dróplet formation with increased precipitation of the drug in the microsponge. This leads to increased %EE [2, 21]. It was also observed by positive value for the interaction terms . The value of has a positive influence on the %EE. This may be due to the higher concentration of DCM which provides more solvent action. Moreover the polymer-drug association was also delayed molecular evaporation of the solvent which leads to increased drug precipitation in the microsponge [1]. However the interaction term has a negative influence on the %EE. This may be due to the leaching of the drug into the aqueous phase from more spongy and porous microsponges.

The interaction term has a negative influence on the EE. This may be observed due to increased intramolecular cohesive forces which cause the densification of core part of the microsponge. This leads to leaching of drug towards periphery of microsponge and in the external phase [14, 22].

### 3.3.3. Effect of Variable on Drug Release

The second most important parameter which needs to be monitored during microsponge preparation for its best performance was the release of the drug from the microsponge. The oxybenzone should be released slowly over the extended period of time to modulate low concentration gradient for skin transport. Therefore, multiple regression analysis for the drug release as per the factorial design revealed the good fit with the following equation:

$$Y3 = 12.96 - 4.33X_1 + 0.76X_2 + 4.36X_1X_1 - 0.04X_2X_2 + 0.013X_1X_2, \quad R^2 = 0.99. \qquad (7)$$

As per (7) and Figure 1(c), the correlation coefficient indicates a good fit. The negative value of indicates decrease in the drug release because of increase in the concentration of EC [17]. The higher amount of EC leads to formation of thick layers which may be responsible for the controlled release of drug [22]. The variable has a positive influence on the drug release. This is attributed to the fact that higher concentration of DCM yields more spongy and porous microsponge. The increased amount of DCM also causes the precipitation of the drug at the periphery of the microsponge. This leads to increase in drug release as shown in (7) [2].

The positive value of interaction term can be supported by increase in the intramolecular cohesive forces as explained previously. The migration of drug towards periphery of microsponge may cause faster drug release. The interaction terms and have a negligible effect on drug release. The effect of polymer ratio on the release of the drug from microsponge containing 100 mg, 200 mg, and 300 mg microsponge was shown in Figure 2(a), respectively. Different kinetic models were employed to fit the data relating to the kinetics of oxybenzone from microsponge. The results shown in Table 2 depicted the release kinetics on the basis of the values. The results indicated best fit of Higuchi model for M6 and M9 formulation. The is because M3 has lower ratio of polymer that makes the walls of the microsponge thinner compared to that in M6 and M9 and release takes place by erosion diffusion at a faster rate. M9 was selected for further deposition studies as it has the diffusion release pattern, maximum %EE, and smallest and uniform particle size of 72 μm [22–24].

.

**Table 2.** In vitro release kinetics of optimized formulations.

| Formulation | Kinetic model | $R^2$ value |
|---|---|---|
| M3 | Peppas equation | 0.97 ± 0.09 |
| M6 | Higuchi equation | 0.96 ± 0.12 |
| M9 | Higuchi equation | 0.95 ± 0.11 |

**Table 3.** Skin irritation test.

| Animal number | Reaction | Placebo gel (24 h) | Placebo gel (72 h) | M9 gel (24 h) | M9 gel (72 h) | Marketed lotion (24 h) | Marketed lotion (72 h) |
|---|---|---|---|---|---|---|---|
| 1 | Erythema | 0 | 0 | 0 | 0 | 1 | 1 |
| 2 | Erythema | 0 | 0 | 1 | 0 | 2 | 1 |
| 3 | Erythema | 1 | 0 | 1 | 0 | 1 | 1 |
| 4 | Erythema | 0 | 0 | 1 | 0 | 1 | 1 |
| Primary irritation | — | 1/8 = 0.125 | | 3/8 = 0.375 | | 9/8 = 1.12 | |
| index (PII) | — | Negligible irritation | | Negligible irritation | | Slight irritation | |

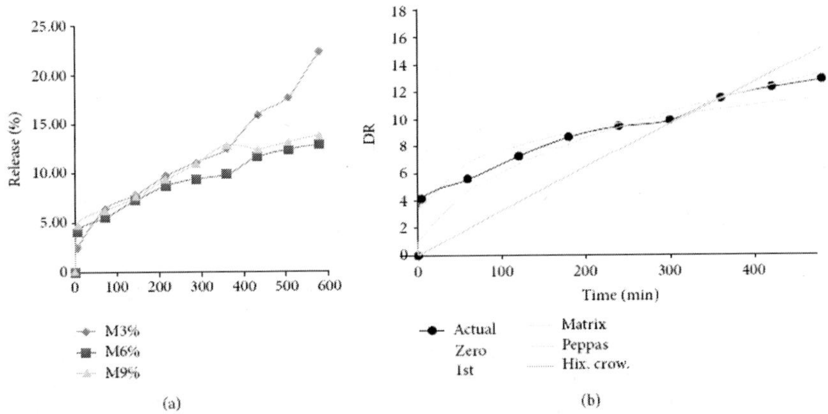


**Figure 2.** (a) Comparative in vitro release profile for M3, M6, and M9 formulations and (b) release kinetics for M9 formulation.

### 3.3.4. Scanning Electron Microscopy

The SEM of microsponge was shown in Figure 3. As shown in the SEM, it revealed spherical microsponge with surface pores. The observed pore size was within the range 0.10–0.22 μm.

### 3.3.5. Differential Scanning Calorimetry

As shown in Figure 4, oxybenzone dispersed in EC showed the same thermal behaviour as drug. The exothermic peak was observed at 64°C which corresponds to the melting point of the pure drug. This report indicates that the thermal properties of oxybenzone were not altered during formulation of microsponge.

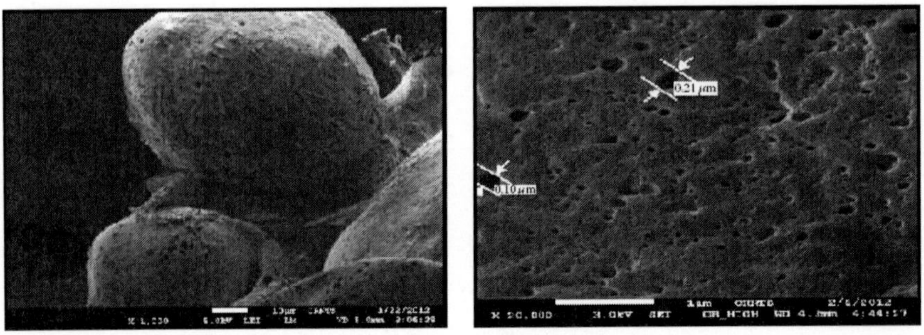


**Figure 3.** Microsponge with surface pore size.

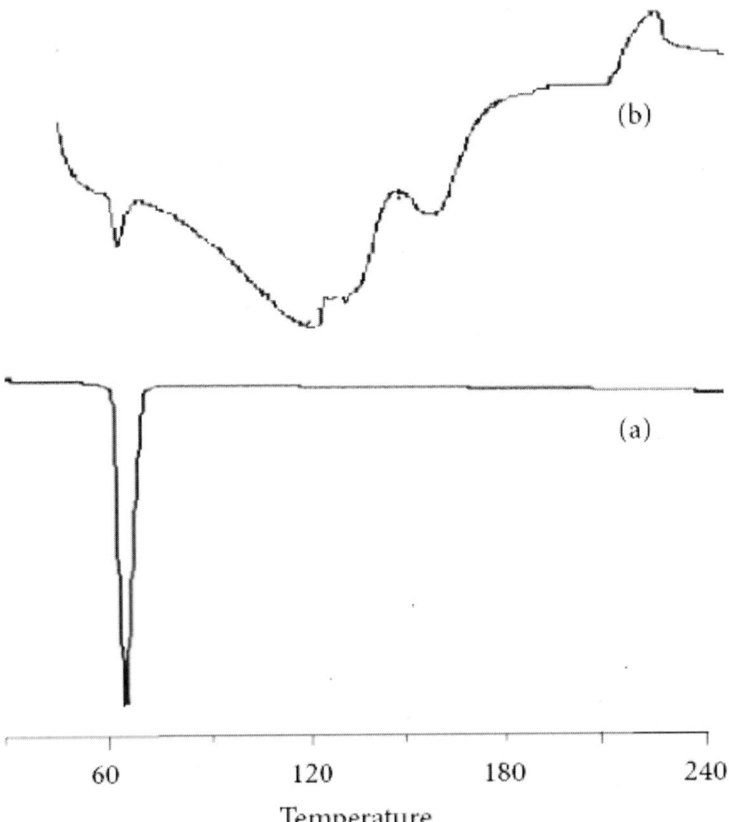


**Figure 4.** DSC plots of (a) pure drug and (b) formulation.

### 3.3.6. Preparation of Microsponge Loaded Gel

The optimized microsponge formulation (M9) was incorporated in 3% w/w HPMC base to obtain the gels. Initially required amount of HPMC was added to water and kept overnight for complete hydration of polymer chains. Microsponge dispersion was added to the hydrated HPMC solution to obtain a final concentration of 2.5% w/w of oxybenzone. The prepared gel was used for drug deposition study.

### 3.3.7. Rheological Characterization

The microsponge gel showed creep recovery of 74.05% compared to 65.11% of blank gel. The same results were depicted in Figure 5. However from the observed results, oxybenzone loaded microsponge gel showed higher elastic contribution than viscous one. In the creep recovery test, it has shown highest creep recovery which was helpful for promising gelling with higher elasticity. This property helps in thinning of the gel under pressure with higher adherence time on the skin.

### 3.3.8. Skin Irritation Test

Skin irritation test of optimized oxybenzone loaded microsponge gel (M9) was compared with the marketed and placebo gel. Erythema with score of 0–2 was observed on all rats. After 72 hours, disappearance of all erythema was observed from test areas applied with placebo gel and microsponge gel as shown in Table 3. The values for PII for placebo gel and microsponge gel were in the range of 0.1–0.4 indicating negligible irritancy. The microsponge gel has shown 0.375 of PII. The PII for marketed lotion was found to be 1.12 indicating slight irritation. From the obtained results it was clear that the microsponge gel for topical delivery has achieved the objectives of controlled drug release. The microsponge is too large to pass through the stratum corneum and hence it would be expected to remain on the skin surface, gradually releasing its contents over time. This reduces higher exposure of oxybenzone to the skin and contact period. This was helpful to reduce the irritation and toxicity of drug.

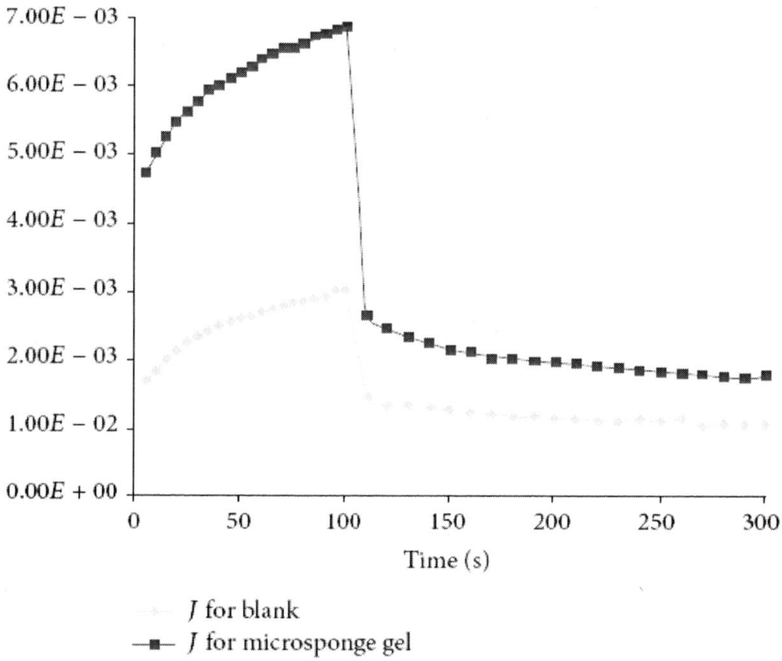


**Figure 5.** Creep recovery of blank and drug loaded microsponge gel.

#### 3.3.9. Determination of Minimal Erythemal Dose

The time required for the development of erythema for the unprotected rats was 7 min. The rats protected by the marketed formulations showed 140 mins for the development of erythema. The microsponge gel showed the 170 min which was more as compared to marketed formulation. This result was maybe observed due to the controlled release of drug from the microsponge loaded gel which helped to avoid excessive deposition of drug.

#### 3.3.10. SPF Testing

The SPF determination of optimized oxybenzone loaded microsponge gel (M9) was compared with the marketed gel. The microsponge gel showed SPF 25 as compared to SPF 20 of the marketed lotion. This was maybe due to slower release of drug from the microsponge gel which provides prolonged retention of oxybenzone. This was reflected in the comparison with marketed lotion where the oxybenzone loaded microsponge gel was found to be more photoprotective. Thus, as shown in Figure 6, topical application of microsponge gel provides more efficacy and safety by overcoming skin irritation and toxicity problem.

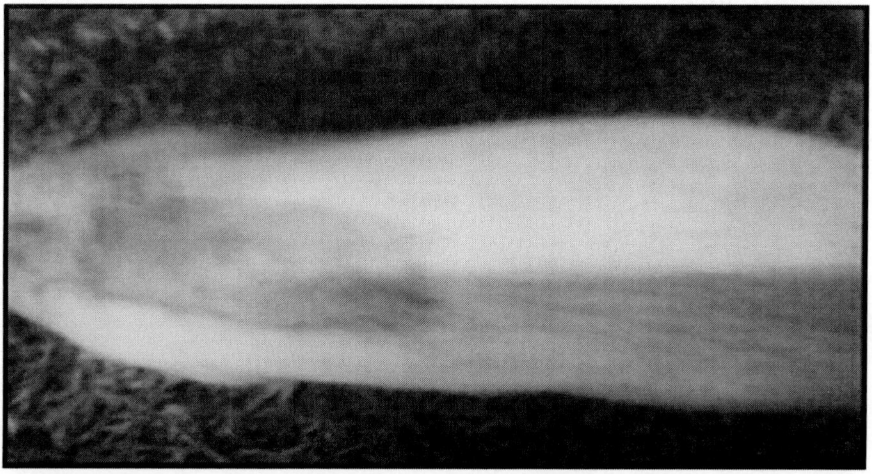

**Figure 6:** Protected skin applied with M9 microsponge gel.

## 4. CONCLUSION

The present study concluded successful preparation and optimization of oxybenzone loaded microsponge gel with the enhanced sunscreening efficiency. In vitro and ex vivo evaluation study of microsponge gel revealed remarkable and enhanced topical retention of drug for prolonged period of time with increased SPF compared to the marketed preparation. A controlled release of oxybenzone onto the skin over a prolonged period of time was beneficial for enhanced UV protection efficacy. This study provides future insights for developing controlled release microsponge gels for topical applications containing sunscreen agents.

## CONFLICT OF INTERESTS

The authors declare that there is no conflict of interests regarding the publication of this paper.

## REFERENCES

1. N. Amrutiya, A. Bajaj, and M. Madan, "Development of microsponges for topical delivery of mupirocin,"AAPS PharmSciTech, vol. 10, no. 2, pp. 402–409, 2009.

2. S. Maiti, S. Kaity, S. Ray, and B. Sa, "Development and evaluation of xanthan gum-facilitated ethyl cellulose microsponges for controlled percutaneous delivery of diclofenac sodium," Acta Pharmaceutica, vol. 61, no. 3, pp. 257–270, 2011.

3. V. Chadawar and J. Shaji, "Microsponge delivery system," Current Drug Delivery, vol. 4, no. 2, pp. 123–129, 2007.

4. M. N. Padamwar and A. P. Pawar, "Preparation and evaluation of sericin gels containing choline salicylate," Indian Drugs, vol. 40, no. 9, pp. 526–531, 2003.

5. A. Nokhodchi, M. Jelvehgari, M. R. Siahi, and M. R. Mozafari, "Factors affecting the morphology of benzoyl peroxide microsponges," Micron, vol. 38, no. 8, pp. 834–840, 2007.

6. J. Jorizzo, R. Grossman, and M. Nighland, "Tretinoin microsphere gel in younger acne patients," Journal of Drugs in Dermatology, vol. 7, no. 8, pp. 9–13, 2008.

7. A. Menter, G. Vamvakias, and J. Jorizzo, "One-week treatment with once-daily fluorouracil cream 0.5% in participants with actinic keratoses," Cutis, vol. 81, no. 6, pp. 509–516, 2008.

8. R. A. Sanad, N. S. Abdelmalak, T. S. Elbayoomy, and A. A. Badawi, "Formulation of a novel oxybenzone-loaded

nanostructured lipid carriers (NLCs)," AAPS PharmSciTech, vol. 11, no. 4, pp. 1684–1694, 2010.

9. S. E. Cross, B. Innes, M. S. Roberts, T. Tsuzuki, T. A. Robertson, and P. McCormick, "Human skin penetration of sunscreen nanoparticles: In-vitro assessment of a novel micronized zinc oxide formulation," Skin Pharmacology and Physiology, vol. 20, no. 3, pp. 148–154, 2007

10. S. Kale, A. Sonawane, A. Ansari, P. Ghoge, and A. Waje, "Formulation and in-vitro determination of sun protection factor of Ocimum basilicum, Linn. leaf oils sunscreen cream," International Journal of Pharmacy and Pharmaceutical Sciences, vol. 2, no. 4, pp. 147–149, 2010.

11. K. S. Shaikh, B. Chellampillai, and A. P. Pawar, "Studies on nonionic surfactant bilayer vesicles of ciclopirox olamine," Drug Development and Industrial Pharmacy, vol. 36, no. 8, pp. 946–953, 2010.

12. U. Rekha and B. P. Manjula, "Formulation and evaluation of microsponges for topical drug delivery of Mometasone furoate," International Journal of Pharmacy and Pharmaceutical Sciences, vol. 3, no. 4, pp. 133–137, 2011.

13. B. V. Mitkari, S. A. Korde, K. R. Mahadik, and C. R. Kokare, "Formulation and evaluation of topical liposomal gel for fluconazole," Indian Journal of Pharmaceutical Education and Research, vol. 44, no. 4, pp. 324–333, 2010.

14. R. L. Campbell and R. D. Bruce, "Comparative dermatotoxicology. I. Direct comparison of rabbit and human primary skin irritation responses to isopropylmyristate," Toxicology and Applied Pharmacology, vol. 59, no. 3, pp. 555–563, 1981.

15. A. K. Mishra, A. Mishra, A. K. Ghosh, and P. Chattopadhyay, "Evaluation of skin irritation of herbal

O/W sunscreen cream on rat model," IJPI's Journal of Pharmaceutics and Cosmetology, vol. 1, pp. 220–226, 2011.

16. N. Singh, "Effect of sorfactants on PVA borax hydrogel rheology and thermal aspects," Indian Journal of Chemistry, vol. 52A, pp. 879–883, 2013.

17. J. I. D'Souza and H. N. More, "Topical anti-inflammatory gels of fluocinolone acetonide entrapped in eudragit based microsponge delivery system," Research Journal of Pharmacy and Technology, pp. 234–245, 2008.

18. V. Jain and R. Singh, "Design and characterization of colon-specific drug delivery system containing Paracetamol microsponges," Archives of Pharmacal Research, vol. 34, no. 5, pp. 733–740, 2011.

19. M. Kiliçarslan and T. Baykara, "The effect of the drug/polymer ratio on the properties of the verapamil HCl loaded microspheres," International Journal of Pharmaceutics, vol. 252, no. 1-2, pp. 99–109, 2003.

20. A. Swetha, M. Gopal Rao, K. Venkata Ramana, B. Niyaz Basha, and V. Koti Reddy, "Formulation and in-vitro evaluation of etodolac entrapped in microsponge based drug delivery system," International Journal of Pharmacy, vol. 1, no. 2, pp. 73–80, 2011.

21. M. Jelvehgari, M. R. Siahi-Shadbad, S. G. Azarmi, A. Nokhodchi, and G. P. Martin, "The microsponge delivery system of benzoyl peroxide: preparation, characterization and release studies," International Journal of Pharmaceutics, vol. 308, no. 1-2, pp. 124–132, 2006.

22. N. S. Abdelmalak and S. F. El-Menshawe, "A new topical fluconazole microsponge loaded hydrogel: preparation and characterization," International Journal of Pharmacy and Pharmaceutical Sciences, vol. 4, no. 1, pp. 460–469, 2012.

23. R. C. Wester, R. Patel, S. Nacht, J. Leyden, J. Melendres, and H. Maibach, "Controlled release of benzoyl peroxide from a porous microsphere polymeric system can reduce topical irritancy," Journal of the American Academy of Dermatology, vol. 24, no. 5, pp. 720–726, 1991.

24. T. Çomoğlu, N. Gönül, and T. Baykara, "Preparation and in vitro evaluation of modified release ketoprofen microsponges," Farmaco, vol. 58, no. 2, pp. 101–106, 2003.

# Chapter 9

# Fliposomes: pH-Sensitive Liposomes Containing a *trans*-2-morpholinocyclohexanol-Based Lipid That Performs a Conformational Flip and Triggers an Instant Cargo Release in Acidic Medium

**Nataliya M. Samoshina [1,2], Xin Liu [2], Barbora Brazdova [2], Andreas H. Franz [2], Vyacheslav V. Samoshin [2,*] and Xin Guo [1,*]**

[1]*Department of Pharmaceutics and Medicinal Chemistry, University of the Pacific, 751 Brookside Road, Stockton, CA 95211, USA*

[2]*Department of Chemistry, University of the Pacific, 3601 Pacific Ave., Stockton, CA 95211, USA*

## ABSTRACT

Incorporation of a pH-sensitive conformational switch into a lipid structure enables a drastic conformational flip upon protonation that disrupts the liposome membrane and causes rapid release of cargo specifically in areas of increased acidity. pH-sensitive liposomes containing the amphiphile (**1**) with *trans*-2-morpholinocyclohexanol conformational switch, a phospholipid, and a PEG-lipid conjugate were constructed and characterized. The optimized composition—**1**/POPC/PEG-ceramide (50/4/5)—could be stored at 4 °C and pH 7.4 for up to 1.5 years, and was stable in blood serum *in vitro* after 48 h at 37 °C. Liposomes loaded with ANTS/DPX or methotrexate demonstrated an unusually quick content release (in a few seconds) at pH below 5.5, which was independent of inter-liposome contact. The pH-titration curve for the liposome leakage paralleled the curve for the acid-induced conformational flip of **1**studied by $^{1}$H-NMR. Freeze-fracture electron microscopy images showed budding and division of the bilayer at pH 5.5. A plausible mechanism of pH-sensitivity involves an acid-triggered conformational flip of **1**, shortening of lipid tails, and membrane perturbations, which cause the content leakage. The methotrexate-loaded liposomes demonstrated much higher cytotoxicity in HeLa cells than the free drug indicating that they can serve as viable drug delivery systems.

**Keywords:** pH-sensitive liposomes; fliposomes; polyethyleneglycol (PEG); conformational switch; controlled drug release; triggered release

## 1. INTRODUCTION

pH-triggered release is an attractive approach to improving liposomes as drug/gene delivery systems because proton concentration is elevated under numerous physiological and pathological conditions including endosome processing, inflammation, ischemia, and solid tumor growth [1-13]. However, it is still a considerable challenge to develop liposomes that promptly respond to small variations of pH while preserving other attributes that are important for drug delivery such as sufficient stability in blood circulation and on shelf.

Recently we suggested a novel strategy to render liposomes pH-sensitive: a protonation-induced conformational switch of lipid tails in the liposome membrane (for the preliminary communication see [14]). For proof of concept, an amphiphile **1**based on *trans*-2-morpholinocyclohexanol was introduced as a pH-sensitive conformational switch of liposome bilayer (Figure 1). The pH-induced flip of its chair conformation was demonstrated by NMR data [14]. In the original conformational equilibrium **1A** ⇆ **1B** (Figure 1), the morpholine and the hydroxy groups of **1** were predominantly in axial positions while both lipidic *trans*-dodecyloxycarbonyl groups

$COOC_{12}H_{25}$ adopted equatorial positions (**1A**). The protonation of the amine nitrogen upon addition of acid resulted in a strong hydrogen bond between the morpholine and the hydroxy groups, forcing both groups to adopt equatorial positions. This impulse was mechanically transmitted via the conformational flip of the cyclohexane ring to force both ester groups into axial positions (**1B**H$^+$ on Figure 1), thereby drastically increasing the spatial separation of the lipid tails and perturbing the structure of bilayer. After incorporation into liposome membranes, lipid **1** enhanced significantly the release from both the traditional liposomes based on phospholipids and the sterically hindered liposomes containing mPEG2000-ceramide (PEG-ceramide) upon exposure to lowered pH [14].

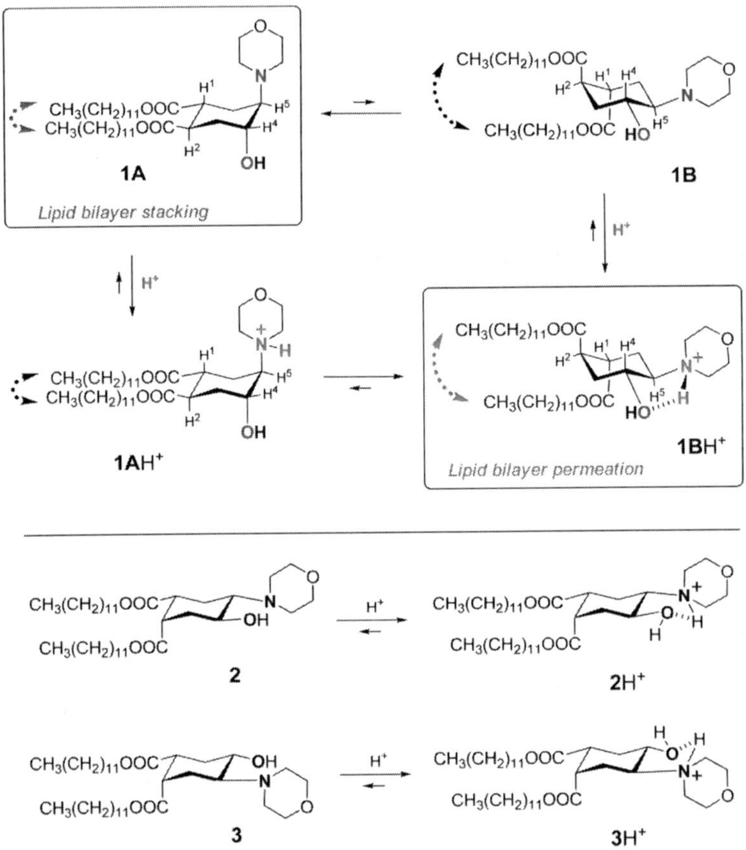


**Figure 1.** Protonation-induced conformational switch of lipid tails in amphiphile **1**, and an absence of such a switch in amphiphiles **2** and **3**.

This approach is different from the previous design of pH-sensitive liposomes in which peptides were used as conformational switches to induce leakage in acidic medium [13,15-17]. pH-sensitive synthetic peptides were added to a lipid composition in a very small quantity, at ratios varying from 1/30 to 1/300000 [13]. In our studies the pH-responsive amphiphile **1** constituted from 25% to 90% of the lipid composition. Apparently, the mechanism of triggering the leakage must be different. It is also different from the pH-sensitivity mechanism of the polymer-modified liposomes [2,7,18].

The preliminary results encouraged us to study in more details the physicochemical and biological properties of this novel type of liposomes including compatibility of the pH-sensitive conformational trigger with commonly used lipids, ability to control the rate and extend of liposome content release, mechanism of lipid membrane destabilization, and viability of liposomes for drug delivery. Of special interest is the ability of **1** to trigger the PEGylated liposomes due to their prolonged half life in blood circulation and successful applications in drug/gene delivery [7,19-23].

To address these issues, we designed, prepared and characterized a series of PEGylated liposomes equipped with the molecular device **1**. The pH-driven conformational flip of **1** was studied by $^{1}$H NMR titration. The pH-triggered release of the liposomes was measured using the ANTS/DPX fluorescent assay [16,24]. The mechanism of the acid-triggered lipid membrane destabilization was probed by freeze-fracture electron microscopy (FFEM) [25-28]. Selected lipid compositions were utilized to construct liposomes encapsulating a widely used anticancer drug methotrexate [29,30], followed by the characterization of their pH-triggered drug release by equilibrium microdialysis [31] and anticancer activity in HeLa cells (human cervical cancer).

## 2. EXPERIMENTAL SECTION

### 2.1. Materials

The lipids 1-palmitoyl-2-oleoyl-*sn*-glycero-3-phosphocholine (POPC), 1,2-dipalmitoyl-*sn*-glycero-3-phosphocholine (DPPC), 1-palmitoyl-2-oleoyl-*sn*-glycero-3-phosphoethanolamine (POPE), N-palmitoylsphingosine-1-(succinyl[methoxy(polyethylene glycol)2000]) (PEG-ceramide), 1,2-dipalmitoyl-*sn*-glycero-3-phosphoethanolamine-N-[methoxy(polyethylene glycol)-2000] (PEG-DPPE) were purchased from Avanti Polar Lipids, Inc. (Alabaster, AL, USA) and used without further purification. The fluorophores aminonaphthalene-1,3,6-trisulfonic acid disodium salt (ANTS) and *p*-xylene-bis-pyridinium bromide (DPX) were purchased from Invitrogen-Molecular Probes (Eugene, OR, USA). Methotrexate (MTX), detergent $C_{12}E_8$ (octaethyleneglycol monododecyl ether), the folate-deficient medium (FDMEM) and all other chemicals were purchased from Sigma-Aldrich or Fisher Scientific. Fetal bovine serum was obtained from Tissue Culture Biologicals (Tulare, CA, USA). HeLa cells were received from American Type Culture collection (Rockvile, MA, USA). CellTiter 96AQueous One Solution reagent was purchased from Promega (Madison, WI, USA). The 24-well and 96-well plates were obtained from TPP (Switzerland). The morpholinocyclohexanol-based amphiphiles **1**, **2** and **3** (Figure 1) were prepared according to the reported procedures [14] with modifications (see Supplementary Data).

## 2.2. NMR analysis of the pH-dependent conformational equilibrium of lipid 1

To characterize the pH-induced change of conformational equilibrium, the lipid **1** was dissolved in $CD_3OD$ (0.03 M), and the changes of its $^1H$ NMR spectra (600 MHz) were monitored during titration of the solution with *d*-trifluoroacetic acid (*d*-TFA) and with a base—1,8-diazabicyclo[5.4.0]undec-7-ene (DBU). Acid or base were dissolved in $CD_3OD$ (1 M) and added to the solution of **1** in NMR tube (0.6 mL) in small portions (1–5 μL). After every addition the solution was thoroughly mixed by gentle shaking, and its pH (pD) was measured using a micro combination pH electrode for NMR cells (9826BN, Thermo Scientific). Shaking and measuring was repeated 3–4 times until a constant value of pD was achieved. After recording the $^1H$ NMR spectrum, pD was measured again: the original and final values matched within 0.05 units. The spin-spin coupling constants between several couples of vicinal protons attached to the cyclohexane moiety are strongly conformation-dependent, which allowed an assignment of a predominant conformation and an estimation of a position of the conformational equilibrium (see section 3.1) as described previously [14,32-36].

## 2.3. Liposome preparation

Liposomes were prepared by the freeze-thawing method based on the procedure of Monnard and co-workers [37]. Both the purchased lipids (POPC, DPPC, POPE, PEG-ceramide and PEG-DPPE) and the synthesized lipids **1–3** were dissolved in dichloromethane before being used for liposome preparation. Ratios of lipid components in liposomes were in mole units. For each liposome preparation, appropriate amounts of lipids in dichloromethane solution were mixed in a Pyrex brand glass test tube (25 mm × 125 mm) to give 10 umol total lipids. Dichloromethane was evaporated under reduced pressure at room temperature (RT) to form a lipid film at the bottom of the tube. The lipid film was subjected to high vacuum for 5–6 h to remove residual solvent. The lipid film was then hydrated in 2 mL of buffer containing either the fluorophores ANTS/DPX (50 mM ANTS, 50 mM DPX, and 5 mM HEPES, pH 7.4) or the anticancer drug MTX (12.5 mM in 5 mM HEPES, pH 7.4) on a bench top vortex machine under argon. The lipid suspension was then frozen by submergence into acetone/dry ice, followed by melting in water bath. The freeze-thawing cycle was repeated ten times and the resultant liposome suspension with encapsulated contents (ANTS/DPX or MTX) was extruded eleven times through a 0.2-μm polycarbonate membrane (Nucleopore, Pleasanton, CA, USA) with a hand-held extrusion device (Avanti Polar Lipids, Alabaster, AL, USA). The extruded liposomes (the opaque fraction) were separated from the unencapsulated materials on a Sephadex G-75 size exclusion column equilibrated in a pH 7.4 buffer (5 mM HEPES and 145 mM NaCl). For storage, the liposome preparations were kept in darkness at 4 °C, under argon in sealed Pyrex glass tubes. Placebo liposomes that contained no encapsulated agents were also prepared as described above.

## 2.4. Physicochemical characterization of liposomes

The hydrodynamic diameter and the ζ-potential of the liposomes were measured with a Malvern Zeta 3000 dynamic light scattering instrument (Malvern Instruments Ltd., Worcester-shire WR14 1XZ, UK), using the automatic algorithm mode. POPC concentrations were determined by a lipid phosphorous assay based on the procedures of Bartlett [38].

The lipid composition of **1**/POPC/PEG-ceramide liposomes was confirmed by $^1$H NMR as we reported recently [39]. Briefly, aliquots (10 μmol total lipids in 2 mL) of the liposome preparations were evaporated to dryness in high vacuum. The lipid components of the residue were extracted by 4 × 0.25 mL $CHCl_3$, evaporated and re-dissolved in 0.7 mL of CDCl3 or CDCl3-DMSO. The $^1$H NMR spectra of the solutions were acquired and the signature peaks of the lipid components were integrated and compared.

## 2.5. ANTS/DPX liposome leakage assays

The liposomes contained a fluorescent dye, 8-aminonaphthalene-1,3,6-trisulfonic acid disodium salt (ANTS), and a quencher, *p*-xylene-*bis*-pyridinium bromide (DPX). Upon release of these compounds from liposomes, the increase of fluorescence ($\lambda_{ex}$ = 350 nm, $\lambda_{em}$ = 550 nm) was monitored on a QuantaMaster Fluorometer (Photon Technology International, Lawrenceville, NJ, USA) based on procedures of prior studies [14,40-42]. A small aliquot of an appropriately diluted liposome preparation (100 μL) was injected into a magnetically stirred quartz cuvette containing 3 mL of a pH 7.4 buffer (5 mM HEPES and 145 mM NaCl). The total lipid concentration in the cuvette was 0.12 mM unless indicated otherwise. Once the fluorescence was stable, 50 μL 1M acetic acid was injected into the cuvette to decrease the pH and the fluorescence was monitored until it plateaued. The liposomes were then permeated by the detergent $C_{12}E_8$ (20 μL of 10% solution in water) to achieve exhaustive leakage (100% leakage). Fluorescent intensity was recorded continuously during the experiment and the raw fluorescent intensity data were converted to ASCII format. The ASCII data was then processed to percentage of contents leakage with Windows Excel software as previously described [41].

To study the pH-dependence of the liposome leakage we used a series of buffers with pH 8.4, 7.2, 6.5, 6.0 (5 mM HEPES, 145 mM NaCl) and pH 5.5, 4.9, 4.5, 4.0, 3.6 (50 mM acetic buffer, 145 mM

NaCl). After injection of a liposome preparation into a buffer and stabilization of the fluorescence as described above, the detergent was added to completely permeate the liposomes, and the fluorescence intensity was determined as "100% leakage".

## 2.6. Freeze-fracture electron microscopy of liposomes

Two liposome samples were characterized by freeze-fracture electron microscopy [25-28] at Nano Analytical Laboratory (San Francisco, CA). Sample 1: the **1**/POPC/PEG-ceramide (50/45/5) liposomes (5 mM total lipids) prepared in 5 mM HEPES buffer, pH 7.4. Sample 2: the pH of an aliquot of Sample 1 was adjusted to 5.5 by acetic acid 5 min prior to freeze-fracturing.

The liposome samples were quenched in liquid nitrogen-cooled propane, using the sandwich technique, which reached a cooling rate of 10,000 K/s to prevent ice crystal formation or artifacts from the cryofixation process. The cryo-fixed samples were stored in liquid nitrogen for less than 2 h before fracturing with a JEOL JED-9000 freeze-etching instrument. The exposed fracture planes were shadowed with Pt for 30 s at an angle of 25-35 degrees and then with carbon for 35 s (2 kV/60–70 mA, $1 \times 10^{-5}$ Torr). The replicas thus produced were cleaned with concentrated, fuming $HNO_3$ for 24 h followed by agitation with fresh chloroform/methanol (1/1, v/v) at least 5 times. The cleaned replicas were examined with a JEOL 100 CX electron microscope.

## 2.7. Equilibrium microdialysis assay for methotrexate leakage

The leakage of the anticancer drug MTX from the liposomes was measured by equilibrium microdialysis [31] using the Rapid Equilibrium Dialysis Device (Thermo Scientific) according to the manufacturer's recommendations (inserts with membrane, MWCO = 8,000). For samples without detergent, 50 μL of 1 M acetic acid and 20 μL of HEPES buffer (pH 7.4; 5 mM HEPES, 140 mM NaCl) were added to 300 μL of a liposome preparation (3 mM total lipid concentration) to adjust pH to 5.5. In control experiments (no acid, pH 7.4), 70 μL of HEPES buffer was added to the liposome preparation. For samples to be permeated by detergent, 50 μL of 1 M acetic acid and 20 μL of 2% $C_{12}E_8$ were added to 300 μL of a liposome preparation (3 mM total lipid concentration) to adjust pH to 5.5. The mixture was transferred into a sample chamber of the Rapid Equilibrium Dialysis Device, and HEPES or acetic buffer (500 μL with the same pH as the sample) was added into a buffer chamber. The sample was dialyzed at room temperature for 4 hours. An aliquot of the aqueous media in the buffer chamber was diluted 5-fold and its UV absorbance (A) was measured at 306 nm. The extinction coefficient of MTX was confirmed to be identical at pH 5.5 and pH 7.4. The percentage of leakage of MTX (Leakage %) due to the drop of pH from 7.4 to 5.5 was calculated according to the formula, Leakage % = $(A_{5.5} - A_{7.4})/(A_d - A_{7.4}) \times 100\%$, where A was the UV absorbance after the sample had been dialyzed at the corresponding pH. $A_d$ was the UV absorbance after the liposomes had been permeated by $C_{12}E_8$ and then dialyzed at pH 5.5.

## 2.8. MTS cytotoxicity assay on HeLa cells

To test the anti-proliferation effect of the MTX-loaded liposomes we used CellTiter 96 $AQ_{ueous}$ One Solution cell proliferation assay (MTS reduction) [43]. The folate-deficient medium (FDMEM) was used, because MTX is a competitive inhibitor of dihydrofolate reductase [29,30]. HeLa (human cervical cancer) cells were continuously cultured in FDMEM containing 10% heat-inactivated fetal bovine serum, penicillin (50 I.U./mL), streptomycin (50 μg/mL), 2% $NaHCO_3$, 2 mM L-glutamine and non-essential amino acids in a humidified atmosphere (T75 flasks, 37 °C, 5% $CO_2$). At 80–90% confluency, the cells were detached by trypsin, diluted with FDMEM, and seeded in 24-well plates (100 μL suspended cells at $5 \times 10^5$ cells/mL plus 400 μL FDMEM for each well). The cells were cultured for another 24 h to reach 70–75% confluency. FDMEM in the well plates were replaced with serum-free FDMEM (400 μL/well), and into each well was added 100 μL of a liposome formulation appropriately diluted by serum-free FDMEM, followed by gentle agitation. The final total concentration of MTX was 1 μM. After 24 h of incubation, the medium was aspirated and the cells were washed twice with phosphate buffered saline (PBS). The cells were then supplemented with FDMEM and cultured for another 6 h.

The cell viability agent MTS [3-(4,5-dimethylthiazol-2-yl)-5-(3-carboxymethoxyphenyl)-2-(4-sulfophenyl)-2H-tetrazolium, inner salt, 100 µL/well] was added and the cells were incubated for 2 h at 37 °C, 5% $CO_2$. To stop the redox reaction, sodium dodecylsulfate (10%, 150 µL/well) was added, and the absorbance of the media at 490 nm ($A_{490}$) was measured with an automated plate reader (Tristar, Brethold Technology, Austria). All data were normalized by the $A_{490}$ of HeLa cells treated with serum-free FDMEM into percentage of viability and reported as mean ± SD of at least eight replicate wells.

# 3. RESULTS AND DISCUSSION

## 3.1. pH-Triggered conformational flip of lipid 1

The key concept of our liposome design is the incorporation into lipid molecules of a pH-responsive switch that performs a drastic conformational flip upon protonation, thus disturbing the lipid bilayer and inducing contents release.

We explored the conformational chair-flip of lipid **1** (Figure 1) by $^1H$ NMR (600 MHz). The vicinal coupling constants $^3J_{HH}$ between several protons attached to the cyclohexane moiety of **1** are strongly conformation-dependent, which allows an assignment of a predominant conformation and an estimation of a position of conformational equilibrium. The conformer populations ($n_A$, $n_B$) in the fast equilibrium [**1A** + **1A**H$^+$] ⇆[**1B** + **1B**H$^+$] (Figure 1) were calculated as described before for (amino)cyclohexanol derivatives [14,32-36] from an averaged signal width ($W = \Sigma J_{HH}$) measured as the distance between terminal peaks of a multiplet in $^1H$ NMR: $\boldsymbol{W_{observed} = W_A \cdot n_A + W_B \cdot n_B}$. We used mainly the signal of H4 (geminal to the hydroxy group, Figure 1), which was usually better resolved and located in a region apart from other signals. The limiting parameter $W_B$ was assumed to equal $W_{BH+}$, *i.e.*, the value observed in presence of excess acid ($\Sigma J_{HH}$ = 10.55 + 10.55 + 4.4 = 25.5 Hz), and the parameter $W_A$ was estimated as 9.0 Hz [14,32-36] from reported data for the related conformationally biased aminocyclohexanols. The estimated share of the conformer **1A** H$^+$ includes both the non-protonated form **1A** and the protonated form **1A**·H$^+$ (the latter being apparently the minor one due to conversion into **1B**·H$^+$). The share of the conformer **1B** ($n_B$) includes both the protonated form **1B**·H$^+$ (apparently the major one in access acid) and the non-protonated form **1B**. The coupling constants for other protons of the cycle, e.g. H5, were used when possible to confirm the conformational assignment.

During the incremental addition of acid, the signal width of H4 in **1** increased from the original 13.2 Hz at apparent pD 7.9 to eventually 25.5 Hz at pD 1.85 (Figure 2A), indicating a strong protonation-induced shift of the conformational equilibrium from **1A** (~75% in original solution) to **1B**H$^+$ (~100% in excess acid). The H5 signal of **1** ($W$ = 13.8 Hz at pH 7.9) also widened upon acidification to $W$ = 26.5 Hz, and migrated from δ 2.23 downfield to δ3.26 because of the deshielding effect of the positive charge at the geminal nitrogen. On the contrary, the multiplet H4 shifted *upfield* from δ3.99 to δ3.90 despite of the deshielding effect of the neighboring morpholinium group. Because *axial* protons typically give a signal at higher field than the otherwise equivalent *equatorial* protons, this observation confirms an *equatorial*-to-*axial* change of H4, and thus the *axial*-to-*equatorial* change of the hydroxy group. Further, the originally well-resolved signals of H1 (δ2.98; $W$ = 22.5 Hz) and H2 (δ3.08; $W$ = 23.3 Hz) in **1** became narrow and unresolved, and both shifted downfield to δ 3.3-3.4 upon the drop of pD. This attests to an *axial*-to-*equatorial* switch of H1 and H2, and thus to the *equatorial*-to-*axial* switch of the ester groups with lipid tails (Figure 1).

The NMR titration curve (Figure 2A) revealed an interesting peculiarity: the change in a conformer population did not occur gradually upon addition of acid, but took place rapidly between pD 5.5 and 4.0. We observed previously such a rapid conformational switch within a certain range of acidity for the simple model *trans*-2-aminocyclohexanols [35] and in the preliminary study of lipid **1** [14].

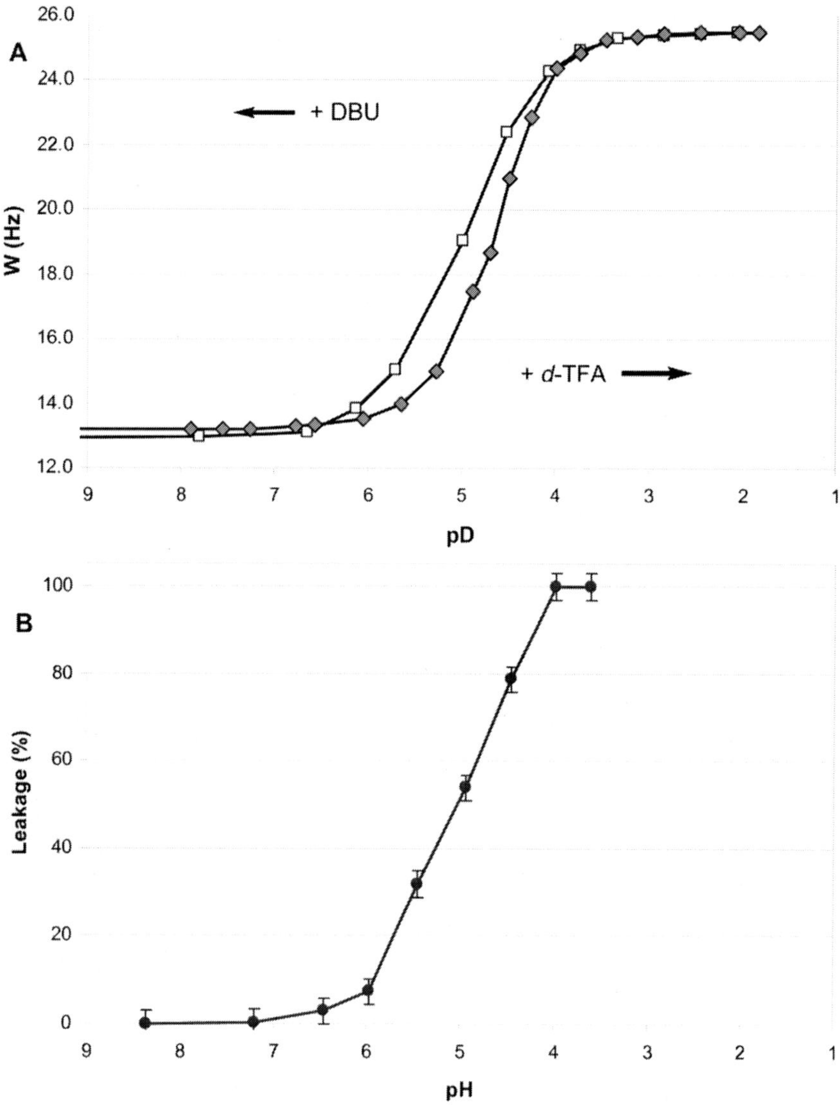


**Figure 2.** (A) Change of the signal width ($W = \Sigma J_{HH}$) for the proton H4 in $^1$H NMR due to the conformational switch of flipid **1** in $CD_3OD$ solution caused by titration with *d*-TFA (◆) and then by backward titration of the resulting acidic solution with DBU (□). (B) pH-Dependence of the ANTS/DPX leakage from liposomes with 50 mol% of flipid **1**.

In order to confirm that the observed pH-triggered conformational flip is reversible and nondestructive, we back-titrated the resulting acidic solution of lipid **1** in $CD_3OD$ with a strong base DBU (Figure 2A). As the apparent pD increased above 4.0, an opposite conformational switch occurred rapidly. Upon addition of excess base, the conformational equilibrium returned finally to the predominance of the conformer **1A** (Figure 1). The base-titration curve is similar to the acid-titration curve but its central part is somewhat shifted to the left of the pD-axis. Thus the backward change of equilibrium happens over a wider range of pD - from 4.0 to 6.0, meaning that it takes a somewhat more basic environment than the original one to achieve the original ratio of conformers. Along the W-axis, the backward curve is above the forward curve indicating a higher population of the form $\mathbf{1B}H^+$ (up to 16% additionally) at the same pD values during the base-titration as compared to the acid-titration. Such a "hysteresis" may result from an increased polarity of solution due to accumulation of the ionic $DBU{\cdot}H^+$ $CF_3COO^-$ when TFA is neutralized by DBU in the course of base-titration.

The $^1H$ NMR spectrum of the fully back-titrated **1** did not show a significant difference from the original one before the titrations (except for additional signals of DBU and its salt), confirming that the lipid survived this pH-induced forward-backward conformational flip.

Thus the $^1H$ NMR titration demonstrated the ability of lipid **1** to perform a dramatic conformational flip in response to variation of pH (pD), and such a flip would substantially affect the packing of liposome bilayers (see the further discussion). Therefore, it is justified to underscore this unusual feature of a quick and reversible alteration of lipid properties by the term *'flipid'*.

Contrary to flipid **1**, the lipids **2** and **3** (Figure 1) were designed not to perform a pH-induced conformational flip: the previous studies confirmed that the formation of intramolecular hydrogen bond in **2** or **3** upon protonation does not require an interconversion of the originally predominant (~95% by NMR) conformation **A** [14].

### 3.2. Preparation and characterization of liposomes

PEGylated liposomes that encapsulated either ANTS/DPX or methotrexate were prepared by the freeze-thawing method [37]. Starting with any particular lipid composition, this method yielded liposomes of reproducible colloidal properties and thus allowed studies on the relationship between the lipid composition of the liposomes and their pH-triggered release of contents. $^{1}H$ NMR analyses of the chloroform extract of the **1**/POPC/PEG-ceramide liposomes also confirmed that the molar ratio of the lipid components remained constant after the liposome preparation.

Liposome formulations containing the amphiphile **1**, different neutral phospholipids [phosphatidyl choline (PC) or phosphatidyl ethanolamine (PE)], and different PEG-lipid conjugates (PEG-ceramide or PEG-DPPE) in various mole percentages were prepared at pH 7.4, and their colloidal properties were characterized (Table 1).

**Table 1.** Size, ζ-potential and pH-triggered leakage of PEGylated liposomes.

| Lipid Formulations | Molar Ratio | Upon Preparation | | | After Storage | | Leakage at pH 5.1[4] (%) |
|---|---|---|---|---|---|---|---|
| | | D[1] (nm) | P.I.[2] | ζ[3] (mV) | D[1] (nm) | P.I.[2] | |
| 1/DPPC/PEG-ceramide | 25/70/5 | 138.9 | 0.08 | −7.1 | 139.7[5] | 0.09[5] | 27 |
| 1/DPPC/PEG-ceramide | 50/45/5 | 141.2 | 0.18 | −3.4 | 204.1[5] | 0.29[5] | 42 |
| 1/POPC/PEG-ceramide | 25/70/5 | 146.3 | 0.13 | −6.5 | 141.5[6] | 0.09[6] | 35 |
| 1/POPC/PEG-ceramide | 50/45/5 | 162.4 | 0.069 | −2.8 | 154.5[6] | 0.01[6] | 67 |
| 1/POPC/PEG-ceramide | 75/20/5 | 158.5 | 0.138 | N.D. | 164.9[6] | 0.18[6] | 95 |
| 1/POPC/PEG-ceramide | 90/5/5 | 233.4 | 0.41 | +4.1 | 229.5[5] | 0.29[5] | 100 |
| 1/POPC/PEG-DPPE | 25/70/5 | 167.8 | 0.01 | −4.9 | 158.8[6] | 0.03[6] | 27 |
| 1/POPC/PEG-DPPE | 50/45/5 | 160.1 | 0.04 | −2.2 | 172.7[6] | 0.14[6] | 46 |
| 1/POPC/PEG-DPPE | 75/20/5 | 184.6 | 0.18 | −4.6 | 184.5[6] | 0.14[6] | 75 |
| 1/POPC/PEG-DPPE | 90/5/5 | 233.1 | 0.11 | −3.7 | N.D. | N.D. | 100 |
| 1/POPE/PEG-ceramide | 25/70/5 | 145.1 | 0.12 | +3.5 | 139.1[5] | 0.23[5] | 23 |
| 1/POPE/PEG-ceramide | 50/45/5 | 175.9 | 0.01 | +6.4 | 183.5[7] | 0.06[7] | 47 |
| 2/POPC/PEG-ceramide | 25/70/5 | 197.3 | 0.14 | −3.1 | Prp.[8] | N.D. | 28[9] |
| 3/POPC/PEG-ceramide | 25/70/5 | 282.6 | 0.34 | −11.9 | N.D. | N.D. | 5[9] |
| 3/POPC/PEG-ceramide | 50/45/5 | 332.0 | 0.42 | −4.7 | N.D. | N.D. | 10[9] |
| DPPC/PEG-ceramide | 95/5 | 151.0 | 0.07 | −7.2 | 149.3[7] | 0.08[7] | < 3 |
| POPC/PEG-ceramide | 95/5 | 146.8 | 0.17 | +3.7 | 146.3[7] | 0.05[7] | < 3 |
| POPE/PEG-ceramide | 95/5 | 194.2 | 0.16 | +1.4 | 178.5[7] | 0.11[7] | < 3 |

All the listed liposomes contain the fluorophores ANTS/DPX. Six control liposomes are also listed at the bottom of the table for comparison. [1] Hydrodynamic diameter, representation of two to three separate liposome preparations with less than 10 nm variation; [2] PI = polydispersity index; [3] ζ-potential, representation of two to three separate liposome preparations with less than 3 mV variation; [4] Percentage of ANTS released from the liposome after lowering pH from 7.4 to 5.1, average of two to three separate liposome preparations with less than 5% variation; [5] After storage at pH 7.4, 4 °C for 70 days; [6] After storage at pH 7.4, 4 °C for 1.5 years; [7] After storage at pH 7.4, 4 °C for 50 days; [8] Precipitation observed at the bottom of the tube; [9] Percentage of the ANTS release after lowering pH from 7.4 to 5.2–5.3.

After freeze-thawing and extrusion through 200 nm polycarbonate membranes, all the liposomes showed a homogeneous hydrodynamic diameter below 200 nm (polydispersity index < 0.2) except for those whose membranes contained the highest mole percentage of **1** (90 mol%). This observation indicates that **1** by itself is not satisfactory for lipid bilayer formation at pH 7.4 unless other types of lipids are incorporated at sufficient mole percentage.

Knowledge of liposomal ζ-potential can help to predict the fate of liposomes *in vivo* [44,45]. All liposome preparations showed near-zero ζ-potential values at pH 7.4 (Table 1) as expected from the neutrally charged lipids used for liposome construction, which suggest a potentially low toxicity [45].

After storage at 4 °C for about 18 months, the best liposome formulations - **1**/POPC/PEG-ceramide and **1**/POPC/PEG-DPPE (all ratios, except 5/90/5) – did not show noticeable changes in hydrodynamic diameter or polydispersity index, and kept a near-zero ζ-potential. The **1**/DPPC/PEG-ceramide (50/45/5) liposomes revealed some aggregation after 2.5 months storage. The liposomes comprising lipids **2** and **3** showed significant precipitation after 2–3 weeks storage.

The **1**/POPC/PEG-ceramide (50/45/5) liposomes containing ANTS/DPX were also stable in serum. After incubation with serum (1/3 = v/v) at 37 °C for 48 h, they leaked only 6% of the total content.

### *3.3. pH-Triggered leakage of liposomes as a result of conformational flip*

The amphiphile **1** was designed to change its predominant conformation in acidic environment thus causing disturbance in the structure of a lipid bilayer, which in turn allows leakage of liposome content. The $^1$H NMR studies demonstrated that flipid **1** does indeed change its conformation when acidity increases, and this flip occurs in $d_4$-methanol solution between apparent pD 5.5 and 4.0 for the acidic titration and between pD 4.0 and 6.0 for the basic back-titration (section 3.1). To further validate the concept, we studied the pH-dependence of the leakage from liposomes containing flipid **1** in their bilayer.

We measured the leakage of ANTS/DPX from the **1**/POPC/PEG-ceramide liposomes (molar ratio 50:45:5) after injecting a small aliquot of the liposome preparation into buffer solutions with pH varying from 8.4 to 3.6 (Figure 2B). After stabilization of fluorescence, its value was measured and normalized by subtraction of the fluorescence at pH 8.4 (0% leakage at Figure 2B). The percent leakage was calculated by comparing to the maximal value obtained after addition of detergent (100% leakage at Figure 2B). We obtained practically the same values of the percent leakage in three sets of measurements, one of which was done for the liposome preparation stored at 4 °C for 7 months.

As the initial horizontal part of the titration curve shows, the liposome leakage does not occur in basic or neutral medium. However, the increase of acidity brings about a dramatic jump of leakage between pH 6.0 and 4.0. The resulting diagram is strikingly similar to the NMR-titration curve for the conformational flip of **1** (Figure 2A), especially to the backward titration of the acidic solution of **1** in $CD_3OD$ with DBU. One may hypothesize that the methanol solution with ionic species accumulated in the course of the back-titration is a better model for the polar environment of liposomes in the aqueous buffer solutions. We consider the similarity between the titration curves (A) and (B) (Figure 2) as an evidence of the intrinsic dependence of the pH-induced liposome leakage on the pH-triggered conformational flip of the amphiphile **1**.

Another important evidence for the role of conformational flip in the liposome leakage was obtained from the comparison of lipids **1** and **3**. Lipid **3** differs from flipid **1** only in the configuration of one lipid tail substituent, and for this reason it is unable to noticeably change its conformation after protonation (Figure 1) [14]. Thus the results for the control**3**/POPC/PEG-ceramide liposomes (Table 1) allowed observation of all possible effects of the protonation of morpholine group on the liposome permeability (change of headgroup radius, change of hydrogen bondings, *etc.*), except for the effects caused by the change of conformation. Therefore, the much larger and faster leakage of **1**/POPC/PEG-ceramide liposomes than of **3**/POPC/PEG-ceramide liposomes at pH 5.1 (Table 1) can be attributed to the pH-triggered conformational change of the lipid tails in **1**. As expected, the control liposomes containing neither **1**, nor **3** (last three entries in Table 1) were not responsive to lowered pH.

To highlight the key role of the conformational flip of the cyclohexane ring in the pH-triggered liposome leakage, we would like to introduce the term *'fliposomes'* for the liposomes comprising lipids equipped with such a pH-sensitive conformational switch.

## 3.4. The effect of the mole percentage of 1 on the pH-sensitivity of fliposomes

We performed most liposome leakage assays using the standardized procedures of prior studies [14,40-42], in which a small aliquot of liposome preparation was injected into pH 7.4 buffer, then acetic acid was added to decrease the pH, and the fluorescence was monitored until it plateaued. The exhaustive leakage (100%) was estimated after addition of detergent.

When incorporated into the lipid membranes at 25 mol%, flipid **1** induced substantial leakage (23–35%) of a variety of PEGylated liposomes at lowered pH (Table 1), including those consisting of saturated lipids, unsaturated lipids, PEs or PCs, and two different types of PEG-lipid conjugates. Since the liposomes containing POPC showed greater pH-triggered release than those consisting of other phospholipids, such liposomes were selected for further studies. In order to examine whether the pH-sensitivity of the liposomes can be improved by incorporating higher mole percentage of **1** into the liposome membrane, the **1**/POPC/PEG-ceramide liposomes containing 25–90 mol% of **1** were prepared and characterized (Figure 3,Table 1). Upon exposure to pH 5.1, the liposomes containing 25 mol% **1** released about 20% of ANTS instantly (in a few seconds), and up to 30% in approximately 5 min. As the mole percentage of **1** was increased, both the rate and the extent of the release of contents were increased. At 50 mol% of **1**, about 70% of ANTS was released in a few seconds. As the mole percentage of **1** was further increased (75 mol% and 90 mol%), the liposomes released all the contents in even fewer seconds. However, at higher than 50 mol% of **1**, the encapsulation efficiency of the liposomes deteriorated severely as shown by much lower fluorescence of ANTS after its exhaustive release in the presence of the detergent $C_{12}E_8$. It appears that 50 mol% of **1** is optimal for balancing efficient release from PEGylated, POPC-containing liposomes at pH 5.1 and high encapsulation capacity at pH 7.4.

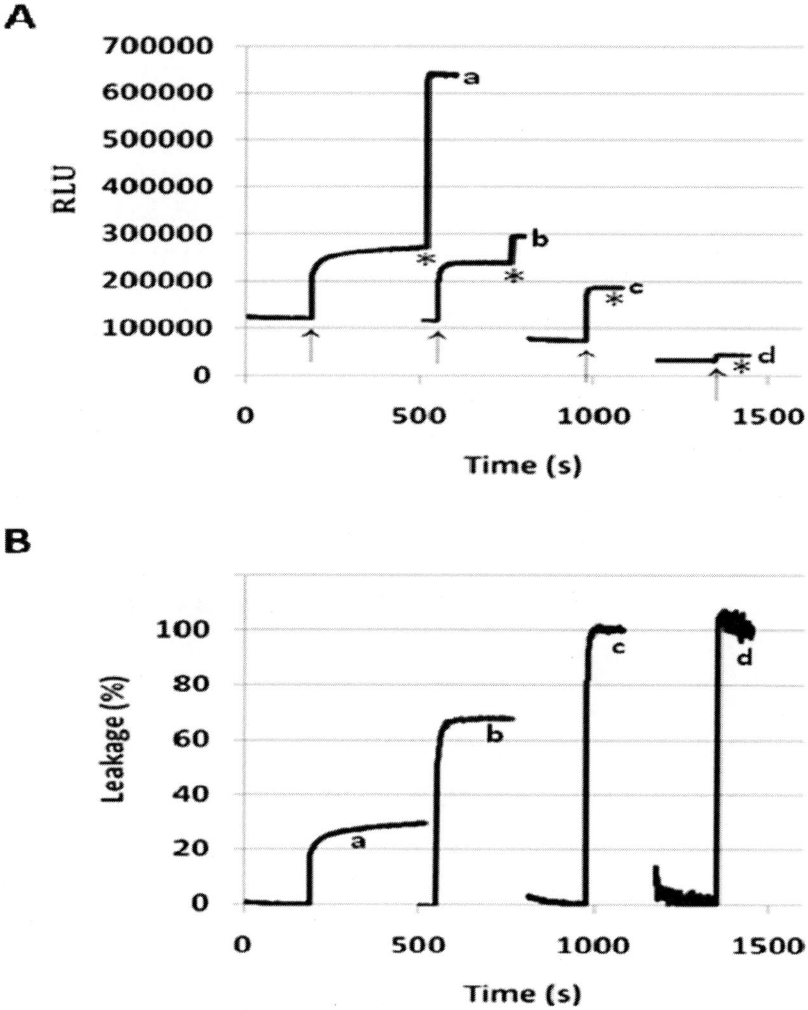


**Figure 3.** Effect of the mole percentage of **1** on the pH-triggered release of ANTS from**1**/POPC/PEG-ceramide fliposomes. The release is presented: (**A**) in relative light units (RLU) and (**B**) in percent of leakage. The molar ratio **1**/POPC/PEG-ceramide: a, 25/70/5; b, 50/45/5; c, 75/20/5; d, 90/5/5. Arrows indicate addition of acid to lower pH from 7.4 to 5.1; asterisks indicate addition of $C_{12}E_8$ for fliposomes permeation. The *x*-axes are in relative time scales to fit all the traces into the figure.

### 3.5. Effect of PEG-lipid conjugates on the pH-triggered release of fliposomes

In our preliminary report on flipid **1** [14], the neutrally charged PEG-lipid conjugate, PEG-ceramide was incorporated into the liposome membrane as a means of grafting the liposome surface with PEG. PEG-ceramide was chosen over PE-PEG conjugates [46–48] to avoid potential ionic interactions between the negatively charged phosphate group of PE-PEG and the positively charged ammonium group of protonated **1**. To further determine whether **1** is capable of triggering liposomes consisting of PE-PEG conjugates, which have been much more widely used in long-circulating drug/gene delivery systems [7,49,50], the **1**/POPC/PEG-DPPE liposomes containing different mole percentages of **1** were constructed and their pH-dependent leakage characterized in comparison with **1**/POPC/PEG-ceramide liposomes (Figure 4). Similar to the**1**/POPC/PEG-ceramide liposomes, the **1**/POPC/PEG-DPPE liposomes quickly released the encapsulated ANTS in response to the lowered pH. The higher the mole percentage of **1** in the liposomes, the higher was the percentage of the leakage. All other conditions being equal, the incorporation of PEG-DPPE in place of PEG-ceramide decreased the percentage of leakage at pH 5.1. For example, approximately 70% of ANTS was released from **1**/POPC/PEG-DPPE liposomes with 75 mol% of **1**, compared to 100% ANTS release from the corresponding **1**/POPC/PEG-ceramide liposomes.

### 3.6. pH-Triggered release from 1/POPC/PEG-ceramide fliposomes does not rely on inter-liposome bilayer contact

To better understand the mechanism of fliposome leakage, the hydrodynamic diameters of the **1**/POPC/PEG-ceramide fliposomes were measured before and after exposure to pH 5.1 for 1 h (Table 2). Regardless of the mole percentage of **1** or the extent of the leakage, the fliposomes retained their averaged hydrodynamic diameters after being triggered by the lowered pH, indicating that liposome aggregation/fusion is not significantly involved in the triggering process. Furthermore, when the **1**/POPC/PEG-ceramide (50/45/5) liposome was triggered at five times lower concentration (0.024 mM, pH lowered from 7.4 to 5.1), the rate and the extent of ANTS leakage (%) (Figure 5) were similar to those at the default lipid concentration

(0.12 mM). This observation confirmed that the liposome content release did not rely on the lipid concentration, and thus did not rely on the inter-liposome bilayer contact, in contrast with most other reported pH-sensitive liposomes [24].

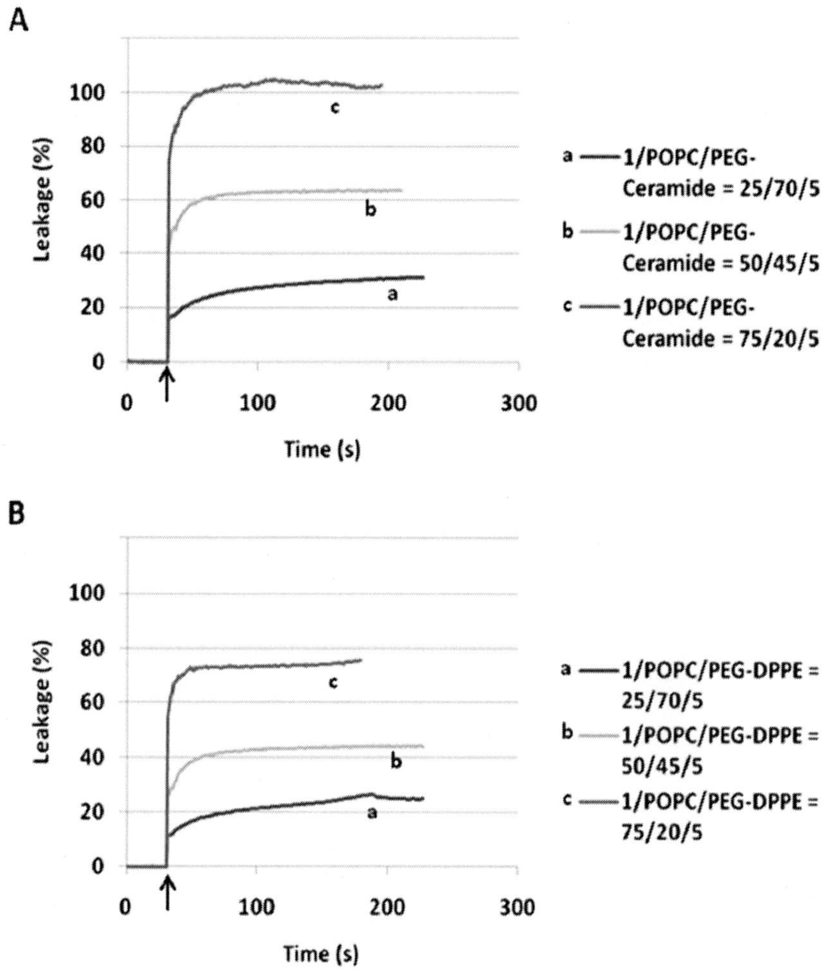


**Figure 4.** Release of ANTS from fliposomes containing (**A**) **1**/POPC/PEG-ceramide or (**B**) **1**/POPC/PEG-DPPE upon lowering pH from 7.4 to 5.1 (arrows). The *x*-axes are in relative time scales to fit all the traces into the figure.

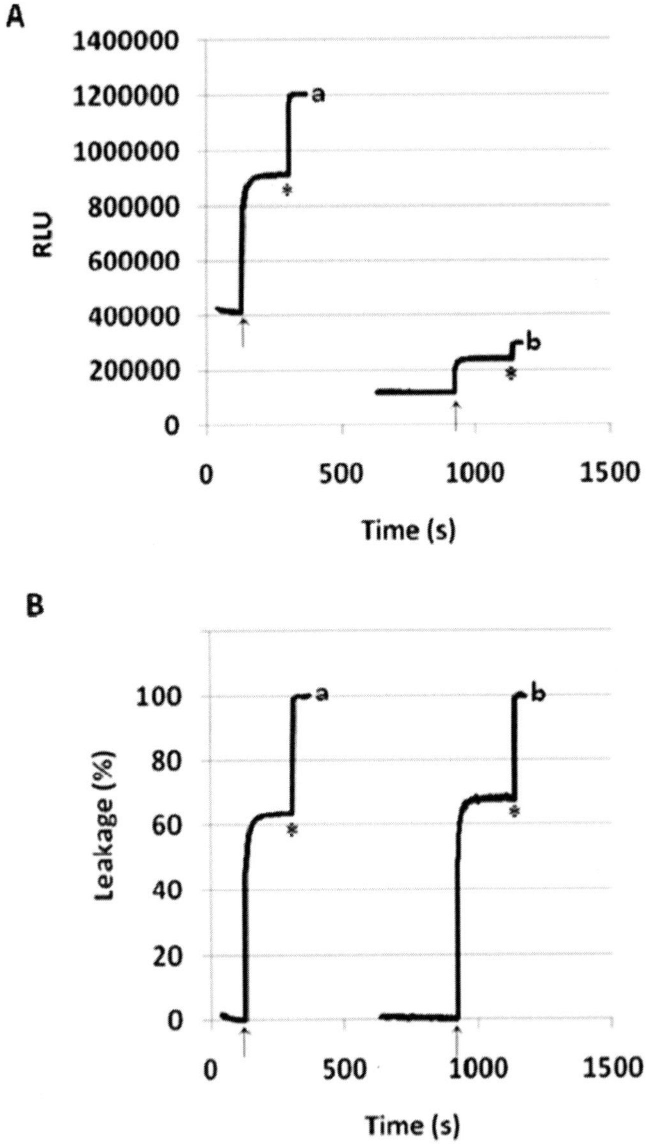


**Figure 5.** pH-triggered release of ANTS from **1**/POPC/PEG-ceramide fliposome (50/45/5) at (a) 0.12 mM and (b) 0.024 mM total lipid concentrations. Arrows: pH lowered from 7.4 to 5.1; asterisk: fliposome permeated by the detergent $C_{12}E_8$. The release is expressed: (**A**) in relative light units (RLU), and (**B**) in percent of leakage. The x-axes are in relative time scales to fit all the traces into the figure.

**Table 2.** Hydrodynamic diameter of **1**/POPC/PEG-ceramide fliposomes at pH 7.4 and after exposure to pH 5.1 for 1 h.

| Lipid Composition (molar ratio) | pH 7.4 | | 1 h at pH 5.1 | |
|---|---|---|---|---|
| | Diameter (nm) | P.I. | Diameter (nm) | P.I. |
| 1/POPC/PEG-ceramide (25/70/5) | 146.3 | 0.130 | 144.5 | 0.135 |
| 1/POPC/PEG-ceramide (50/45/5) | 162.4 | 0.069 | 161.2 | 0.132 |
| 1/POPC/PEG-ceramide (75/20/5) | 158.5 | 0.138 | 152.1 | 0.190 |
| POPC/PEG-ceramide (95/5) | 146.8 | 0.170 | 142.8 | 0.241 |

All the liposomes listed in the table contained the fluorophore ANTS/DPX; P.I.: polydispersity index.

For the purpose of drug delivery, the contact-independent pH-sensitive fliposomes may offer certain advantages. For instance, the fliposomes can retain their pH-sensitivity in the presence of PEG-lipid conjugates, which have been well documented to improve stability in blood circulation and to hinder the inter-liposome bilayer contact. Another potential advantage would be the robust drug release from each fliposome after it reaches certain acidic target sites (e.g., core of solid tumors) where the number of available liposomes may be too low for contact-dependent lipid phase changes.

## 3.7. Morphological changes of the 1/POPC/PEG-ceramide fliposomes in response to lowered pH

We applied freeze-fracture electron microscopy (FFEM) to gain more insight in the mechanism of triggered release from fliposomes because this powerful technique can not only image structures of lipid colloids at nanometer resolution, but also take snapshots of lipid phase transformation by rapid freezing [25-28]. The unloaded **1**/POPC/PEG-ceramide (50/45/5) fliposome formulation was studied both at pH 7.4 and after exposure to pH 5.5 for 5 min. Electron micrographs were taken from several freeze-fracture preparations of each sample and are presented on Figure 6. At both pH values, the samples contained vesicles. Since these vesicles

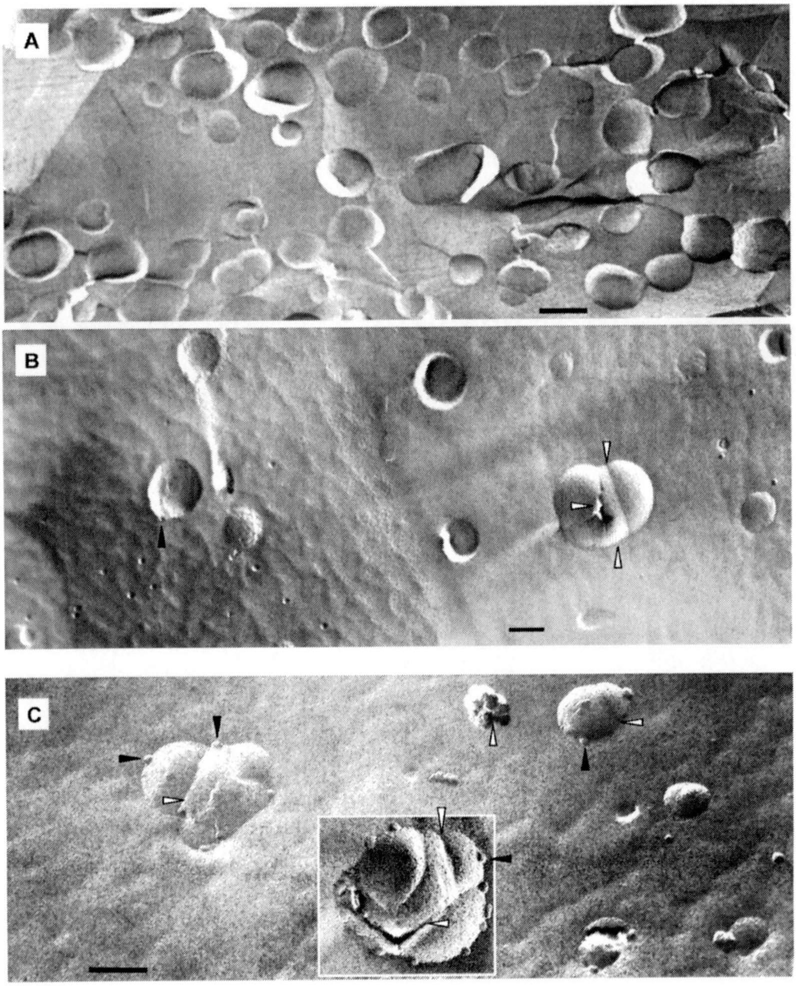


**Figure 6.** Freeze-fracture electron microscopy of the **1**/POPC/PEG-ceramide fliposome formulation at pH 7.4 (**A**) and 5 minutes after adjusting the pH to 5.5 with diluted acetic acid (**B**, **C**). Examples of division, buds, and stripes are shown with white, black, and yellow arrows respectively. The bars represent 100 nm.

displayed their shadows both in front of (concave fracture surfaces) and behind their structures (convex fracture surfaces), they are confirmed as liposomes with a shell of lipid bilayer. The diameters of the fliposomes measured on the electron micrographs range from 20 to 230 nm with an average diameter of about 100 nm. They are smaller than determined by photon correlation spectrometry (PCS), possibly for two reasons: one is that FFEM does not reflect the PEGylated outer lipid monolayer, and the other is that the averaged diameter by PCS usually over-represents the lager particles because they scatter light much more efficiently than their smaller counterparts [51].

At pH 7.4 the **1**/POPC/PEG-ceramide fliposome formulation appeared to be composed mostly of unilamellar vesicles together with a few vesicles displaying two bilayers (Figure 6A). At 5 mM total lipid concentration, the fliposomes were close to one another in the micrographs. Occasionally, small aggregates of a few vesicles were also observed. Upon decrease of pH from 7.4 to 5.5, the **1**/POPC/PEG-ceramide fliposomes underwent drastic morphological transformations (Figures 6B, C) that fell roughly into two categories: division and budding. Division frequently took place in larger vesicles, where stripes were observed in the dividing areas. Defects of lipid packing that resembled long and deep cracks were also observed on some of the dividing fliposome membranes. Budding was frequently observed in both smaller and larger vesicles, where small domains of lipids (<9 nm in diameter) protruded out of the fliposome membranes (Figure 6C). It appears that a large number of such lipid domains already pinched off the fliposomes as freely suspended small spherical particles (Figures 6B, C). Some fliposomes showed all of the above-described morphological features (division, stripes, and buds), indicating that the division and the budding events could take place simultaneously on the same fliposome (the complex fliposomes at Figures 6B, C).

The results of size distribution measurements (Figure 7) conform in general to the data of electron microscopy. The PCS-estimated average size of particles changed very little with addition of acid (from ~180 nm to ~187 nm). However, the maximum of the distribution curve shifted to somewhat greater sizes (from ~216 to ~243), and a broad small-size shoulder emerged at around 60 nm.

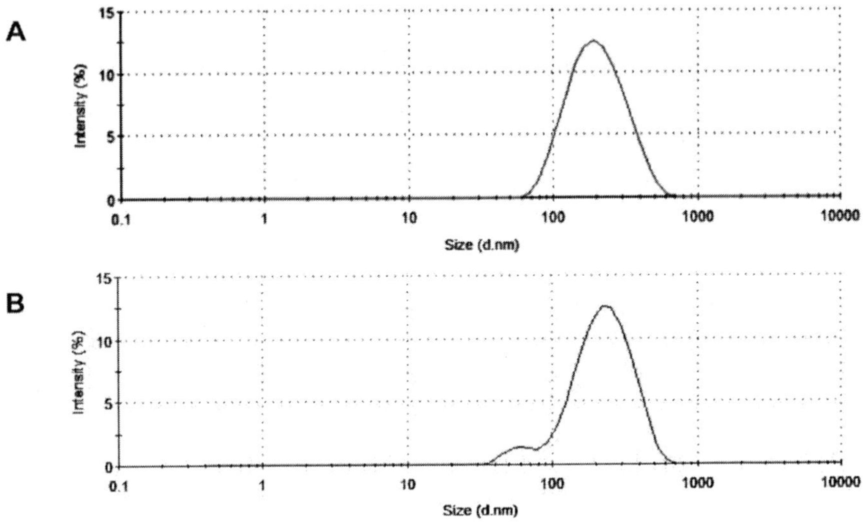


**Figure 7.** The PCS-estimated size distribution for the unloaded **1**/POPC/PEG-ceramide fliposome formulation at pH 7.4 (**A**) and pH 5.5 (**B**).

## 3.8. pH-Triggered release of the anticancer drug methotrexate from PEGylated fliposomes

Up to date, many reported pH-sensitive lipids managed to trigger liposomes only in cooperation with a high mole percentage of fusogenic PEs [10,11]. In contrast, the flipid **1** successfully destabilized a large variety of liposome membranes at lowered pH, including saturated membranes containing DPPC, unsaturated membranes containing POPC or POPE, membranes containing small (PE) or large (PC) lipid head groups, and membranes grafted with either PEG-ceramide or PEG-DPPE. Such versatility suggests that the aminocyclohexanol-based conformational switches may find applications in diverse delivery systems of therapeutic or diagnostic agents such as saturated, long-circulating liposomes for anticancer drug delivery [52,53], and unsaturated, PE-rich liposomes for gene delivery [54,55] across cellular membranes.

In order to confirm that PEGylated fliposomes are capable of releasing encapsulated drugs in response to lowered pH [56,57], we constructed the **1**/POPC/PEG-ceramide (50/45/5) and the **1**/POPC/PEG-DPPE fliposomes (50/45/5) containing the anionic anticancer drug methotrexate (MTX) [29,30]. After exposure to pH 5.5, both fliposome formulations were subjected to equilibrium micro-dialysis [31] as a more versatile method to quantify drug release regardless of its fluorescence. The percentage of MTX release was determined by measuring the UV absorbance (λ = 306 nm) of the free drug in the solution outside the dialysis bag after the micro-dialysis had reached equilibrium. As shown in Table 3, none of the fliposome formulations released significant amount of MTX after dialysis at pH 7.4 for 4 hours. Upon dialysis at pH 5.5, both fliposome formulations containing flipid **1** released most of the encapsulated MTX. The concentration of MTX generated in the buffer chamber exceeded by far the typical levels of MTX in patients' plasma and serum [58,59]. Interestingly, the percentage of MTX released was higher than that of ANTS from the corresponding fliposome formulations (Table 1), probably due to the much longer duration of the micro-dialysis assay (4 hours *versus* minutes), which would allow the detection of additional slower release of MTX after the initial fast release. For comparison, liposomes containing the diastereomeric amphiphiles **2** or **3** released much less MTX after micro-dialysis at pH 5.5 (Table 3). Such observations confirm that pH-triggered release of contents from fliposomes (ANTS, MTX, *etc.*) results mainly from the conformational change of the lipid tails, which takes place in **1** but not in its diastereomers **2** or **3**.

**Table 3.** pH-Triggered release of methotrexate from PEGylated liposomes.

| | MTX concentration (μM) | | | | Leakage (%) |
|---|---|---|---|---|---|
| | pH 7.4 | pH 7.4 + $C_{12}E_8$ | pH 5.5 | pH 5.5 + $C_{12}E_8$ | |
| **1**/POPC/ PEG-ceramide (50/45/5) | 61 | 601 | 560 | 642 | 86 |
| **1**/POPC/ PEG-DPPE (50/45/5) | 42 | 461 | 380 | 469 | 79 |
| **2**/POPC/ PEG-ceramide (50/45/5) | 45 | 382 | 85 | 411 | 11 |
| **3**/POPC/ PEG-ceramide (50/45/5) | 42 | 457 | 100 | 427 | 15 |

The pH of the liposome samples (300 μL) was adjusted with acetic acid (0–50 μL) with or without the detergent $C_{12}E_8$, followed by micro-dialysis. The **2**/POPC/PEG-ceramide (50/45/5) and **3**/POPC/PEG-ceramide (50/45/5) liposomes were characterized in parallel as conformationally non-switchable controls. The optical density of the buffer in the outer chamber (500 μL) was used to calculate the MTX concentration and the percentage of leakage (Leakage%).

### 3.9. Anticancer activity of fliposomes against HeLa cells

Finally, to test whether the fliposomes can serve as a viable drug delivery system, selected liposome formulations encapsulating the anticancer drug MTX were applied to the HeLa cells (human cervical cancer) followed by assessment of the cell viability using the MTS assay [43]. Methotrexate is an active drug in the first-line treatment of the cell carcinoma of the cervix [60,61]. The MTS assay works on the principle that the mitochondrial dehydrogenase of the live HeLa cells reduces the active compound MTS (inner salt) to colored formazan product that can be measured directly at 490 nm. The reduction of MTS by HeLa cells treated with free MTX or with the liposomes was compared to reduction by untreated HeLa cells and reported as relative viability in percentage (Figure 8).

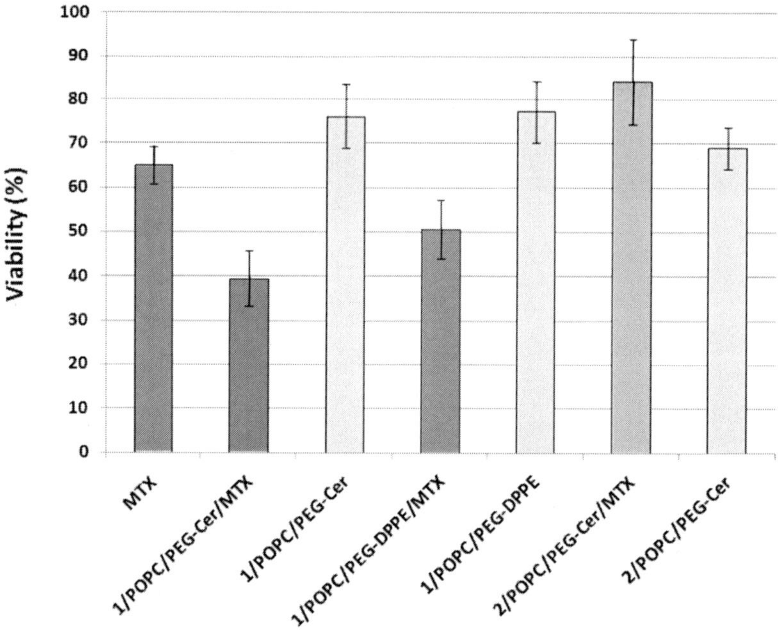


**Figure 8.** Cytotoxicity of MTX, of the liposome-encapsulated MTX, and of placebo liposomes against HeLa cells. The anticancer cytotoxicity is determined by the MTS assay as the decrease of viability *vs.* untreated cells (100% viability).

HeLa cells treated with 1 μM (final concentration) of MTX solution retained 65.0 ± 4.3% viability, consistent with prior reports [62-64] on the anticancer activity of the free drug. In comparison, the HeLa cells treated with MTX-loaded fliposomes containing the flipid **1** (**1**/POPC/PEG-ceramide = 50/45/5, and **1**/POPC/ PEG-DPPE = 50/45/5) showed a significantly lower viability (39.4 ± 4.3% and 50.5 ± 6.8%; $p < 10^{-6}$ and $10^{-3}$ by two-tailed Student's T-test, respectively), indicating the superior anticancer cytotoxicity of such liposomal formulations of MTX compared to the free drug at the same dosage.

In contrast, the HeLa cells treated with MTX-loaded liposomes containing the diastereomeric analogue **2** instead of **1**retained most of the viability (84.3 ± 9.9%), thus highlighting the importance of the flipid **1** in enhancing the cytotoxicity of the payload MTX.

As negative controls, the placebo fliposomes (**1**/POPC/PEG-ceramide = 50/45/5, and **1**/POPC/ PEG-DPPE = 50/45/5) without the MTX payload caused much less cytotoxicity (higher viability of 76.1 ± 7.3% and 77.2 ± 7.0%, respectively) than their MTX-loaded counterparts. This result confirmed that the anticancer activity of MTX-loaded fliposomes resulted mostly from the payload drug rather than the vector.

Because the cell culture media were buffered at ~pH 7.4, the discharge of the **1**/POPC/PEG-ceramide/MTX fliposomes most likely took place in the acidic endosomal compartment of the HeLa cells after their cellular uptake. Because MTX is too hydrophilic to passively diffuse across biomembranes, it is likely that the **1**/POPC/PEG-ceramide/MTX fliposomes not only released MTX in response to the lowered pH in the endosome, but also facilitated the diffusion of the released MTX from the endosome to the cytosol. One possible mechanism of such facilitated diffusion could be a destabilization of the endosomal membranes by the micelles generated from the destruction of fliposomes.

Thus in the HeLa cell culture, the **1**/POPC/PEG-ceramide fliposomes encapsulating MTX demonstrated the highest cytotoxicity. Comparisons with the negative controls (**2**/POPC/PEG-ceramide/MTX and empty **1**/POPC/PEG-ceramide liposomes) confirmed that most of the cytotoxicity resulted from the enhancement of the MTX release by the conformational flip of compound **1**.

## 3.10. Plausible *mechanism* of the pH-triggered cargo release by fliposomes

Many reported pH-sensitive liposomes are rich in phosphatidylethanolamine (PE) and require inter-liposome bilayer contact in order to respond to the decrease of pH [24,40,41]. In contrast, the lack of aggregation after pH-triggering (Table 2), as well as the concentration-independent release of ANTS (Figure 5), indicates that the **1**/POPC/PEG-ceramide fliposomes do not rely on the inter-liposome contact to undergo pH-sensitive leakage. The fliposomes are also different from most of the reported pH-sensitive liposomes in their extraordinarily fast response: a sufficient decrease of pH releases the fliposome cargo within seconds (Figures 3–5), compared to minutes or even hours that were required for most of the reported pH-sensitive liposomes [24,40,41]. Only some pH-sensitive polymers (e.g., EALA peptide) have been reported to start liposome leakage at a similar rate [13].

Based on the NMR studies on the pH-triggered conformational flip of **1**, the fluorometric and UV-studies on the pH-induced leakage of fliposomes, FFEM images of the morphological changes of **1**/POPC/PEG-ceramide fliposomes (division and budding), and the prior reports on lipid phase transitions, we propose the following unique mechanism of the pH-triggered content release from fliposomes: conformational shortening of the flipid **1** followed by lipid phase separation.

As the flipid **1** is protonated at lowered pH, its headgroup assumes a positive charge and hence a larger hydrodynamic size due to higher hydration. The protonation also generates a strong intramolecular hydrogen bond between the morpholine amine and the neighboring hydroxyl group, which flips the chair conformation of the cyclohexane ring and switches its two remote ester groups from the equatorial to the axial positions, thereby increasing the spatial separation of the two dodecyl groups of **1** (Figure 9). Such spatial separation would be more at the proximal end of the hydrocarbon chains than at their distal end, where conformational freedom and hydrophobic interactions would allow the chains to partially fold back and re-pack in the lipid bilayer. Such curved conformation of the two dodecyl groups (Figure 9) would decrease the packable length of the hydrophobic moiety of **1** in the fliposome membrane, which we refer to as “conformational shortening”.

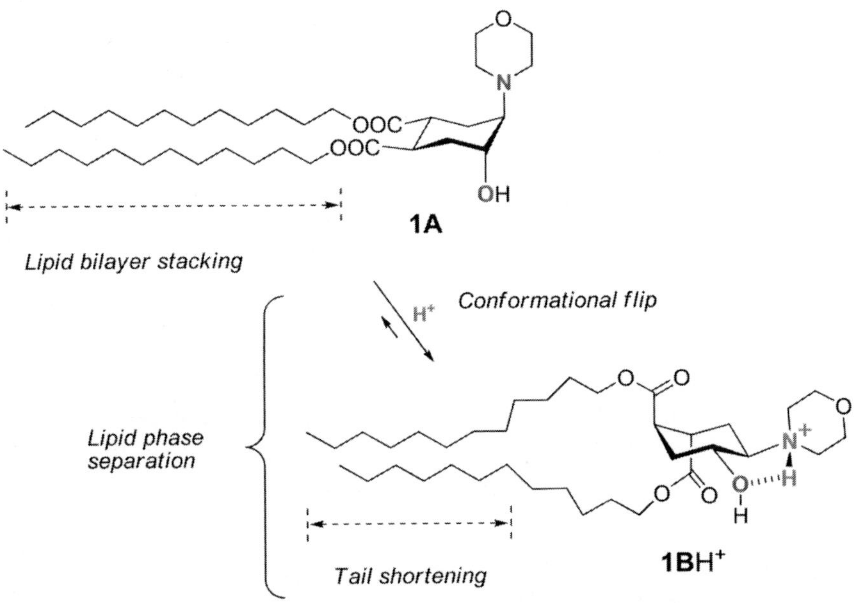


**Figure 9.** Protonation-induced conformational shortening of flipid **1** causes a quick perturbation of the lipid bilayer, lipid phase separation, and a fast fliposome leakage.

Such “conformational shortening” of the hydrophobic moiety of **1**, which constitutes in most experiments 50 mol% of the whole lipid composition, could directly perturb the lipid bilayer to cause the fliposome leakage. More likely, the conformational shortening would induce phase separation of the fliposome membrane, e.g. into thinner domains that are rich in **1** and thicker domains that are rich in POPC molecules, which carry a longer hydrophobic moiety. The encapsulated contents of the fliposomes would then quickly leak through defects between the domains. The domains of monolayers that are rich in **1** would subsequently bud from the fliposome membranes as small micelles [65,66], as observed in FFEM. Conversely, the remaining of the fliposome would carry minimal charges but retain a much larger size. Such larger particles would scatter photons much more strongly than the small micelles and therefore dominate the readings of photon correlation spectrometry [51] to show a relatively stable apparent size of the fliposomes after adjusting the pH from 7.4 to 5.1. The formation of micelles from larger **1**/POPC/PEG-ceramide fliposomes would be slower because their outer lipid monolayer carries less positive curvature than the smaller fliposomes. This allows the small domains that are rich in **1** to merge into larger lipid phases such as stripes, which would eventually disperse as micelles to leave defects on the fliposome surface. The kinetically competitive nature of the budding and the processes of the lipid phase separation would explain why both events could be observed in the same fliposome.

Although a lipid translocation (flip-flop) was involved in many reported pH-sensitive lipid phase changes [66-68], it is unlikely to significantly contribute to the pH-triggered release from the fliposomes because of its much slower kinetics (hours for flip-flop [68] *versus* seconds for fliposome leakage).

## 4. CONCLUSIONS

By incorporation of the conformationally switchable *trans*-2-morpholinocyclohexanol-based amphiphile (flipid) into lipid compositions, we designed pH-triggerable liposomes (fliposomes) with extraordinary characteristics: high stability in storage and in serum *in vitro* combined with instant release of their cargo in response to a weakly acidic medium. The acid-induced release from fliposomes can be modulated by the mole percentage of the flipid, and is independent of inter-liposome contact. Based on fluorometric, NMR and electron microscopy studies, a mechanism of pH-sensitivity has been proposed that starts with an acid-triggered conformational flip and is followed by a set of membrane perturbations, which cause the leakage. Anticancer activities of selected methotrexate formulations in HeLa cells demonstrate that fliposomes can serve as viable drug delivery systems.

## ACKNOWLEDGMENTS

We thank Brigitte Papahadjopoulos-Sternberg at Nano Analytical Laboratory in San Francisco, CA, for acquiring the electron microscopy images and helpful discussion. We thank Roshanak Rahimian at the Department of Physiology and Pharmacology, UOP, for the use of the QuantaMaster Fluorometer and Silvio Rodriguez at the Department of Chemistry, UOP, for the use of the Perkin Elmer Lambda 35 UV/vis Spectrometer. This work is supported by Teva US Scholar Grant (2009-2012) administered by the American Chemical Society, and by the National Science Foundation Major Research Instrument Grant (CHE-0722654).


## REFERENCES


1. Torchilin, V. Liposomal nanomedicines. Pan Stanford Ser. Biomed. Nanotechnol. 2011, 1, 315–382.
2. Yuba, E.; Harada, A.; Sakanishi, Y.; Kono, K. Carboxylated hyperbranched poly(glycidol)s for preparation of pH-sensitive liposomes. J. Control. Release 2011, 149, 72–80.
3. Musacchio, T.; Torchilin, V.P. Recent developments in lipid-based pharmaceutical nanocarriers. Front. Biosci. Landmark Ed. 2011, 16, 1388–1412.
4. Tarahovsky, Y.S. "Smart" liposomal nanocontainers in biology and medicine. Biochemistry (Moscow) 2010, 75, 811–824.
5. Sawant, R.R.; Torchilin, V.P. Liposomes as 'smart' pharmaceutical nanocarriers. Soft Matter 2010, 6, 4026–4044.
6. Gao, W.-W.; Chan, J.M.; Farokhzad, O.C. pH-Responsive nanoparticles for drug delivery. Mol. Pharm. 2010, 7, 1913–1920.

7. Kale, A.A.; Torchilin, V.P. "Smart" drug carriers: PEGylated TATp-modified pH-sensitive liposomes. J. Liposome Res.2007, 17, 197–203.

8. Karanth, H.; Murthy, R.S.R. pH-Sensitive liposomes - principle and application in cancer therapy. J. Pharm. Pharmacol.2007, 59, 469–483.

9. Guo, X.; Szoka, F.C., Jr. Chemical approaches to triggerable lipid vesicles for drug and gene delivery. Acc. Chem. Res.2003, 36, 335–341.

10. Fattal, E.; Couvreur, P.; Dubernet, C. "Smart" delivery of antisense oligonucleotides by anionic pH-sensitive liposomes. Advan. Drug Deliv. Rev. 2004, 56, 931–946.

11. Simoes, S.; Moreira, J.N.; Fonseca, C.; Duzgunes, N.; Pedroso de Lima, M.C. On the formulation of pH-sensitive liposomes with long circulation times. Advan. Drug Deliv. Rev. 2004, 56, 947–965.

12. Leung, K.C.-F.; Chak, C.-P.; Lo, C.-M.; Wong, W.-Y.; Xuan, S.; Cheng, C.H.K. pH-Controllable supramolecular systems. Chem. Asian J. 2009, 4, 364–381.

13. Li, W.; Nicol, F.; Szoka, F.C. GALA: a designed synthetic pH-responsive amphipathic peptide with applications in drug and gene delivery. Advan. Drug Deliv. Rev. 2004, 56, 967–985.

14. Brazdova, B.; Zhang, N.; Samoshin, V.V.; Guo, X. trans-2-Aminocyclohexanol as a pH-sensitive conformational switch in lipid amphiphiles. Chem. Commun. 2008, 4774–4776.

15. Lee, H.M.; Chmielewski, J. Liposomal cargo unloading induced by pH-sensitive peptides. J. Pept. Res. 2005, 65, 355–363.

16. Parente, R.A.; Nir, S.; Szoka, F.C., Jr. Mechanism of leakage of phospholipid vesicle contents induced by the peptide GALA. Biochemistry 1990, 29, 8720–8728.

17. Vogel, K.; Wang, S.; Lee, R.J.; Low, P.S.; Chmielewski, J. Peptide-mediated release of folate-targeted liposome contents from endosomal compartments. J. Am. Chem. Soc. 1996, 118, 1581–1586.

18. Ng, L.-T.; Yuba, E.; Kono, K. Modification of liposome surface with pH-responsive polyampholytes for the controlled-release of drugs. Res. Chem. Intermed. 2009, 35, 1015–1025.

19. Allen, T.M. Long-circulating (sterically stabilized) liposomes for targeted drug delivery. Trends Pharmacol. Sci. 1994,15, 215–220.

20. Gabizon, A.A.; Shmeeda, H.; Zalipsky, S. Pros and cons of the liposome platform in cancer drug targeting. J. Liposome Res. 2006, 16, 175–183.

21. Allen, T.M.; Cullis, P.R. Drug delivery systems: entering the mainstream. Science 2004, 303, 1818–1822.

22. Ichihara, M.; Shimizu, T.; Imoto, A.; Hashiguchi, Y.; Uehara, Y.; Ishida, T.; Kiwada, H. Anti-PEG IgM response against PEGylated liposomes in mice and rats. Pharmaceutics 2011, 3, 1–11.

23. Patel, S.; Bhirde, A.A.; Rusling, J.F.; Chen, X.; Gutkind, J.S.; Patel, V. Nano delivers big: designing molecular missiles for cancer therapeutics. Pharmaceutics 2011, 3, 34–52.

24. Ellens, H.; Bentz, J.; Szoka, F.C. pH-Induced destabilization of phosphatidylethanolamine-containing liposomes: role of bilayer contact. Biochemistry 1984, 23, 1532–1538.

25. Papahadjopoulos-Sternberg, B. Freeze-fracture electron microscopy on domains in lipid mono-and bilayer on nano-resolution scale. Methods Mol. Biol. 2010, 606, 333–349.

26. Sternberg, B. Liposomes as a model for membrane structures and structural transformations: A liposome

album. InHandbook of Nonmedical Applications of Liposomes; CRC: Boca Raton, FL, USA, 1996; pp. 271–297.

27. Hope, M.J.; Rodrigueza, W.V. Membrane lipids and model membrane systems. In Rapid Freezing, Freeze Fracture, Deep Etching; Wiley-Liss: New York, NY, USA, 1995; pp. 235–253.

28. Sternberg, B. Freeze-fracture electron microscopy of liposomes. In Liposome Technology, 2nd ed.; CRC Press: Boca Raton, FL, USA, 1993; pp. 363–383.

29. Hagner, N.; Joerger, M. Cancer chemotherapy: targeting folic acid synthesis. Cancer Manage. Res. 2010, 2, 293–301.

30. Chan, E.S.L.; Cronstein, B.N. Methotrexate-how does it really work? Nat. Rev. Rheumatol. 2010, 6, 175–178.

31. Waters, N.J.; Jones, R.; Williams, G.; Sohal, B. Validation of a rapid equilibrium dialysis approach for the measurement of plasma protein binding. J. Pharm. Sci. 2008, 97, 4586–4595.

32. Brazdova, B.; Tan, N.S.; Samoshina, N.M.; Samoshin, V.V. Novel easily accessible glucosidase inhibitors: 4-hydroxy-5-alkoxy-1,2-cyclohexanedicarboxylic acids. Carbohydr. Res. 2009, 344, 311–321.

33. Samoshin, V.V.; Chertkov, V.A.; Gremyachinskiy, D.E.; Dobretsova, E.K.; Shestakova, A.K.; Vatlina, L.P. trans-2-Aminocyclohexanols as pH-triggers for conformationally controlled crowns and podands. Tetrahedron Lett. 2004, 45, 7823–7826.

34. Samoshin, V.V.; Brazdova, B.; Chertkov, V.A.; Gremyachinskiy, D.E.; Shestakova, A.K.; Dobretsova, E.K.; Vatlina, L.P.; Yuan, J.; Schneider, H.-J. trans-2-Aminocyclohexanols as pH-triggered molecular switches. ARKIVOC 2005, 129–141.

35. Wong, Y.S.; Brazdova, B.; Koo, S.; Samoshin, A.V.; Franz, A.H.; Samoshin, V.V. trans-2-Alkylaminocyclohexanols as pH-triggered molecular switches. J. Undergrad. Chem. Res. 2007, 6, 81–85.

36. Samoshin, V.V.; Chertkov, V.A.; Vatlina, L.P.; Dobretsova, E.K.; Simonov, N.A.; Kastorsky, L.P.; Gremyachinsky, D.E.; Schneider, H.-J. trans-1,2-Cyclohexanedicarboxylic acid derivatives as pH-trigger for conformationally controlled crowns. Tetrahedron Lett. 1996, 37, 3981–3984.

37. Monnard, P.-A.; Oberholzer, T.; Luisi, P. Entrapment of nucleic acids in liposomes. Biochim. Biophys. Acta Biomembr.1997, 1329, 39–50.

38. Bartlett, G.R. Phosphorus assay in column chromatography. J. Biol. Chem. 1959, 234, 466–468.

39. Franz, A.H.; Samoshina, N.M.; Guo, X.; Samoshin, V.V. NMR investigation of phospholipid/PEG-ceramide liposomes. In International Symposium: Nuclear Magnetic Resonance in Condensed Matter; "Solo" Publisher: Saint Petersburg, Russia, 2010; p. 74.

40. Chen, H.; Zhang, H.; Szoka, F.C.; Guo, X. Unsaturated cationic ortho esters for endosome permeation in gene delivery. J. Med. Chem. 2007, 50, 4269–4278.

41. Guo, X.; MacKay, J.A.; Szoka, F.C., Jr. Mechanism of pH-triggered collapse of phosphatidylethanolamine liposomes stabilized by an ortho ester polyethyleneglycol lipid. Biophys. J. 2003, 84, 1784–1795.

42. Huang, Z.; Guo, X.; Li, W.; MacKay, J.A.; Szoka, F.C., Jr. Acid-triggered transformation of diortho ester phosphocholine liposome. J. Am. Chem. Soc. 2006, 128, 60–61.

43. CellTiter 96® AQueous Non-Radioactive Cell Proliferation Assay; Promega Co.: Madison, WI, USA, 2009.

44. Blume, G.; Cevc, G. Molecular mechanism of the lipid vesicle longevity in vivo. Biochim. Biophys. Acta Biomembr. 1993,1146, 157–168.

45. Mahato, R.I. Water insoluble and soluble lipids for gene delivery. Advan. Drug Deliv. Rev. 2005, 57, 699–712.

46. Klibanov, A.L.; Maruyama, K.; Beckerleg, A.M.; Torchilin, V.P.; Huang, L. Activity of amphipathic poly(ethylene glycol) 5000 to prolong the circulation time of liposomes depends on the liposome size and is unfavorable for immunoliposome binding to target. Biochim. Biophys. Acta Biomembr. 1991, 1062, 142–148.

47. Klibanov, A.L.; Maruyama, K.; Torchilin, V.P.; Huang, L. Amphipathic polyethylene glycols effectively prolong the circulation time of liposomes. FEBS Lett. 1990, 268, 235–237.

48. Woodle, M.C.; Matthay, K.K.; Newman, M.S.; Hidayat, J.E.; Collins, L.R.; Redemann, C.; Martin, F.J.; Papahadjopoulos, D. Versatility in lipid compositions showing prolonged circulation with sterically stabilized liposomes. Biochim. Biophys. Acta Biomembr. 1992, 1105, 193–200.

49. Park, J.W.; Kirpotin, D.B.; Hong, K.; Shalaby, R.; Shao, Y.; Nielsen, U.B.; Marks, J.D.; Papahadjopoulos, D.; Benz, C.C. Tumor targeting using anti-HER2 immunoliposomes. J. Control. Release 2001, 74, 95–113.

50. Zalipsky, S.; Brandeis, E.; Newman, M.S.; Woodle, M.C. Long circulating, cationic liposomes containing amino-PEG-phosphatidylethanolamine. FEBS Lett. 1994, 353, 71–74.

51. Segota, S.; Tezak, D. Spontaneous formation of vesicles. Advan. Colloid Interface Sci. 2006, 121, 51–75.

52. Allen, T.M.; Martin, F.J. Advantages of liposomal delivery systems for anthracyclines. Semin. Oncol. 2004, 31, 5–15.

53. Needham, D.; Dewhirst, M.W. The development and testing of a new temperature-sensitive drug delivery system for the treatment of solid tumors. Advan. Drug Deliv. Rev. 2001, 53, 285–305.

54. Duan, Y.; Zhang, S.-B.; Wang, B.; Yang, B.-L.; Zhi, D.-F. The biological routes of gene delivery mediated by lipid-based non-viral vectors. Expert Opin. Drug Delivery 2009, 6, 1351–1361.

55. Wasungu, L.; Hoekstra, D. Cationic lipids, lipoplexes and intracellular delivery of genes. J. Control. Release 2006, 116, 255–264.

56. Hong, M.-S.; Lim, S.-J.; Lee, M.-K.; Kim, Y.B.; Kim, C.-K. Prolonged blood circulation of methotrexate by modulation of liposomal composition. Drug Delivery 2001, 8, 231–237.

57. Hong, M.-S.; Lim, S.-J.; Oh, Y.-K.; Kim, C.-K. pH-sensitive, serum-stable and long-circulating liposomes as a new drug delivery system. J. Pharm. Pharmacol. 2002, 54, 51–58.

58. Ramsay, C.S.; Xie, H.; Ozaeta, P.; Smith, D.; Bacani, M.; Fishpaugh, J. LC/MS/MS quantitation of methotrexate levels in human plasma and serum. Proceedings of 239th ACS National Meeting, San Francisco, CA, USA, 21–25 March 2010; ACS: Washington, DC, USA, 2010; p. ANYL-84.

59. Xie, J.-p.; Feng, L.-l.; Kuang, X. Determination of methotrexate level in serum using higher doses methotrexate by HPLC. Zhongguo Shiyan Fangjixue Zazhi 2010, 16, 69–72.

60. Markman, M. Systemic therapy for gynecologic cancer. Curr. Opin. Oncol. 1992, 4, 939–945.

61. Chauvergne, J.; Rohart, J.; Heron, J.F.; Ayme, Y.; Berlie, J.; Fargeot, P.; George, M.; Lebrun-Jezekova, D.; Pigneux, J.; Chenal, C. Randomized trial of initial chemotherapy in 151 locally advanced carcinoma of the cervix (T2b-N1, T3b, MO). Bull. Cancer 1990, 77, 1007–1024.

62. Zhu, L.; Huo, Z.; Wang, L.; Tong, X.; Xiao, Y.; Ni, K. Targeted delivery of methotrexate to skeletal muscular tissue by thermosensitive magnetoliposomes. Int. J. Pharm. 2009, 370, 136–143.

63. Dhanikula, R.S.; Argaw, A.; Bouchard, J.-F.; Hildgen, P. Methotrexate loaded polyether-copolyester dendrimers for the treatment of gliomas: enhanced efficacy and intratumoral transport capability. Mol. Pharm. 2008, 5, 105–116.

64. Yoon, S.Y.; Choi, H.I.; Choi, J.E.; Sul, C.A.; Choi, J.M.; Kim, D.H. Methotrexate decreases PP2A methylation and increases tau phosphorylation in neuron. Biochem. Biophys. Res. Commun. 2007, 363, 811–816.

65. Hurley, J.H.; Boura, E.; Carlson, L.-A.; Rozycki, B. Membrane budding. Cell 2010, 143, 875–887.

66. Schreier, S.; Malheiros, S.V.P.; de Paula, E. Surface active drugs: self-association and interaction with membranes and surfactants. Physicochemical and biological aspects. Biochim. Biophys. Acta Biomembr. 2000, 1508, 210–234.

67. Contreras, F.X.; Sanchez-Magraner, L.; Alonso, A.; Goni, F.M. Transbilayer (flip-flop) lipid motion and lipid scrambling in membranes. FEBS Lett. 2010, 584, 1779–1786.

68. Demina, T.; Grozdova, I.; Krylova, O.; Zhirnov, A.; Istratov, V.; Frey, H.; Kautz, H.; Melik-Nubarov, N. Relationship between the structure of amphiphilic copolymers and their ability to disturb lipid bilayers. Biochemistry 2005, 44, 4042–4054.

# Chapter 10

# Influence of the Vehicle on the Penetration of Particles into Hair Follicles

**Alexa Patzelt [1,*], Heike Richter [1], Lars Dähne [2], Peter Walden [3], Karl-Heinz Wiesmüller [4], Ute Wank [4], Wolfram Sterry [1] and Jürgen Lademann [1]**

[1]*Center of Experimental and Applied Cutaneous Physiology (CCP), Department of Dermatology and Allergology, Charité – Universitätsmedizin Berlin, 10117 Berlin, Germany*

[2]*Surflay Nanotec GmbH, Schwarzschildstr. 8, 12489 Berlin, Germany*

[3]*Department of Dermatology and Allergology, Charité – Universitätsmedizin Berlin, Tumorimmunology, 10117 Berlin, Germany*

[4]*EMC microcollections GmbH, Sindelfinger Str. 3, 72070 Tübingen, Germany*

## ABSTRACT

Recently, it has been demonstrated that particulate substances penetrate preferentially into the hair follicles and that the penetration depth depends on the particle size. In the present study, the influence of the vehicle of the particulate substances on the penetration depth was investigated. Four different formulations (ethanolic suspension, aqueous suspension, ethanolic gel and aqueous gel) containing peptide-loaded particles of 1 µm in diameter were prepared and applied on porcine ear skin. After penetration, punch biopsies were taken and the penetration depths of the particles were investigated by laser scanning microscopy. The deepest penetration was achieved with the gel formulations demonstrating an influence of the vehicle on the penetration depth of particulate substances.

**Keywords:** hair follicle; penetration; particle; vehicle; formulation

## 1. INTRODUCTION

Particulate substances are increasingly utilized as carriers for active ingredients in dermatological and cosmetic products to improve efficacy of delivery. Whereas, intercellular penetration of particulate substances via the lipid layers of the stratum corneum can be considered implausible because of size, the hair follicles have been demonstrated to be the main target for topically applied particles in undamaged skin [1]. Hair follicles are breaks in the otherwise highly efficient skin barrier and, therefore, act as pit traps for topically applied particles [2]. Effective delivery of active agents, however, is also strongly related to its efficient release from the delivering particles subsequent to the transport into the hair follicle allowing their independent penetration through the skin barrier into the living tissue and, if desired, their diffusion to the target structures. Several release mechanisms are being explored such as external stimulation or enzymatic release [3].

The hair follicle itself can be divided into at least four target areas for topical application: the sebaceous gland, the bulge region, the hair matrix cells and the hair follicle infundibulum [4]. The latter provides an interrupted barrier with increased permeability and is surrounded by a high density of immune cells and an extensive capillary network important for penetration and systemic absorption of active agents [5,6].

Recently, it could be demonstrated that selective delivery of particulate substances to the desired target sites can be realized by modification of the particle size [2]. Deepest penetration was found for particles between 300 and 600 nm, which corresponds to the thickness of the keratin scales of the hair [7]. For smaller and larger particles significantly lower penetration depths were determined. Based on these findings it was hypothesized that the moving hair and the hair follicle might act as an active transport system shuffling the particles into the hair follicles.

Moreover, it is established that efficacy, tolerability and application properties of topically applied products are clearly related to the type of vehicle used [8]. The variety of vehicles available can be distinguished by their galenic properties such as rheological properties, polarity and physicochemical features according to the guideline of the European Pharmacopoeia [8], all having an impact on the penetration properties of substances. Aqueous suspension is considered to be the standard vehicle, whereas ethanol is known as a penetration enhancer through extracting the lipids from the stratum corneum [8]. Also, hydrophilic gel preparations are known to improve drug delivery of substances into the skin [9].

Therefore, the aim of the present study was to investigate the influence of the vehicle on the penetration of $SiO_2$ particles reversibly loaded with a model peptide. For this purpose, four different vehicles were selected: an aqueous and an ethanolic suspension, an aqueous agarose gel and an ethanolic gel. For identification and tracing, the particles and the peptide were labeled with different fluorescence dyes. The investigations were performed on porcine skin as a model for human skin [10,11]. After application and penetration, follicular penetration depths of the particles and the loaded model peptide were investigated.

## 2. EXPERIMENTAL SECTION

### 2.1. Skin samples

The porcine ears were obtained immediately after slaughtering from the butcher. Pre-treatment of the porcine ear skin included rinsing with cold water, drying with paper towels and carefully shortening of the bristles. Approval for these experiments had been obtained from the Government Office of Veterinary Medicine in Berlin-Treptow, Germany.

## 2.2. Particle preparation and formulations

For reversible coupling of the peptide, monodisperse silica particles of 1 µm in diameter (FUSO, Japan) were coated by the Layer-by-Layer® process [12] with alternating layers of the polycation poly(allylamine hydrochloride) PAH and the polyanions poly(styrene sulfonate) PSS and poly(methacrylic acid sodium salt) PMAA. All polyelectrolyte solutions were prepared as 1 g/L polymer, 200 mM salt and 50 mM acetate buffer pH 5.6 in MilliQ water. The coating sequence was silica/PAH/PSS/(PAH-Cy5/PSS)$_2$/PAH/PMAA. For the third and fifth layers, PAH covalently linked at every 180th monomer unit with the fluorescence dye Cy5 was used. Thickness of the polymer layers was around 20 nm in sum as reported in several publications [12]. The polymer-coated particles were carefully washed with water and the pH was set to 8 by addition of 50 mM Tris-buffer in order to load them with the peptides.

A synthetic peptide modified by a positively charged amino acid tag and labeled with rhodamine B (6 mg) was added overnight to the suspension of polymer-coated particles (100 mg) for adsorption to the negatively charged polymer surface of the particles. After incubation, excess of peptide was washed off. The amount of peptide loaded on the particles was determined by UV/Vis spectroscopy ($\lambda_{abs\,(Cy5)}$ = 643 nm) of the collected supernatants as 41 µg peptide/mg particles.

The peptide-loaded particles were diluted to a 1% suspension in 10 mL Tris-buffer and divided into 4 aliquots. The suspensions were centrifuged, the supernatants removed and the deposited particles thoroughly mixed with 2.5 mL of the following media for a 1% suspension resp. gel-mixture:

-MilliQ water

-20% ethanol in water

-low melting agarose gel (45 °C) at 0.5% in the liquid state

-low melting ethanolic gel (Actensa, Berlin, Germany)

For preparation of the aqueous gel, 0.5% Agarose (m.p. 45 °C) was dissolved in water at 60 °C. After cooling down to 45 °C, a concentrated particle suspension (10%) in water was mixed with the gel at a ratio of 1:10. The ethanolic gel contains 80% ethanol, water and gel constituents in the 1–2% range and could be used as is.

## 2.3. Application protocol

The experiments were performed on six porcine ears in parallel. Preparation of the skin included marking of 4 areas A–D of 2 × 3 cm in size (one for each formulation) on each porcine ear and the application of a silicone barrier around the marked skin areas in order to avoid lateral spreading. Subsequently, 120 μL of each of the 4 formulations were applied homogeneously onto the skin areas A–D using a massage appliance for 3 minutes (Massage Gerät PC60, Petra electric, Burgau, Germany). After a penetration time of one hour, punch biopsies of 3 mm in diameter were collected from the porcine tissue. The samples were shock-frozen in liquid nitrogen and longitudinal cryo sections of 10 μm thickness were prepared using the cryotome HM 560 Cryo-Star, Microm International GmbH, Walldorf, Germany.

## 2.4. Sample analysis

The sections were analyzed using a laser scanning microscope LSM 2000 (Carl Zeiss, Jena, Germany). To avoid double excitation of both dyes, the respective excitation wavelengths had to be shifted out of the absorption maximum. Therefore, rhodamine was excited at 488 nm and Cy5 at 568 nm. Emission was measured at 515 nm for rhodamine and 665 nm for Cy5, respectively, for identification of the stained particles and peptides. Intensities were not used for evaluation.

The same samples were additionally imaged in transmission mode in order to identify the follicular structure. By superposition of the images from both visualization modes, the maximal penetration depths of the fluorescent particles and of the fluorescent peptide were determined. In Figure 1, a longitudinal section of a hair follicle taken in the transmission and the fluorescent mode is exemplarily depicted.

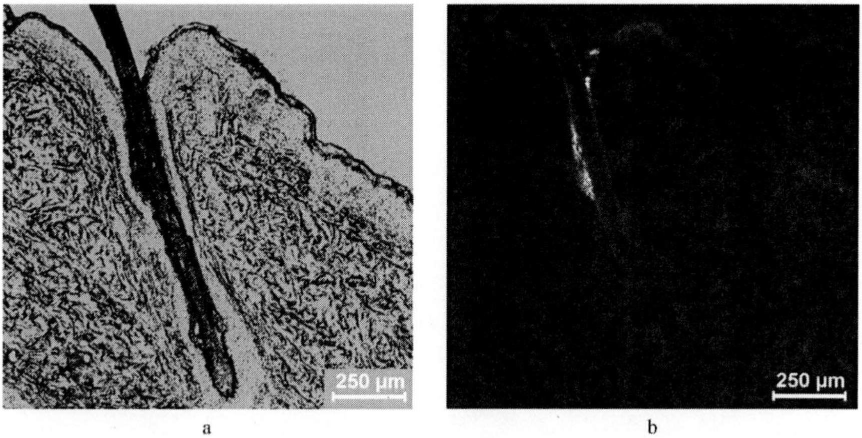


**Figure 1.** Images of a longitudinal section of a hair follicle taken in the transmission (**a**) and the fluorescence mode (**b**) by laser scanning microscopy.

### 2.5. Statistical analysis

For statistical analysis, the distances covered by the deepest penetrating fluorescent particles resp. peptide molecules were measured. Mean values and standard deviations were calculated from different hair follicles and compared using Microsoft Excel®. Further statistical analysis was done with the software program SPSS® 16.0. To compare the follicular penetration depths of the different particle preparations, the t-test was utilized at a significance level of $p < 0.05$.

## 3. RESULTS AND DISCUSSION

Polymer coated $SiO_2$ particles labeled with Cy5 were reversibly loaded with a rhodamine-labeled peptide. These peptide-loaded particles were formulated with four different vehicles. The penetration depths of the particles and the loaded peptide in the porcine ear skin hair follicles were investigated separately and are summarized in Figure 2. The results revealed differences in the penetration depths with the different formulations as well as between the particles and peptide.

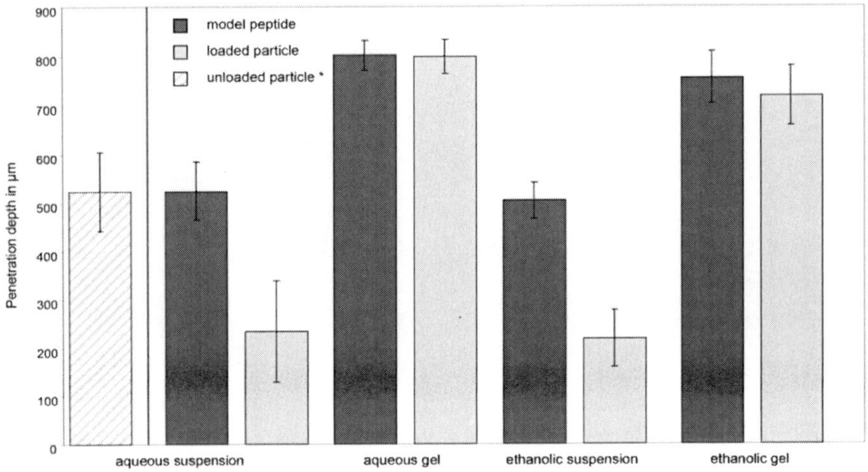


**Figure 2.** Follicular penetration depths of the loaded particles and the model peptide applied in four different vehicles. (* penetration depth of unloaded bare $SiO_2$ particles in aqueous suspension for comparison, data utilized from previous study [2]).

The penetration depths of the particles and peptide were significantly deeper ($p < 0.05$) with the gel preparations than with the suspensions. Whereas with the gel formulations comparable penetration depths were observed for particles and peptide ($p > 0.05$), with suspensions the peptide penetrated significantly deeper into the hair follicles than the particles ($p < 0.05$). No differences were observed between ethanolic and aqueous formulations.

The penetration efficacy of topically applied substances potentially depends on the properties of the active agent, the carrier and the vehicle in combination. While previous investigations showed that the penetration of bare $SiO_2$ particles mainly depends on particle size when applied in aqueous suspension [2], the present study demonstrates that in addition the vehicle, *i.e.*, formulation, influences the penetration of particulate substances.

With the gel preparations, significantly increased penetration depths could be achieved when compared to the suspensions. This suggests that aggregation tendency of the particles might be reduced in a viscous gel preparation by stabilizing a homogeneous dispersion of carriers in the matrix as described in literature [9].

Related observations have been reported by other investigators. Hydrophilic gels were shown to serve as effective and inert environments for carriers including nanocapsules [13], liposomes [14], solid lipid nanoparticles [15] and microemulsions [16]. Sintov and colleagues [17] performed an *in vitro* diffusion study of flutamide gel combined with a penetration enhancer. They demonstrated the beneficial effect of the gel in comparison to a hydroalcoholic solution or a gel containing no penetration enhancer.

The release of the peptide from the delivering particles could clearly be demonstrated. In aqueous and ethanolic suspensions, the peptide penetrates significantly deeper into the follicles than the particles. Efficient release of the peptide triggered by the physiological conditions in the hair follicles and its independent diffusion responsible for this outcome. The release effect was less impressive for the gel preparations and especially for the aqueous gel. Using the ethanolic gel preparation, the peptide also penetrated slightly deeper into the hair follicles than the delivering particles, although here the differences were not significant ($p > 0.05$).

Compared to our previous study, the peptide-loaded particles applied in aqueous suspension penetrated less far into the hair follicles than the bare $SiO_2$ particles (234 ± 105 *versus* 524 ± 81 μm). As the application protocol, study conductor, skin model and particle preparation were identical, loading of the particles with the model peptide seems to have an effect. The increased size of the particles due to the coating (40 nm increase in diameter in the dry state but up to 100 nm when swollen in the suspension), and also the state of aggregation, because of the physico-chemical properties of the peptide, may affect the penetration of the particles.

The present study revealed no penetration-enhancing effect of ethanol, neither for the suspension and nor for the gel formulations. Even though ethanol is described as classical penetration enhancer for intercellular penetration, explained with the extraction of lipids from the stratum corneum [8], this might not be applicable to follicular penetration processes. This observation supports our hypothesis of a simple mechanical mechanism for particle transport into the hair follicles.

## 4. CONCLUSION

In conclusion, in addition to the particle size, the loading and the vehicle can also significantly impact the follicular penetration depth of particulate substances. This effect may be related to altered aggregation states of the particles which may indirectly influence particle size and the efficiency of the mechanical transport mechanism.

## ACKNOWLEDGEMENTS

This work was conducted in context of the BMBF-funded project "Topische Vakzinierung mit funktionalen Nanopartikeln". The authors acknowledge that the work was supported by a grant from the German Ministry of Education and Research (BMBF Grant Nos 13N9196, 13N9197, 13N9198).

## CONFLICT OF INTERESTS

The authors declare no conflicts of interests.

## REFERENCES

1. Lademann, J.; Richter, H.; Teichmann, A.; Otberg, N.; Blume-Peytavi, U.; Luengo, J.; Weiss, B.; Schaefer, U.F.; Lehr, C.M.; Wepf, R.; Sterry, W. Nanoparticles - an efficient carrier for drug delivery into the hair follicles. *Eur. J. Pharm. Biopharm.* **2007**, *66*, 159–164.

2. Patzelt, A.; Richter, H.; Knorr, F.; Schaefer, U.; Lehr, C.M.; Daehne, L.; Sterry, W.; Lademann, J. Selective follicular targeting by modification of the particle sizes. *J. Control. Release* **2011**, *150*, 45–48.

3. Mak, W.C.R.H.; Patzelt, A.; Sterry, W.; Lai, K.K.; Renneberg, R.; Lademann, J. Drug delivery into the skin by degradable particles. *Eur. J. Pharm. Biopharm.* **2011**. In Press.

4. Patzelt, A.; Knorr, F.; Blume-Peytavi, U.; Sterry, W.; Lademann, J. Hair follicles, their disorders and their opportunities. *Drug Discov. Today: Dis. Mech.* **2008**, *5*, 173–181.

5. Vogt, A.; Blume-Peytavi, U. Biology of the human hair follicle. New knowledge and the clinical significance. *Hautarzt* **2003**, *54*, 692–698.

6. Vogt, A.; Mandt, N.; Lademann, J.; Schaefer, U.; Blume-Peytavi, U. Follicular targeting - a promising tool in selective dermatotherapy. *J. Investig. Dermatol. Symp. Proc.* **2005**, *10*, 252–255.

7. Lademann, J.; Patzelt, A.; Richter, H.; Antoniou, C.; Sterry, W.; Knorr, F. Determination of the cuticula thickness of human and porcine hairs and their potential influence on the penetration of nanoparticles into the hair follicles. *J. Biomed. Opt.* **2009**, *14*, 021014.

8. Daniels, R.; Knie, U. Galenics of dermal products - vehicles, properties and drug release. *J. Dtsch Dermatol. Ges.* **2007**,*5*, 367–383.

9. Batheja, P.; Sheihet, L.; Kohn, J.; Singer, A.J.; Michniak-Kohn, B. Topical drug delivery by a polymeric nanosphere gel: Formulation optimization and in vitro and in vivo skin distribution studies. *J. Control. Release* **2011**, *149*, 159–167.

10. Jacobi, U.; Kaiser, M.; Toll, R.; Mangelsdorf, S.; Audring, H.; Otberg, N.; Sterry, W.; Lademann, J. Porcine ear skin: an *in vitro* model for human skin. *Skin Res. Technol.* **2007**, *13*, 19–24.

11. Meyer, W.; Schwarz, R.; Neurand, K. The skin of domestic mammals as a model for the human skin, with special reference to the domestic pig. *Curr. Probl. Dermatol.* **1978**, *7*, 39–52.

12. Peyratout, C.S.; Daehne, L. Tailor-made polyelectrolyte microcapsules: from multilayers to smart containers. *Angew. Chem. Int. Ed. Engl.* **2004**, *43*, 3762–3783.

13. Alvarez-Roman, R.; Barre, G.; Guy, R.H.; Fessi, H. Biodegradable polymer nanocapsules containing a sunscreen agent: preparation and photoprotection. *Eur. J. Pharm. Biopharm.* **2001**, *52*, 191–195.

14. Glavas-Dodov, M.; Goracinova, K.; Mladenovska, K.; Fredro-Kumbaradzi, E. Release profile of lidocaine HCl from topical liposomal gel formulation. *Int. J. Pharm.* **2002**, *242*, 381–384.

15. Pople, P.V.; Singh, K.K. Development and evaluation of topical formulation containing solid lipid nanoparticles of vitamin A. *AAPS Pharm. Sci. Tech.* **2006**, *7*, 91.

16. Chen, H.; Chang, X.; Du, D.; Li, J.; Xu, H.; Yang, X. Microemulsion-based hydrogel formulation of ibuprofen for topical delivery. *Int. J. Pharm.* **2006**, *315*, 52–58.

17. Sintov, A.; Serafimovich, S.; Gilhar, A. New topical antiandrogenic formulations can stimulate hair growth in human bald scalp grafted onto mice. *Int. J. Pharm.* **2000**, *194*, 125–134.

# Chapter 11

# Semi-solid Sucrose Stearate-Based Emulsions as Dermal Drug Delivery Systems

**Victoria Klang [1], Julia C. Schwarz [2], Nadejda Matsko [3], Elham Rezvani [4], Nivine El-Hagin [1], Michael Wirth [1] and Claudia Valenta [1,2,*]**

[1]*Department of Pharmaceutical Technology and Biopharmaceutics, Faculty of Life Sciences, University of Vienna, Althanstraße 14, 1090 Vienna, Austria*

[2]*Research Platform "Characterisation of Drug Delivery Systems on Skin and Investigation of Involved Mechanisms", University of Vienna, 1090 Vienna, Austria*

[3]*Institute for Electron Microscopy and Fine Structure Research, Graz University of Technology and Centre for Electron Microscopy Graz, 8010 Graz, Austria*

[4]*Department of Food Sciences and Technology, BOKU-University of Natural Resources and Applied Life Sciences Vienna, 1190 Vienna, Austria*

## ABSTRACT

Mild non-ionic sucrose ester surfactants can be employed to produce lipid-based drug delivery systems for dermal application. Moreover, sucrose esters of intermediate lipophilicity such as sucrose stearate S-970 possess a peculiar rheological behavior which can be employed to create highly viscous semi-solid formulations without any further additives. Interestingly, it was possible to develop both viscous macroemulsions and fluid nanoemulsions with the same chemical composition merely by slight alteration of the production process. Optical light microscopy and cryo transmission electron microscopy (TEM) revealed that the sucrose ester led to the formation of an astonishing hydrophilic network at a concentration of only 5% w/w in the macroemulsion system. A small number of more finely structured aggregates composed of surplus surfactant were likewise detected in the nanoemulsions. These discoveries offer interesting possibilities to adapt the low viscosity of fluid O/W nanoemulsions for a more convenient application. Moreover, a simple and rapid production method for skin-friendly creamy O/W emulsions with excellent visual long-term stability is presented. It could be shown by franz-cell diffusion studies and *in vitro* tape stripping that the microviscosity within the semi-solid formulations was apparently not influenced by their increased macroviscosity: the release of three model drugs was not impaired by the complex network-like internal structure of the macroemulsions. These results indicate that the developed semi-solid emulsions with advantageous application properties are highly suitable for the unhindered delivery of lipophilic drugs despite their comparatively large particle size and high viscosity.

**Keywords:** sucrose stearate S-970; O/W emulsion; semi-solid; nanoemulsion; particle size; skin penetration

## 1. INTRODUCTION

Sucrose fatty acid esters have been known as additives in the fields of nutrition, cosmetics and pharmacy for a long time [1-4]. However, it is only recently that their potential as mild non-ionic surfactants in the production of topical lipid-based drug delivery systems has been investigated more thoroughly. Different sucrose esters of various HLB values have been investigated for their potential to form O/W nanoemulsions [5-7] and to increase [8-10] or retard [11] the skin permeation of incorporated drugs. We have recently demonstrated the superiority of sucrose stearate S-970 over a comparable lecithin mixture to produce highly stable and homogeneous O/W nanoemulsions for dermal application [7]. In this context we found that the employed emulsifier sucrose stearate S-970 exhibited a peculiar rheological behavior when processed in a specific way. The astonishing gel-forming ability of sucrose stearate mixtures of intermediate hydrophilic/lipophilic balance (HLB value) around 9 to 11 has been reported in earlier literature [12,13] as well as recently [11,14,15]. However, no attempt has been made so far to design semi-solid multiphase vehicles which are stabilized in this fashion and can be used for incorporation of lipophilic drugs. The properties of a sucrose stearate/water dispersion were recently investigated [15], but no approach to incorporate additional excipients has been reported. However, incorporation of oil or model drugs may have a significant effect on the gelling properties of the sucrose ester and thus the microstructure of the resulting vehicles. Likewise, the drug release properties of such viscous sucrose ester-stabilized formulations have not been explored yet. Since these aspects are of great practical interest for the development of new formulations, the present work addresses these points.

A simple and skin-friendly sucrose stearate-based O/W emulsion was developed. Optical light microscopy, cryo transmission electron microscopy, rheological investigations and laser diffractometry were employed to characterize the microstructure of the novel system. Three lipophilic model drugs were incorporated and the effect of formulation microstructure and viscosity on the release profile of the system was investigated *in vitro* using franz-type diffusion cells and tape stripping experiments on porcine ears. Since a large particle size and high viscosity of a topically applied formulation are frequently associated with decreased or sustained drug release, we decided to compare the novel systems to corresponding O/W nanoemulsions. Through a slight alteration of the production process and subsequent high-pressure homogenization it was possible to develop fluid O/W nanoemulsions of the exact same composition as the novel macroemulsions and the same content of sucrose stearate, namely 5% (w/w). Microscopic and rheological investigations were performed on these systems as well. Dynamic light scattering and laser Doppler electrophoresis were employed to further characterize the nanoemulsions.

Overall, the aim of the present study was to explore the astonishing gel-forming properties of sucrose stearate S-970 in colloidal multiphase drug delivery systems and to characterize the nature of the resulting semi-solid vehicles. In addition, the drug release profile of these novel O/W emulsions was evaluated by comparing them to fluid nano-sized emulsions of identical chemical composition.

# 2. EXPERIMENTAL SECTION

## 2.1. Materials

Sucrose stearate (Ryoto Sugar Ester® S-970) was supplied by Mitsubishi-Kagaku Food Corporation (Tokyo, Japan). PCL-liquid (cetearyl ethylhexanoate, isopropyl myristate) was purchased from Dr.Temt Laboratories (Vienna, Austria). The preserving agent potassium sorbate was obtained from Herba Chemosan Apotheker-AG (Vienna, Austria). Flufenamic acid (CAS: 530-78-9, Batch No. 1619) and diclofenac acid (CAS: 15307-86-5, Batch No. 080304) were obtained from Kemprotec Limited (Middlesbrough, UK). Curcumin (CAS: 458-37-7, Batch No. 079K1756) was purchased from Sigma Aldrich (St. Louis, USA). Standard Corneofix® adhesive films with a square area of 4.0 $cm^2$ were obtained from Courage + Khazaka GmbH (Cologne, Germany). All further chemicals used were of analytical reagent grade and used without further purification.

## 2.2. Formulations

Different concentrations of 1 to 5% w/w sucrose stearate S-970 were tested for their emulsifying potential in O/W emulsions. An increase in viscosity in dependence of the preparation method had been noticed especially for 5% w/w of sucrose stearate. At surfactant concentrations above 5% w/w, highly viscous creamy emulsions had been obtained irrespective of the preparation method, *i.e.* the emulsion microstructure had been too viscous to pass it through a high-pressure homogenizer even if heated. Therefore, an amount of 5% w/w of sucrose stearate was chosen for the final formulations.

The produced viscous macroscopic emulsions and the corresponding fluid nanoemulsions were identical in their composition, which is given in Table 1.

**Table 1.** Basic composition of macroemulsions (E) and nanoemulsions (NE).

| Excipients | Emulsion composition (% w/w) E = NE |
|---|---|
| PCL-liquid | 20 |
| Sucrose stearate S-970 | 5.0 |
| Potassium sorbate | 0.1 |
| Model drug | 0.5 |
| Distilled water to | 100 |

The preparation of a separate water and oil phase was the same in both cases. The aqueous phase, consisting of freshly distilled water and potassium sorbate, as well as the oil phase, consisting of the cosmetic oil PCL-liquid, were respectively stirred at 50 °C. Blank and drug-loaded formulations were prepared. The lipophilic model drugs flufenamic acid, diclofenac acid and curcumin were respectively dissolved in the oil phase at a concentration of 0.5% (w/w).

In case of the macroemulsions, sucrose stearate S-970 was dissolved in the oil phase. A highly viscous macroemulsion was obtained upon slow admixture of the aqueous phase, further stirring for 10 minutes and subsequent treatment with an ultra-turrax (Omni 500, 2500 rpm, 4 minutes). Refrigerated storage appeared to favor the observed gelling effect.

In case of the nanoemulsions, sucrose stearate S-970 was dissolved in the aqueous phase in order to maintain low viscosity of the system. The oil phase was subsequently added slowly to the aqueous phase for the same reason. The mixture was stirred for further 10 minutes, then pre-homogenized with an ultra-turrax (Omni 500, 2,500 rpm, 4 minutes). The mixture was stirred and heated to 50 °C before homogenization with a high-pressure homogeniser (EmulsiFlex C3, Avestin) for 16 homogenization cycles at 750 bars. Process parameters such as homogenization pressure and homogenization time had been optimized during previous studies [7]. Care was taken to process the mixture under mildly pre-heated conditions to avoid any sudden cooling and associated gelling within the device.

## 2.3. Emulsion Characterization

### 2.3.1. Visual characterization

Both macroemulsions and nanoemulsions were investigated for the presence of structures visible to the eye as well as for their texture and skin feeling.

### 2.3.2. Particle size

The macroemulsions were investigated for their particle size and particle size distribution by laser diffractometry (laser diffraction, static laser light scattering). Measurements were performed in triplicate on a Mastersizer 2000 (Malvern, UK). The instrument was operated with the HydroS 2000 sample dispersion unit (Malvern, UK) and software version 5.60 at 25 °C. The samples were diluted with distilled water (1:1000 v/v) and stirred slightly prior to analysis. All samples were analyzed in triplicate (n = 3). No sonification of the samples was performed prior or during the measurements to avoid the destruction of possible aggregates which may provide information about the microstructure as well as destabilization phenomena [16,17]. Laser diffraction measurements yield volume-weighted diameters as results for droplet sizes up to 2000 µm [16]. The parameters obtained in the present experiments were the d(v, 0.1), d(v, 0.5) and d(v, 0.9). Likewise, the volume weighted mean D [4,3] and the surface weighted mean D [3,2] were obtained. The d(v, 0.5) or volume median diameter marks the size where 50% of the distribution is above and 50% is below this value. The d(v, 0.1) represents the point where 10% of the volume distribution is below this value. In analogy, the d(v, 0.9) marks the point where 90% of the volume distribution is below this value. The d(v, 0.9) can be employed to quantify larger droplets which might be present in the sample such as aggregates formed due to internal processes or destabilization [16]. The volume weighted mean or volume mean diameter D [4,3] corresponds to the mean diameter of spheres with the same volume as the analyzed droplets and is calculated by $d_{4,3} = \sum n_i d_i^4 / \sum n_i d_i^3$, where $n_i$ is the number of particles with diameter $d_i$ [17]. In analogy, the surface weighted mean D [3,2] represents the mean diameter of the spheres with the same surface area as the analyzed droplets. In addition, the span was automatically calculated for all samples. This dimensionless number represents the width of the droplet size distribution based on the 10%, 50% and 90% quantile. A wide particle size distribution will yield a comparatively large span. All parameters were calculated automatically using the Mie theory with a refractive index of 1.52 and a particle absorption value of 0.1. Measurements were conducted immediately after production and after six months of storage time.

The nanoemulsions were investigated for their particle size and particle size distribution by dynamic light scattering (DLS, photon correlation spectroscopy) using a Zetasizer Nano ZS (Malvern, UK) at 25 °C. Samples were diluted with freshly distilled water 1:100 (v/v) to diminish opalescence. The obtained parameters were the hydrodynamic diameter expressed as z-average value of the samples as well as the polydispersity index (PDI). The z-average value is an intensity weighted mean diameter of the bulk population of the sample while the PDI represents the particle size distribution within the formulations. PDI values below 0.2 indicate a narrow size distribution and thus good long-term stability [18]. The approximate measuring range of this instrument is from 3 nm to 3 µm [19]. All samples were analyzed in triplicate (n = 3). Each individual result was automatically calculated as the average of 3 measurements with 20 sub-measurements each. The particle size and PDI of the nanoemulsions were measured immediately after preparation and in regular intervals over a period of six months. In order to detect the presence of potential larger droplets or aggregates, both optical light microscopy and cryo TEM were employed.

### 2.3.3. Particle surface charge (zeta potential)

The particle surface charge of the nanoemulsions was determined by laser Doppler electrophoresis using a Zetasizer Nano ZS (Malvern, UK). The electrophoretic mobility of the droplets was determined and automatically converted into the zeta potential using the Helmholtz-Smoluchowski equation by the Malvern data analysis software [16]. Zeta potential (ZP) values of the formulations were determined at 25 °C. Samples were diluted with distilled water (1:100 v/v) containing sodium chloride (0.01 mmol) in order to ensure constant conductivity below 0.05 ms/cm and thus reproducible measurement conditions [16,18,20]. The ZP roughly characterizes the surface charge of the emulsion droplets in solution. High absolute values above 30 mV lead to repulsive forces between the droplets which may improve the physical stability of multiphase systems [20]. Absolute ZP values above 60 mV indicate excellent electrochemical stability [16]. Zeta potential values were determined in triplicate for all nanoemulsions (n = 3) after production and in regular intervals over six months.

#### 2.3.4. Physical stability

The physical stability of both macroemulsions and nanoemulsions was compared by determination of the particle size after an observation period of six months. All formulations were stored at 4 °C. A visual control was regularly performed to detect any signs of instability. In case of the nanoemulsions, additional control measurements were performed in regular intervals over the whole observation period as well.

### 2.3.5. Drug content, chemical stability and pH value

The drug content of all formulations was analyzed immediately after preparation to ensure appropriate drug incorporation. Briefly, 10 mg of the emulsion were dissolved in 1 mL of methanol, centrifuged for 6 minutes at 12,000 rpm (Hermle Z323K, MIDSCI, USA) and analyzed by HPLC or UV/Vis spectroscopy. Samples were taken at least in triplicate (n ≥ 3). In case of flufenamic acid and diclofenac acid, further samples were taken in regular intervals over three months to obtain a rough overview about the chemical stability of the acidic drugs and their homogeneous dispersion within the systems. Since curcumin is known to undergo a variety of degradation processes which would require more specific methods of analysis, no attempt was made to cover this aspect in the scope of the present work. The obtained data should merely ensure the use of representative and intact formulations for all further studies.

The pH value of the formulations was determined using a pH meter (Orion 420A, Bartelt, Austria). The pH of all formulations was determined at room temperature (25 °C) in regular intervals to detect destabilization phenomena induced by chemical degradation through hydrolysis or oxidation, which result in a decrease of pH [21].

### 2.3.6. Optical light microscopy

Optical light microscopy was employed to obtain an overview about the presence of structures within the micrometer size range, which was especially interesting in the case of the macroemulsion morphology. In case of nanoemulsions, optical light microscopy served as a quality control to ensure the absence of larger structures. The microscopic analysis was carried out using a photo microscope (Zeiss Axio Observer.Z1 microscopy system, Carl Zeiss, Oberkochen, Germany) equipped with phase contrast and differential interference contrast (DIC) and using LD Plan-Neofluar objectives. A small amount of fresh or stored sample of the macroemulsions and nanoemulsions was respectively placed on an object slide, covered and analyzed immediately. Images were taken in conventional bright field mode, with phase contrast and with DIC while 5, 10, 20 and 40-fold magnifications were employed for all samples.

#### 2.3.7. Transmission electron microscopy (TEM): Cryo TEM and negative staining for conventional TEM

The structure of blank macroemulsions and nanoemulsions containing 5% (w/w) sucrose stearate was visualized using cryo TEM. To this end, several vitrified specimens were prepared for each formulation type. In case of the macroemulsion, a fresh glow-discharge copper grid covered with a perforated carbon film was placed on the sample, polished by filter paper in order to remove excess material and immediately plunged into liquid ethane. The macroemulsion samples were observed in an undiluted state so as not to destroy the internal structure. In case of the nanoemulsion, the sample was dissolved in distilled water (1:10 v/v). Subsequently, a 4 µm drop of the solution was placed on a fresh glow-discharge TEM copper grid covered with a perforated carbon film (Pelco International) and blotted with a filter paper to form a thin liquid film of the sample (thickness of 100–250 nm). The thinned sample was plunged into liquid ethane at its freezing temperature (−183 °C) to form a vitrified specimen, and was then transferred to liquid nitrogen (−196 °C) for storage until examination. Vitrified specimens were examined in a Philips T12 transmission electron microscope (Philips) operating at an accelerating voltage of 120 kV using an Oxford CT3500 (Oxford Instruments) cryo holder that maintained the vitrified specimens at −160 °C during sample observation. Images were recorded digitally on a cooled Gatan BioScan CCD camera (Gatan) using the DigitalMicrograph 3.4 software (Gatan) in low-dose imaging mode to minimize beam exposure and electron beam radiation damage.

In addition, conventional TEM analysis was performed for both samples after negative staining with uranyl acetate as previously described [22]. To this end, a carbon coated mesh was hydrophilized by glow discharge and a drop of the respective undiluted emulsion was deposited on the mesh. An aqueous solution of 1% (v/v) of the negative staining agent uranyl acetate was subsequently applied on the mesh to facilitate observation.

### 2.3.8. Rheological characterization

The rheological properties of both macroemulsions and nanoemulsions were investigated. All experiments were performed on a Bohlin CVO Rheometer (Malvern Instruments, UK) with a thermostatic control system (Bohlin KTB30, Malvern, UK). The employed rheometer tools were a thermostatically controlled cone and plate tool with 40 mm in diameter and a 4° angle (CP 4°/40 mm) for the macroemulsions and a coaxial cylinder system with 25 mm in diameter (cup and bob C25) for the nanoemulsions. The temperature for both tools was maintained at 25 ± 0.5 °C throughout all experiments. The applied amount of sample was around 2 g for macroemulsions and around 15 g for nanoemulsions. Both blank and drug-loaded formulations were investigated. All measurements were performed at least in triplicate (n ≥ 3). Values given in figures and tables are the average values.

Flow curves were established for all systems. The flow properties of both blank and drug-loaded macroemulsions and nanoemulsions were investigated by measuring the dynamic viscosity η (in Pa·s) under shear stress. Rheological experiments in a controlled-rate mode were performed. A controlled shear rate $\gamma$ was employed at a constant temperature of 25 ± 0.5 °C to determine the viscosity of the samples as a function of the shear rate ranging from 0.1 $s^{-1}$ to 100 $s^{-1}$. The obtained flow curves of both macroemulsions and nanoemulsions were compared to the power law model (Ostwald model) defined as $\eta = m\ \gamma^{(n-1)}$ where $\eta$ represents the shear viscosity, $m$ equals the consistency coefficient, $\gamma$ represents the shear rate and $n$ is the flow behavior index. Values of n = 1 are indicative for Newtonian fluids while values of n < 1 are representative for shear-thinning, *i.e.* pseudoplastic fluids. Values of n > 1 are found for shear-thickening dilatant fluids [23,24].

Moreover, oscillatory shear experiments were performed for all systems. In the oscillatory mode, a sinusoidal stress is applied to the sample and the response in form of the induced strain is measured [25,26]. To this end, the rheometer tool is moved forward and backward in a defined sinusoidal motion. After identification of the linear viscoelastic region the samples were investigated over a frequency of 1–10 Hz. Crucial parameters were determined as a function of the oscillatory frequency ($v$, in Hz). The parameters obtained in this fashion are the elastic modulus G′, the viscous modulus G″, the complex modulus G* and the dynamic viscosity $\eta'$.

The elastic modulus or storage modulus G′ is defined as G′ = G* cos (δ) and describes the recoverable energy that is stored within an elastic system. The viscous modulus or loss modulus G″ is calculated by G″ = G* sin (δ) and represents the energy that is dissipated in the viscous flow and transformed into heat. These moduli represent the real and imaginary parts of the complex dynamic shear modulus G* [25–27]. The dynamic viscosity $\eta'$ is defined as $\eta' = G''/\omega$, where ω is the angular velocity of the oscillatory stress which is in turn related to the oscillatory frequency by the relationship $\omega=2\pi v$. The related phase angle is expressed as δ [25,26].

## 2.4. Skin permeation experiments using franz-type diffusion cells

*In vitro* skin permeation studies were performed using standard franz-type diffusion cells (Permegear, USA). Thus, the potential influence of the different formulation properties of macroemulsions and nanoemulsions on the skin permeation of the three model drugs flufenamic acid, diclofenac acid and curcumin was investigated. Porcine abdominal skin was chosen as model membrane because of its morphology and permeability, which are similar to those of human skin [9,28]. The porcine abdominal skin was freed from hair and treated with a dermatome (GB 228R, Aesculap) set at 1.2 mm. The skin was stored at −20 °C until use and thawed prior to the experiments. Appropriate skin patches were clamped between the donor and the receptor chamber of the diffusion cells having a permeation area of 1.13 $cm^2$. The receptor compartment was filled with 2 mL of phosphate buffer (pH 7.4, 0.012M) in case of flufenamic acid and diclofenac acid [29]. In case of curcumin, a mixture of distilled water/ethanol (50/50 % v/v) was employed to ensure sink conditions [30,31]. The diffusion cells were kept at skin surface temperature (32 °C) and stirred with magnetic bars for 24 hours. The formulation (0.6 g) was placed on the excised skin in the donor chamber. Samples of 200 µL were removed at defined time intervals for analysis and were replaced by fresh receptor medium. At least five parallel experiments were performed for each formulation ($n > 5$). The samples were analyzed for their drug content by HPLC in case of flufenamic acid and diclofenac acid or by UV/Vis spectroscopy in case of curcumin. Permeation profiles of the drugs were constructed by plotting time (hours) against the cumulative amount of the drug (µg/$cm^2$) as measured in the receptor solution. In addition, the steady state flux (J, $\mu g \cdot cm^{-2} \cdot h^{-1}$) was calculated by linear regression after the respective lag-times.

## 2.5. Skin penetration experiments via in vitro tape stripping

In order to obtain penetration profiles of the three model drugs from both macroemulsions and corresponding nanoemulsions at least six individual tape-stripping experiments were performed for each formulation ($n \geq 6$) on porcine ear skin. Fresh porcine ears were donated by the Clinic for Swine, University of Veterinary Medicine, Vienna. Since previous studies had shown that frozen storage does not alter the skin barrier function or the stratum corneum properties in the context of tape stripping experiments [32,33], the ears were stored at −24 °C and thawed prior to the respective experiments. After defrosting, the ears were cleaned carefully with purified water and blotted dry with soft tissue. The skin was subsequently freed from hair with scissors and intact, representative skin areas were indicated with a permanent marker. In addition, the transepidermal water loss (TEWL) of the skin was determined using the closed-chamber device AquaFlux® (Biox Ltd., London, UK) to confirm an intact skin barrier function and to monitor the defrosting process [33]. The software program AquaFlux® V6.2 was used for analysis of these data. When the TEWL reached values between 15 and 20 g $m^{-2}$ $h^{-1}$ the experiment was started. To this end, the porcine ears were stretched out on styrofoam plates and fixed with needles if necessary. The respective formulation was applied onto the marked skin area at a concentration of 6 mg·$cm^{-2}$ with a saturated vinyl glove finger and was gently distributed and massaged for 30 seconds. After a penetration time of 1 hour the tape stripping procedure was started.

The adhesive films employed to remove the superficial stratum corneum layers were standard Corneofix® tapes. Care was taken to ensure a reproducible working procedure. After placing the first adhesive film on the skin its outline was indicated with a permanent marker to ensure subsequent tape stripping on the exact same location. Pressure was applied with the thumb covered in a vinyl glove as previously reported [34] to ensure a rolling movement and thus minimize the influence of wrinkles [35]. The experiment was performed on a balance to ensure a constant pressure of 49 N (5 kg) which is a prerequisite for the removal of reproducible amounts of stratum corneum proteins [33]. After applying pressure for 3 seconds, the tape was removed in a single rapid movement. In this fashion, 20 sequential adhesive films were removed per experiment. The amount of adherent corneocytes was subsequently determined by IR-densitometry using the infrared densitometer SquameScan™ 850A (Heiland electronic GmbH, Wetzlar, Germany) [36]. Briefly, the optical pseudo-absorption of the adhesive films at a wavelength of 850 nm is employed to quantify the amount of stratum corneum proteins on the tapes. The absorption values in % can be read from the display and the corresponding mass of proteins can be determined using the correlation factor of 0.41 which was previously established for analysis of porcine ear skin [33]. This value can be employed to calculate the mass of SC proteins (*m*) after determination of their pseudo-absorption at 850 nm (*A*) for a normalized tape area of 1 $cm^2$ by employing the equation m = A/0.41 (in $\mu g \cdot cm^{-2}$).

The mean cumulative amount of removed stratum corneum proteins was employed to establish the penetration depth of the applied drugs in relation to the complete stratum corneum thickness. The latter was determined by continuous stripping of the complete stratum corneum in four of the experiments (n = 4) until the detection limit of the IR-densitometer was reached.

## 2.6. HPLC analysis

The formulations or samples containing flufenamic acid or diclofenac acid were analyzed for their drug content by HPLC (Series ISS-200, Perkin Elmer, USA), consisting of an auto sampler, a lc pump and an UV-diode array detector (235C). Previously reported methods were used using a Nucleosil 100-5 C18 column (250 mm × 4 mm, Macherey-Nagel, USA) plus a Nucleosil 100-5 C18 pre-column (CC8/4, 40 mm × 4 mm, Macherey-Nagel, USA). For all analyses, the oven temperature was set at 50 °C and the injection volume was 20 µL. The analysis of the data was performed using the TotalChrom Navigator 6.2.0 software. Standard solutions of the drugs were prepared and calibration curves were calculated by plotting the analyzed drug concentrations against the obtained peak area values.

The quantification of flufenamic acid and diclofenac acid was conducted according to previously described methods [29,37]. For both drugs, the mobile phase consisted of methanol/water (75/25 w/w); glacial acetic acid was added until a pH value of 3.2 was reached. The flow rate was 1.0 mL/min in both cases. For flufenamic acid, the detection wavelength was set at 245 nm with a retention time of 4.5 minutes. A calibration curve was calculated based on peak area measurements of diluted standard solutions ranging from 0.09 µg/mL to 110.50 µg/mL with a coefficient of determination $R^2$ = 0.9999. The limit of detection for flufenamic acid was found to be around 0.04 µg/mL; the limit of reasonable quantification was set at 0.09 µg/mL. For diclofenac acid, the detection wavelength was set at

280 nm with a retention time of 10 minutes. The measurement range of the diluted standard solutions employed for the calibration curve was between 0.06 µg/mL and 28.97 µg/mL with $R^2 = 1$. The limit of detection for diclofenac acid was, likewise, around 0.04 µg/mL; the limit of quantification was set at 0.06 µg/mL.

### 2.7. UV/VIS spectroscopic analysis

The quantification of curcumin was performed as previously reported [30] using a double beam UV/Vis spectrophotometer (Spectrophotometer U-3010, Hitachi, Japan). A correlation curve was established for standard solutions of curcumin in pure ethanol (96% v/v) ranging from 0.31 µg/mL to 5.01 µg/mL with $R^2 = 0.9952$. The curcumin content of the samples filled into quartz cuvettes was determined at 425 nm. Samples containing a higher curcumin content were diluted prior to the analysis until values within the linear range of the calibration curve were obtained. This was frequently the case for samples extracted from the first two adhesive films of the tape stripping experiments.

### 2.8. Statistical data analysis

Results are expressed as means of at least three experiments ± SD. Statistical data analyses were performed with the software program GraphPadPrism3. Parametric data were analyzed using the Student's t-test with $P < 0.05$ as minimum level of significance while non-parametric data were analyzed using the Mann-Whitney test or the Wilcoxon signed rank test with $P < 0.05$, respectively.

## 3. RESULTS AND DISCUSSION

### 3.1. Formulations and production aspects

The optimal surfactant concentration to produce both highly viscous macroemulsions and fluid nanoemulsions was found to be 5% w/w. Despite the increasing viscosity, considerate sample preparation still allowed for high-pressure homogenization of the mixture in case of the anoemulsions. Thus, the physicochemical properties of emulsions stabilized by 5% w/w of sucrose stearate could be varied by modification of the production process.

As anticipated, conductivity measurements confirmed the nature of the obtained emulsions as being of the O/W type. The temperature seemed to play a crucial role during processing of the sucrose stearate-based emulsions. If the fluid mixture was kept at 40–50 °C, further homogenization was feasible. If the mixture was cooled, some sort of gelling effect took hold and transformed the system into a semi-solid emulsion. This was especially pronounced if the mixture was cooled down rapidly. Similar behavior has been reported for aqueous sucrose stearate dispersions [15]. Moreover, the different ways of emulsion preparation as described in the literature [22] may have had an additional influence on the properties of the resulting mixture and thus either allowed for further high-energy processing or not. The variation in the mixing protocol of the compounds apparently influenced the viscosity of the pre-emulsion, which plays an important role for later processing [19].

### 3.2. Visual characterization

Creamy, thick macroemulsions were produced by dissolving the sucrose ester in the oil phase. The low density of the emulsions suggested that large amounts of air were incorporated to provide a fluffy appearance. All formulations had an appealing, homogeneous appearance which was retained over the whole observation period.

In contrast, fluid if slightly gel-like nanoemulsions were produced by dissolving the surfactant in the aqueous phase and subsequent high-pressure homogenization. Figure 1 shows the visual appearance of the viscous macroscopic emulsions in contrast to the fluid nanoemulsions. Upon closer inspection, small white aggregates could be detected in the otherwise homogeneous whitish to bluish nanoemulsions. These were most likely composed of surfactant aggregates formed during or after high-pressure homogenization and can be ascribed to the comparatively high surfactant concentration as opposed to our previous studies [7]. These structures did however not impair the performance or physical stability of the formulations in any way. Upon cooled storage at 4 °C, they appeared to contribute to the increasingly gel-like texture of the nanoemulsions. Indeed, low storages temperatures have previously been reported to cause gelation of nanoemulsions of certain compositions [38].

**Figure 1.** Visual appearance of a sucrose stearate-based macroemulsion (E) and a corresponding nanoemulsion (NE). Age of the presented formulations: 9 months.

### 3.3. Particle size

In case of the macroemulsions, the mean particle sizes were in the micrometer range as shown in Table 2A and 2B.

All parameters of importance are given, namely the D [4,3], D [3,2], d(v, 0.1), d(v, 0.5) and d(v, 0.9) values as well as the span. The span, which describes the width of the particle size distribution, was comparatively large for both blank and drug-loaded formulations. This indicates that various emulsion droplet sizes, ranging from the nanometer up to the micrometer scale, were present in the mixture. This could also be derived from a visual observation of the obtained distribution curves, which indicated a highly polydisperse nature of the samples with droplet sizes ranging from 0.7 up to several hundred micrometers. This was especially pronounced after 6 months of storage. In particular the strong increase in d(v, 0.9) values points to a small population of increasingly large individual droplets.

**Table 2.** Physicochemical properties of fresh **(2A)** and stored **(2B)** blank and drug-loaded macroemulsions (E) after high-shear dispersion with an ultra-turrax. Measurements were performed in triplicate on a Mastersizer 2000 (Malvern, UK) at 25 °C. The samples were diluted with distilled water (1:1000 v/v) and stirred slightly prior to analysis. The parameters shown are the mean particle size expressed as volume weighted mean D [4,3], surface weighted mean D [3,2] and volume median diameter d(0.5) as well as the d(0.1) and d(0.9) values and the span. All values represent the mean of three formulations (n = 3) in µm and are given ± SD.

| **(2A) Freshly prepared samples** | | | | |
|---|---|---|---|---|
| *Parameters* | E blank | E curc | E fluf | E diclo |
| D [4.3] | 06.94 ± 0.97 | 09.72 ± 1.92 | 08.56 ± 0.05 | 11.80 ± 0.42 |
| D [3.2] | 03.70 ± 0.15 | 04.14 ± 0.04 | 04.46 ± 0.02 | 05.43 ± 0.36 |
| d (v, 0.1) | 01.74 ± 0.04 | 01.73 ± 0.01 | 01.72 ± 0.01 | 02.04 ± 0.16 |
| d (v, 0.5) | 05.16 ± 0.26 | 06.80 ± 0.07 | 08.26 ± 0.04 | 11.29 ± 0.45 |
| d (v, 0.9) | 12.58 ± 2.25 | 14.55 ± 0.41 | 15.44 ± 0.09 | 22.09 ± 0.42 |
| Span | 02.09 ± 0.31 | 01.89 ± 0.04 | 01.66 ± 0.01 | 01.78 ± 0.05 |
| **(2B) After 6 months of storage** | | | | |
| *Parameters* | E blank | E curc | E fluf | E diclo |
| D [4.3] | 25.81 ± 2.44 | 26.46 ± 08.27 | 35.33 ± 2.35 | 33.03 ± 3.89 |
| D [3.2] | 08.71 ± 0.38 | 06.57 ± 00.72 | 11.25 ± 0.88 | 08.79 ± 0.41 |
| d (v, 0.1) | 04.18 ± 0.25 | 02.56 ± 00.25 | 06.88 ± 0.65 | 03.41 ± 0.18 |
| d (v, 0.5) | 20.04 ± 2.29 | 13.41 ± 02.57 | 21.53 ± 1.49 | 23.54 ± 1.57 |
| d (v, 0.9) | 55.31 ± 5.96 | 49.66 ± 16.30 | 77.37 ± 3.01 | 73.61 ± 6.74 |
| Span | 02.55 ± 0.05 | 03.45 ± 00.51 | 03.28 ± 0.13 | 02.98 ± 0.08 |

Since the samples were diluted prior the measurements, it is unclear whether these data merely give an overview about the oil droplet size distribution within the emulsion, or also about remnants of the hydrophilic network which provides the basis for the high viscosity of the systems. Likewise, since the results obtained with this technique are volume-based, the presence of a few individual larger droplets may skew the correlation considerably since the presence of very small droplets may easily be outweighed by the far more voluminous larger droplets. Thus, an additional microscopic analysis was performed.

In case of the nanoemulsions, the mean particle sizes as determined by DLS were in the lower submicron range for both blank and drug-loaded formulations (Table 3).

**Table 3.** Physicochemical properties of blank and drug-loaded nanoemulsions (NE) after 16 cycles of high-pressure homogenization. Measurements were performed in triplicate on a Zetasizer Nano ZS (Malvern, UK) at 25 °C. Samples were diluted with distilled water (1:100 v/v) containing sodium chloride (0.01 mmol) before the experiments to ensure constant conductivity below 0.05 ms/cm. Parameters shown are mean particle size (MPS), zeta potential (ZP), conductivity (cond) and polydispersity index (PDI). Values represent the mean of at least three formulations (n ≥ 3) and are given ± SD.

| *Parameters* | **NE blank** | **NE curc** | **NE fluf** | **NE diclo** |
|---|---|---|---|---|
| Particle size (nm) | 116.40 ± 10.22 | 124.69 ± 2.58 | 128.33 ± 11.34 | 114.44 ± 2.42 |
| Zeta potential (mV) | −58.89 ± 14.48 | −47.11 ± 1.49 | −51.36 ± 2.71 | −54.12 ± 4.83 |
| Conductivity (mS/cm) | 0.024 ± 0.005 | 0.017 ± 0.004 | 0.025 ± 0.005 | 0.023 ± 0.003 |
| PDI | 0.11 ± 0.03 | 0.25 ± 0.03 | 0.09 ± 0.01 | 0.11 ± 0.02 |

The narrow intensity-based distribution curves indicated a monodisperse nature of the samples. The PDI values were below 0.2 except for curcumin-loaded formulations, which indicates a narrow droplet size distribution and thus good long-term stability. Individual whitish aggregates detected among visual inspection were not detected with these measurements since they were most likely dissolved upon dilution of the samples. It is likewise known that DLS alone may fail to detect the presence of individual larger oil droplets or vesicles and may thus provide incomplete information [39]. Therefore, as for the macroemulsions, an emphasis was placed on microscopic examination techniques to obtain more accurate information about the actual microstructure of the formulations.

In context with the DLS measurements it has to be mentioned that the highly lipophilic drug curcumin was rather dispersed than dissolved within the oil phase. The presence of undissolved drug did not disturb the particle size measurements, as previously reported [40]. Merely a slight increase of the PDI value was noticed. Homogeneous distribution of the drug could be obtained after rehomogenization of the system by slight shaking. In case of the corresponding macroemulsions with curcumin the drug was homogeneously distributed within the system and no dispersed drug aggregates were visible within the homogeneous orange emulsion.

Overall, the droplet size in equilibrated emulsions is mainly determined by the intensity of mechanical agitation, the amount and interfacial properties of the surfactants, the interfacial tension and the physical properties of the oil and aqueous phases [17,41]. The properties of an emulsion will change significantly with the type of emulsification process used [41], as was impressively demonstrated in the present study. Thus, care should be taken to ensure an exact mixing procedure, since any irregularity may lead to changes in formulation microstructure.

### 3.4. Particle surface charge of nanoemulsions

The ZP values of blank and drug-loaded nanoemulsions are given in Table 3. The surface charge of sucrose stearate-based nanoemulsions was in the range around −50 to −60 mV, which indicates high electrochemical stabilization of the system. These high negative values are most likely caused by the presence of residual free fatty acids at the interface [7].

### 3.5. Physical stability

The physical long-term stability of all systems was highly satisfying. As anticipated in case of the macroemulsions, a notable increase in mean particle size after six months was observed (Figure 2A). However, the formulation remained visually stable and showed no signs of phase separation or microbial contamination upon conventional storage at 4 °C in a receptacle for ointments.

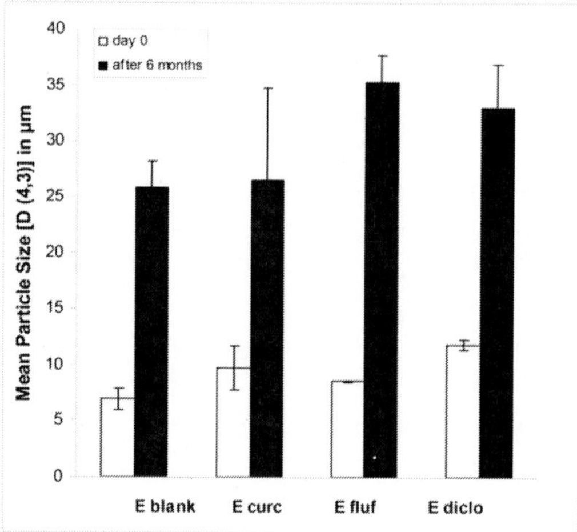


**(2A)**

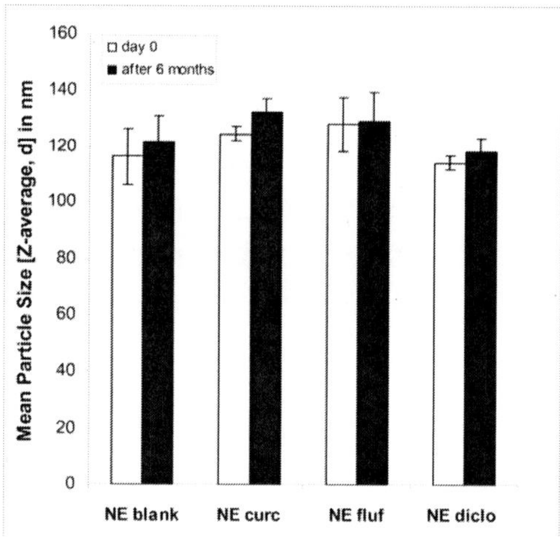


**(2B)**

**Figure 2.** Mean droplet size of blank and drug-loaded macroemulsions (E, **2A**) and corresponding nanoemulsions (NE, **2B**) as determined immediately after production and after 6 months. The diluted samples were analyzed in triplicate at 25 °C on a Mastersizer 2000 (Malvern, UK) in case of the macroemulsions and a Zetasizer Nano ZS (Malvern, UK) in case of the nanoemulsions. The parameters shown are the volume weighted mean D [4,3] for macroemulsions and the mean droplet diameter as z-average for nanoemulsions. Values represent the mean of at least three formulations ($n \geq 3$) and are given ± SD.

In case of the nanoemulsions (Figure 2B), the mean particle sizes remained highly constant in the course of six months as confirmed by regular measurements.

As can be seen in Table 4, this was the case for both blank and drug-loaded nanoemulsions, shown on representative formulations containing flufenamic acid. The mean ZP values of the nanoemulsions increased slightly (Table 4A and 4B), most likely due to chemical changes within the formulations such as hydrolysis of surfactant molecules or excipients of the oil phase. This process results in the release of free fatty acids and thus an increased amount of negative charges at the interface. Since a certain surplus of surfactant was employed, the chemical degradation of the latter may have been more apparent than in our previous studies [7]. At the same time, this surplus of surfactant might be responsible for the individual whitish aggregates that were observed within the nanoemulsions. The number of these aggregates visible to the eye increased over time.

In summary, particle size measurements of submicron-sized emulsions by light scattering techniques are not always sufficient to monitor the actual physical stability of such formulations. Visible destabilization phenomena such as separation of oil droplets or formation of a precipitate might remain undetected [40]. Thus, carefully visual inspection of the samples is necessary. Additional and more precise information can be gained by microscopic investigations.

## 3.6. Drug content, chemical stability and pH value

The initially determined drug contents of all formulations as well as the chemical stability of flufenamic acid and diclofenac acid remained satisfying over the course of a limited observation period of three months. No further attention was devoted to this topic since a more thorough analysis of the chemical stability of the incorporated drugs, especially in case of curcumin, was not an emphasis of this study.

**Table 4.** Physical stability of blank **(4A)** and drug-loaded nanoemulsions (**4B**, shown on systems containing flufenamic acid). Similar results were obtained for all drug-loaded formulations. Experiments were performed in triplicate (n = 3) in regular intervals over an observation period of six months. The indicated parameters are the mean particle size (MPS), polydispersity index (PDI) and zeta potential (ZP). Numbers are given as means ± SD.

**(4A)**

| time (weeks) | **NE blank** MPS (nm) ± SD | PDI ± SD | ZP (mV) ± SD |
|---|---|---|---|
| 0 | 116.40 ± 10.22 | 0.11 ± 0.03 | −61.73 ± 10.50 |
| 4 | 116.07 ± 09.93 | 0.12 ± 0.03 | −64.13 ± 07.10 |
| 8 | 116.53 ± 08.56 | 0.13 ± 0.02 | −60.91 ± 04.08 |
| 12 | 118.31 ± 08.28 | 0.12 ± 0.02 | −61.27 ± 16.41 |
| 16 | 117.28 ± 08.05 | 0.13 ± 0.01 | −60.70 ± 06.09 |
| 20 | 120.11 ± 08.93 | 0.13 ± 0.02 | −64.69 ± 04.00 |
| 24 | 121.71 ± 09.61 | 0.15 ± 0.04 | −64.76 ± 06.03 |

**(4B)**

| time (weeks) | **NE fluf** MPS (nm) ± SD | PDI ± SD | ZP (mV) ± SD |
|---|---|---|---|
| 0 | 128.28 ± 09.61 | 0.09 ± 0.01 | −49.03 ± 00.37 |
| 4 | 128.01 ± 10.01 | 0.10 ± 0.01 | −49.86 ± 02.05 |
| 8 | 125.06 ± 10.06 | 0.10 ± 0.01 | −49.73 ± 04.38 |
| 12 | 126.55 ± 09.16 | 0.09 ± 0.01 | −50.77 ± 04.64 |
| 16 | 129.94 ± 10.47 | 0.09 ± 0.01 | −52.16 ± 05.13 |
| 20 | 132.92 ± 11.46 | 0.09 ± 0.02 | −48.38 ± 02.13 |
| 24 | 129.12 ± 10.78 | 0.08 ± 0.01 | −55.20± 04.40 |

The pH values of blank formulations were around 6.80 ± 0.04 for macroemulsions and 6.89 ± 0.01 for nanoemulsions (n = 3, respectively). Drug incorporation led to slightly lower pH values in case of flufenamic acid and diclofenac acid (data not shown). However, all pH values were in an acceptable range for dermal application.

Interestingly, chemical degradation processes appeared to affect the nanoemulsions to a greater extent than the corresponding macroemulsions irrespective of drug incorporation. After a storage time of 6 months, the overall mean pH value of all formulations was 6.40 ± 0.20 in case of the macroemulsions and 6.01 ± 0.11 in case of the nanoemulsions (n = 13, respectively). This observation is in agreement with previously reported data which indicate that lipid oxidation in nanoemulsions proceeds more rapidly than in conventional emulsions due to the increased surface area of the nano-sized droplets [17].

### 3.7. Optical light microscopy

Optical light microscopy was conducted to obtain an overview about larger structures present in the different formulations. The images were in good agreement with the visual observations of the samples as well as the particle size measurements.

In case of freshly prepared blank macroemulsions a complex network of hydrophilic spherical structures presumably composed of sucrose ester/water aggregates was observed (Figure 3A to 3C). Large spherical interconnected aggregates formed a net-like structure which surrounded the darker oil droplets. In between the large "meshes" of this network, smaller spherical aqueous structures were observed which filled up the space. Likewise, it may be assumed that large amounts of air are incorporated as well. Overall, the particle sizes observed for the different surfactant aggregates varied from around 30 µm for the large network-forming structures down to 0.6 µm for the smaller aggregates filling up the spaces in between. The oil droplets were of variable size and their diameter ranged mostly within the micrometer range, as already indicated by the laser diffraction measurements. Although these particle size measurements were conducted with highly diluted samples, it is unclear whether the sucrose ester aggregates were included in the analysis. If this was the case, it would account for the high polydispersity of the analyzed samples. Particle sizes as small as 600 nm have likewise been reported for the structural compounds of aqueous gel-like dispersions of sucrose stearate [15]. However, the values reported by Ullrich and co-workers were based on DLS analysis of highly polydisperse and undiluted samples, which renders an interpretation difficult.

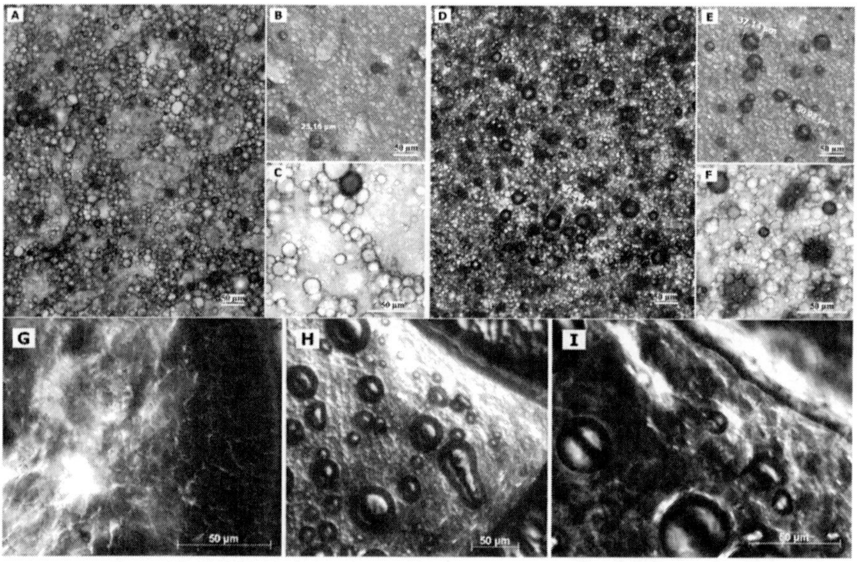


**Figure 3.** Images of fresh as well as stored macroemulsions as observed by optical light microscopy. Images **3A, 3B and 3C** show a blank macroemulsion directly after preparation while the corresponding images **3D, 3E and 3F** show the same formulation after 6 months of storage. The employed microscopic modes were 10× magnification/bright field (3A, 3D), 20× magnification/DIC (3B, 3E and 3G, 3H, 3I) and 40× magnification/bright field (3C, 3F). The indicated scale bars represent 50 µm. Images **3G, 3H and 3I** represent artefacts of fresh macroemulsions obtained after 20 minutes of storage of the object slide.

Interestingly, the nature of the viscous macroemulsions changed upon storage. Images that were taken after a storage time of over 6 months revealed an increasingly dense aggregate network with less free space between the aggregate "meshes" of the network (Figure 3D to 3F). This increase in density of the network might have been caused by a minor separation of water condensation on the lid of the storage receptacle. Likewise, the influence of gravity might have caused incorporated air to escape from the emulsion bulk phase. As anticipated by particle size measurements, the average size of the dispersed oil droplets showed a definite increase with oil droplet diameters frequently larger than 30 µm. Individual oil droplets of up to 160 µm in diameter were observed as well. It may be assumed that the presence of such individual large droplets remained undetected in the laser diffraction measurements due to methodological limitations [42]. Despite this obvious change in the internal formulation structure, the visual appearance of the semi-solid vehicles remained intact.

Interesting additional information was gained from observation of changes in formulation microstructure upon manipulation on an object plate. After prolonged presence of the macroemulsions on the object plate, a dried network became visible which covered the dried out area around residual water droplets (Figure 3G). In addition, the potential of the sucrose ester mixture to form liquid crystalline structures became more apparent as increasingly large areas, also along the dried network structure, showed birefringence under polarized light (Figure 3G, 3H, 3I). These observations indicate that the network structure of the viscous formulation might be at the margin of a weak liquid crystalline matrix.

Overall, the observed network of unilamellar vesicles bears a certain resemblance to a cubic gel phase observed in previous studies [43,44]. Despite the apparent differences in formulation composition and size range when compared to our macroemulsions, similar general observations were reported. A system of high viscosity was obtained with no other compounds than a dispersed phase fraction of 5–15% w/w. The vesicular unilamellar spheres responsible for the system's properties consisted of amphiphilic material only. Dilution of the gel phase led to the formation of a viscous, but not gel-like phase which was unfortunately not further characterized. The fact that the macroemulsion structure is not as ordered as the cubic gel structure might be due to the fact that much larger amounts of water and less surfactant are present. Our system might thus be comparable to the described diluted cubic phase system. Another explanation might point to a resemblance to self-standing gel-like emulsions. However, larger amounts of internal phase are usually reported for such systems [45].

In case of the freshly prepared nanoemulsion (Figure 4A), constant background movement indicated the presence of nano-sized oil droplets subjected to Brownian motion [22]. The samples were highly homogeneous except for a few larger vesicular structures and individual surfactant aggregates. These structures which were visible to the naked eye as whitish flakes appeared as irregularly shaped "islands" within the formulation. However, their number was highly limited after production. These aggregates remained undetected during the DLS measurements of the diluted samples.

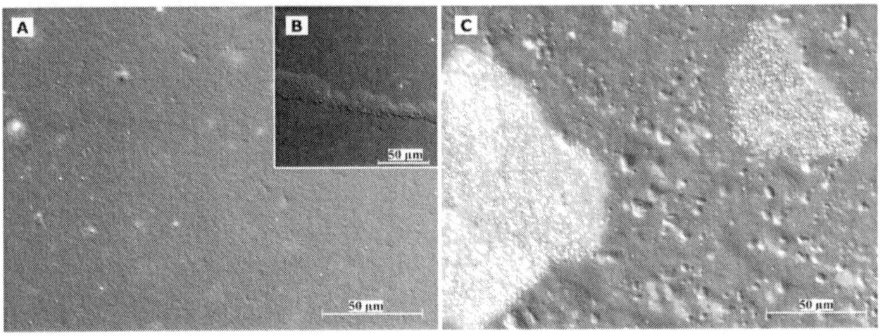


**Figure 4.** Images of fresh, as well as stored, nanoemulsions as observed by optical light microscopy. All images were taken with 40 × magnification/DIC. Image **4A**shows the blank nanoemulsion directly after preparation. Figure **4C** shows the same formulation after 6 months of storage. Image **4B** shows an artefact obtained with a fresh nanoemulsion sample due to evaporation effects on the object slide. The indicated scale bars represent 50 µm.

The nature of the fluid nanoemulsions changed upon storage. Images that were taken of samples after 6 months of storage time (Figure 4C) revealed a much larger number of the described shapeless aggregates. It may be assumed that these aggregates represent separated fractions of surplus sucrose ester. For blank nanoemulsions, the viscosity of the sample appeared to be increased as compared to the fresh one due to gelling effects of the surfactant. No such gelling effect upon storage was observed for the more fluid nanoemulsions with flufenamic acid and diclofenac acid. This aspect is currently being investigated in rheological studies over prolonged observation periods and will be reported in a separate context. Overall, nanoemulsions apparently suffered notable changes in formulation microstructure despite the fact that the particle size measurements suggested otherwise.

Again, observation of the sample's behavior on the object plate provided useful information. The nanoemulsion droplet started gelling immediately upon application on the plate. After covering of the sample, a structured dispersed film remained at the edges of the droplet (Figure 4B). Again, this rather ordered structural network may be situated at the margin of a weak liquid crystalline network [15]. Similar behavior can be observed upon positioning of a microemulsion on an object plate, where growth of liquid crystals can be observed at the margin of the sample due to evaporation of volatile compounds.

Although the peculiar rheological behavior of colloidal sucrose ester suspensions in water has recently attracted attention [11,14], the microstructure of these systems is still somewhat unclear [15]. Microscopic data exists mostly for suspensions with higher concentrations of sugar surfactant, which consequently contain increasing amount of liquid crystalline structures [13]. Interestingly, for a suspension of another sucrose stearate mixture with a slightly higher HLB value of 12, liquid crystalline structures were already observed at a concentration of 4% w/w [46]. Although information on the structure of O/W emulsions co-stabilized by alkylpolyglucosides, a frequently employed type of sugar surfactant, can be found [47], no such data exist for O/W emulsions stabilized by a sucrose ester mixture alone.

### 3.8. Cryo TEM and TEM after negative staining

Cryo TEM investigations of freshly prepared formulations were additionally performed to visualize the structural differences between the two original systems on a nano-scale level. In case of the macroemulsion (Figure 5A), a dense structural network was observed which appeared to consist of closely located or connected spherical aggregates with mean diameters as small as a few hundred nanometers (marked areas). These aggregates formed the larger droplets which had been visualised by light microscopy. Since the sample was observed in its original state without dilution and the TEM image is merely a 2D projection, the borders of the smaller aggregates could not be clearly distinguished. However, the images serve to confirm the rich internal structure of the macroemulsion. The structural network appeared to be remarkably homogeneous, since the ice crystals commonly observed during cryo-preparation emerged in a highly ordered and regular fashion. Additional analysis with conventional TEM sample preparation and negative staining confirmed these observations (Figure 5B). Droplets of various sizes could be distinguished.

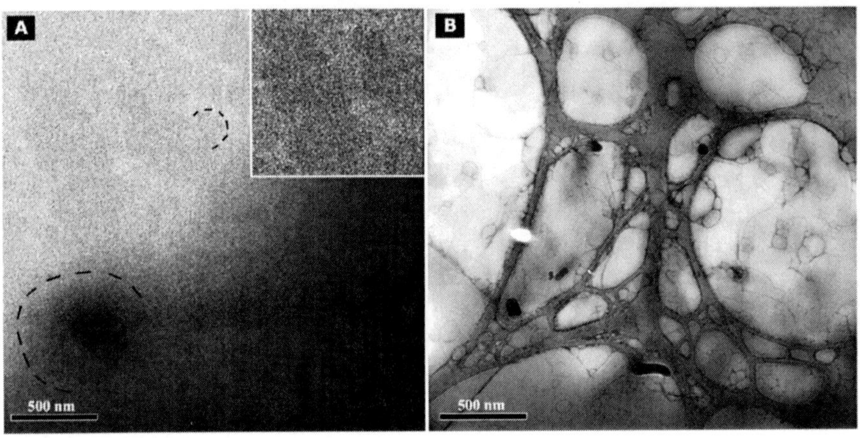


**Figure 5.** Analysis of the microstructure of blank macroemulsions by cryo TEM **(5A)**and conventional TEM after negative staining with uranyl acetate **(5B)**. The magnification is illustrated by the black scale bars.

In case of the nanoemulsion, a common if highly crowded internal structure was revealed despite the dilution of the sample (Figure 6A). The nano-sized oil droplets appeared to be partially deformed or collapsed, which is not entirely unexpected given the high surfactant concentration and resulting high viscosity of the formulation. Likewise, the shape of the deformable nanodroplets can be influenced by the oil volume fraction [48]. At high oil volume fractions, the surfaces of the crowded droplets strongly repel each other. This can cause the droplets to deform and become non-spherical [49]. In addition, individual shapeless aggregates most likely composed of sucrose stearate/water were detected in the nanoemulsion sample, which confirmed the optical light microscopy data. The rheological properties of the sample influence the processing conditions during high-pressure homogenization. The equilibrium between the rupturing of oil droplets and coalescence events which occur within the device are governed by the viscosity of the processed colloidal system [50,51]. In terms of viscosity, the employed pre-homogenized mixture surely resides at the margin of the device's working capacity. The surplus of surfactant which is subjected to the high-pressure homogenization procedure is apparently united in the described shapeless aggregates. Conventional TEM analysis after negative staining confirmed the above observations (Figure 6B). A noteworthy observation regarding the conventional TEM analysis is the fact that a largely intact emulsion structure could be visualized despite the high vacuum and the potential risk of beam damage imminent to this technique. This aspect will be the subject of further investigations.

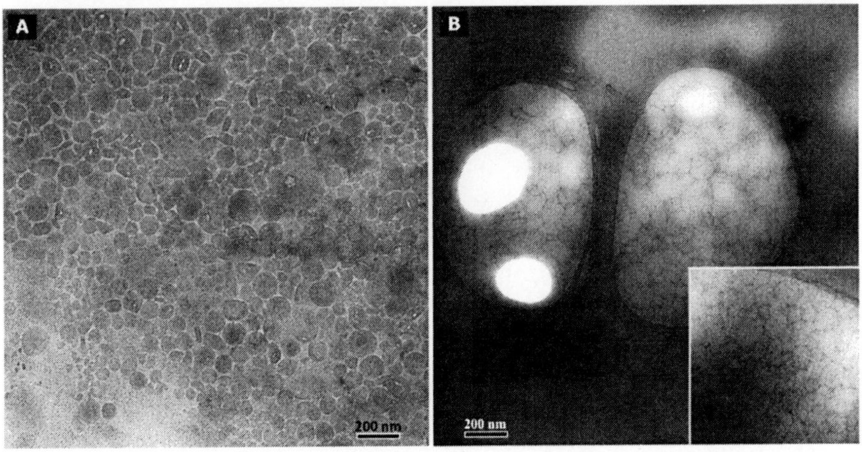


**Figure 6.** Analysis of the microstructure of blank nanoemulsions by cryo TEM **(6A)**and conventional TEM after negative staining with uranyl acetate **(6B)**. The magnification is illustrated by the black scale bars.

Summarizing the main conclusions of the microscopic observations, it may be assumed that the highly viscous and dense structure of the macroemulsions is caused by a network of excess surfactant. In case of the nanoemulsion, smaller droplet sizes are created which possess a larger surface area covered by surfactant molecules. Thus, only a small amount of surplus surfactant is left after production which subsequently leads to the observed aggregates which increase in number and size during storage. In case of the macroemulsion, the droplet sizes remain in the micrometer range, thus providing less surface area to be covered by surfactant molecules. Consequently, a larger amount of free surfactant is left which then forms the network-like structure via self-assembly into vesicles or similar structures, possibly approaching a weak liquid crystalline state.

### 3.9. Rheological investigations

The rheological properties of a colloidal system strongly depend on its composition and, more importantly in this case, on the processing conditions. The analysis of these properties is a simple tool to characterize the macroscopic properties of a formulation in an objective way and thus to confirm visual observations [52]. The rheological properties of emulsions are crucial for their application on skin as well as their physical stability. Especially in case of the presented macroemulsions, it may be assumed that the coalescence of oil droplets or other potential destabilization phenomena strongly depend on the rheological properties of the system. These properties are influenced by the oil volume fraction, the droplet size and particle charge as well as by colloidal interactions [53]. In order to obtain an overview about the rheological properties of the different systems, the flow behavior as well as the viscoelastic properties of both blank and drug-loaded systems were analyzed.

In case of the macroemulsions, the flow curves revealed that the dynamic viscosity of the systems decreased with increasing shear rates. This pseudoplastic or shear-thinning flow behavior was found for both blank and drug-loaded macroemulsions. The incorporation of the model drugs led to an increase in viscosity at all shear rates. Figure 7demonstrates the advantageous effect of drug incorporation on the viscosity of the macroemulsions in an exemplary manner at a shear rate of 15 $s^{-1}$. The apparent viscosity of the macroemulsions at this shear rate was between 2.26 ± 0.10 and 7.92 ± 0.02 Pa·s.

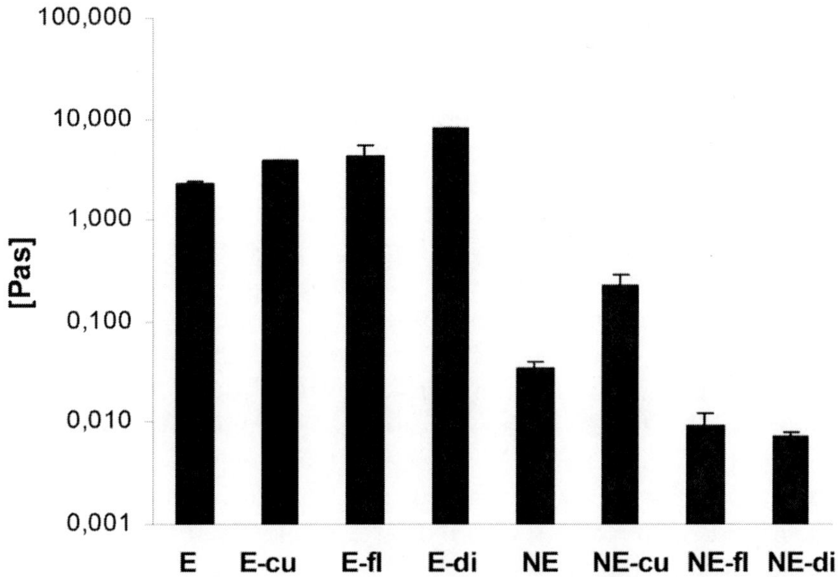


**Figure 7.** Comparison of the apparent viscosity of macroemulsions (E) and corresponding nanoemulsions (NE) with and without incorporated drug at a shear rate of 15 $s^{-1}$. The effect of the incorporated drugs curcumin (cu), flufenamic acid (fl) and diclofenac acid (di) is demonstrated. Values represent the mean of three formulations (n = 3) and are given ± SD.

A minor shear-thinning effect was also observed for blank nanoemulsions and nanoemulsions with curcumin. As already indicated, curcumin was partly dispersed in the system, thus changing its overall properties and leading to an increased viscosity and shear-thinning behavior of the nanoemulsion. For all other drug-loaded nanoemulsions, the dynamic viscosity was entirely independent of the applied shear rate which is characteristic for Newtonian flow behavior. Except in the case of curcumin, the incorporation of drugs into the sucrose stearate nanoemulsion led to a decrease of viscosity at all shear rates (Figure 7): nanoemulsions with flufenamic acid and diclofenac acid exhibited an apparent viscosity of 0.01 ± 0.001 Pa·s at all shear rates.

Overall, it was apparent that the viscosity of the macroemulsions was several orders of magnitude higher than that of the nanoemulsions. The apparent viscosity of the blank nanoemulsion was 0.03 ± 0.001 Pa·s at the presented shear rate, while the viscosity of the corresponding blank macroemulsion was 2.26 ± 0.10 Pa·s, which corresponds to a 64-fold increase in viscosity.

An analysis of the flow curves of both macroemulsions and nanoemulsions using the power law model confirmed the above discussed observations. In case of the nanoemulsions, the value of the flow behavior index n was in the order NE diclo > NE fluf > NE blank > NE curc, where especially the values of the nanoemulsions with diclofenac acid and flufenamic acid were close to 1 (n = 0.98 ± 0.03 and n = 0.92 ± 0.08), thus confirming Newtonian flow behavior. In contrast, the flow behavior index n of blank macroemulsions was 0.10 ± 0.01 and was decreased further by incorporation of either drug. A value of n close to zero indicates pronounced shear-thinning behavior of the samples.

Overall, the shear-thinning effect observed for macroemulsions and, to a minor extent, for blank and curcumin-loaded nanoemulsions is consistent with literature. The pseudoplastic nature of the macroemulsions can be explained by the deformation of the emulsion droplets under increasing shear which facilitates their flow. Likewise, nanoemulsions may exhibit shear-thinning behavior due to changes in the droplet shape along the flow channel [22]. In this case, the incorporation of flufenamic acid and diclofenac acid apparently eliminated any such effect by lowering the viscosity of the blank nanoemulsion system, possibly by interacting with surplus amounts of surfactant.

In addition, oscillatory measurements were performed. In case of the macroemulsions, the elastic modulus G′ was strongly dominating over the viscous modulus G″ at all oscillatory frequencies, which is favorable in terms of physical stability. A comparison of G′ and G″ for all systems at a frequency of 1 Hz is given in Figure 8. The elastic modulus G′ ranged from approximately 250 to 1300 Pa while the viscous modulus G″ ranged from 70 to 380 Pa. Drug incorporation generally increased the values of G′ and G″. The only exception was the curcumin-loaded formulation where G″ was decreased. Overall, both parameters increased at an increasing oscillatory frequency. An increase in the elastic modulus with increasing frequency has been related to the closer packing of microgelled colloidal particles and the resulting larger friction forces between the droplets subjected to shear [54].

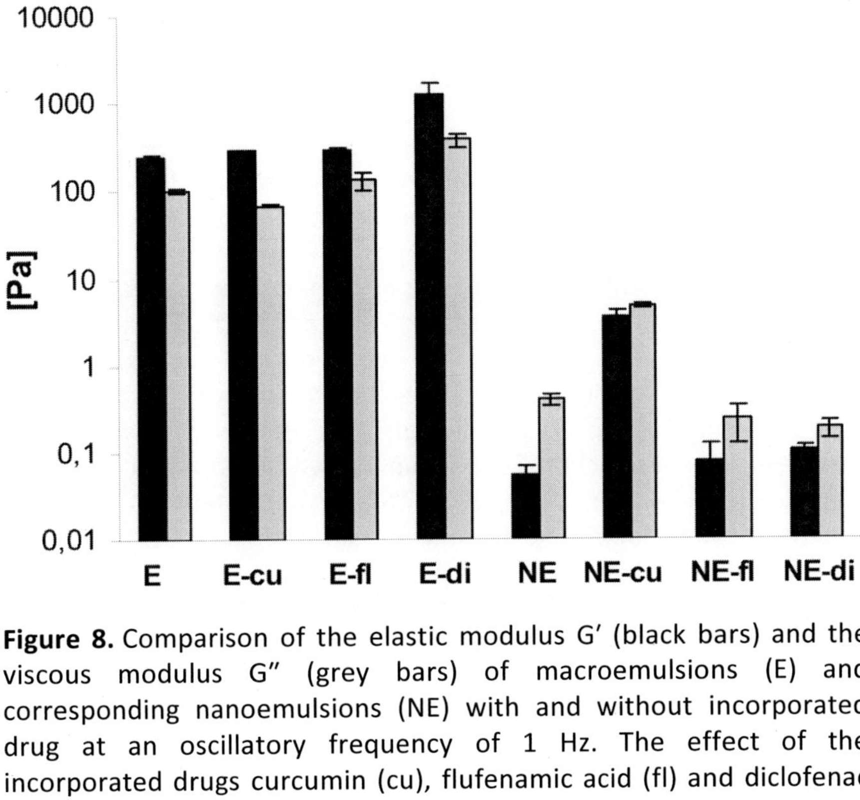


**Figure 8.** Comparison of the elastic modulus G′ (black bars) and the viscous modulus G″ (grey bars) of macroemulsions (E) and corresponding nanoemulsions (NE) with and without incorporated drug at an oscillatory frequency of 1 Hz. The effect of the incorporated drugs curcumin (cu), flufenamic acid (fl) and diclofenac acid (di) is demonstrated. Values represent the mean of three formulations (n = 3) and are given ± SD.

In case of the nanoemulsions, the viscous modulus G″ clearly dominated over the elastic modulus G′ (Figure 8). In case of flufenamic acid and diclofenac acid, drug incorporation led to a decrease of the viscous modulus G″, thus confirming their fluidizing effect on the nanoemulsions. In case of curcumin, incorporation led to an increase of the viscous modulus G″ due to undissolved drug.

The elastic modulus G′ was increased by drug incorporation in all cases. Again, both parameters G″ and G′ increased with increasing oscillatory frequency. Needless to say, both the elastic and viscous modulus were again several orders of magnitude larger for macroemulsions than for nanoemulsions. While the elastic modulus G′ of blank nanoemulsions was 0.06 ± 0.01 Pa, the corresponding value for blank macroemulsons was 248.01 ± 14.97 Pa. This corresponds to a 4409-fold increase in the formulation's elasticity. Likewise, the viscous modulus G″ of blank macroemulsions was 256 times larger than for blank nanoemulsions (0.40 ± 0.05 *versus* 101.83 ± 3.68 Pa).

Overall, the rheological data confirmed that the employed sucrose stearate mixture led to the formation of entirely different emulsion bulk structures by alteration of the production process. A thorough understanding of the bulk structure of an emulsion is necessary to accurately describe its macroscopic mechanical properties. If the droplets within an emulsion are concentrated enough to be deformed, as is obviously the case for the present systems, the mechanical properties of the system can change from viscous to elastic during production due to increased deformation through osmotic pressure [55]. The application of a small shear strain works against the interfacial tension and causes the packed droplets to deform, thereby creating additional interfacial area and storage energy [55]. Likewise, as indicated by the cryo TEM experiments, the macroemulsion structure appeared to be highly symmetrical in terms of distribution of water and oil phase, which may contribute to increasing viscosity and elasticity [56].

The potential of the sucrose ester mixture to stabilize highly elastic macroemulsions is worthy of further investigation. So far, it may be assumed that the ability of the employed sucrose ester to increase the viscosity of emulsions may be related to its potential to self-assembly and the ability of sucrose to form hydrogen bonds and bind water [17].

### 3.10. In vitro skin permeation: franz-cells

The cumulative permeated drug amounts after 24 hours as well as the corresponding drug fluxes for all three model drugs are given in Table 5.

**Table 5.** Skin permeation rates of curcumin (curc), flufenamic acid (fluf) and diclofenac acid (diclo) from macroemulsions (E) and nanoemulsions (NE) expressed as cumulative permeated drug amounts (µg·cm$^{-2}$) and mean drug fluxes (J, µg·cm$^{-2}$·h$^{-1}$). At least five experiments were performed for each formulation (n ≥ 5); indicated values are means ± SD.

| Formulation | Cumulative drug amount after 24h ± SD (µg·cm$^{-2}$) | Mean drug flux ± SD (J, µg·cm$^{-2}$·h$^{-1}$) |
|---|---|---|
| E curc | n.d. | n.d. |
| NE curc | 0.71 ± 0.96 | 0.04 ± 0.06 |
| E fluf | 27.27 ± 7.18 | 1.28 ± 0.34 |
| NE fluf | 24.48 ± 5.13 | 1.15 ± 0.24 |
| E diclo | 140.30 ± 27.36 | 6.66 ± 1.28 |
| NE diclo | 147.37 ± 31.05 | 6.92 ± 1.44 |

As can be seen, the corresponding macroemulsions and nanoemulsions performed equally well in this experimental setup, leading to highly similar release profiles in all three cases. No statistically significant differences between the different formulation types were obtained in terms of either cumulative drug amounts or drug fluxes ($P > 0.05$, respectively). In case of curcumin, the achieved permeation rates were negligible despite the adapted acceptor medium. This can be ascribed to the high lipophilicity of curcumin, which is known to be problematic in terms of formulation development and drug delivery [30,31]. However, the skin permeation experiments were not perpetuated for a longer time span so as not to allow maceration effects to take hold.

The small droplet size of the nanoemulsions is associated with a large surface area, which has frequently been reported to result in an enhanced or accelerated release of incorporated drugs and thus an increased biological effect [51,57,58]. Interestingly, no such effect was observed in the present experiments. Indeed, literature shows that a smaller particle size is not necessarily associated with improved drug delivery [59]. In this case, the skin penetration of the model drugs rather appears to be governed by the employed excipients.

Another interesting aspect in this context is the fact that the skin permeation rates of the drugs were not influenced by the strongly increased viscosity of the macroemulsion systems. The microviscosity of the macroemulsions appeared to be comparable to that of the fluid nanoemulsions despite the significant difference in macroviscosity. This phenomenon has been investigated and confirmed in a recent study dealing with gel-like colloidal dispersions of a comparable sucrose stearate mixture [15]. It may thus be assumed that the loose interconnected hydrophilic network observed for the macroemulsions in our study is of a similar nature despite the presence of additional oil droplets. The release of all three model drugs remained impaired by the complex network-like macroemulsion structure.

### 3.11. In vitro skin penetration: tape stripping

The results of the tape stripping experiments were in good agreement with the results obtained with the franz-cell studies. In summary, neither the particle size nor the viscosity appeared to exert any influence on the penetration behavior of the three model drugs. The penetration depth of the drugs was found to be highly similar for corresponding macroemulsions and nanoemulsions in case of all three model substances ($P > 0.05$, respectively). The same tendency was observed for the accumulated amounts of drug in the SC as determined by summarizing the drug quantities recovered from the individual tape strips ($P > 0.05$, respectively). Merely in case of diclofenac acid, slightly if significantly larger drug amounts were recovered from the skin treated with the macroemulsion due to a surplus of drug on the first adhesive film ($P < 0.05$). Table 6 shows a comparison of the macroemulsions and nanoemulsions in terms of penetrated drug amounts and the penetration depth of the drugs. The latter is expressed both in absolute values (μm) and as percentage of the entire SC thickness, which was found to be 6.59 ± 0.47 μm for the employed porcine ears after removal of the entire SC via tape stripping ($n = 4$).

A graphical illustration of the penetration profiles for flufenamic acid from both macroemulsions and nanoemulsions is given in Figure 9A/9B as a representative example.

**Table 6.** Skin penetration data of curcumin (curc), flufenamic acid (fluf) and diclofenac acid (diclo) from macroemulsions (E) and nanoemulsions (NE) as determined by tape stripping. At least six experiments were performed for each formulation ($n \geq 6$); indicated values are means ± SD.

| Formulation | Penetrated drug amount [µg/cm²] | Penetration [µm] | depth [% of SC] |
|---|---|---|---|
| E curc | 45.22 ± 6.61 | 3.75 ± 0.53 | 56.79 ± 08.01 |
| NE curc | 51.07 ± 4.17 | 3.21 ± 0.81 | 48.61 ± 12.24 |
| E fluf | 21.93 ± 6.29 | 3.08 ± 1.29 | 46.65 ± 19.62 |
| NE fluf | 24.02 ± 7.03 | 3.61 ± 0.95 | 54.67 ± 14.36 |
| E diclo | 27.98 ± 4.43 | 5.62 ± 0.65 | 85.22 ± 09.83 |
| NE diclo | 20.72 ± 2.58 | 4.79 ± 0.95 | 72.70 ± 14.40 |

The highest skin penetration depth was achieved by by diclofenac acid, which was in good agreement with the results of the franz-cell studies. Concerning curcumin it is interesting to note that unlike the results derived from the franz-cell diffusion studies, satisfying skin penetration was reached in this experimental setup which was comparable to that of flufenamic acid. It may thus be assumed that *in vitro* tape stripping is a more suitable approach to investigate the skin penetration of highly lipophilic drugs such as curcumin. Additional *in vivo* tape stripping studies will be conducted with the curcumin-loaded formulations to confirm these results.

## 3.12. Comparison of in vitro studies: franz-cells vs. tape stripping

Since the classical experimental set-up using franz-type diffusion cells may be influenced by interactions between the receptor medium and the model skin which may affect the barrier properties [60], additional tape stripping experiments were performed to avoid the influence of the receptor medium and to provide a more practically orientated experimental setup with a short finite-dose application.

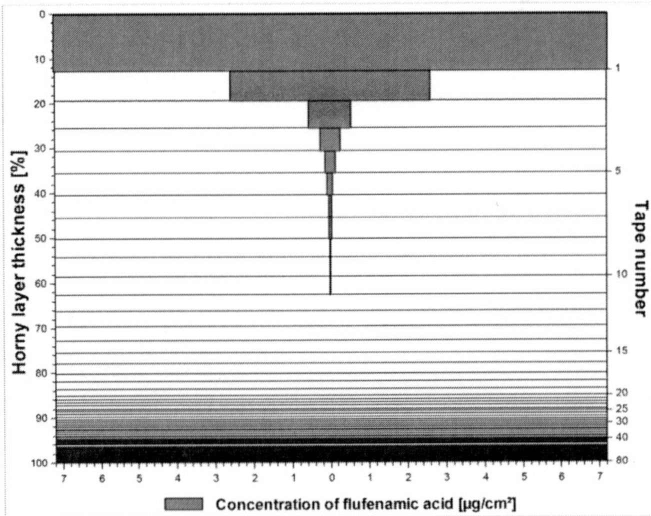


**(9A)**

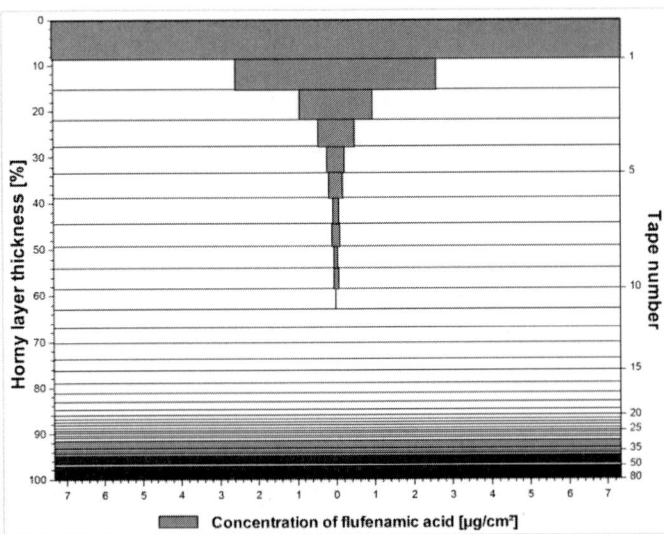


**(9B)**

**Figure 9.** *In vitro* skin penetration profiles of flufenamic acid applied topically in macroemulsions **(9A)** and nanoemulsions **(9B)**. The data were obtained via tape stripping using porcine ear skin (n = 8, respectively).

Under *in vivo* conditions, there is of course a high tissue clearance due to the bloodstream which cannot be simulated with the excised porcine ear. However, the results of our study showed that in the case of curcumin, hardly any skin diffusion was obtained with franz-type diffusion cells over the course of 24 hours despite the presence of a large amount of ethanol in the receptor medium, which offers a high solubilizing capacity for curcumin. In contrast, a penetration profile similar to that of the other drugs was achieved by *in vitro* tape stripping.

As expected, the skin penetration and skin permeation data obtained by the different experimental setups were not entirely comparable in terms of numerical values. In case of curcumin, a reasonable penetration into the stratum corneum was determined by tape stripping (around 50 µg $cm^{-2}$) while no transdermal permeation was observed with franz-type diffusion cells despite the adapted receptor medium. In case of flufenamic acid, the amounts detected in the skin by tape stripping and in the receptor medium after 24 hours were of a similar order of magnitude (around 25 µg $cm^{-2}$, respectively). In case of diclofenac acid, a comparatively smaller amount of drug was obtained by tape stripping (around 25 µg $cm^{-2}$) than was recovered from the receptor medium (around 145 µg $cm^{-2}$). Since it is well-known that diclofenac as an acid is difficult to deliver, it may be assumed that as for curcumin, the results obtained with franz-type diffusion cells are not representative of the *in vivo* situation. In case of curcumin, an underestimation of the skin penetration potential resulted while in case of diclofenac, an overestimation was obtained. The inconsistent experimental results for diclofenac might be related to the different types of setup, the different types of skin employed for the experiments and related differences in pH gradients across the skin [61]. Overall, it may be concluded that tape stripping experiments deliver by far more realistic data than franz-type diffusion cell studies. Comparative *in vivo* tape stripping experiments are envisioned in order to confirm the relevance of the data obtained by *in vitro* tape stripping.

## 4. CONCLUSIONS

Sucrose stearate of an intermediate HLB value can be employed to design innovative lipid-based drug delivery systems which possess improved texture for dermal application while at the same time providing unimpeded drug release properties. The exact nature of the fluffy hydrophilic network surrounding the O/W emulsion droplets of various sizes should be subject to further investigations in order to specifically create desired properties of similar new vehicles. In the context of our investigations, additional *in vivo* tape stripping experiments are planned to gain a more realistic estimation of the penetration behavior of the newly developed formulations.

## ACKNOWLEDGEMENTS

The authors would like to thank Wolfgang Sipos and the Veterinary University of Vienna for providing fresh porcine ears and Gerhard Schleining for valuable discussion. The financial support of the research platform "Characterisation of Drug Delivery Systems on Skin and Investigation of Involved Mechanisms" is gratefully acknowledged.

## REFERENCES AND NOTES

1. Desai, N.B. Sucrose esters - an interesting class of substances for cosmetics. Parfuemerie Kosmet. 1985, 66, 629–632.

2. Thevenin, M.A.; Grossiord, J.L.; Poelman, M.C. Sucrose esters/cosurfactant microemulsion systems for transdermal delivery: Assessment of bicontinuous structures. Int. J. Pharm. 1996, 137, 177–186.

3. Hill, K.; Rhode, O. Sugar-based surfactants for consumer products and technical applications. Fett/Lipid 1999, 101, 25–33.

4. Carlotti, M.E.; Sapino, S.; Ugazio, E.; Peira, E.; Gallarate, M. O/W Moisturizing Emulsions with Saccharose Palmitate and Saccharose Stearate. J. Disp. Sci. Technol. 2008, 29, 375–386.

5. Takegami, S.; Kitamura, K.; Kawada, H.; Matsumoto, Y.; Kitade, T.; Ishida, H.; Nagata, C. Preparation and characterization of a new lipid nano-emulsion containing two cosurfactants, sodium palmitate for droplet size reduction and sucrose palmitate for stability enhancement. Chem. Pharm. Bull. (Tokyo) 2008, 56, 1097–1102.

6. Klang, V.; Matsko, N.; Zimmermann, A.M.; Vojnikovic, E.; Valenta, C. Enhancement of stability and skin permeation by sucrose stearate and cyclodextrins in progesterone nanoemulsions. Int. J. Pharm. 2010, 393, 152–160.

7. Klang, V.; Matsko, N.; Raupach, K.; El-Hagin, N.; Valenta, C. Development of sucrose stearate-based nanoemulsions and optimisation through gamma-cyclodextrin. Eur. J. Pharm. Biopharm. 2011. in press.

8. Calderilla-Fajardo, S.B.; Cazares-Delgadillo, J.; Villalobos-Garcia, R.; Quintanar-Guerrero, D.; Ganem-Quintanar, A.; Robles, R. Influence of sucrose esters on the in vivo percutaneous penetration of octyl methoxycinnamate formulated in nanocapsules, nanoemulsion, and emulsion. Drug Dev. Ind. Pharm. 2006, 32, 107–113.

9. Cazares-Delgadillo, J.; Naik, A.; Kalia, Y.N.; Quintanar-Guerrero, D.; Ganem-Quintanar, A. Skin permeation enhancement by sucrose esters: A pH-dependent phenomenon. Int. J. Pharm. 2005, 297, 204–212.

10. Csoka, G.; Marton, S.; Zelko, R.; Otomo, N.; Antal, I. Application of sucrose fatty acid esters in transdermal therapeutic systems. Eur. J. Pharm. Biopharm. 2007, 65, 233–237.

11. Szuts, A.; Budai-Szucs, M.; Eros, I.; Ambrus, R.; Otomo, N.; Szabo-Revesz, P. Study of thermo-sensitive gel-forming properties of sucrose stearates. J. Excipients Food Chem. 2010, 1, 13–20.

12. Gallegos, C.; Calahorro, C.; Munoz, J.; Berjano, M.; Guerrero, A. High-HLB sucrose esters: A peculiar viscous behaviour. Comun. Jorn. Com. Esp. Deterg. 1991, 22, 283–295.

13. Calahorro, C.; Munoz, J.; Berjano, M.; Guerrero, A.; Gallegos, C. Flow behavior of sucrose stearate/water systems. J. Am. Oil Chem. Soc. 1992, 69, 660–666.

14. Szuts, A.; Budai-Szucs, M.; Eros, I.; Otomo, N.; Szabo-Revesz, P. Study of gel-forming properties of sucrose esters for thermosensitive drug delivery systems. Int. J. Pharm. 2010, 383, 132–137.

15. Ullrich, S.; Metz, H.; Maeder, K. Sucrose ester nanodispersions: Microviscosity and viscoelastic properties. Eur. J. Pharm. Biopharm. 2008, 70, 550–555.

16. Mishra, P.R.; Al Shaal, L.; Mueller, R.H.; Keck, C.M. Production and characterization of Hesperetin nanosuspensions for dermal delivery. Int. J. Pharm. 2009, 371, 182–189.

17. Lee, S.J.; Choi, S.J.; Li, Y.; Decker, E.A.; McClements, D.J. Protein-stabilized nanoemulsions and emulsions: Comparison of physicochemical stability, lipid oxidation, and lipase digestibility. J. Agr. Food Chem. 2011, 59, 415–427.

18. Yilmaz, E.; Borchert, H.H. Design of a phytosphingosine-containing, positively-charged nanoemulsion as a colloidal carrier system for dermal application of ceramides. Eur. J. Pharm. Biopharm. 2005, 60, 91–98.

19. Saupe, A.; Gordon, K.C.; Rades, T. Structural investigations on nanoemulsions, solid lipid nanoparticles and nanostructured lipid carriers by cryo-field emission scanning electron microscopy and Raman spectroscopy. Int. J. Pharm. 2006, 314, 56–62.

20. Mueller, R.H. Zetapotential und Partikelladung in der Laborpraxis; Wissenschaftliche Verlagsgesellschaft mbH: Stuttgart, Germany, 1996; Band 37, Paperback APV.

21. Wabel, C. Influence of Lecithin on Structure and Stability of Parenteral Fat Emulsions. PhD Thesis, Friedrich-Alexander-Universität, Erlangen-Nürnberg, Germany, 1998.

22. Schalbart, P.; Kawaji, M.; Fumoto, K. Formation of tetradecane nanoemulsion by low-energy emulsification methods.Int. J. Refr. 2010, 33, 1612–1624.

23. Rao, M.A. Rheology of Fluid and Semisolid Foods: Principles and Applications; Aspen Publishers Inc: Gaithersburg, MD, USA, 1999.

24. Taherian, A.R.; Fustier, P.; Ramaswamy, H.S. Effect of added oil and modified starch on rheological properties, droplet size distribution, opacity and stability of beverage cloud emulsions. J. Food Eng. 2006, 77, 687–696.

25. Valenta, C.; Kast, C.E.; Harich, I.; Bernkop-Schnuerch, A. Development and in vitro evaluation of a mucoadhesive vaginal delivery system for progesterone. J. Control. Release 2001, 77, 323–332.

26. Valenta, C.; Schultz, K. Influence of carrageenan on the rheology and skin permeation of microemulsion formulations. J. Control. Release 2004, 95, 257–265.

27. Klang, S.H.; Baszkinb, A.; Benita, S. The stability of piroxicam incorporated in a positively-charged submicron emulsion for ocular administration. Int. J. Pharm. 1996, 132, 33–44.

28. Michniak-Kohn, B.B.; Wertz, P.W.; Al-Khalili, M.; Meidan, V.M. Skin: Physiology and Penetration Pathways. InDelivery System Handbook for Personal Care and Cosmetic Products; Rosen, M.R., Ed.; William Andrew Inc.: New York, NY, USA, 2005; pp. 77–100.

29. Hoeller, S.; Valenta, C. Effect of selected fluorinated drugs in a "ringing" gel on rheological behaviour and skin permeation. Eur. J. Pharm. Biopharm. 2007, 66, 120–126.

30. Lin, C.; Lin, H.; Chenc, H.; Yu, M.; Lee, M. Stability and characterisation of phospholipid-based curcumin-encapsulated microemulsions. Food Chem. 2009, 116, 923–928.

31. Maiti, K.; Mukherjee, K.; Gantait, A.; Saha, B.P.; Mukherjee, P.K. Curcumin-phospholipid complex: Preparation, therapeutic

evaluation and pharmacokinetic study in rats. Int. J. Pharm. 2007, 330, 155–163.

32. Hahn, T.; Hansen, S.; Neumann, D.; Kostka, K.H.; Lehr, C.M.; Muys, L.; Schaefer, U.F. Infrared densitometry: A fast and non-destructive method for exact stratum corneum depth calculation for in vitro tape-stripping. Skin Pharmacol. Physiol. 2010, 23, 183–192.

33. Klang, V.; Schwarz, J.C.; Hartl, A.; Valenta, C. Facilitating in vitro tape stripping: Application of infrared densitometry for quantification of porcine stratum corneum proteins. Skin Pharmacol. Physiol. 2011. in press.

34. Breternitz, M.; Flach, M.; Prassler, J.; Elsner, P.; Fluhr, J.W. Acute barrier disruption by adhesive tapes is influenced by pressure, time and anatomical location: Integrity and cohesion assessed by sequential tape stripping. A randomized, controlled study. Br. J. Dermatol. 2007, 156, 231–240.

35. Lademann, J.; Jacobi, U.; Surber, C.; Weigmann, H.J.; Fluhr, J.W. The tape stripping procedure--evaluation of some critical parameters. Eur. J. Pharm. Biopharm. 2009, 72, 317–323.

36. Voegeli, R.; Heiland, J.; Doppler, S.; Rawlings, A.V.; Schreier, T. Efficient and simple quantification of stratum corneum proteins on tape strippings by infrared densitometry. Skin Res. Technol. 2007, 13, 242–251.

37. Hanyšová, L.; Mokrý, M.; Kastner, P.; Klimeš, J. HPLC Evaluation of Diclofenac in the Various Forms of Therapeutic Preparations. Chem. Pap. 2005, 59, 103–108.

38. Rao, J.; McClements, D.J. Stabilization of phase inversion temperature nanoemulsions by surfactant displacement. J. Agr. Food Chem. 2010, 58, 7059–7066.

39. Benita, S.; Levy, M.Y. Submicron emulsions as colloidal drug carriers for intravenous administration: Comprehensive physicochemical characterization. J. Pharm. Sci. 1993, 82, 1069–1079.

40. Sznitowska, M.; Janicki, S.; Dabrowska, E.; Zurowska-Pryczkowska, K. Submicron emulsions as drug carriers. Studies on destabilization potential of various drugs. Eur. J. Pharm. Sci. 2001, 12, 175–179.

41. Jahanzad, F.; Josephides, J.; Mansourian, A.; Sajjadi, S. Dynamics of Transitional Phase Inversion Emulsification: Effect of Addition Time on the Type of Inversion and Drop Size. Ind. Eng. Chem. Res. 2010, 49, 7631–7637.

42. Keck, C.M.; Mueller, R.H. Size analysis of submicron particles by laser diffractometry--90% of the published measurements are false. Int. J. Pharm. 2008, 355, 150–163.

43. Gradzielski, M.; Bergmeier, M.; Mueller, M.; Hoffmann, H. Novel Gel Phase: A Cubic Phase of Densely Packed Monodisperse, Unilamellar Vesicles. J. Phys. Chem. B 1997, 101, 1719–1722.

44. Gradzielski, M.; Mueller, M.; Bergmeier, M.; Hoffmann, H.; Hoinkis, E. Structural and Macroscopic Characterization of a Gel Phase of Densely Packed Monodisperse, Unilamellar Vesicles. J. Phys. Chem. B 1999, 103, 1416–1424.

45. Kawada, H.; Kume, T.; Matsunaga, T.; Iwai, H.; Sano, T.; Shibayama, M. Structure and Rheology of a Self-Standing Nanoemulsion. Langmuir 2009, 26, 2430–2437.

46. Sadtler, V.M.; Guely, M.; Marchal, P.; Choplin, L. Shear-induced phase transitions in sucrose ester surfactant. J. Colloid. Interface Sci. 2004, 270, 270–275.

47. Savic, S.D.; Savic, M.M.; Vesic, S.A.; Vuleta, G.M.; Mueller-Goymann, C.C. Vehicles based on a sugar surfactant: Colloidal structure and its impact on in vitro/in vivo hydrocortisone permeation. Int. J. Pharm. 2006, 320, 86–95.

48. Mason, T.G.; Graves, S.M.; Wilking, J.N.; Lin, M.Y. Extreme emulsification: Formation and structure of nanoemulsions. Condens. Matter Phys. 2006, 1, 193–199.

49. Graves, S.; Meleson, K.; Wilking, J.; Lin, M.Y.; Mason, T.G. Structure of concentrated nanoemulsions. J. Chem. Phys.2005, 122, 134703-1–134703-16.

50. Cortés-Muñoz, M.; Chevalier-Lucia, D.; Dumay, E. Characteristics of submicron emulsions prepared by ultra-high pressure homogenisation: Effect of chilled or frozen storage. Food Hydrocolloid. 2009, 23, 640–654.

51. Tadros, T.; Izquierdo, P.; Esquena, J.; Solans, C. Formation and stability of nano-emulsions. Adv. Colloid Interface Sci.2004, 108-109, 303–318.

52. Heuschkel, S. Untersuchungen zum Mechanismus der Penetrationserhöhung durch Mikroemulsionen und neue Enhancer bei der dermalen Applikation von Wirkstoffen. PhD Thesis, Martin-Luther-University, Halle-Wittenberg, Germany, 2009.

53. McClements, D.J. Food Emulsions: Principles, Practices, and Techniques; CRC Press: Boca Raton, FL, USA, 2005.

54. Valdez, M.A.; Acedo-Carrillo, J.I.; Rosas-Durazo, A.; Lizardi, J.; Rinaudo, M.; Goycoolea, F.M. Small-deformation rheology of mesquite gum stabilized oil in water emulsions. Carbohyd. Polym. 2006, 64, 205–211.

55. Mason, T.G.; Graves, S.M.; Wilking, J.N.; Lin, M.Y. Effective structure factor of osmotically deformed nanoemulsions.J. Phys. Chem. B 2006, 110, 22097–22102.

56. Lee, C.H.; Moturi, V.; Lee, Y. Thixotropic property in pharmaceutical formulations. J. Control. Release 2009, 136, 88–98.

57. Friedman, D.I.; Schwarz, J.S.; Weisspapir, M. Submicron emulsion vehicle for enhanced transdermal delivery of steroidal and nonsteroidal antiinflammatory drugs. J. Pharm. Sci. 1995, 84, 324–329.

58. Bouchemal, K.; Briancon, S.; Perrier, E.; Fessi, H. Nano-emulsion formulation using spontaneous emulsification: Solvent, oil and surfactant optimisation. Int. J. Pharm. 2004, 280, 241–251.

59. Wu, X.; Biatry, B.; Cazeneuve, C.; Guy, R.H. Drug delivery to the skin from sub-micron polymeric particle formulations: Influence

of particle size and polymer hydrophobicity. Pharm. Res. 2009, 26, 1995–2001.

60. Wagner, H.; Kostka, K.H.; Lehr, C.M.; Schaefer, U.F. Drug distribution in human skin using two different in vitro test systems: Comparison with in vivo data. Pharm. Res. 2000, 17, 1475–1481.

61. Stracke, F.; Weiss, B.; Lehr, C.M.; Koenig, K.; Schaefer, U.F.; Schneider, M. Multiphoton microscopy for the investigation of dermal penetration of nanoparticle-borne drugs. J. Invest. Dermatol. 2006, 126, 2224–2233.

# Index


## C

carboxymethyl, 33, 34, 35, 54, 55

complex coacervation, 33, 34, 35, 37, 38, 41, 53, 55, 56, 58

conformational switch, 203, 235

controlled drug release, 196, 204

## D

drug analysis, 96

Drug delivery, 32, 59, 163, 236, 252, 301

## E

Emulgents, 59, 61

## F

fliposomes, 204, 219, 233

formulation, 9, 11, 12, 13, 14, 289, 290, 292, 301

## G

gelatine, 33, 34, 35, 37, 38, 39, 51, 53

## H

hair follicle, 17, 244, 245, 247, 248, 252

High-pressure, 59, 63

homogenization, 59, 62, 63, 274, 284

## I

ibuprofen, 33, 34, 35, 37, 38, 105, 253

illicit drugs, 96, 102, 103, 104, 114

## M

microencapsulation, 34, 54, 58

microsponge gel, 181, 183, 187, 188, 196, 197, 198

## N

nanoemulsion, 59, 60, 61, 62, 285, 286, 287, 296, 297, 298

Nanoemulsion, 59, 67, 69, 70, 300

## O

O/W emulsion, 256, 257, 295

penetration, 2, 5, 7, 8, 11, 12, 294, 295, 296, 302

## P

pH-sensitive liposomes, 203, 204, 206, 222, 231, 234, 235

polyethyleneglycol, 204, 238

PRONIOSOMES, 4

PSORIASIS, 10

## R

Raman spectroscopy, 95, 96, 114, 297

## S

sustained release, 6, 14, 20, 34, 51, 163, 175

## T

triggered release, 88, 204, 206, 228, 233

## V

vehicle, 2, 69, 243, 244, 245, 249, 251, 301